Inequality, Globalization, and World Politics

Edited by

ANDREW HURRELL

and

NGAIRE WOODS

OXFORD
UNIVERSITY PRESS

OXFORD

UNIVERSITY PRESS

Great Clarendon Street, Oxford OX2 6DP

Oxford University Press is a department of the University of Oxford.
It furthers the University's objective of excellence in research, scholarship,
and education by publishing worldwide in

Oxford New York

Athens Auckland Bangkok Bogotá Buenos Aires Calcutta
Cape Town Chennai Dar es Salaam Delhi Florence Hong Kong Istanbul
Karachi Kuala Lumpur Madrid Melbourne Mexico City Mumbai
Nairobi Paris São Paulo Shanghai Singapore Taipei Tokyo Toronto Warsaw
with associated companies in Berlin Ibadan

Oxford is a registered trade mark of Oxford University Press
in the UK and in certain other countries

Published in the United States
by Oxford University Press Inc., New York

British Library Cataloguing in Publication Data
Data available

Library of Congress Cataloging in Publication Data
Inequality, globalization, and world politics / edited by Andrew
Hurrell and Ngaire Woods; [contributors, Albert Berry . . . et al.].
Includes bibliographical references (p.   ) and index.
1. International relations.   2. Equality of states.   3. World
politics—1989-   .   I. Hurrell, Andrew.   II. Woods, Ngaire.
III. Berry, R. Albert.
JZ1305.154 1999 327—dc21 98-44963
ISBN 0-19-829567-7 (hbk.)
ISBN 0-19-829566-9 (pbk.)

3 5 7 9 10 8 6 4

Printed in Great Britain
on acid-free paper by
Biddles Ltd
Guildford and King's Lynn

INEQUALITY, GLOBALIZATION,
AND WORLD POLITICS

CONTENTS

NOTES ON CONTRIBUTORS

ALBERT BERRY is Professor of Economics at the University of Toronto and has published extensively on inequality and income distribution, particularly in Latin America. Most recently, he has published *Poverty, Economic Reform and Income Distribution in Latin America* (1998).

CHRISTINE CHINKIN is Professor of International Law at the London School of Economics and Political Science. Her teaching and research interests are in international law, including international dispute settlement processes, human rights, and the application of feminist theories to the international legal process. She is the author of *Third Parties in International Law* (1993) and *Halsbury's Laws of Australia: Title on Foreign Relations and Dispute Resolution in Australia* (1993).

BOB DEACON is Professor Associate at the Department of Sociological Studies, University of Sheffield and Director of the Globalism and Social Policy Programme (GASPP). His publications include *The New Eastern Europe: Social Policy Past, Present and Future* (1992) and *Global Social Policy* (1989).

ANDREW HURRELL is University Lecturer in International Relations and a Fellow of Nuffield College. His major interests include international relations theory and the international relations of Latin America, with particular reference to the foreign policy of Brazil and US–Latin American relations. Publications include *The International Politics of the Environment* (co-editor with Benedict Kingsbury, 1992) and *Regionalism in World Politics* (co-editor with Louise Fawcett, 1995).

BENEDICT KINGSBURY is Professor of Law at New York University Law School. He is working on a book on indigenous peoples in international law. He has edited *United Nations, Divided World* (with Adam Roberts, 2nd edn., 1993), *The International Politics of the Environment* (with Andrew Hurrell, 1992), *Hugo Grotius and*

International Relations (with Hedley Bull and Adam Roberts, 1990), and *Indigenous Peoples of Asia* (with R. H. Barnes and Andrew Gray, 1995).

DAVID MILLER is Official Fellow in Social and Political Theory at Nuffield College, Oxford. At present he is working mainly on problems of nationality and citizenship, and on ideas of social justice and equality. Among his books are *On Nationality* (1995); *Pluralism, Justice and Equality* (co-edited with Michael Walzer, 1995); and *Principles of Social Justice* (forthcoming).

CHARLES OMAN is Head of the Research Programme at the Development Centre of the Organization for Economic Cooperation and Development (OECD) in Paris. His recent publications include *Globalization and Regionalization: The Challenge for Developing Countries* (1994).

MICHAEL REDCLIFT is Professor of International Environmental Policy and Head of the Department of Environmental Social Sciences at Keele University. He is the author or co-author of numerous books on environmental issues, including *Sustainable Development* (1987), *Refashioning Nature* (1991), *Social Theory and the Global Environment* (1994), and *Wasted Earth: Counting the Costs of Global Consumption* (1996).

COLIN SAGE is College Lecturer in the Department of Geography at University College Cork, National University of Ireland. His research interests lie in the intersection of development and the environment, in operationalizing local sustainability in an era of globalization, and in managing the consequences of consumption in hyper-developed industrialized societies.

FRANCES STEWART is the Director of the International Development Centre and Professor of Development Economics at Oxford University. She is a co-author of *Adjustment with a Human Face* (1988) and *Adjustment and Poverty: Options and Choices* (1995).

NGAIRE WOODS is Fellow in Politics at University College and Lecturer in International Relations at Oxford University. Her present research is concerned with international institutions and, in particular, the IMF and the World Bank. Her recent publications include articles about international institutions and good governance and *Explaining International Relations since 1945* (1996).

LIST OF FIGURES

LIST OF TABLES

Introduction

Andrew Hurrell and Ngaire Woods

Inequality has long been a defining feature of world politics. This volume draws together evidence that it has been increasing, both within and across states, and examines the consequences. Immense and increasing disparities of wealth, of power, and of security shape the world in which we live. Economic liberalization is exacerbating the gap between rich and poor within virtually all developing regions. At the same time, other elements of globalization are increasing the inequalities of political power and influence, as well as highlighting new dimensions of inequality. For one group of countries globalization is eroding the cohesion and viability of the state. However, other countries and actors are empowered by processes of globalization, since they are better placed to adapt and exploit its new opportunities. Equally, the disparity of power among states is becoming more marked and more visible as an increasing volume of ever more far-reaching rules, rights, and values are being asserted and imposed at the global level. New rules and norms, whether about investment, military security, environmental management, or social policy, are being made by those countries with the power to shape outcomes and to control international institutions. Less powerful states are, even more than in the past, becoming 'rule-takers'. Equally, technological advances, far from creating more equality among states and other groups, are in fact widening gaps among states and regions. In the military sphere, for example, advanced technologies and the so-called revolution in military affairs may be leading to a recentralization of military and coercive power around the United States and its core allies. Overall, then, globalization is exacerbating inequalities of resources, capabilities, and, perhaps most importantly, the power to make and break rules in the international arena.

Within weak states globalization and widening inequality are

eroding the capacity of governments to deal with an increasing set
of social, economic, and political conflicts. At the level of world
politics, the consequences are still more profound. As globalization
creates sharper and more urgent problems for states and international institutions, increasing inequality reduces their capacity to
manage these problems effectively.[1] In this context, it is unsurprising that the sense of unease about globalization has increased
and that political and media attention has come to highlight its
negative consequences.[2] Indeed, even the more 'technocratic' international institutions, such as the International Monetary Fund and
the Bank for International Settlements, are beginning to address
more directly issues of poverty, inequality, and equity.[3] At the same
time, debates about more equal representation of states in international organizations such as the United Nations Security Council
and the World Trade Organization are once again emerging centre-
stage.[4] Yet academic discussion of these issues has remained uneven
and limited. It has tended to concentrate on a narrow range of
economic issues. The political, institutional, and security dimensions of inequality have been played down, as have the combined
effects of all dimensions of inequality on the practices of world
politics. This volume attempts to address this lacuna by examining
inequality in relation to eight central issues.

In the first chapter, Ngaire Woods defines inequality and traces
the changing place of inequality on the agenda of world politics.
Traditional conceptions of world order assume that stability is
best maintained through hierarchy or entrenched inequality among
states. Yet in the 1970s this vision faced a normative challenge.
Developing countries argued that a more just world order would
ensure greater equality among states. Since the 1970s, however, the
moral argument has shifted towards a more focused concern for
poverty within states, and for ameliorating the position of the
poorest states. In other words, inequality slipped off the agenda of
world politics, to be replaced by a greater regard for poverty and
the poorest in the world. In the late 1990s, however, globalization
is presenting a new set of challenges which force us to rethink
inequality. In managing and facilitating globalization, international
institutions are needing to probe deeply into domestic politics,
ensuring compliance with agreements on issues ranging from the
environment to trade and arms control. To do this effectively,
they need full participation and commitment from a wide range of

members. Yet existing multilateral organizations are still hierarchically arranged. Order is still maintained through inequality and the will of their most powerful members. The present dilemma for powerful states is whether to accept losing some of their own control in order to reap the advantages of stronger and more effective institutions. The alternative is to maintain their place in the old hierarchical order, even in the face of its ineffectiveness in dealing with new challenges and problems.

In Chapter 2, Charles Oman turns to the question of whether globalization can be managed so as to minimize increasing inequality and exclusion. The chapter details the driving forces behind globalization. These include: deregulation in OECD countries which is also fostering regionalism; the emergence of technologies which have altered the way in which firms organize production (from Taylorism to flexible production); financial globalization which has increased governments' vulnerability to financial markets; and the opening up of non-OECD countries which have entered the global market place. The last process is described by Stewart and Berry in Chapter 6. In several cases, these challenges of globalization are being managed by greater regional cooperation and integration. However, increasing regionalism is also opening up two additional threats. First, there is a risk that non-OECD countries will become excluded from the 'deep' policy integration among OECD countries. In Chapter 3 this risk is described in terms of the emergence of a 'zone of peace' among OECD countries with 'the rest' excluded on the margins. The dangers of such a development are also described in Chapter 5 in respect of environmental policy. A second risk of regionalism is that as trade opens up within regions, so too pressures for global free trade become muted. Multinationals, for instance, acquire a foothold within the region and then push for continued intra-regional free trade and stop pressing for inter-regional reductions in barriers. In this case the 'zone of peace' is better described as a fortress from which all others continue to be excluded. Charles Oman concludes that each of these threats underlines the importance of constructively managing globalization now.

In Chapter 3, Benedict Kingsbury elaborates on the way in which inequality is entrenched within existing international order, examining the inseparable way in which sovereignty and inequality are intertwined in international law. He explains why the principle of sovereignty has long relieved international lawyers from thinking about inequality, permitting them to assume that all states are formally equal and leaving actual inequalities to be sorted out at the state level. Yet, underneath the guise of formal equality, international law has always reconciled sovereign equality with manifest actual inequalities among states, both by narrowly defining the group to whom rules and laws apply and by selectively applying the laws and principles. Yet today, that exercise in careful application and legal definition is becoming more difficult. Globalization, democratization, privatization, and the growth of transnational civil society have all contributed to a new pressure to dissolve some of the traditional boundaries between domestic law and international law. Internationalists argue that by diluting sovereignty one can ensure a wider reach of normative principles—whether of human rights, or of environmental protection. However, sovereignty, as traditionally defined, has at least offered protection against intervention or recolonization and a locus for group identity and loyalty. Any dilution of such sovereignty could further entrench inequality both among and within states. In particular, it could lead to a zone of peace in which a particular standard of conduct (defined by powerful states) is upheld, leaving 'the rest' to cope with turmoil and marginalization.

In Chapter 4, Christine Chinkin assesses the efficacy of international law as an instrument to promulgate a more equal and participatory international system. She critically surveys efforts made to use international law to promulgate greater gender equality. The chapter begins by examining the reality of women's global inequality. Several changes have occurred in international legal standards of equality between men and women and international strategies and programmes have been introduced. However, there continues to be an enormous disparity between legal regulation and reality. In particular, the gap is evinced by: flaws within the legal framework; defects in the concept of equality used to promote women's advancement; and the inadequacies of law to amend behaviours that are deeply rooted within tradition and culture and supported by global economic structures. Christine Chinkin concludes by questioning whether legal prescription, and in particular international legal prescription, can ever generate fundamental societal change.

In Chapter 5, Michael Redclift and Colin Sage examine interna-

tional policy on environmental degradation, highlighting implications for inequality as well as the potential ineffectiveness of policy
in this area. They highlight the dangers of policies and principles
formulated by the OECD countries and applied to the rest. In the
first place, a highly critical account of Northern policies and institutions is given, underlining the persistent tolerance in OECD countries for high levels of poverty and inequality in the world economy.
The chapter then argues that environmental degradation highlights
the short-sightedness of this neglect. Clearly, definitions of environmental degradation vary. Developing countries give priority to
problems of access to clean drinking water and the treatment of
sewage. By contrast, OECD governments give priority to the issue
of global warming. Yet for global warming to be managed, the
industrialized countries need the cooperation of the developing
countries. Indeed, the most rational strategies for OECD countries
to pursue in order to manage the problem they rate as the most
important would be to transfer technology and resources to the
South to prevent environmentally degrading industrialization there
which mirrors the North. Yet such strategies are not being
adopted—and nor does there seem to be much likelihood that they
will be in the future. Rather, policy is being shaped by inequalities
of bargaining power, corporate interests, and a lack of will to
change, both in Northern governments and the international institutions which they dominate.

The inequalities mentioned in the first section of Chapter 5 are
further expounded and explained in Chapter 6. Frances Stewart
and Albert Berry examine economic inequality and the impact of
globalization and liberalization not just among but more particularly *within* states. Their analysis charts the coincidence of economic liberalization and increases in inequality both in primary and
in secondary incomes across countries in several regions, including
Africa, Latin America, Asia, and countries in transition. The
authors underline the difficulties in relying on the data available,
but they do manage to identify the conditions in which liberalization has been most likely to exacerbate inequality. They also manage to draw out broader conclusions about global economic
inequality. In particular, the chapter demonstrates that over the
1980s inequalities within countries tended overall to worsen—
more so than in any previous post-war decade. Furthermore, this
fact alters the picture of global inequality since, if inequalities

within states had not worsened in the 1980s, overall global inequalities (within states) would have been diminished.

The moral significance of the inequalities described in Chapter 6 is analysed by David Miller in Chapter 7. The chapter examines the arguments as to whether or not inequalities among states matter morally. Not all inequality in international relations can be said to be 'unjust'. Indeed, this chapter criticizes the two most prominent kinds of argument which purport to demonstrate that existing inequalities are unjust. In the first place, the author dismisses the notion of a 'global community of states' in which equality implies recognition and respect. In the second place, he rejects arguments based on a notion of an equal right to natural resources. In their place, the author leaves us with two bases on which inequalities can be viewed as unjust: first, where they entail violating 'basic rights'; and second, where the inequalities derive from 'exploitative' transactions.

In Chapter 8, Bob Deacon analyses the relationship between globalization and social policy, raising once again the question as to how globalization can be constructively managed and, more specifically, what its effects are on social policy. Whilst inequality and social policy were once the preserve of national governments, globalization has brought them into the arena of international relations. Furthermore, a new range of actors has been brought into international relations, including individuals with rights at the international level. This exemplifies the way sovereignty is being redefined in the domain of international politics—as Benedict Kingsbury highlights in Chapter 3—and the way international institutions are moving beyond their old mandates, as Ngaire Woods argues in Chapter 1. The result in the area of social policy is that international organizations such as the IMF, the World Bank, the OECD, the ILO, the WTO, the European Union, and others have taken on different aspects of welfare and social policy. At the same time, these organizations now exert significant influence on national governments' social policies. Bob Deacon argues that these changes imply a need for large-scale reform of global management of social policy, including: greater social regulation of economic competition, greater accountability of international organizations, and a strengthening of global political, legal, and social rights in pursuit of global justice.

Finally, in Chapter 9, Andrew Hurrell examines the paradoxical and problematic relationship between inequality and security. He begins by looking back to the classical state system, in which inequality was central not only to the generation of insecurity (above all as the 'natural' inequalities among states fostered power-political competition and fuelled the security dilemma that inevitably resulted), but also to its management and limitation. The chapter then considers how this traditional picture has been challenged. Whilst old-style threats have by no means wholly disappeared (especially at the regional level), the security agenda has expanded. Inequality has come to play a critical role, first in the generation of a wide range of new threats and sources of social violence; second, in deciding whose security counts politically and should become the source of international attention; and third, in the highly differentiated capacity of states to respond to this expanded range of security challenges. The final section returns to the role of inequality in the management of international security. It considers but rejects the argument that the recentralization of military power can provide the basis for a stable and sustainable security order. But whilst the old bases for the management of security, in which inequality played such a central role, have been undermined, they have not been replaced by anything more secure or reliable.

1

Order, Globalization, and Inequality in World Politics

Ngaire Woods

I. WHY INVESTIGATE INEQUALITY?

Traditional investigations into world order have tended to neglect the issue of inequality. They have confined themselves to questions such as: how relations are ordered among states?; who comprises the 'society of states'?; who makes the rules?; and what kinds of leverage and coercion are available to enforce the rules? In other words, they have eschewed investigating the role that equality and inequality have played in promulgating and influencing international order.[1] Yet there are powerful reasons for investigating inequality in any discussion of order in international relations today. Although traditionally great powers or super-powers have provided stability and order through leadership or the balance of power, today these rudimentary institutions will not suffice. Processes of globalization are challenging the bases of order in profound ways: first, as the evidence presented in this book demonstrates, by exacerbating inequalities both within and among states; and second, by eroding the capacity of traditional institutions to manage the new threats.

This chapter introduces these arguments in the following way. Section II defines inequality and argues that emerging inequalities in world politics challenge the traditional conception that order is best maintained through hierarchy among states. Yet inequality has been absent from the agenda of world politics for a long time. As charted in the third section, since the 1970s there has been a shift in normative arguments away from a concern about inequality among and within states, and towards a more focused concern with poverty and the poorest states. However, as the fourth section of this chapter argues, globalization presents new challenges which, for practical reasons, force us to think once again about inequality. Globalization, it is argued, transforms the processes, the actors and capabilities, and the agenda of world politics, necessitating more effective international institutions of management. Today institutions need to probe deeply into domestic politics, ensuring compliance with agreements on issues ranging from the environment to trade and arms control. To do this effectively, they need full participation and commitment from a wide range of members. Yet, as argued in the fifth section of the chapter, existing multilateral organizations are still hierarchically arranged. Their authority and effectiveness depends upon the will and actions of their most powerful members and, as the most powerful states balance up the advantages of stronger and more effective institutions against possible losses in their own control and sovereignty, they repeatedly come down on the side of the latter. This means, as is argued in the sixth and concluding section of the chapter, that international institutions are committing themselves to maintaining the old hierarchical order, even in the face of its ineffectiveness in dealing with new challenges and problems.

II. INEQUALITY AND THE TRADITIONAL VIEW OF INTERNATIONAL ORDER

Order in international relations carries many meanings and many interpretations. At a conference on 'Conditions of World Order' thirty years ago, several leading academic lights in international relations were brought together in Bellagio, Italy. They defined 'order' as 'the minimum conditions for coexistence',[2] eschewing any wider definition of order which would open up discussions of necessary conditions for a 'good life' or any other set of deeper values. And indeed, this is a traditional vision of international order. It begins with a European conception of the 'Westphalian system',[3] the key actors within which are sovereign states who are in a formal sense equal—each is accorded an equal 'formal' sovereignty. However, order among these states is traditionally understood to be a product of *hierarchy*. A balance of power among the major states, such as that prescribed in the Treaty of Utrecht (1713), prevents any one state from predominating or extinguishing the sovereignty of all others.

Inequality within the traditional conception of world order is a positive, restraining, and ordering force. It permits the operation of a balance of power as a substitute for the centralized authority of a Hobbesian Leviathan in domestic politics. At the same time, hierarchy in the international system, or the imbalance of power, has never meant a strict imposition of the absolute will of the most powerful state or states. Rather, within the hierarchical system institutions have emerged which permit limited accommodation and change. The Concert of Europe, for example, or the League of Nations, were institutions which reflected the need of the most powerful to accommodate those directly beneath them—to ensure that they have a stake in the system so that they will assist in preserving the status quo. However, the scope of this type of accommodation within traditional realist views of international relations has been strictly limited.[4]

Similarly, in contemporary accounts of international relations the comfortable relationship between power and accommodation is continued in theories that assume that 'hierarchy' breeds order. In the realist tradition, inequality simply describes the status quo in international relations and not a deeper set of normative concerns.[5] Order is provided by a powerful state which sets up institutions and rules in the international system.[6] The real debate within the recent literature has been about whether or not a hegemon is required to maintain and enforce the rules. It has certainly not focused on the degree to which a particular regime will cement or alleviate inequalities. Neo-realists argue that a hegemon is essential.[7] The institutionalist critics of neo-realism argue that a hegemon is not required for the institutions to acquire a driving force of their own.[8] However, even within the institutionalist view, the role of norms and institutions can only be explained *after* a power-political framework has been ascertained.[9] Hierarchy and inequality are thus asserted as a precondition for subsequent kinds of order.

In brief, the traditional view of order assumes that 'right depends largely on might'.[10] In making any accommodation to the less powerful, the most powerful must beware that they do not diminish their own capacity to maintain order. The normative concern is to ensure order, and concessions to justice or distributional equality, we are told, do not breed the conditions for order. By contrast, the more brutal reality of unequal states does produce order.[11] Hence, for example, Robert Tucker's 1970s attack on the Carter Administration for listening to developing countries' demands for justice. Tucker argued that by accommodating Third World states' claims for equality and justice, the United States caused their claims to escalate and at the same time reduced its own control over world politics.[12] In modern realist and neo-realist accounts of international relations, the way to deal with increasing disorder is to reinforce the traditional hierarchy of power.[13]

Yet the experience of the 1990s suggests that traditional hierarchy does not maintain order in the face of new challenges. Although immediately after the end of the Cold War there was a brief euphoric period during which a 'New World Order' led by the United States was trumpeted,[14] the idea was short-lived. The United States and its close allies soon found that a global agenda of democratization, liberalization, peace, and self-determination would often be self-contradictory. In transition or democratizing countries, difficult choices had to be made between either economic liberalization or democratization, with governments often forced to give priority to one or the other.[15] Self-determination, on the other hand, often seemed to lead to civil war and conflict, nowhere as starkly as in the former Yugoslavia.[16] A clearer hierarchy of power in the international system—the new 'leadership' of the United States—did not offer solutions to these problems. Rather, a second wave of policy since the end of the Cold War has highlighted the shortcomings of existing international institutions (as will be discussed in the fifth section of this chapter).

Today, in order for countries to achieve the myriad goals of wealth, environmental protection, and a wide range of forms of security (see Chapter 9), a more sophisticated order is required. Yet while the most powerful states in the system resist any reform of the institutions they dominate, it is difficult to imagine any such new order evolving. For at least twenty years, normative arguements for greater equality in international institutions have been advanced. Yet, as analysed in the next section of this chapter, these arguements have had very little effect.

III. JUSTICE, ORDER, AND INEQUALITY

At the end of the twentieth century, there is little evidence of any widespread consensus or acceptance of a moral case for alleviating inequalities within or among states, or for reforming the international system in the name of justice. Such arguments against inequality have virtually disappeared from the agenda of world politics. At the same time, however, more limited formal arguments about equality still retain currency.

The widely accepted notion of a formal kind of equality among states borrows from ideas about the rights of 'man'.[17] This principle is not concerned with the unequal natural attributes of states, such as their population, territorial expanse, or natural resources. Rather, equality in this formal sense means that all states should be treated as equal members of international society.[18] It is this kind of 'foundational equality' which has underpinned support for decolonization and self-determination,[19] as well as the post-war international institutions organized on the basis of one state, one vote, such as the United Nations General Assembly and the World Trade Organization.

Yet poorer, developing states soon became disillusioned with this formal notion of equality in world politics which they achieved in the aftermath of the Second World War. Decolonization, and access to international institutions, did not result in a more substantive equality. For this reason, from the 1960s onwards, developing countries presented the issue of inequality to the world community in more exacting terms, arguing their case for greater 'distributional equality' on the grounds of justice.[20] 'Distributional equality' is concerned with the configuration of economic goods, social opportunities, and political powers in a society. In international relations 'distributional equality' implies a need to transfer wealth and power from wealthy, powerful states to poorer states,[21] but poses a problem about the relationship between poor individuals (who are the catalysts of moral duties of redistribution) and states (to whom the principles of equality are applied by analogy). These debates continue today, as analysed by David Miller in Chapter 7. But since the 1970s the divide between the ethical debate and actual politics has widened dramatically. Arguments for redistribution and wealth transfers disappeared from the agenda of world politics in the 1980s, overwhelmed by the debt crisis and new neo-liberal interpretations of inequalities both within and among countries. As a result, international institutions are no longer primarily fora within which North–South inter-state inequalities are debated.

Inequality and redistribution in the 1970s

Inequality shifted to centre stage in world politics, alongside 'North–South politics', in the 1970s. Southern coalitions of decolonized and developing states emerged, sharing a collective identity cemented by a shared sense of historical injustice and significant material inferiority to the industrialized world.[22] North–South negotiations, which had commenced with the formation of the Non-aligned Movement in the United Nations, expanded into the Group of 77 within the UN economic system, and into the formation of UNCTAD.[23] Overcoming inequality became a key tenet of demands for a new international economic order, and later in the negotiations for a new Law of the Sea.[24]

At the same time, inequality also became a central concern of domestic politics within much of the industrialized world. During the 1960s political movements and policies emerged which strove to overcome inequalities rooted in race, gender, or poverty, such as President Johnson's Great Society, and welfare and education reforms within Britain. In conjunction with this trend, a lively theoretical debate about justice, equality, and inequality took centre stage in the study of politics, spilling over into the study and rhetoric of international relations.[25] At both domestic and international levels, the effectiveness of political systems came to be defined not merely in terms of 'order', but equally in terms of 'justice'. The very fact of inequality in international relations—the fact that some states were so rich, whilst others were so poor—grounded claims for a more equal sharing of resources among rich and poor and, specifically, greater transfers of resources from North to South, preferential terms for trade and investment, and a negotiated share of any new international resources—such as the fruits of the deep-sea bed.[26] What became known as the North–South debate was fed by three very different kinds of arguments about the injustice of inequalities among states.

Underpinning one case for redistribution among states was the argument of historical injustice. Colonialism, it was argued (particularly in Africa), had exploited and stripped resources from developing countries: justice demanded redress and transfers back of some of the wealth and technology accrued through exploitation.[27] A different emphasis ran through arguments coming predominantly from Latin America, where underdevelopment was blamed on the structure of the world economy, which integrated countries in such a way as to keep them on the periphery—an underclass of primary producers.[28] Finally, a more theoretical argument for redistribution emerged in the wake of John Rawls's 1973 work *A Theory of Justice*, which set out a robustly egalitarian standard of justice for politics within the borders of the state.[29] Inequalities, it was argued, are only acceptable in so far as 'they are to be to the greatest benefit of the least advantaged members of society'. Writing in the early 1980s, Charles Beitz extended these principles to international society, arguing for transfers from rich to poor states on the grounds that interdependence has bound them into a community analogous to domestic political society.[30] His argument reflects a style of argument and standard of justice which ran through many writings at the time.[31]

All three accounts of international inequality in the 1970s—neo-colonialism, dependency theory, and theories of distributive justice—put inequality at the top of the agenda of world politics and posited that the evolution and continuation of international order depended upon a greater degree of 'justice'. This transformed universal organizations into fora of the North–South debate. The *Zeitgeist* was summed up in the Brandt Report, an independent investigation of development by internationally renowned politicians and intellectuals, which recommended an immediate 'large-scale transfer of resources to developing countries', an international energy strategy, a global food programme, and a start on some major reforms in the international economic system.[32] Yet by the time the report was published, the international community had changed dramatically.

Inequality and neo-liberalism in the 1980s

In the early 1980s new leaders had come to power in the United States, the United Kingdom, and Germany, each bringing a new harder rhetoric to both domestic and international politics. Ronald

Reagan, Margaret Thatcher, and Helmut Kohl soon made the Brandt Report look anachronistic. Inequality was pushed off both domestic and international agendas, replaced by theories of self-help, and the notion that individuals and poorer countries should take responsibility for their own choices and actions. Underdevelopment in the South was soon being explained in terms of the policy failures within each of the developing countries, which were highlighted by the debt crisis. The demands of 'justice' would be met, argued these new 'neo-liberals', by ensuring that processes of distribution and economic exchange were just,[33] and this meant ensuring the unfettered operation of free markets wherever possible. In political rhetoric the argument was framed as ensuring that corrupt regimes would be disciplined by the market. At the same time, a concerted attempt was made to curtail and discipline international organizations which had become fora for the debate about inter-state inequality.[34]

The consequences of the shift in ideology were several. In the first place, aid flows to developing countries were cut back as the rationale for such redistribution was rewritten. In the second place, assistance offered to developing countries became conditional on adherence to policy prescriptions largely being written in Washington.[35] Overall, the impetus was to cut back the role of the state, reducing the extent to which governments would or could actively play a role in redistribution (whether with positive or negative results) within the economy. In many countries this period of liberalization was accompanied by a marked exacerbation of inequality (as charted by Stewart and Berry in Chapter 6 of this volume). Finally, the shift in ideology led to an overhauling of theories of development.

Neo-liberals had little truck with the argument that developing countries faced structural constraint. They pointed to the newly industrializing countries (NICs) of East Asia (such as Japan, Singapore, Hong Kong, Korea, and Taiwan), arguing that these economies succeeded in spite of the alleged structural bias of the world economy, because governments had made good policy choices, and relied on markets. The shift in the argument about inequality from 'structural barriers' to 'policy choices' removed inequality from the realm of international politics and cast it instead into that of economics and public administration. Yet, as we will see below, not only is there still debate about why the NICs flourished,[36] there are

also still strong barriers in the world economy which inhibit growth
and welfare in developing countries.

'Just' and 'unjust' inequalities in the 1990s

Today justice-claims based on the inequality of resources among
states have all but disappeared. Dependency and structuralist explanations and prescriptions have not been revived. The liberal
arguments for redistribution have been significantly watered down.
John Rawls himself, in turning to apply his argument for redistribution to the international system, seems to have been influenced
by the subsequent anti-egalitarian spirit of the 1980s and early
1990s.[37] In his application of justice to world politics, we find no
demand for distributive justice. In his *Law of Peoples* Rawls stops
short at the suggestion of mutual assistance in times of famine and
drought and ensuring, if feasible, that in 'all reasonably developed
liberal societies' people's basic needs are met. This statement reflects a much wider watering-down of concerns about inequality
among states in world politics.

By the 1990s just one kind of inequality remained prominent on
political agendas (both domestic and international), and that was,
and still is, poverty. Previously 'equality' was promulgated as the
goal of a just society, and this required attempts to reduce resource
differences between individuals or groups of people. Now, 'poverty
alleviation' has replaced it and that requires reducing or eliminating
some supposedly absolute standard of deprivation.[38] Practically,
this shift is seen in policy prescriptions which require governments
to remove across-the-board benefits (be they pensions or food
subsidies) and to 'target' welfare measures towards the poorest.
This shift is highlighted in two other chapters of this volume
(Deacon and Stewart and Berry). As Stewart and Berry note, the
problems with targeting are not just practical (that the poor are
often not in a position to access the benefits), but also political: if
only the poorest benefit from state welfare policies, there is a
danger that the benefits can subsequently be cut back with no
strong political protest, since the poor usually have the weakest
capacity to influence policy.

A further element of the increased attention to poverty is a new
categorization of the South. In the 1980s, institutions dealing with

the debt crisis began to distinguish among different categories of poor and developing countries, using descriptions such as 'middle-income', 'lower-middle-income', 'low-income', and 'highly indebted'. Most institutions have now agreed that they ought to focus their most concessional lending or assistance on the poorest countries, as pronounced by the G7 at their London Summit in July 1991.[39] Indeed, since 1996, the International Monetary Fund and the World Bank have put together a debt relief initiative for the poorest and most highly indebted poor countries, offering relief on portions of debt.[40]

Finally, in the early 1990s the new focus on poverty alleviation has been accompanied by a desire to reduce the role of the state, including its role in delivering aid and administering development projects. In practice, this aim was partly achieved by an increased reliance on non-governmental organizations (NGOs). In the late 1990s, however, the multilateral institutions and their powerful industrialized country members have found that the market-oriented development blueprint has wrongly neglected the role of institutions. As a result, conditional lending today reflects an aspiration to 'strengthen and modernize' the state and its capacity to deliver.[41] However, the renewed focus on institutions and the state has carefully proscribed any revival of arguments for strongly redistributive taxation and fiscal policies. Similarly, at the international level, there is continuing rhetoric against inter-state redistribution and a dampening of all arguments for greater equality among states. Yet this discourse hides continuing deep and deepening inequalities in the world political and economic systems.

Remaining barriers to equal treatment

The rules governing the world economy were a source of major discontent to developing countries seeking to overcome inequality in the 1960s and 1970s. In the 1990s it may still be said that developing and industrialized countries do not compete on a level playing field. This reality contrasts sharply with the theory that globalization will open up new opportunities for countries who make good policy choices. Developing countries have been persuaded to liberalize and deregulate their economies so as more fully to exploit opportunities in a global world economy. Yet, if we take international trade rules as an example, a study of the rules demonstrates that the opportunities developing countries might exploit are far from equal.

The Uruguay Round of trade negotiations promised to liberalize rules for all countries, yet the negotiations have left intact a system which is biased against developing countries. Overall, developing countries are still disproportionately affected by tariff barriers. It has been estimated (in 1997) that developing countries face tariffs 10 per cent higher than the global average, and the least-developed countries face tariffs 30 per cent higher (because tariffs remain so high on textiles, leather, and agricultural commodities). Whilst the Uruguay Round achieved substantial tariff reductions, these reductions have been much more advantageous to the industrialized countries (reducing tariffs on 45 per cent of what they export) than developing countries (for whom the reduced tariffs affect only 20–25 per cent of their exports).[42]

The clearest examples of unequal treatment relate to textiles, clothing, and agriculture. Since 1961 textiles and clothing have been the subject of restrictive quotas (set out in the Multi-fibre Arrangement) beyond which high tariffs apply. These goods account for a large proportion of what developing countries produce: for Bangladesh and Sri Lanka it represents half their export earnings, for Sub-Saharan Africa 24 per cent of exports, for Asia 14 per cent of exports, and for Latin America and the Caribbean 8 per cent of exports. The Uruguay Round agreement will phase out the quotas over a ten-year period and reduce tariffs, but only to an average tariff of 12 per cent—which is three times the average levied on industrial country imports.

Agriculture is the other great unbalancer of the playing field of international trade. The United States and the European Union dominate world markets in agriculture and each gives heavy subsidies to their own farmers. It has been estimated that these subsidies amount to roughly half the value of agricultural output in these economies.[43] This protectionism is having three devastating effects on developing countries: first, it keeps world prices for agricultural commodities artificially low; second, it excludes developing countries from markets in the main industrialized countries; and finally, it exposes developing country producers to 'dumping' of (artificially) cheap produce from industrialized countries.

Developing countries are also still affected by tariff escalation. In other words, tariffs are still higher on processed goods than on raw materials. For example, for leather, oilseeds, textile fibres, and beverages, tariffs continue to be 8–26 per cent higher on the final product than on the underlying raw materials. The result is that developing countries cannot afford to 'move up the ladder' of industrialization. Rather, they become locked into producing primary commodities. The problem with producing primary commodities is that world markets for them are volatile, their prices are declining, and world demand for them does not increase significantly as income increases or as their price decreases.

A third hindrance to developing country exports has been the use of non-tariff barriers by industrialized countries. Quotas, 'voluntary' export restraints, and anti-dumping measures all curtail the export opportunities of developing countries. Anti-dumping measures theoretically protect countries from exporters who sell below cost to drive competitors out of business and then exploit their larger market shares. However, a recent OECD study found that in 90 per cent of US and EU anti-dumping actions there was little or no threat to national industries.[44] The results of the Uruguay Round should effect a decrease in the use of anti-dumping measures. But there is a dangerous trend that must be reversed: it has been estimated that between 1989 and 1994 the use of anti-dumping actions and penalties more than doubled in number.[45]

Finally, a core part of the 1970s agenda for a fairer world economy was for a greater transfer of technology from the industrialized North to the developing South. In the 1970s this was expressed in terms of multinationals' duties to transfer technology at the same time as they introduced production and investment into a developing country. Yet here there has been no easing of transfer to developing countries, who claim that until they have access to technology they cannot hope to compete in a global economy in which profits are skewed sharply towards high-technology products. The Uruguay Round introduced a regime of intellectual property rights which extends the life of patents and other intellectual property rights and enforces protection of them. In this way technology transfer has, if anything, been made all the more difficult and costly for developing countries. Furthermore, in respect of more general rules governing investment, negotiations on a Multilateral Agreement on Investment have proceeded among OECD

countries without the formal participation or representation of
developing countries.[46]

Overall, the fact that developing countries still face greater trade
barriers than industrialized countries poses problems for the neo-
liberal normative framework which has prevailed in the 1980s and
1990s. Neo-liberals rejected the notion that unequal outcomes are
unjust in the world economy, on the assumption that equality of
opportunity exists. Yet the evidence shows that equal opportunity
in the international economy does not exist. Furthermore, the fact
that so many barriers remain highlights the costs to developing
countries of their political inequality in international relations.
Most developing countries have not participated in setting the rules
of global trade or investment or the like, and in various groupings
they suffer from unevenly and unfairly drawn regulations. Furthermore, as will be argued in the next section, as globalization proceeds apace, both political and economic inequality are likely to
increase.

IV. THE IMPACT OF GLOBALIZATION

In the market-based economists' account, globalization opens up
opportunities and advantages to all states. Yet the existing evidence
highlights that the process is a much more uneven one than the
theory suggests. Globalization describes dramatic changes in the
transactions and interactions taking place among states, firms, and
peoples in the world. It describes both an increase in cross-border
transactions of goods and services, and an increase in the flow of
images, ideas, people, and behaviour. Economistic views treat the
process as technologically driven. Yet globalization has also been
driven by deregulation, privatization, and political choices made by
governments. Whilst flows of goods, services, people, and capital
are increasing, they are, at the same time, often barred or blocked
by regulations. In other words, the impact of globalization has been
strongly shaped by those with the power to make and enforce the
rules of the global economy.[47] At the same time, however, to create
rules which are enforceable, rule-makers are increasingly having
to rely upon a wider group of actors and a wider range of institutions. This creates a real tension between increases in inequality
caused by processes of globalization and the necessary increase in

participation required to regulate the processes. In this section, the key elements of globalization are analysed to highlight these tensions.

A first core aspect of globalization is technological change, which has transformed the possibilities of global economic activity. Firms can now organize production globally using new means of communication, and new, more flexible techniques of production. This has led to what Charles Oman (in Chapter 2) calls 'global localization'. Increasingly, multinational firms (MNCs) produce goods as close to their markets as they can. This means they have a presence in several regions or areas of the world economy. The political implications are manifold and, importantly for our purposes, they do not all point to deregulation and an opening up of possibilities. Rather, those who benefited first (and most) from technological change have also been very quick in seeking to protect their position, pushing for international rules which may well hinder others wishing to emulate them.

Where once MNCs were a force for liberalization and the opening up of trade barriers (so that they could trade into regions and countries), today, having situated themselves within regions or countries in which they wish to trade, they no longer need to press for the opening up of borders. Life inside a 'fortress' Europe or NAFTA might be quite comfortable. Furthermore, rather than diffusing technological advances worldwide, leading companies have pushed for increasingly strict international rules on intellectual property.[48] Competition today is not just for a competitive edge in technological or economic terms. Rather, firms also compete for control of the rules of the game at international and at regional levels. Yet, for the rules to have an impact they must be enforced by governments not all of whom firms can influence. Globalization is cementing old economic inequalities between 'haves' and 'have-nots'—not just in the sense of having technology or not, but also in the sense of having the capacity to make rules or not. Yet at the same time, globalization is creating a new set of requirements for regulation and enforcement which requires the cooperation of the so-called 'have-nots'. This cannot be achieved through the hierarchical arrangements of old.

International trade is another aspect of globalization which has had highly uneven consequences. While there is a dispute as to how much world trade has increased,[49] there is clear evidence that high levels of trade in today's world economy are strongly concentrated in trade among industrialized countries.[50] For this reason, although globalization suggests that world markets are opened up and the flow of transactions among all states is thereby increased, in fact we find that the effects of change are vastly unequal. Although many developing countries have liberalized their trade policies, some are being marginalized. In Chapter 6, Stewart and Berry point out that exporters of primary commodities, minerals, and manufacturing goods have each fared differently. Yet more generally, they adduce evidence that where liberalization (which has often been trade-led) has been undertaken, inequality within countries has grown.[51] We are forced to consider the terms on which trade liberalization has proceeded and here Deacon (in Chapter 8) points to the critical role of institutions such as the IMF, the World Bank, and the OECD, in which poorer countries have little voice. In brief, trade liberalization has cemented inequalities among states. Yet it has also resulted in increasing demands for regulation, for example from industrialized countries who argue that where countries flout international labour, environmental, and safety standards, they present 'unfair' competition. The demand for an 'even playing field' requires greater regulation and enforcement at a global level.

Yet greater demands for regulation do not translate solely into efforts to strengthen global institutions. On the contrary, globalization has been accompanied by a surge of new regional and bilateral arrangements.[52] In some ways regionalism cements the old hierarchy, yet in others it loosens it. In theory, regional organizations offer small and less powerful states a way to unite and exercise more influence in setting trade rules and in enjoying open access to a wider market than their national market.[53] Furthermore, the prospect of regional trade arrangements and integration offers a useful lever to governments who need to dismantle powerful domestic vested interests: new policies offer both the carrot of wider markets and the stick of stiffer regional competition.[54] In these ways, the 'new regionalism' could well be seen as an even and powerful way of opening up trade. However, increasing regionalism may also cement inequalities by marginalizing less powerful states—for example, by excluding developing countries from the 'fortresses' mentioned above. Furthermore, regional institutions can provide powerful states with excuses for not using global institutions: they might, for example, choose to take their disputes to the forum in which they feel they have the most power to ensure a particular outcome.[55]

International finance is a further arena of globalization which has powerful implications for traditional notions of hierarchy and order. Technology and US policies in the post-war period[56] have unleashed powerful forces in financial markets, as international banks and investment funds expand their global operations. Today financial markets and investment funds shift capital so fast that governments in both industrialized and developing countries fear capital flight and speculative attacks by the market. In some ways this has a levelling effect: all governments live in some fear of the markets and all are susceptible to a speculative attack. Yet the tendency of capital markets to punish governments occurs in an uneven way which highlights both weaknesses and vulnerabilities in developing countries as well as in the institutions upon which they rely for assistance.[57] Industrialized countries in the more global economy can borrow to ease the monetary costs of fiscal expansion[58] and the evidence suggests that this does not necessarily heighten the risks of capital flight and market fear of default.[59] By contrast, in developing countries, high public debt, and indeed even high private debt (as in Mexico in 1994, and South Korea in 1997) can trigger markets into withdrawing, leading to a run on both investment and the currency.[60] Yet paradoxically, the threat of this kind of crisis means that previously less significant countries can now pose a systemic threat to international economic stability: the tail can now wag the dog. So whilst financial globalization reinforces old inequalities, at the same time it creates new challenges and crises which the old unequal order cannot deal with particularly effectively.

Finally, globalization has included the spread of policy ideas. Global economic order is not founded on state power and rules alone, but also on sets of policy ideas and beliefs. These are promulgated both formally through international organizations (see below and Chapter 8), and informally through networks of education and research which 'globalize' particular orthodoxies. Both the 1980s and the 1990s provide powerful examples of this. In the 1980s 'structural adjustment' was urged on developing countries the world over,[61] and in the 1990s a similar set of liberalizing policies were urged on the former Eastern bloc countries—the so-called 'transition economies'. The impact of these policy changes was mostly to increase income inequality within these countries.[62] In the late 1990s, there have been some changes in the prescriptions being written in Washington. The reform of the economy is now being followed up with second and third phases of reform, described as 'modernizing the state'. Good governance, transparency, accountability, and participation are now being advocated by the international financial institutions.[63] In theory, of course, if these ideas were applied to these institutions themselves, the result might well be a more egalitarian and participatory international economic order.[64] In reality, however, their application is being strictly limited.[65] Nevertheless, for the international institutions the new agenda reflects a recognition that to succeed, their reforms need greater commitment and participation by recipient governments—a top-down model of incentives and leverage exercised from Washington will not succeed.

Globalization, it has been argued, is changing both competition among, and policies within, countries. It is also affecting the nature of actors and institutions in world politics. In a system created for 51 countries, 193 states now enjoy a sovereignty which is becoming ever more diffuse. Control over policy in certain areas is increasingly passing either 'down' to local bodies, or 'up' to regional or international bodies.[66] Alongside states, new actors are striding the stage of world politics: the 'stateless' multinational in the 'borderless world';[67] national groups without a state (such as Quebec, Scotland, Chiapas, Palestine, and Chechnya); rebels and terrorists enjoying a greater capacity to publicize themselves and gain an audience.[68] These new actors cut across the traditional structures of state sovereignty and inter-state order, challenging governments and demanding access to the inter-state organizations charged with global governance.[69] Indeed, the very principles on which sovereignty is recognized and respected are changing, so that, in the words of an international law scholar, we are faced with an 'impossibility of reconciling the notions of sovereignty which prevailed even as recently as fifty or sixty years ago with the contemporary state of global interdependence'.[70] As constructivist theorists of international relations remind us, globalization is transforming our understanding of sovereignty as well as core identities in international relations.[71]

Particularly noticeable in their demands for a status in international organizations are the non-governmental organizations (NGOs) claiming a transnational or sub-national constituency.[72] NGOs have carved out a role for themselves in many multilateral organizations,[73] not to mention taken a lead in international relations on some issues such as the environment.[74] It is now the case that NGOs can participate within some international fora, such as the World Bank's Panel of Inspection hearings on environmental issues.[75] Yet, before heralding the rise of a 'transnational civil society', the limitations on NGO claims to greater legitimacy or accountability must also be recognized.[76]

Traditional conceptions of order not only fail to take new actors into account in portraying international order, they also fail to explain how and why these actors have emerged onto the stage of world politics. It is assumed that actors change as the configuration of power changes. Yet the new actors and the changing authority of old actors also reflects a shift in beliefs and understandings about representation and legitimacy, as we will see in the following section.

In summary, globalization is challenging the traditional state-centred and hierarchical world order.[77] Yet few of the forces analysed here have altered the structure of institutions of management. Rather, technological change, trade liberalization, regionalism, the globalization of international finance, and policy ideas are all proceeding within the rules and institutions which reflect the traditional hierarchy of power. However, that hierarchical order is becoming less effective as new 'global' issues, such as environmental problems, trade rules, and concerns about transnational crime or movements of people, demand greater levels of cooperation among states.

V. INTERNATIONAL INSTITUTIONS AND THE MANAGEMENT OF ORDER

The above discussion of globalization underlines that inequality is not just about starting positions and outcomes in international relations. It is also, crucially, about 'meta-power' or who gets to make the rules within which international relations proceed and who decides how and where to enforce them. During the 1970s

North–South debate, the South pressed for more of a say in the rules governing international economic order and, for the most part, they failed. The rules governing trade, investment, finance, and monetary order continued largely to be written by Northern countries. Today, this top-down approach to making and enforcing rules is being questioned even within the North. The question being posed is: what makes international institutions effective?

In international relations various theories compete to account for the strengths and limitations of global institutions, and these are analysed below before examining specific areas in which globalization is creating a need for deeper rules—such as in trade, banking, and security. In these areas effective international rules require powerful compliance by states. In theory, this might be achieved either through coercion and greater inequality, or through more equal participation and accountability. Yet in practice, globalization has created new limitations to achieving compliance through coercion, and at the same time there is little evidence that international organizations are being opened up to greater degrees of participation and accountability.

In the first section of this chapter we saw that traditional views of international order present inequality as a positive ordering element in the international system: an order created and maintained through hierarchy or hegemony, relegating the role of international institutions to the sidelines. This view re-emerged triumphantly in the 1930s as a response to the perceived failure of the League of Nations as an international organization.[78] From the realist point of view, institutions are a way for powerful states to reduce or share the costs of maintaining a particular order. The effectiveness of a multilateral organization will depend primarily upon the relative power and commitment of its more powerful members.[79]

In opposition to this view, scholars have argued that international organizations reflect shared purposes and interests, not just of states, but of peoples, and of interest groups within states.[80] In the early post-war years, the emerging European Economic Community was proffered as one such case.[81] The continuation of international institutions in spite of a decline in US hegemony in the 1970s was later offered as another.[82] On this view, multilateral institutions exist to promulgate rules which reflect shared aims, and to ensure that rules are enforced through the participation and mutually recognized interests of all parties. The effectiveness of an institution, in this view, depends on the commitment of all members to the institution's aims, and their willingness to participate in the enforcement of them.

Between these two views, one can situate much of the work done by scholars examining specific international organizations. Effectiveness, in practice, seems to depend upon an institution's capacity to fulfil a particular role,[83] to be adaptive,[84] and to reflect adequately the range of stakes in the institution. Recent work by Abbott and Snidal, for example, examines how multilateral institutions deal with international conflicts and demonstrates that because international organizations can centralize policy and can act with some degree of autonomy, they can achieve goals which states could not accomplish on an individual basis.[85] Taking this point further, Young argues that any such autonomy requires a basic equality among members: 'the more symmetrical the distribution of power, the harder it is to establish institutional arrangements initially but the more effective they are once formed' (since powerful states—or groups of states—will not be able simply to flout the rules of the institution).[86] All authors agree that the autonomy of any international institution is strictly limited by member states and by the need to require compliance from them. Studies of specific institutions, however, highlight trade-offs between hierarchy and effectiveness that are neglected in either the realist or institutionalist analyses of institutions.

Effective institutions in a global post-Cold War order

For many policy-makers and academics alike, the end of the Cold War held out possibilities for a new role and contribution of international organizations, such as the United Nations, NATO, the European Union, the WTO, and the IMF, in forging a new world order.[87] Strengthening and broadening international organizations seemed a natural correlate to a new raft of foreign policy goals which, in the case of the United States, included democracy, good governance, economic stability, and growth, in regions as diverse as Latin America, Africa, the Middle East, East Asia, Russia, and the former USSR. Many of these broad goals were shared with other countries and, taken together, the new post-Cold War aims implied the need for costly economic and security interventions. Stronger institutions would be an essential way not just of sharing the burden but also of ensuring that the new mandate was not seen as a new imperialism, but rather as a set of universally attractive norms. From a more realist perspective, stronger institutions were perceived as a necessary way to ensure continuing US predominance, as reflected in a paper written for the Bush Administration in 1992, which argued that the new order would need to account 'sufficiently for the interests of the [other] advanced industrial nations to discourage them from challenging our leadership', while also maintaining a military dominance capable of 'deterring potential competitors from even aspiring to a larger regional or global role'.[88]

Yet the initial post-Cold War euphoria was soon quashed. In its place emerged an impasse in respect of international organizations. Within the United States, a furious debate has taken place, catalysed by a Congressional majority wanting to stamp a unilateral agenda on the above-mentioned organizations, including: reducing US contributions and continuing to refuse to pay those owed to the United Nations; increasing US control over their structure and size; and at the same time dictating what the institutions should be doing and where.[89] Meanwhile, in the rest of the world there has been a curious acquiescence to US demands while at the same time many countries have increasingly sought to fulfil security and economic objectives through regional rather than multilateral organizations.[90] Yet this leaves a significant problem for world order. Globalization is posing challenges which require increasingly effective international organizations, as authors in this volume substantiate in the fields of transnational investment and production (Oman); security (Hurrell); the environment (Redclift and Sage); social policy (Deacon); and law (both Kingsbury and Chinkin). The remainder of the chapter details the arguements in respect of trade rules, capital markets, and the role of the Security Council.

International trade

Until 1992, international trade was regulated globally under the auspices of the GATT, a very loose institution whose rules and procedures were developed in an ad hoc way.[91] Within this arrangement there was a clear inequality of power, with the 'Quad' (the

US, the European Union, Japan, and Canada) able to work behind the scenes to shape most decisions. The results were trading rules which had a very uneven impact on countries, which has already been discussed. Importantly, these results reflected a process which magnified inequalities among members. The GATT operated as a club with a core membership empowered to decide who to admit and on what conditions.[92] Several attempts were made to change the structure of representation and decision-making within the GATT: developing countries tried unsuccessfully in the 1970s to create a powerful Executive Committee within which they would have a voice; and in the other direction, the United States tried to push the idea of an IMF-style Executive Board with weighted voting during the Uruguay Round.

Yet the unequal 'club' approach of the GATT has become unsatisfactory as globalization, or more specifically trade liberalization, proceeds apace. Trading nations both large and small require an institution which can regulate in areas such as non-tariff barriers and domestic practices, and which can deal with a raft of new issues, including services, intellectual property, trade-related investment, and labour and environmental standards.[93] For these reasons, even the United States needs a multilateral organization, for its strongest regional arrangement—NAFTA—accounts for less than a third of its trade.[94] In a globalizing world, compliance with an international trade regime requires a high level of participation, commitment, and confidence from all members. Hence, the decentralized framework of the GATT was inadequate: the resolution of disputes, for example, was held hostage to the consensus required of panels making decisions. Yet the replacement for the GATT, the World Trade Organization (WTO), has not resolved the problem of participation and compliance.[95]

The new organization has a structure and enforcement mechanisms which transform it into a more powerful international institution. The WTO is now the administrator of all multilateral trade agreements, an overseer of national trade policies, and has a disputes settlement procedure which, unlike that of the GATT, can make rulings on disputes which are automatically accepted by the organization unless there is a consensus *against* acceptance. At least in theory, developing countries are better served by this step towards more legalized and institutionalized procedures, since it restrains the capacity of large trading countries to veto Panel decisions. Certainly, developing countries seem already to be using the new WTO processes more: whereas the GATT mechanisms tended to be used mainly by the 'Quad', about half the requests before the WTO in mid-1996 were from developing countries.[96]

However, for the WTO to be effective in upholding an international rule of law, it needs compliance from its largest and most powerful member. Yet the United States had the worst record of compliance with GATT panel judgements of any country,[97] and further 'retreated from multilateralism' in the 1980s, adopting policies which were 'increasingly aggressive and bilateral'.[98] The trend towards unilateral trade policy was reflected in Congress during its debate on ratifying the Uruguay Round results (and the new WTO),[99] and yet more obviously since then, as the US has boycotted the WTO dispute settlement proceedings triggered by the Helms–Burton Act's penalties on other countries' dealings with Cuba.[100] One might also mention other US extra-territorial sanctions legislation, such as the Iran–Libya Sanctions Act. Each of these actions of the United States detracts from an international rule-based system.

The World Trade Organization has been created in recognition of the need for powerful rule-based institutions to facilitate global trade. Yet alongside the WTO, unilateral and bilateral actions are continuing, such as those of the US. This means that the credibility and effectiveness of the new system is being constantly undermined by assertions of the old power-political hierarchy as the basis for order in international trade. Yet that power-political order, which had been so clearly reflected in the GATT, simply cannot deal effectively with the new issues mentioned above. The tension is a simple one. Although a strong rule-based international regime is increasingly in the interests of the US in a global world economy, it remains to be seen whether the US is prepared to give up the rights of its special position as *primus inter pares* in order to reap the benefits of a multilateral regime.

The international financial system

The international financial and monetary system has changed dramatically with the emergence of ever-larger global capital markets, investment funds, and floating exchange rates. From the end of the

Second World War, the rules of the system were very much set by the United States, conferring at various stages with Western Europe and Japan.[101] The fora within which decisions have been taken include the G7, the Bank for International Settlements (BIS), and the IMF (within which the United States is the largest voter and shareholder). During the 1970s developing countries made repeated attempts to increase their voice on the international financial and monetary system, with very limited success.[102] However, over the past two decades, the success and ongoing stability of the international financial and monetary system has come to rely much more heavily on the behaviour of less powerful countries, who have traditionally been marginalized.

Recent crises show the vulnerabilities of an increasingly globalized international financial and monetary system. At the end of 1994, the Mexican currency collapsed, sending reverberations through the system which have been dwarfed by the more recent crises in East Asia 1996–7 and in Russian 1998. Overall, all actors now agree that international financial and monetary stability requires a much deeper and broader level of cooperation than ever before—in order to deal with issues of capital account liberalization, financial sector reforms, exchange rate policies, and sound banking regulation and supervision. The costs of inadequate cooperation are clear. When financial crisis erupted in East Asia, the International Monetary Fund provided some US$36 billion in financial support, and mobilized a further US$77 billion from multilateral and bilateral sources. In Russia, the IMF provided US$11.2 billion in financial support and likewise coordinated an even larger relief package. The policies associated with both 'resources' have subsequently been heavily criticized.[103]

Yet even aside from the question of resources, the solution to the crisis is proving extremely difficult to implement. The Fund is attempting to require 'forceful, far-reaching structural reforms' from the countries in crisis. The aim is to correct weaknesses in their financial systems and 'to remove features of the economy that had become impediments to growth (such as monopolies, trade barriers and nontransparent corporate practices)'.[104] These conditions go far beyond those imposed on debtors in the 1980s. They drive deep into a country's domestic economic policies.

Politically, the depth of conditions being required of East Asian countries has caused many commentators to ask fundamental

questions about how legitimate it is for the IMF to do this. For
example, Marty Feldstein recently wrote in *Foreign Affairs*: 'The
legitimate political institutions of the country should determine the
nation's economic structure and the nature of its institutions. A
nation's desperate need for short-term financial help does not give
the IMF the moral right to substitute its technical judgements for
the outcomes of the nation's political process'.[105]

The issue here is a difficult one. The IMF is charged with the role
of safeguarding the stability of the international monetary system.
Yet in a globalizing world, this is difficult to do without incursion
into the domestic policies of countries. An alternative approach is
to accept that stability requires deeper international standards
and to ask how the Fund might bolster its legitimacy in entering
into this new terrain. The answer here surely lies in rethinking the
representation and participation of those whose compliance is
required—so as to lessen the sense of unequal 'imposition' or the
impingement on democratic processes.[106] Already the IMF has
made some effort to open up its way of working, such as by
publishing an increasing number of background papers to bilateral
negotiations, by rethinking the role 'external evaluation' might play
in its work, and by opening up the issue of 'governance' in its
dealings with member countries. These changes, however, do not
alter the representation and ownership structure which underpins
the Board of the organization, and as a result do not imbue the
organization with any greater degree of legitimacy in propounding
'deep' interventions and reforms such as we have seen in East Asia.

The IMF has not been the only institution in the firing line over
East Asia. Early on in the crisis, ideas flourished about the possibilities of an Asian institution which would replace the IMF and/or the
BIS, the latter of which was drawn in alongside the IMF to deal
with prudential regulation and supervision.[107] Prior to 1996 the BIS
had comprised only the G10 countries, yet it had operated as an
international lender of last resort. In September 1996, it opened its
doors to Brazil, China, Hong Kong, India, Mexico, Russia, Saudi
Arabia, Singapore, and South Korea. However, this has not affected the way policy is formulated or applied. The real work of the
BIS is still done by the Supervisory Committee, which comprises
just the G10 Central Bankers. Similarly, although the G7 can claim
to have opened up to permit the Managing Director of the IMF and
the President of the World Bank to attend its summits as observers,

and indeed to meet with Russia in a G8 format, these are extremely modest changes that do not redress the legitimacy concerns highlighted in the recent East Asian crisis.

International financial institutions have been undergoing some changes in the 1990s. However, for the most part, these have been refinements on 'work as usual' in these organizations. It is doubtless useful for the institutions to open themselves up to greater scrutiny and wider membership. However, decision-making processes have remained the same and rely on a hierarchy which reflects fifty-year-old inequalities. Yet the evidence suggests that effectively to manage a globalizing world economy, these institutions need-greater legitimacy, and a greater degree of representation and participation. This requires change of a more fundamental kind, which is unlikely given the persistence of the old hierarchy.

The United Nations Security Council

Finally, the United Nations Security Council has sprung into action since the end of the Cold War.[108] Yet its membership today seems anachronistic with respect to the work it is trying to do. The victors of the Second World War took permanent seats on the Council in an attempt to institute a system of collective security managed by the Great Powers. Those original five members still have permanent seats, and their concurring vote is still required for the Council to pass any substantive resolution. This gives each of China, Russia, the US, France, and the UK a veto over Security Council decisions. The other ten seats on the Council rotate around different groupings of countries. Like other institutions this chapter has analysed, the Security Council institutionalized a hierarchy of states which existed at the end of the Second World War. Yet the Council remained virtually inactive during the Cold War, marginalized by balance-of-power politics between the super-powers. This has now changed.

Between August 1990 and May 1995 the Council adopted 325 resolutions (as well as some 82 'Presidential statements'), giving an average of 80 resolutions per year. This compares with an average of 14 per year over the preceding 44 years. The new high level of Security Council activity brings prominently to the fore several issues of governance. Developing countries have been quick to point out that the Council's new level of activity involves intervention in an unprecedented way into the affairs of (almost exclusively) developing countries. This has focused attention sharply on the core inequality of the institution. The power inequality was amply demonstrated in the 1980s, when the United States bullied the UN as a whole into de facto altering its Constitution so as to give the US a veto over critical budget decisions.[109]

In the 1990s, some very modest changes have occurred in the United Nations Security Council.[110] Beyond this, many members have accepted that the membership of the Council should be enlarged, to include at least Germany and Japan as permanent members and probably also representatives of developing countries.[111] However, there is great unwillingness on the part of the existing permanent members to permit any dilution of their rights in the institution. Leading the opposition but not alone is the United States.[112] The Republican majority in Congress expressed its implacable opposition to the United Nations in its Contract with America in 1994,[113] and it is unlikely to permit the payment to the United Nations of any of the $1 billion in dues that the US currently owes. There is, as John Gerard Ruggie suggests to us, 'a political time warp in the US Congress'.[114] However, the time warp may well extend to other members, for amid wider paralysis there is a broader impasse within the Security Council whereby virtually no one is prepared to relinquish the privileges of their place in the time-bound hierarchy of power that the institution reflects.

VI. CONCLUDING THOUGHTS

Inequality and effective institutions in a globalizing world

Although the traditional view of international order placed great weight on the hierarchy of power, when modern international institutions were created fifty years ago it was appreciated that a balance had to be struck between 'efficiency' wrought through great-power management and 'legitimacy', which was necessary to ensure the cooperation of the rest. The latter required that some basic notion of 'equality' be respected. Within the United Nations the balance was felt to be struck by a General Assembly in which all states would have an equal vote, and a Security Council in which the most powerful states would have a veto. Even in the IMF, where most voting power was apportioned according to economic power, 'basic votes' were apportioned to symbolize the equality of member states. As Joseph Gold explains, 'the authors of the plans for the Fund and the negotiators felt that the bold step of weighting the voting power . . . should be combined with the political considera- tion of the traditional equality of states in international law. The basic votes were to serve the function of recognizing the doctrine of the equality of states'.[115] What theorists have referred to as the 'trappings of universality'[116] have been vital to the place and role of international organizations.

In the 1990s, for international institutions to be effective they will have to reflect more than ever a wide range of members and to embody commitments that all members are prepared to implement. On some issues, this has already been recognized. Although many believed the era of global summitry to be over at the end of the 1970s, in fact the 1990s has seen North–South Summits on issues including: the environment and development (Rio de Janeiro, 1992); population and development (Cairo, 1994); women (Beijing, 1995); and global climate change (Kyoto, 1997). These summits reflect a recognition that effective action in these areas will depend vitally upon commitments from a range of governments—rich, poor, weak, and strong—and that compliance is unlikely to be forthcoming unless parties each have a stake in the final agreement and a clear stake in abiding by it. Yet outside of these summits, in the organizations and institutions which are needed to regulate and facilitate international issues, there is little indication that powerful member states have any intention of altering the hierarchical basis on which order has traditionally been maintained, even though that hierachy will not serve to meet the more complex challenges of order in a globalizing world.

2

Globalization, Regionalization, and Inequality

Charles Oman

I. OVERVIEW

Since the late 1970s, a new wave of globalization has been facilitated and stimulated by market deregulation and economic policy liberalization, by the new microelectronics-based information and communications technologies, and by the globalization of financial markets. Globalization is driven today, as it was in earlier periods, by the dynamics of inter-firm competition in the leading economies. The principal microeconomic force shaping those dynamics, and driving globalization in the 'real' (non-financial) economy, is the ongoing development, formidable competitive strength, and gradual spread (despite much resistance to that spread) of post-Taylorist 'flexible' approaches to the organization of production within and between firms—just as in the 1950s and 1960s globalization was driven by the then ongoing development, competitive superiority, and rapid international diffusion of Taylorist or 'scientific management' approaches to the organization of production.

The current wave of globalization is accompanied by a crisis in Taylorist organizations in the leading economies—organizations which still account for the majority of output and employment in those economies. That crisis, much more than globalization per se, is a central cause of the 'structural' labour-market problems that now plague Europe and the United States, which many blame on 'globalization'. Financial globalization, much more than globalization in the real economy, is in turn primarily responsible for the

The author writes here in his personal capacity.

perceived weakening of national governments' ability to assert their policy autonomy vis-à-vis the global market, i.e. the weakening of national economic policy sovereignty, which is also widely blamed on globalization.

Globalization today is accompanied by growing inequality, both within and between countries, and by a threat of exclusion faced by many people. Amplified by the crisis of Taylorism, that growing inequality is visible in the United States in the stagnation or decline in the real wages of many workers (hence the growing number of 'working poor') along with growing job insecurity and income disparities in that country—the end of the 'American dream' for many Americans. In Europe the problem, above all, is high levels of 'structural' unemployment, especially long-term unemployment, and the virtual demise of the 'welfare state'.[1] In both the United States and Europe, a further result has been to look for scapegoats, and to blame 'globalization' and imports, if not migratory pressures, from developing countries.

In many developing countries the main threats are exclusion from globalization (except perhaps through emigration) and growing poverty. Even in the more dynamic developing, 'emerging-market', or 'newly industrializing' economies, which are less likely to be excluded from globalization, there are growing internal income disparities, and stagnant or declining real incomes and increased economic insecurity for many people.

II. THE CONCEPTS

'Globalization' can be defined as the growth, or more precisely the accelerated growth, of economic activity that spans politically defined national and regional boundaries. It finds expression in greater cross-border movement (for a given level of domestic activity) of tangible and intangible goods and services, including ownership rights, via trade and investment, and often of people, via migration. It can be, and normally is, facilitated and stimulated by a lowering of impediments to cross-border activity both via technological progress (notably in transportation and communications) and via a lowering of policy or political impediments (e.g. tariffs, investment restrictions, conflicting national standards or regulations on the environment, labour, etc.). But globalization is driven by the actions of individual actors—firms, banks, people—usually in the pursuit of profit, and often spurred by the pressures of competition. Globalization is thus best understood as a micro-economic phenomenon.

'Regionalization' is the movement of two or more economies, i.e. two or more societies, toward greater integration with one another. It can be a de facto process, driven by the same microeconomic forces that drive globalization (as remains predominantly the case in Pacific Asia for example), or it can be a de jure process, driven by political forces, which may in turn be motivated by security, economic, or other objectives. While de jure regionalization can take a variety of forms,[2] what those different institutional arrangements have in common are (1) participating governments' use of extra-economic powers ('powers of state') to lower impediments to intra-regional economic activity, and (2) those governments' movement, to a greater or lesser degree, to pool their policy sovereignty, usually with the aim of collectively strengthening that sovereignty vis-à-vis the global market.

III. THE ECONOMISTS' VIEW: A FOCUS ON TRADE ISSUES

Economists tend to see globalization as enhancing global welfare. While few economists understand globalization as a micro-economic phenomenon (most see it simply as an increase in the level of international activity, especially trade and investment flows, relative to that of domestic activity), they see the process as giving freer rein to the forces of competition within and between countries—forces which all market-based societies need to help channel their resources, and people's energies, into activities where they are likely to be most productive. Some economists also see globalization as increasing the possibilities for efficiency gains through greater international specialization. Despite the cost to individuals, and society, of the inevitable dislocation of people and resources, economists thus tend to see globalization, on balance, as inherently a good thing.

Much of the economic policy debate over globalization and re-gionalization since the mid-1980s has therefore tended to focus not on globalization, but on regionalization. The reason is that economists tend to see de jure regional agreements as good only in so far as they are 'trade-creating', i.e. reinforce globalization by lowering policy impediments to trade between countries and stimulate competition within a region. They see such agreements as bad in so far as they are 'trade-diverting', i.e. work against globalization by favouring trade between countries inside a region at the expense of trade with countries outside the region. Economists thus see regionalization as capable of being either good or bad, with the outcome also more directly dependent on the action of policy-makers.

In addition to the risk of global welfare loss due to trade diversion per se—a loss that could be expected to fall disproportionately on the many developing countries excluded from the major regional groupings—some economists have also pointed out the danger of degenerate regionalism, i.e. an escalation of regionalization that leads, as during the inter-war period, to a fragmentation of the global trading system into a number of relatively closed and hostile regional blocs.[3] Here again, the costs could be expected to fall very heavily, first of all, on weaker countries left outside the main blocs; and one should not ignore the risk, for all countries, that economic frictions among the blocs could eventually escalate into military conflict, of immeasurable cost.

Much of the economic policy debate over globalization and regionalization has therefore focused on two closely related questions: (1) Do the major recent regional integration agreements, notably Europe's Single Market programme and NAFTA, tend, on balance, to be trade-creating or trade-diverting? (2) Do they tend to work for, or against, a more open world trading system? The answers, moreover, remain inconclusive. While the data on actual trade patterns are consistent with a benign (not trade-diverting) interpretation because they show inter-regional trade growing strongly—and the 1993 signing of the Uruguay Round and the 1994 creation of the World Trade Organization should help guard against markedly trade-diverting regional agreements as well—debate over the second question, in particular, remains inconclusive.[4]

Though formally inconclusive, the debate over regionalization is not without importance from both a policy and a political perspective. First, it draws attention to the importance for policy-makers, particularly in OECD countries, of remaining vigilant to ensure that regional agreements do not somehow become instruments for increasing protection at the regional level—in response, for example, to political pressures created by domestic unemployment. In stressing the dangers of protection, the debate also highlights the fact that trade, even with an export powerhouse like China, is a positive-sum game for the countries that trade.

Second, the debate points up the fact that maintaining an open world trading system has recently become a much more critical concern for developing countries. This is because many of those countries have recently shifted from inward- to outward-oriented industrial growth strategies—and have done so at a time, during the 1980s, when OECD countries increased their use of non-tariff barriers to imports, often targeted against products in which developing countries have, or seek to acquire, significant export capabilities.

Third, because bargaining power in multilateral trade negotiations depends largely on domestic market size, interest in the debate also reflects the fact that a de jure regional grouping should have greater bargaining power than any of its members individually vis-à-vis countries outside the group.

The last two of these observations also go far to explain the strong interest shown today by policy-makers in developing countries for joining one of the big regional integration schemes, and/or for creating a scheme of their own (examples of the latter include Mercosur and AFTA, and the controversial Malaysian proposal to create an East Asian Economic Caucus). They also point up the sharp contrast between the logic of the largely unsuccessful regional integration schemes among developing countries during the period from the 1950s to the 1970s, when many Latin American and African countries sought to reduce their dependence on manufactures trade with the developed countries, and the logic of regional integration in developing countries today, which is one of strengthening their participation in that trade.

A further reason why de jure regionalization is important for policy-makers, perhaps the single most important reason, is one which the debate, with its strong focus on trade, has nevertheless tended to miss. It is that, as a policy instrument for individual countries, a de jure regional agreement can, and generally must, have an internal objective as well: to weaken, disrupt, or dilute the often considerable growth-retarding powers of domestically entrenched special-interest groups—oligopolies, rent-seekers, what

Mancur Olson has called 'distributional cartels'—whose actions, both in the market and through politics, tend to dampen an economy's competitiveness at home and abroad.[5] Whether or not diluting or disrupting the powers of such groups is a declared objective of regional agreements—often it is not—weakening those powers is often required to stimulate the forces of domestic competition. Weakening those powers through de jure regional integration can thus be a key to strengthening domestic growth and competitiveness, as well as to strengthening the economy of the region vis-à-vis the rest of the world.

IV. A BROADER VIEW: THE SPECIFICITY OF GLOBALIZATION TODAY

The tendency to focus the economic policy debate over globalization and regionalization on trade and trade-related policy issues has, however, come at a cost: it has made it difficult to grasp the specificity of globalization today, relative to earlier waves of globalization. In fact, the last one hundred years alone have witnessed three distinct periods, or waves, of strong globalization.

We are in the midst of one wave of globalization today, in the 1980s and 1990s. The previous wave was during the 1950s and 1960s: then, as now, barriers to trade fell significantly (especially in the advanced countries), and world trade growth outpaced world output growth; then, as now, international investment—including to many developing countries—grew even faster than trade (that investment, mainly foreign direct investment, was driven by the remarkable expansion of multinational corporations (MNCs), notably US MNCs, at the time). That wave of globalization weakened in the 1970s, as productivity growth fell markedly in the advanced countries, and stagflation emerged in the latter half of the decade in the United States and Europe.

Prior to the wave of the 1950s and 1960s, it was the fifty years or so leading up to World War I that witnessed a strong wave of globalization. Then, as now, trade grew rapidly; and international investment—including to many less developed countries and colonies—grew even more spectacularly (those investments, mainly in the form of financial flows, were, relative to output levels, as large as or larger than they are today). That wave of globalization—remarkably similar to the current wave in important respects—ended in the Great War, the beggar-thy-neighbour policies that led to the disasters of the 1920s and 1930s, and to World War II.

So, one must ask, what is so special about globalization today? It is important to grasp the similarities between the current and previous waves of globalization, and how the current wave follows on and builds upon the legacy of earlier waves. It is equally if not more important, from a policy perspective, to understand the specificity of the current wave, relative to earlier waves. Both require, above all, a grasp of the dynamics of change at the level of the microeconomic forces that drive globalization, to which I turn in Section V below.

First, however, brief comments on four other sets of factors which have contributed since the late 1970s, individually and in combination, to facilitate and shape the current wave of globalization: the deregulation of markets in the advanced countries; the advent and spread of the new microelectronics-based information and communications technologies; the globalization of finance; and the sea change in policy orientation in the developing and many ex-socialist countries.

Deregulation in the advanced countries

In the late 1970s the Carter Administration launched a two-pronged policy response to stagflation and stagnant productivity growth in the US—one prong was monetary 'shock treatment' to halt inflation, which drove up real interest rates, further squeezed US corporate profits, induced the recession of the early 1980s, and triggered the Third World debt crisis in 1982. The other prong was a move towards greater market deregulation was followed in the UK by the newly elected Thatcher government, and in the US during the 1980s by the Reagan Administration. It put strong pressure on continental Europe to follow suit. This deregulation combined with the effects of 'Eurosclerosis' in the late 1970s (and recession in the early 1980s), and widespread perceptions in Europe at the time that the centre of world economic gravity was shifting from the North Atlantic to the Pacific, led the European

Community to launch the Single Market programme in 1985 (to be completed in 1992).

The latter in turn gave impetus to the US decision to pursue regionalization in the Americas (leading to the Canada–US Free Trade Agreement, NAFTA, and the Bush and Clinton Administrations' 'Enterprise for the Americas' and 'Free Trade Agreement for the Americas' initiatives). The combination of regional agreements in Europe and North America has in turn stimulated such regional initiatives as Mercosur, AFTA, the APEC process, and others. Deregulation in the advanced countries has thus been a major stimulus both to the current wave of globalization, and to regionalization—whether as a vehicle for collective deregulation, as in Europe, as a means to lock in unilateral policy liberalization, as in Mexico under NAFTA, or as a response to regionalization by others.

New technologies

Much has been written about the pervasive impact of the new microelectronics-based information and communications technologies. Suffice it here to warn against two views that have gained widespread currency, but are largely mistaken. One, common even among economists, is that thanks to the new technologies we have reached the age of truly global, 'borderless' production. In fact, if anything, physical proximity between firms and both their customers ('global localization') and suppliers has become more, not less, important. Truly global production, in the sense of a firm's sourcing intermediate goods and services from around the globe for production in a given location or locations, is carried out by only a few firms in a small number of activities. Truly international production (cross-border sourcing) is growing, but, for reasons discussed below, much of that growth is within, not between, each of the major regions (greater Europe, Asia, the Americas).[6]

The other mistaken but widely held view (though not by most economists who are familiar with aggregate figures on productivity growth[7]) is that the new technologies have greatly enhanced productivity levels in firms across manufacturing and service industries. The truth is that while the new technologies have been, and increasingly are, widely applied by firms across manufacturing and services—and those technologies have almost certainly had a greater impact than imports from developing countries on unemployment rates in Europe and on the wages of low-skilled workers in the United States[8]—only a limited number of firms have proved capable of taking advantage of those technologies in order significantly to enhance total factor productivity and, hence, their competitive strength. Much more than the relatively rigid Taylorist firms, it is the flexible post-Taylorist firms (discussed below) which have benefited most from the new technologies, especially the new flexible automation technologies.[9]

Financial globalization

It was only in the 1960s that international financial activity began, slowly, to pick up again—after its collapse during the inter-war period—with the creation of the Eurodollar and other unregulated 'offshore' financial markets. It gained considerable momentum after the collapse of the Bretton Woods system of fixed-but-adjustable exchange rates in 1971–3 (speculative activity in the offshore markets was itself a major catalyst of that collapse) and with the recycling of petrodollars after 1973. Its growth has been most spectacular since the late 1970s, to which the deregulation of financial markets and the application of the new information and communications technologies have given strong impetus. The value of cross-border assets held by banks more than tripled between 1983 and 1993, for example, and global foreign-exchange transactions, which tripled between 1986 and 1992 alone, now amount on average to more than \$1,200 billion per day—well over fifty times the value of total world-wide trade in manufactures and services combined—even after allowing for double-counting due to local and cross-border inter-dealer transactions.

The globalization of financial markets, and financial deregulation, are in turn largely responsible—much more than globalization in the real economy—for the widely perceived weakening of the sovereignty of national economic policy. One reason is that the sheer volume of funds circulating in the financial markets makes it more difficult for central banks to control exchange rates. But, in policy terms, that is the tip of the iceberg. It has become much more difficult to tax capital, which weakens governments' revenue base, and shifts the fiscal burden more towards the less mobile factor of production, i.e. labour (governments' attempts to shore up their revenue bases have also tended to lead them to increase consumption taxes). A further effect of financial globalization has been to reinforce the trend towards more regressive income distribution while increasing the relative price of labour. Moreover, as governments have increasingly used interest rates to try to stabilize exchange rates—a stabilization which becomes more important as economies become more open to trade and investment flows—interest rates have become less available as a tool to facilitate or stimulate growth. While major capital inflows have caused problems for some countries, pushing up the exchange rate and threatening to undermine export competitiveness, many countries have had to raise interest rates, which tends to weaken growth. And events in one country can very quickly affect other countries, while big 'mood swings' in global financial markets tend to affect many countries independently of local conditions. Because highly mobile financial capital is responsive to regulatory differentials among countries, as well as to interest-rate differentials, there has also been some tendency toward competitive deregulation—compared by some to the competitive devaluations of the 1930s[10]—which further weakens governments' economic policy sovereignty vis-à-vis the global market. While this weakening arguably contributes, along with financial globalization per se, to enhancing the efficiency of financial markets—some also see it as a useful discipline on governments, because it reduces politicians' and government bureaucrats' ability to tax and spend, and to distort markets—it means that countries without efficient and profitable financial markets tend to suffer.

Finally, it is worth noting, financial deregulation and the globalization of financial markets have contributed to amplifying the size and volatility of exchange-rate fluctuations among the major currencies—fluctuations which have been far greater in the 1980s and 1990s than anyone anticipated at the time of the demise of the Bretton Woods system. Those fluctuations, and that volatility, have in turn helped induce a growing number of firms that compete in global markets to move to establish relatively complete production capabilities within each major region in order more closely to match revenues and outlays in each major currency area. This movement is one reason for the trend towards the regionalization of production, noted earlier.

While few economists would propose a return to the financial controls that prevailed during the 1970s, there are strong arguments for restoring a greater degree of policy autonomy to governments—perhaps collectively, on a regional basis, as in Europe—vis-à-vis global financial markets; several have proposed 'throwing sand in the wheels of international finance'.[11] For developing countries, in particular, the issue also raises important questions about the sequencing of policy reforms, notably as regards internal versus external liberalization, and about finding the right policy mix to ensure growth and vigorous inter-firm price competition on the domestic market.

Opening of non-OECD countries

The move by non-OECD countries, both developing and ex-socialist, to privatize, liberalize, and deregulate their economies over the last decade has been massive and far-reaching—for many a sea change. Until the 1980s many pursued inward-oriented growth strategies, relied heavily on state-owned enterprises, and had highly protected and regulated economies. Only a handful of relatively small economies—the Asian newly industrializing economies NIEs—successfully pursued strategies of export-oriented industrialization, and even they were relatively protected and regulated (Hong Kong and to some extent Singapore were more the exceptions than the rule even among the NIEs). Today most non-OECD countries hope to emulate the manufacturing export success of the NIEs, and have moved to reduce import barriers, attract foreign investment, privatize state-owned companies, and carry out domestic regulatory reform. China since 1979, India since the mid-1980s and especially since 1991, Indonesia and most of Latin America since the mid-1980s (the latter especially in response to the debt crisis), and Eastern Europe since 1989 are all important cases in point. Korea and Taiwan are also moving to deregulate and liberalize their economies.

The remarkable shift by non-OECD countries to greater reliance on, and exposure to, global markets is accompanied in many by democratization or political liberalization (China remains a notable exception). The process thus increases not only their economic vulnerability, but in many cases their political vulnerability, to events in the global market. It also raises their exposure to protectionist pressures in OECD countries (thereby heightening as well their concern about the risk of exclusion from the major de jure regional groupings) at a time when those pressures have risen. Simultaneously, the process of economic policy reform can tend to widen domestic wage and income disparities; and the domestic costs of deregulation and liberalization can generate resistance from entrenched special-interest groups, whom domestic governments may find difficult to resist. The actions of special-interest groups, alongside growing inequality, can generate political instability that may threaten not only democratization, where it is occurring, but the very process of economic reform.

From an OECD perspective, the massive opening-up of non-OECD countries is seen by some as stimulating competition and opening vast new areas for investment and growth. Unfortunately, many others see it mainly as a threat, especially in so far as they believe, largely mistakenly, that trade with and investment in those countries are syphoning off jobs and depressing living standards at home.

V. FLEXIBLE PRODUCTION AND THE CRISIS OF TAYLORISM

The preceding features of globalization—deregulation in OECD countries, new technologies, globalization of financial markets, the opening of non-OECD countries—all facilitate and spur the process, and contribute to its specificity relative to earlier waves of globalization. For policy-makers, however, it is particularly important to understand the microeconomic forces that are driving the process, and how they differ from those that drove globalization in the 1950s and 1960s. Put simply, the microeconomic foundation of globalization in the 1950s and 1960s was the ongoing development and rapid international diffusion, at that time, of Taylorism or what Frederick Taylor himself liked to call 'scientific management'. Today Taylorism is in crisis, and it is the ongoing development and international diffusion, despite resistance, of flexible post-Taylorist organizations that is driving and shaping globalization.

It was during the 1950s and 1960s that Taylorism, invented in the United States on the eve of World War I, first spread widely outside the United States. It was then that 'scientific management' took root and spread in Europe, as well as to the so-called 'modern' manufacturing sector in many developing countries, and was widely implemented in the centrally planned economies. As an approach to organizing activity, it combined three main features: (1) a tendency to separate 'thinking' and 'doing', i.e. to separate the responsibilities of conception (largely incumbent on managers and specialized engineers) from those of execution (performed by workers), throughout an organization; (2) a tendency toward a very high degree of specialization, which also meant very narrowly defined job responsibilities, at all levels of an organization (even today, many economists also seem to conceive of the benefits to be derived from ever greater specialization as if they were the product of an inexorable law of nature, independent of any particular paradigm of work organization—when in fact they are not so independent); and (3) belief in 'one best way' of doing things (whence the term 'scientific').

Taylorism served greatly to raise productivity levels, worldwide, as well as to drive globalization during the 1950s and 1960s. Over time, however, it also built serious rigidities into the organization of production (and the fabric of society), especially in the OECD countries, where it was most developed and widespread. Those rigidities were a central cause of the slowing of productivity growth in the 1970s, and of the emergence of stagflation in the latter half of that decade in the United States and Europe.

At the same time, a growing number of European and Japanese firms were rapidly closing or had closed the 'technology gap' between them and their US counterparts, and began successfully to compete in the US market. More and more US firms, squeezed between slowed domestic productivity growth and growing competition in their home market, moved to relocate some of the more labour-intensive segments of production for their home market to production sites in a few low-wage countries, mainly in Asia, Mexico, and the Caribbean. Japanese firms' relocation of some of their more labour-intensive production to lower-wage countries in Asia also grew rapidly during this period, though much of it was for the US market, and later also for Europe. This relocation occurred largely in response to rapid wage increases in Japan, revaluation of the yen, and growing US and European non-tariff barriers against Japanese exports. To a lesser degree European firms, especially German firms, followed a pattern similar to US firms, with production relocated mainly to North Africa and the Mediterranean, Central and Eastern Europe (under communism), and Asia.

This relocation of production destined for OECD consumers, via foreign direct investment (FDI) but also via sub-contracting and other 'new forms' of investment,[12] contributed substantially to the rapid growth during the 1970s of US and European imports of manufactures from a few relatively low-wage non-OECD countries, notably in Asia—countries which, as a result, gained the appellation 'NICs' (newly industrializing countries) in 1979. Those imports became a source of concern in the latter half of the 1970s, especially in the United States but also in Europe, because just as they reached a level that was no longer trivial (and US trade with the NICs turned to a deficit) stagflation and high unemployment hit the US and European economies.

The relocation of production for OECD consumers to non-OECD countries carried into the 1980s, but with flagging momentum. Contrary to popular perceptions in many OECD countries today, the relocation of production for OECD markets to low-wage production sites in other regions has not accelerated, overall, but has actually decelerated since the early to mid-1980s.[13] And this notwithstanding a few well-publicized cases to the contrary (e.g. Swissair's relocation of back-office operations to Bombay) as well as China's phenomenal growth of manufactured exports over the last decade.

One reason for this deceleration is the OECD countries' partial recovery of productivity growth in manufacturing at home (though, it must be stressed, productivity growth remains far below the levels attained in the 1950s and 1960s). Another reason is the very strong recovery, overall, of OECD corporate profits. A third is the downward trend in the share of variable low-wage labour costs in OECD firms' total operating costs—crudely estimated to have fallen from an average of about 25 per cent in the 1970s to less than 10 per cent by the late 1980s.[14] A fourth and very important reason is the combined impact of the growth of flexible post-Taylorist organizations, the resulting increased importance of proximity between firms and both their customers and their suppliers—particularly in assembly-type production, which is most prone to relocation—and advances in automation technologies that give a new measure of flexibility to production in OECD countries (especially when they are used in flexible organizations).

The rigidities of Taylorism are still a problem in OECD countries. They are a major cause of the severe 'structural' labour-market problems both in the United States and in Europe, noted earlier—not least because Taylorist organizations still account for a large share of activity in OECD countries, and resistance to change in those organizations, often starting with top management, can be very strong.[15] That resistance, and the very real effects of domestic labour-market problems, particularly when growth slows, feed protectionist pressures in the United States and Europe. In combination with perceptions of diminished national economic policy sovereignty, a further consequence has been to nourish mistaken perceptions that 'globalization' in general, and imports from low-wage non-OECD countries in particular, are a major threat to US and European jobs and living standards. OECD policy-makers, business leaders, and economists all have a responsibility to correct those mistaken perceptions, which cannot be ignored.

It is therefore crucial to distinguish between the crisis of Taylorism, on the one hand, and the microeconomic forces that are driving globalization today, on the other. Since the 1980s, a growing number of firms in OECD countries—across manufacturing and services—have moved to adopt flexible post-Taylorist forms of organization. These flexible organizations take many forms—ranging from industrial 'clusters' that comprise large numbers of relatively small firms, to large firms like Toyota, Motorola, and Hewlett Packard—which often involve complex networking arrangements among firms that compete and cooperate simultaneously.[16] These organizations nevertheless have a common denominator, which is that they invert the logic of Taylorism: (1) they tend to integrate thinking and doing in production; (2) they tend to define job responsibilities broadly, and to use much more teamwork; and (3) they emphasize continuous improvement and innovation in the way things are done, as well as in what is produced.

To a significant degree, flexible organizations successfully combine the strengths of craft production (flexibility, high product quality, and a degree of customization) with the strengths of Taylorist mass production (speed, low unit costs) while avoiding the main drawbacks of both (the high unit costs and slow speed of craft producers; the rigidity, bureaucracy, and standardization of Taylorist firms). Whereas Taylorist producers of goods and services can attain productivity levels far superior to craft producers through standardization and economies of scale, post-Taylorist flexible organizations can attain productivity levels significantly superior to the best Taylorist producers. They do so by greatly reducing waste of capital and other resources, by greatly improving information management and flows, and by generating economies of scope in the production of a diversity of more customized products or services without sacrificing economies of scale. They do so, above all, by more successfully exploiting the human intelligence, creativity, flexibility, and knowledge based on experience of their workers. Compared to Taylorist organizations, they are learning organizations, which often show much greater sensitivity to change, and the potential for change, on both the demand and the supply sides of the markets in which they operate.

The fact that most successful flexible post-Taylorist organizations can achieve productivity levels (of capital and labour) clearly superior to those attainable by the best Taylorist organizations, combined with flexible organizations' significantly greater responsiveness to market demands, and to change in those demands, make successful flexible organizations the leading competitive force in global markets today—in industry and modern services alike. It is this competitive strength of flexible post-Taylorist organizations in the OECD economies which, more than any other factor, is driving and shaping globalization today in the real economy, at the microeconomic level. That competitive strength, not exports from low-wage countries, is 'changing the rules of the game' in global competition across manufacturing and modern services.[17]

VI. IMPLICATIONS FOR DEVELOPING COUNTRIES

The tremendous jump in productivity levels achieved by Taylorist organizations over craft organizations around the turn of the century was due above all to the perfection of interchangeable parts, which eliminated the need for skilled fitters in advanced manufacturing industries and opened the way for the development of assembly-type production employing large numbers of relatively unskilled workers. Enhanced by Taylor's 'scientific management' techniques and Ford's invention of the moving conveyor belt, economies of scale in production gave rise to economies of scale in plant size. With increasing returns to scale in production and plant size came the importance of market share, oligopoly, and the competitive advantages of large firm size. Because these three dimensions of scale—production, plant size, firm size—have grown together with the development of corporate capitalism in the leading economies, there is a tendency to see them as necessarily linked. Flexible production is changing this relationship as well, with important consequences for developing countries.

Flexible organizations are generally able efficiently to produce a much wider range of products in a single plant than are Taylorist organizations, and their minimum-efficient level of output for a given product is often significantly lower.[18] The result is of great potential importance to developing countries, especially because of those countries' often limited market size: flexible organizations offer considerably greater possibilities to adapt both product features and output levels to demand requirements specific to relatively small markets, without sacrificing quality or efficiency—both of which tend to be sacrificed by Taylorist organizations when they operate behind high protectionist walls to serve segmented local markets in developing countries (often producing standardized products designed for developed-country consumers). Smaller minimum-efficient scales of production can also favour healthy price competition in smaller markets, in so far as they reduce the number of 'natural monopolies',[19] thereby favouring domestic productivity growth as well.

Also important is the fact that the key to flexible production is organizational, not technological per se. It means that the essential changes required in firms, and countries, that seek to make the transition from Taylorist to flexible production, or to develop flexible production, are neither capital-intensive, nor therefore, for developing countries, foreign-exchange-intensive.[20]

The relative instability and, in recent years, high real interest rates in many developing countries also put a premium on flexibility, hence on flexible producers' greater ability to produce in response to actual demand rather than to (unreliable) demand forecasts, and on their much smaller inventories and reduced wastage.

Finally, it should be noted, the fact that Taylorist production has not constituted a foundation for economic development in developing countries the way it has in the developed countries means that

Taylorist organizations, and Taylorist thinking, may not be as entrenched in developing countries. Indeed, many developing countries may benefit from greater flexibility, both in mentality and in the economy, than exists in many developed countries. The good news, then, is that in important respects flexible production is well suited to developing countries, especially in production for local markets, where low minimum-efficient scales of production are important. But there are caveats, and bad news, too.

First, one should not underestimate the extent to which developing countries suffer from the rigidifying actions of entrenched rent-seekers, oligopolists, and 'distributional cartels', which are often considerably more powerful in developing countries, relative to the size of the local economy, than in developed countries.

Second, while minimum-efficient levels of production tend to be significantly lower under flexible production than under Taylorist production, those levels often remain high relative to effective levels of demand for many products in developing countries. Export-oriented development strategies and access to OECD markets thus remain important for successful flexible producers in developing countries, though the advantages gained from proximity between firms and both their customers and suppliers also point to advantages for developing countries in pursuing greater integration among themselves, as a complement to—or as a means to help strengthen—greater integration with developed countries.

Third, lower minimum-efficient scales of production and plant size do not mean that there is a reduction in the advantages to be derived from large firm size, or that there is a trend towards smaller firm size per se. Flexible production means, first of all, a shift towards the network enterprise, away from the simple dichotomy of 'markets' and 'hierarchies', which makes it problematic to compare the size of Taylorist and flexible organizations. But the importance of economies of scope under flexible production means that the advantages of large firm size apply to network enterprises, and the often large size of fixed costs—in R&D or in gaining access to technology, in marketing, in worker training, etc.—means that those advantages are often significant. They point to the importance for flexible organizations of size in financial and marketing terms, while avoiding the internal rigidities typical of large Taylorist organizations. Industrial clusters may provide the solution in some cases. But for many firms in developing countries and newly industrializing economies (NIEs) that aspire to become, or remain, successful competitors in the current context of globalization, the solution may lie in establishing tie-ups with or attracting investment by flexible organizations in OECD countries.

Fourth, and perhaps even more serious than the two preceding points, successful flexible production tends to be demanding both in terms of its need for a well-functioning modern transportation and communications infrastructure and in terms of its human-resources requirements. Many developing countries find it difficult to meet the infrastructure requirements, which raises serious questions about the viability of flexible production in developing countries, notwithstanding the evidence of a number of successful flexible organizations in such countries as Zimbabwe, India, and Indonesia.[21] The human-resources requirements of flexible production can also be a serious constraint on its development, though the importance of on-the-job skill acquisition in flexible organizations means that it is less the paucity of skilled labour than of workers with basic numeracy and literacy skills ('trainability') that is likely to pose the constraint in many developing countries. The more 'consensual' approach to work organization in flexible production also raises difficult questions about the adaptability of the system to social and political as well as economic conditions in countries where extreme social inequality, political instability, and/or undemocratic political institutions prevail.

In contrast, the greater robustness of Taylorist organizations, compared to flexible organizations, is reflected not only in their ability productively to absorb greater quantities of unskilled labour. It also means they tend to be somewhat less demanding in terms of infrastructure requirements, and less vulnerable to certain internal frictions, than flexible organizations. That robustness means, in short, that Taylorist organizations may still be better adapted, in important respects, to conditions in many developing countries.

It is equally true, however, that the development of flexible production in the developed countries raises serious questions about the long-term viability for developing countries of industrial growth strategies based on Taylorist, low-skilled-labour-intensive production of manufactures for global, and especially OECD, mar-

kets. Those strategies are increasingly constrained by the importance for all firms—not just OECD-based firms—of proximity to
their customers ('global localization') and to their suppliers (reflecting the benefits of continuous information exchange, reinforced
under just-in-time systems). Those strategies are also weakened by
the declining share of low-skilled-labour costs in total production
costs and the impact of flexible automation technologies in
enhancing the competitiveness of production in OECD countries.
The result, as flexible production spreads in OECD countries, is
that it becomes more difficult for developing countries and NIEs
successfully to pursue manufacturing export growth on the basis of
comparative advantage in low-skilled-labour-intensive products
alone—at a time when many developing countries have recently
changed strategies and are hoping to do just that. Already, the
importance of proximity, reinforced in some cases by protectionist
pressures in OECD countries, means that firms in NIEs and developing countries that want to compete in OECD markets increasingly find it necessary to invest in the establishment of production
capabilities in those markets.

Combined, these trends suggest that for many developing countries, the risk of exclusion from the growth dynamics of globalization in the developed countries is significant. What remains to be
seen is the extent to which flexible production will take root and
grow in developing countries, whether to serve domestic markets,
OECD markets, or both.

VII. THE RELATIONSHIP BETWEEN GLOBALIZATION AND REGIONALIZATION

The greater importance of proximity between firms and both their
customers and their suppliers under flexible production, relative
to Taylorist production, and the greater pressure today on both
OECD- and non-OECD-based firms to have production capabilities in each of the major regions if they want to sell to OECD
markets in those regions, combined with the volatility of exchange-
rate fluctuations between the major currencies, go far to explain
why globalization today tends to reinforce the trend towards the
regionalization of production, mentioned earlier. That trend in
turn reinforces the political pressure many firms bring to bear on

governments to lower barriers to intra-regional activity, notably
through regional integration agreements. The marked proliferation
of de jure regional agreements since the mid-1980s thus reflects,
as much as it contributes to, the trend for globalization and
regionalization today to be mutually reinforcing.

Indeed, while de jure regionalization can be a political response
to globalization, as noted earlier, it can at the same time help
strengthen the microeconomic forces within a country, and a region, that drive globalization there. It can do this not only by
removing impediments to intra-regional activity, effectively enlarg-
ing the domestic market, but by stimulating domestic competition.
By weakening the power of domestically entrenched special-interest
groups, de jure regionalization has the potential to help member
governments collectively establish, or re-establish, their policy
sovereignty vis-à-vis the market internally, as well as vis-à-vis
global markets. Politically, de jure regionalization can also give
impetus to much needed reform legislation at the national level that
otherwise might not overcome domestic opposition—and in doing
so, it can help open the economy to globalization.

De jure regionalization can also enhance member states' policy
stability and credibility—because it can lead to needed reform
legislation, but also because an international agreement is more
difficult to change than domestic legislation—which can in turn
be good for macroeconomic stability, and the ability to attract
foreign investment. Indeed, the principal motivation behind many
of the recent regional agreements, certainly in developing countries, has precisely been to attract FDI, more than to promote trade
per se. (Free flows of FDI between regions should also offset
whatever small trade-diverting effects the regional agreements may
have.[22])

De jure regionalization can also be an efficient vehicle for
responding to the growing pressure for 'deep' international policy
integration in a way that is difficult or impossible to achieve among
countries, and peoples, that do not share a strong sense of cultural
or historical as well as geographic proximity. Indeed, that pressure
which globalization engenders—for more international integration
or harmonization of traditionally 'domestic' policies—has led in
recent years to a blurring of the distinction between domestic and
international policy instruments.

In short, globalization and regionalization are opposites only in the sense that one is usefully understood as a centrifugal process and the other as a centripetal process, and in the sense that one is driven by microeconomic forces and the other is often a political phenomenon. In practice, globalization and regionalization tend to be mutually reinforcing, especially in so far as regionalization stimulates internal competition.

Policy-makers must nevertheless remain alert to the fact that the same special-interest groups that are most likely to oppose de jure regionalization in so far as it threatens to undermine their domestic rent-seeking powers, if unable to block the process, are also among the political forces most likely to seek to transform a process of regional integration into a tool for regional protection. The inter-war period provides a dramatic illustration of such a possibility.

The message for policy-makers, worldwide, is that when de jure regionalization becomes a tool for regional protection and loses its internal competition-enhancing effects—by failing adequately to disrupt or dilute the rent-seeking powers of domestic oligopolies and special-interest groups—regional integration loses its value as a policy tool for strengthening regional growth and competitiveness in global markets. In this case, moreover, whatever the benefits regional integration may well not even justify the cost to participating countries terms of their reduced national policy autonomy. On the other hand, in so far as de jure regionalization strengthens internal competition, by enhancing 'deep' policy integration among members and/or by weakening the rigidifying powers of entrenched distributional cartels, it can enhance member states' collective policy sovereignty vis-à-vis the market. This in turn will strengthen the potential effectiveness of their policy measures as well as strengthening the region's competitiveness vis-à-vis the rest of the world. In short, globalization and de jure regionalization tend to be mutually reinforcing in so far—but only in so far—as the latter stimulates intra-regional competition.

This policy message is only reinforced by the fact that many powerful OECD-based multinational firms that might once have collectively constituted a strong political force against regional protectionism in OECD countries can no longer be counted on to play that role. Most of those firms still favour a liberal multilateral trade regime, to be sure. But because many have moved, or are moving, to establish or consolidate production capabilities within each of the major regions, they tend to give more importance to the lowering of intra-regional barriers to economic activity as a whole than to any perceived risk of higher inter-regional barriers to trade. (Low investment barriers are important for those firms, between as well as within regions, but even worst-case scenarios, in terms of the formation of relatively closed regional blocs, foresee little danger of increased barriers to inter-regional investment.) Weaker firms, on the other hand, are more likely to be among those seeking either to block regional agreements or to transform them into tools for regional protection.[23]

Globalization is thus also stimulating regionalization today because globally competitive firms have become a strong political force for de jure regionalization as a means to lower policy impediments to intra-regional activity. As 'traditional' trade barriers have been reduced through successive rounds of multilateral trade negotiations, the dynamics of global inter-firm competition in the leading economies lead to increasing corporate pressures on governments to go beyond 'shallow' international policy integration, i.e. to go beyond reducing trade and other policy barriers to international activity 'at the borders', and to engage in 'deeper' policy integration by harmonizing a growing number of policies hitherto seen as essentially 'domestic'. Differences in national (and sometimes sub-national) policies on the rules of competition, financial regulations, product standards, environmental standards, labour standards, public procurement, government subsidies to science and technology, and even fiscal and monetary affairs, as well as different approaches to corporate governance, are all seen today as having an important incidence on a firm's ability to compete in individual markets, and are thus the source of new tensions and conflicts among governments.[24] De jure regional approaches are seen by many as the most effective means to pursue such 'deeper' international policy integration—with multilateral institutions, notably the WTO and the OECD, playing a vital complementary role in seeking to ensure at least minimal harmony or compatibility among the regional approaches.

A further result of globalization is thus the increased importance of industrial clusters or 'districts', mentioned earlier, which are sub-national phenomena that nevertheless sometimes straddle one or more national boundaries.[25] Still another result is that the redeployment of production to lower-wage production sites—a phenomenon that has been tempered but not eliminated by the development of flexible production, by the diminished relative importance of low-skilled-labour costs in firms' total costs, and by the increased importance of proximity to customers and suppliers—tends to consist of production for regional markets, not for global markets. That is, notwithstanding China's impressive extra-regional export performance, production redeployed to a low-wage site but destined to serve European consumers is more likely today to go to Eastern or Southern Europe, or perhaps to North Africa, than to Asia or Latin America. Production to serve the North American market is more likely to go to a lower-wage site in the United States or to Mexico. And while production redeployed to low-wage economies in Asia—by NIE-based firms as well as by Japanese and other OECD-based firms—remains strongly oriented towards extra-regional markets, the trend is clear: that production is increasingly going to those economies to serve the fast-growing Asian market.

A final reason globalization stimulates regionalization today is that some governments, more than others, see de jure regionalization and a (greater) degree of pooling of their policy sovereignty at the regional level as a collective means to reassert that sovereignty and thereby gain, or regain, a measure of policy autonomy vis-à-vis the global market—if only to palliate some of the destabilizing effects of globalization.

Regionalization is nevertheless a very different phenomenon in each of the major regions—in each of the 'poles' of the emerging tripolar world economy. In Europe, the process is very much one of 'deep' policy integration among members of the European Union. The logic of the Single Market, in particular, is clearly not one of protectionism, but of promoting competition within Europe to strengthen European competitiveness at home and abroad. For non-Europeans, the main challenge is to take advantage of whatever stimulus to European growth the Single Market provides. For developing countries and NIEs, the main challenge nevertheless comes not from European integration per se, but from changes in Central and Eastern Europe—and the danger of diversion of EU trade, investment, and aid to the latter. The Central and Eastern European countries benefit from physical and cultural proximity to EU countries, and at least some degree of preferential access to EU markets, and can be expected to develop competitive strength in manufactures that compete directly with those of developing and newly industrializing economies outside the region.

In North America, the process is one of relatively shallow de jure regionalization, under NAFTA, preceded by substantial de facto regionalization between the United States and both Canada and Mexico. For Mexico, a major motivation for NAFTA was nevertheless to 'lock in' the country's far-reaching policy reforms, and to attract foreign investment. For countries outside the region, NAFTA's significance lies primarily in the risk of diminished US commitment to multilateral trade liberalization, and the agreement's potential to divert trade and investment to Mexico. It has also added to incentives for other developing countries to form subregional groupings among themselves, such as Mercosur in South America and AFTA in South-East Asia.

In Pacific Asia, regionalization is basically a de facto process, driven by strong economic growth, particularly in the region's developing countries and NIEs. The main challenge for those outside the region, both countries and firms, is to share in the benefits of that growth—which looks likely to continue for some time—by pursuing policies and strategies to develop their own competitive strengths.

VIII. CONCLUSIONS

Globalization presents the main challenge today for policy-makers in OECD and developing countries alike; the significance of regionalization, though considerable, is subordinate. The challenge, above all, is to pursue globalization in ways that do not weaken, but rather strengthen, social cohesion. All segments of society, within countries and internationally, must share in the benefits, and perceive themselves as standing to benefit, from the raising of productivity levels to which globalization can contribute.

The challenge is amplified by the extent to which globalization today, as prior to World War I, increases the political vulnerability of governments in both the advanced and the less advanced countries to events in the global market. It requires close attention to the microeconomic features of globalization, as well as to the effects of financial globalization, on the one hand, and to the effects of the crisis of Taylorism, on the other.

For OECD countries, the imperative is mainly to increase domestic flexibility, and to do so in ways that favour social cohesion. This is first and foremost a task for firms and managers; but governments and labour organizations face it as well—not least because they, too, are often organized along Taylorist lines. The need is to move beyond Taylorist management and organizational precepts, and the dichotomy of markets and hierarchies, in order to embrace the transition to more flexible forms of organization, which must generally include promoting greater social cohesion and better information flows within organizations, if only to enhance their internal efficiency and flexibility. Resistance to change within the organization, notably at the top, and blindness to the type of change required—often reflected in a fascination with 'downsizing' without understanding the need to change how things are done—often constitute the main impediments. All too often the tendency therefore is to look for scapegoats, notably in 'globalization' and imports, if not migratory pressures, from developing countries.

OECD governments must seek to enhance microeconomic flexibility at home, rather than succumb to pressures to resist change through protection or other measures to restrict competition. They should promote social cohesion, not only because the cost of rapid change without it can be high (demotivation, drugs, crime) but because it fosters creativity and facilitates necessary change; weak or declining social cohesion increases resistance to change, and prolongs and exacerbates the crisis of Taylorism. They may also consider ways to 'throw some sand in the wheels' of global finance, as in the creation of the single European currency and Central Bank, without returning to the constraints that prevailed in the 1970s.

For non-OECD countries, the challenge is even greater. For many, it is a double challenge: open up to global markets and global competition (already a sea change for many) and, at the same time, deal with the problems and policy responses to globalization emanating from OECD countries (regionalization, mounting protectionist pressures, etc.) along with the effects both of financial globalization and the move towards flexible production—including the increased importance of proximity between firms and both their suppliers and their consumers, and the diminished importance of low-skilled-labour costs as a basis for competing in global markets, relative to such factors as proximity, well-functioning infrastructure, etc. Indeed, it is no small irony that just as many developing and ex-socialist countries finally turn outward and seek to become low-cost sites for production to serve global markets, a chorus of protectionist voices has emerged in some OECD countries to blame unemployment and declining wages at home on a massive shift of production to low-wage countries that has not occurred and is unlikely to occur.

The challenge for non-OECD countries, as for OECD countries, is to benefit from the productivity-enhancing features and long-term growth dynamics of globalization, and to do so in ways that strengthen social cohesion. Many of the policy implications for OECD countries broadly apply to non-OECD countries. These include the need to: pursue mutually reinforcing macroeconomic and structural policies; promote the development of human capital, and focus public investment in human resources on strengthening broad-based problem-solving skills, i.e. basic numeracy and literacy skills at the primary and secondary levels, and on developing social and inter-personal communications skills ('trainability'); facilitate the diffusion and absorption of know-how, both technological and organizational; promote the formation of industrial clusters; promote investment in the development of modern infrastructure; create an entrepreneurial climate—which in many developing countries requires a lot of attention to creating and nurturing that all-important public good called the market (often mistakenly assumed to emerge and flourish spontaneously), and to ensure that markets are 'contestable' (characterized by healthy inter-firm price competition). Governments should also ensure that participation in any de jure regional integration schemes serves to strengthen competition within the region, including domestically.

Problems that are more specific to non-OECD countries tend to include low domestic levels of development of human capital and infrastructure, low productivity and income levels, sometimes widespread poverty, perhaps a very small effective domestic market. The combined result, for many non-OECD countries, is the spectre of exclusion from globalization. The question they face, in other words, is whether there will be a globalization of globalization.

Where experience points to a possible yes, notably in Pacific Asia and northern Mexico as regards the development of internationally competitive flexible organizations, it also points up some critical, if unsurprising, policy lessons. One is the importance of macro-economic stability, hence of sound macroeconomic policies, combined with political stability. Another is the importance of policy credibility, vis-à-vis both internal and external economic actors. Also important is public attention to the maintenance of well-functioning transportation and communications infrastructure, as well as human capital formation, and to the question of access to OECD markets.

Recent developing-country successes in manufactured exports—notably, but not only, in China—also confirm, however, that Taylorist organizations have not exhausted their competitive potential in non-OECD countries. They also show that competitive success can sometimes be achieved by combining elements of Taylorist and flexible production in low-wage countries. Clearly, for non-OECD countries and firms—perhaps even more than for OECD countries and firms—there is no 'one best way'.[26]

Successful flexible production in developing countries and NIEs also shows, finally, that flexible production is not something that can be purchased or imported via foreign direct investment like a capital good. More akin to a philosophy of human organization, it is something that can and must be learned and developed locally.

International inter-firm tie-ups and inward FDI nevertheless have a crucial role to play. Indeed, a further implication of globalization for non-OECD countries, especially for firms, is the importance of networking with OECD-based firms, and conceivably with non-OECD-based firms, which are likely to be strong global competitors tomorrow—which is not always the case with today's market leaders.[27]

The importance of FDI also points to the importance of a hospitable investment climate and policies to attract FDI—and at the same time to the danger of 'bidding wars' among governments (within as well as between countries) to attract FDI. Conceivably, such policy competition can induce socially beneficial increases in public investment in human capital formation and infrastructure; but it can easily lead to a costly and socially unwarranted escalation of direct and indirect subsidies to FDI, and/or to a process of competitive deregulation that undermines environmental and/or labour standards, for example. And both 'bidding wars' and competitive deregulation can in turn have substantial perverse effects: escalating subsidies and 'incentives' to FDI can exacerbate fiscal deficits and/or divert resources from public investment in infrastructure and human capital—investment that can often do more to raise economy-wide productivity and even to attract long-term productive investment. Excessive and therefore unsustainable incentives and/or policy competition among governments can also create policy instability and weaken policy credibility, which results in uncertainty that can actually reduce the inflow of valuable long-term investment (it may also attract investment looking mainly for a quick profit).

Another message for governments—national and sub-national—is thus the importance of increased policy coordination and cooperation. The danger of excessive policy competition to attract FDI, and the pressures of competitive deregulation, are but two examples of the growing importance of moving beyond 'shallow integration' to 'deeper' international policy integration in developing countries, as well as in OECD countries.

De jure regional agreements can be a useful vehicle to strengthen such policy coordination among developing countries. They can also help to attract FDI, not least because of the greater steadiness and credibility they can give to member governments' policies, as well as the larger market they offer to investors. They can also be— and the message for policy-makers is that they must be designed to be—means to strengthen internal competition, and thus to stimulate domestic productivity growth. The agreements can involve national governments (e.g. Mercosur, AFTA) but they can also involve sub-national governments (as in several of Asia's 'growth triangles'). And they can be particularly valuable as vehicles for developing 'deeper' economic integration, including the cross-border development of infrastructure, as well as for deeper policy integration.

De jure regionalization can also be important for strengthening relations between developing and developed countries, as in NAFTA. But for relations between OECD and developing countries as a whole, there is clearly no substitute for a strong World Trade Organization. Indeed, for non-OECD countries, perhaps the single greatest threat of exclusion from globalization stems, in policy terms, from the threat of being excluded from the process of 'deep' policy integration among OECD countries. That process, driven by the microeconomic forces of globalization, is moving ahead. It is in the ultimate interest of OECD countries that the process take full account of conditions in non-OECD countries, and integrate them in a way that promotes social cohesion, within and between countries, along with economic efficiency and growth. The collapse of globalization from 1914 to 1945, and all that accompanied that collapse, is a stark reminder of what can happen when market forces lead to a breakdown in social cohesion, and governments fail to respond adequately.

3

Sovereignty and Inequality

Benedict Kingsbury

Sovereignty has been a foundational concept—perhaps *the* foundational concept—throughout the modern history of international law.[1] Inequality, by contrast, has received minimal consideration as a theoretical topic in the recent literature of international law. The reluctance formally to confront inequality has many causes, but it has been made possible by the centrality of sovereignty. The theory of sovereignty has relieved international lawyers from the need for a general theory of the legal management of inequality, in three major ways.

First, the concept of sovereignty underpins a principle of sovereign equality that has attained almost an ontological position in the structure of the international legal system. This ontological status means not only that a very small state such as the Solomon Islands is procedurally on an equal footing with the United States in arguing in the International Court of Justice about the legality of the use of nuclear weapons, but also that groups of very small states can make some difference, whether in legal opinions given by the World Trade Organization Appellate Body, or in the dynamics of multilateral bargaining, for instance over the 1992 Framework Convention on Climate Change and its 1997 Kyoto Protocol. Examples of this sort are held up to vindicate the system of sovereign equality as an effective system for equality before the law. In the same spirit, legal doctrines of the special legal status of great powers have been in the descendant since 1945, and such matters as the structure of the

This chapter owes much to the thought and generosity of Andrew Hurrell. Many thanks also to Laurence Boisson de Chazournes, David Caron, Donald Horowitz, Liam Murphy, Ngaire Woods, and other friends for their helpful comments on earlier drafts.

Non-Proliferation Treaty or the UN Security Council are dealt with by most legal writers as anomalies, however necessary or enduring, in the scheme of sovereign equality. This scheme serves, albeit unevenly, as a counter to the vast inequalities that might otherwise be expected to feature in the formal structure of the legal system.

Second, the concept of state sovereignty allows questions of social and economic inequality among people to be treated in international law as a responsibility of territorial states. International law and legal institutions are able to promote market activity, for example through the WTO or the International Monetary Fund, while in theory leaving largely to states the responsibility of mitigating social and economic inequalities associated with markets. Episodic attempts to address economic and social inequality directly through substantial non-market changes in the international legal order have met with little success outside the established human rights and environmental programmes,[2] and for the time being such concerns about inequality have to a large extent been displaced by contemporary preoccupations with reducing the role of the state in economic activity and in major market-distorting egalitarian redistribution. Although international institutions continue to play important roles in economic development, there is growing incongruence between the increasing market-orientation of international law and the inability of international governance institutions or of many sovereign states to cope with problems of inequality that markets alone do not resolve.[3]

Third, the theory of sovereignty legitimates the application of international legal norms, and international institutional competences, where these might infringe egalitarian principles or otherwise be in doubt. The main device for achieving this legitimation is consent, whether express or tacit. This is of vast importance for the international legal system. It is not clear that, in the present state of heterogeneous international society, any other non-consensual legitimating principle is viable; and sovereignty appears to be a relatively low-cost means to organize 'consent'.

There is thus a relationship of mutual containment between sovereignty and inequality. The system of sovereignty at least notionally precludes some forms of inequality, while helping exclude other forms of inequality from real consideration. Inequality limits sovereignty where hierarchies are established among different political and legal units. Inequality also grounds critiques of sovereignty that weaken sovereignty as a normative concept, including critiques flowing from human rights, self-determination, feminist theory, and critical theory.

Although sovereignty is central to the mainstream tradition of international law, it has always been viewed with ambivalence in that tradition.[4] For mainstream writers, sovereignty is at once the architecture for the present and future international legal system, an obstacle to a deepening rule-of-law system, a legitimation of morally dubious state conduct or social practices, a bulwark against the iniquities of dominance by powerful external forces, and a basis for identity and democratic decision-making.[5] This ambivalence has intensified with globalization, democratization, and the increasing self-assurance of liberal agendas, threatening to destabilize the established function of sovereignty as a device to contain inequality. Substitute theories for the better management of heightened problems of inequality have not emerged, nor even been seriously investigated. This chapter will explore the interplay in international legal doctrine between sovereignty and inequality. Section I will examine the relations between sovereignty and inequality in the mainstream tradition of international law, focusing on the approach charted by Lassa Oppenheim and others at the beginning of the twentieth century that has endured, in its fundamentals, throughout the century. Section II will assess the extent to which challenges of globalization, democratization, and privatization have led during the past century to adaptations in the traditional sovereignty-based account of international law, and will note some implications for the treatment of inequality. Section III will consider whether the mounting critiques of the traditional concept of sovereignty might soon lead to the replacement of the present normative international law view by a functional view, and if so, what the consequences might be for the management of inequality. The conclusion will summarize the principal argument of this chapter, that a radical change in the international law concept of sovereignty will be hazardous without concomitant development of adequate alternative means to manage inequality.

I. MANAGEMENT OF INEQUALITY IN TRADITIONAL SOVEREIGNTY-BASED ACCOUNTS OF INTERNATIONAL LAW

Equality as an incident of sovereignty in traditional international legal doctrine

The system of sovereign equal states has been one of the defining ideas of international relations throughout the twentieth century. On it have been built the modern mainstream projects for a working system of international law. These projects have been based on status: entities of the same status enjoy comparable and reciprocal entitlements. As Oppenheim put it: 'In entering the Family of Nations a State comes as an equal to equals; it demands a certain consideration to be paid to its dignity, the retention of its independence, of its territorial and its personal supremacy . . . The equality before International Law of all member-States of the family of nations is an invariable quality derived from their International Personality.'[6] This system is embedded as the first principle in the architecture of the UN Charter: 'The Organization is based on the principle of the sovereign equality of all its Members.'

The commitment to equality—whether of status, capacity for rights, procedural rights, or even substantive rights—has not been matched by consensus on the justification for equality.[7] Naturalistic, logical entailment, and reciprocity justifications have coexisted uneasily in the mainstream literature and in institutional practice.

The naturalist approach to equality is well represented in Vattel's famous passage:

Since men are by nature equal, and their individual rights and obligations the same, as coming equally from nature, Nations, which are composed of men and may be regarded as so many free persons living together in a state of nature, are by nature equal and hold from nature the same obligations and the same rights. Strength or weakness, in this case, counts for nothing.[8]

For naturalists, the notion of equality of rights remains a powerful one.[9] Vattel's remarkable analogy between equality of individuals and equality of states, which is consistent with Vattel's anthropomorphization of inter-state law more generally,[10] continues to have echoes, as, for example, in assertions that the exclusion of individuals from democratic participation in local and national government is the same injustice as exclusion of large Third World states from permanent membership in the Security Council.

In the positivist doctrine of the beginning of this century, represented by Oppenheim, equality was seen as a logical corollary of sovereignty. Enjoyment of full international personality must be on the basis of equality, for there is no higher status. Dickinson argued in 1920 that while sovereign equality encompassed equality before the law, specifically equality of capacity for rights, it clearly did not and could not mean equality of rights.[11] This made sense to positivist lawyers, but was not easily reconciled with the positivist view that sovereignty encompasses entitlement not to be bound by any rule without some form of consent (a form of equal-rights argument).

The realist view of international relations as inter-state interactions given particular configurations of power among states presupposes mutual acceptance among the units of the system, and formal equality among sovereigns is a predictable outcome of the reciprocity that underpins a non-hierarchical system. Reciprocity is an inherent feature of the international system as thus conceived, and for structural realists explains the otherwise puzzling acceptance by states of formal equality despite disparities of power.[12]

While there was widespread support for sovereign equality as a foundational principle of the international legal system, unease about it persisted. Neither the Concert of Europe nor the Allied and Associated Powers at Versailles operated on the basis of equality among sovereign states, yet these groupings were decisive in the formulation of major legal elements of the public order of Europe. Several prominent international lawyers recognized and endorsed special rights and responsibilities of great powers,[13] and some saw such inequalities as grounds for rejecting the theory that sovereignty entailed equality.[14] In good positivist fashion, Oppenheim treated major inequalities, such as that between the Great Powers and other powers, as political but not legal.[15] But Oppenheim, unlike the vast majority of his successors among international lawyers, regarded the balance of power as a fundamental principle of international order, and took a distinctly realist view in accepting that the use of force could be justified to maintain the balance of power. He showed no sign of believing that the inegalitarian implications of a balance-of-power system ought to result in its subordination to the principle of sovereign equality.

The uncertainties as to the justifications for sovereign equality and the extent to which it negated differences in power are evident also in debates of the period concerning specific international legal doctrines. Recognized sovereign states were equal for such purposes as claiming diplomatic immunity and sovereign immunity and having their laws accepted in other states' courts, but non-recognition could be used to deny the premiss for such equality, as in the case of delayed recognition of the Bolshevik government after the formation of the USSR.[16] The freedoms of the high seas were generally extended to all recognized states without discrimination. Equality among states applied to such matters as access of trade goods and missionaries to territories held under League of Nations mandates, and participation in multilateral treaties on such matters as conditions of workers. Equality was thought by some to ground claims for rights of European states to acquire colonies in Africa and Asia, although by the 1930s such claims were becoming less tenable. Equality was proposed as a foundational principle for international trade law, but this met with only limited success prior to the General Agreement on Tariffs and Trade in 1947. Equality was one of the principles weighed in arms control and disarmament projects in the period between the two World Wars, but it was departed from in specific treaties that were actually adopted, such as the Washington Naval Treaty. Special problems arose in the design of international institutions. After the deadlock in negotiations at the 1907 Hague Peace Conference for a new standing international court, which found no compromise between the insistence of less powerful states that equality meant every state must be permitted to appoint a judge and the insistence of the more powerful states that such a system was unwieldy and that only great powers could always expect to have judges of their nationalities appointed, international lawyers in the US and other powerful states sought to staunch the further extension of equal-rights arguments, which they saw as an obstruction to the progressive growth of effective international legal institutions.[17] In the design of new international organizations, sovereign equality was thought to mandate membership open to all states, equality in voting power, and unanimity rules in certain binding decisions and with respect to reservations to multilateral treaties, but each phase of institutional design in fact involved compromises between sovereign equality, great power primacy, and institutional efficacy.[18]

Racial, religious, and cultural diversity:
to whom does sovereign equality apply?

Confrontation with religious, cultural, and racial difference was a perennial issue in the historical development of what became the Eurocentric international legal order. An earlier tendency in the European natural law tradition to discuss international law in universal terms and by reference to a *civitas gentium maxima*,[19] albeit with important distinctions tending to favour Europeans and Christians over others, was from the eighteenth century gradually displaced by a view of international law as the public law of the European heartland.[20] Europe was established as the original sphere of operation of international law. There was a geographic element to this, in that many of the problems regulated by international law, and much of the relevant practice and law-making activity, arose within or between European states. But the relevant practice and interactions came more and more to involve, especially during the nineteenth century, extra-European states and entities; many of these states and entities accepted and applied much the same set of legal standards, although others did not. This interaction contributed to a second development, the informal doctrinal promulgation of a membership test for international society, sometimes described as the 'standard of civilization'. Extra-European entities with the attributes of statehood were admitted to the family of nations as their degree of civilization and intercourse with the family of nations warranted. The test for membership was a creation of doctrine much more than of practice, and varied among publicists. Writing in 1905, Oppenheim had no hesitation in declaring that Christianity was not a requisite of a civilized state: civilization meant simply whatever was necessary 'to enable the respective State and its subjects to understand and to act in conformity with the principles of the Law of Nations'.[21] Acceptance of the system of sovereign states, and the convenience of the strongest powers, were two elements of the test for membership. This view conditioned a reductionist schematic of the history of international law, of which Oppenheim's account is exemplary: the international law of the family of nations originated amongst the Christian states of Europe, was extended with the independence of the former European colonies of the Americas and the establishment of other Christian states such as Liberia and Haiti, was extended again with the admission in 1856 of the Ottoman Empire to the advantages of the public law and Concert of Europe, and again with the acceptance of Japan as a Great Power after 1895.[22] In Oppenheim's view in 1905, the full members of the Family of Nations were the independent European states (including Turkey and Russia) and the independent states of North, Central, and South America, plus Liberia, the Congo Free State, and Japan. Egypt was half-sovereign owing to Turkish suzerainty. Tunis was half-sovereign owing to the French protectorate. Morocco and Abyssinia were regarded by Oppenheim as 'full-Sovereign States', but as members of the Family of Nations only for some purposes (e.g. diplomacy and treaty-making), and not for other purposes (e.g. restrictions on the conduct of war). Similarly, Oppenheim viewed Persia, China, Korea, Siam, and Tibet as members of the Family of Nations for some purposes only, and not as international legal persons with the same position as 'Christian States'.[23]

The insistence on a European model of statehood and the organization of the state, and the articulation in parochial terms of a 'standard of civilization' which was itself applied in self-serving ways, were all conducive to the structuring and promotion of a great deal of inequality. There was, in Oppenheim's view, no equality for half-civilized and similar States, States under suzerainty and under protectorate, or ('depending on their particular constitutional arrangements') member-states of a federal state. In his opinion—although this view was contested at the time—the law of nations placed no restrictions on the treatment of states or entities that were wholly outside the Family of Nations; such treatment was a matter of discretion, and frequently was 'not only contrary to Christian morality, but arbitrary and barbarous'.[24] The Eurocentric system excluded from its purview entities that powerful recognized states were not willing to treat as 'states', whether because they wished to dominate or colonize these entities, or because these did not closely resemble 'states' as the category had come to be understood, or because they showed little acceptance of the organizing ideas of the system, or because they did not seem likely to uphold international legal obligations. While a weaker entity such as Abyssinia might be excluded on grounds of difference, arguments that Meiji Japan was still too different were eclipsed by Japan's military victories, especially the 1904–5 Russo–Japanese war. While power and interests were central to this system, they do

not represent the whole explanation for the perpetuation of inequalities. The rejection of Japan's proposal for a racial equality
clause in the League of Nations Covenant was evidence not just of
the limited strength of Asian and African states in the Versailles
diplomacy, but also of a deeper cognitive or identity-based resistance to racial equality as a global principle.[25] This was connected
not only with systematic racial discrimination in independent
states, but also with colonial policy in territories where the maintenance of colonial rule had come increasingly to depend on the
structuring of distinctions among ethnic groups.[26]

This membership standard and the Western dominance that
made it possible had the further important effect of establishing a
degree of structural homology among sovereign states. The Western model of the state became established globally as a structural equilibrium or a reference point. Once established, it came to
dominate the normative and ontological landscape, and helped
to delegitimize the possible alternatives. Non-European forms of
political organization that might have attained widespread legitimacy as alternatives to the European-style sovereign state were
subordinated and delegitimized as global models, a situation which
for the time being remains unlikely to be reversed, however important such non-European forms are in contemporary politics. With
its global ascendancy and homologizing tendency, the Western
system of international law provided some basis for the development of minimum standards on such matters as treatment of
foreigners and their property, the law of the sea, recognition of
governments, and perhaps even religious tolerance. Whatever its
limitations and inequalities, this modest structure of international
order was the foundation upon which attempts to regulate state
conduct and establish legal responsibility have thereafter built.

The gatekeeping doctrines of recognition of states and membership in the Family of Nations allowed some consideration of type
of regime, but as between recognized member states the modest
scheme described by Oppenheim in 1905 did not draw legal distinctions on the basis of type of regime. The division of the world into
functionally and juridically similar territorial units implied that,
provided the entity was treated internationally as a state, its domestic structure and type of regime did not matter.[27] This remained an
orthodox view for most of the century, as the International Court
of Justice made clear in 1986 in *Nicaragua* v. *USA*.[28]

Nevertheless, the characterization of the system of sovereign equality embodied in the writings of legal positivists such as Oppenheim as a 'billiard ball' approach is excessively stark. States were expected to be able to keep order, particularly to meet international obligations to foreigners. As international economic law and labour law began to develop, internal decisions of states began to be subject to external standards, as with the attempt in the early 1900s to achieve a level playing field through uniform restrictions on the use of phosphorus in workplaces. There were proposals to apply viability criteria to states, although the practical application of these was limited. Oppenheim acknowledged the strength of the principle of nationality and the desirability of treating minorities within states on a basis of equality. Although the two pre-World War I editions did not contain it, the shattering effects of that conflict prompted the addition to Oppenheim's list of morals derivable from the history of international law the proposition that

the progress of International Law is intimately connected with the victory everywhere of constitutional government over autocratic government, or, what is the same thing, of democracy over autocracy. Autocratic government, not being responsible to the nation it dominates, has a tendency to base the external policy of the State, just as much as its internal policy, on brute force and intrigue; whereas constitutional government cannot help basing both its external and its internal policy ultimately on the consent of the governed. And although it is not at all to be taken for granted that democracy will always and everywhere stand for international right and justice, so much is certain, that it excludes a policy of personal aggrandizement and insatiable territorial expansion, which in the past has been the cause of many wars.[29]

Judicial decisions and arbitral awards of the period also suggested awareness of the importance in international relations of the links between sovereignty and domestic structures. The arbitral tribunal in the North Atlantic Coast Fisheries Arbitration (1910) rejected the implication of a servitude for the USA in the territorial waters of Canada, finding that the creation of such sovereign rights for the United States would involve dividing the sovereignty over the waters. The tribunal acknowledged that this did occur among entities with 'quasi-sovereignty', as in the Holy Roman Empire, but opined that modern states, particularly Britain, had never accepted such partitions of sovereignty, 'owing to the Constitution of a modern State requiring essential sovereignty and independence'.[30]

The doctrine of international servitudes was 'little suited to the principle of sovereignty which prevails in States under a system of constitutional government such as Great Britain and the United States and to the present international relations of sovereign States'.[31] The equivocation in this statement was matched in wider political discourse. Where Woodrow Wilson sought to promote constitutional democracy as a general principle, E. H. Carr attacked the Wilsonian predilection for making American principles the principles of mankind, and Americans into the bearers of a higher ethic.[32]

Practice was often more nuanced than broad doctrinal assertions suggest, but it is nonetheless evident that treatment of issues of equality and inequality in the traditional conceptual structure of international law based on sovereign equality was grossly inadequate as a basis for accommodating the developments of this century; major difficulties have resulted from the simultaneous commitments to Oppenheim's basic structure and to making adequate provision for new realities.[33] Numerous devices have been honed to reconcile the system of sovereign equality and unit homogeneity with challenges posed by the facts of inequality and difference.

Strategies for reconciling the sovereign equality system with existing inequalities

Oppenheim, like many of his leading successors, was an accomplished exponent of devices to reconcile the idea of obligatory international law with the positivist conception of a legal system founded on state sovereignty: including the binding/non-binding dichotomy, the analytical separation of law and politics, and some focus on the then limited sphere of international legal process. These strategies were employed, for example, to enable adherence to the fundamental legal value of formal isonomy while limiting the range of inequalities with which the international legal system concerns itself. Thus Oppenheim, like other legal positivists, separates law from non-law so that the inequalities become social rather than legal facts. Many positivist writers emphasize consent (an analogue to the move from status to contract) as explanation for such phenomena as protectorates, oppressive rules, and voting inequalities. Categories used for distinction or discrimination are defined by neutral-sounding criteria which are less likely to attract strict scrutiny, e.g. 'specially affected states' are deemed to be a relevant category in weighing competing practice to determine the existence or otherwise of a rule of customary international law,[34] but this category operates mainly (albeit not exclusively) for the benefit of powerful states. The theoretical problem arising from the fact that many smaller states may not show any support (in the sense of practice) for a rule is addressed by the move from consent to consensus. This enables responsibilities to be fixed on states that have not in fact accepted them, and is supported by the persistent dissenter rule, which in practice is mainly a negotiating card (or possible outlet) for the powerful.[35]

Apparent inequalities among peoples in achieving independence and statehood were addressed by separating equality of states from equality of peoples, and managing some of the more pressing demands through the principle of nationalities, the principle of self-determination, and minority rights, all formulated as universal principles but applied only selectively in practice.

Progress toward equality has been continuously anticipated in international law: in Wilsonian or Leninist versions of self-determination, in the terms of the Class A Mandates of the League of Nations, in the provisions for trusteeship and decolonization under the UN Charter, in the hopes for general and complete disarmament in UN documents. Shortcomings in the attainment of equality are explained by the relative infancy and temporary weakness of international law.[36] Enduring inequalities among equal sovereigns, such as the structural inequalities in the United Nations Charter, the Nuclear Non-Proliferation Treaty, or the voting arrangements of the International Monetary Fund, are characterized either as special functional exceptions or as temporary accommodations to the realities of power. There are debates as to how equality is most fairly expressed in representative arrangements, such as proposals for the most populous states from particular regions to become permanent members of the Security Council, but accounts of international law that would base it upon the management of inequality, for example through the principle of balance of power recognized by Oppenheim, have virtually disappeared from the literature of international law, although they are more evident in its practice.[37]

II. CHALLENGES TO THE TRADITIONAL INTERNATIONAL LAW SYSTEM OF SOVEREIGNTY AND EQUALITY

The 'traditional' account of international law as law between states uses the notion of 'the sovereign state' as a somewhat artificial organizing device to simplify the complex world, in order to manage it. 'States' represent the carving of the world into non-overlapping territorial units, now virtually exhaustive of the earth's land area, vested with the authority to regulate in their territories, the responsibility not to harm certain interests of others, and the capacity to make claims when they or their nationals are affected by illegality for which other states or international organizations are responsible. A reasonably comprehensive if decentralized effort is made to connect every individual, corporation, vessel, and aircraft with at least one territorial state for these purposes. Even as it was becoming entrenched in the international law framework of the world, this organizing account of the legal system among sovereign states was confronted with numerous glaring problems. Arguments about the suitability of the 'traditional' international law concept of state sovereignty have been a feature of the international legal literature throughout the twentieth century,[38] but the recent perception of a globalizing, democratizing world, no longer dominated by the politics of bipolar confrontation between nuclear alliances, has provided empirical sustenance to normative arguments that have gained ground in the West against excesses of the sovereignty system. Many of the contemporary challenges to the state are considered elsewhere in this volume; this part will briefly note some of their implications for the international law system of sovereignty, as a basis for consideration of possible changes in the relationship of sovereignty and inequality.

Globalization

The amorphous congeries of phenomena loosely denominated 'economic globalization' suggest that transnational industries and markets increasingly require forms of transnational regulation or regulatory cooperation that differ from the methods and institutions of traditional inter-state law-making.[39] In some sectors national laws are converging around standards established in the dominant states. In others important operational norms are shaped by non-governmental groups or by market practitioners, on such matters as forest management practices, labour standards for shoe and apparel exporters, accounting standards, marine insurance terms, and interpretation of international commercial contracts. Forms of 'world law' may be emerging—whether through mimesis, or world culture, or regulatory competition—from which most states are not free to depart except at intolerable cost.[40] These emerging features of rule-making are being replicated, more slowly, in evolving systems of implementation and enforcement. National courts, administrative agencies, and perhaps even legislatures are said increasingly to function not simply as parochial national institutions but as parts of cooperative regulatory and enforcement webs, to interact in transgovernmental networks 'with one another and with supranational tribunals in ways that would accommodate differences but acknowledge and reinforce common values'.[41] Proposals for private schemes of implementation are appearing in diverse areas, from tradeable CO_2 emission permits to private contracting for enforcement of intellectual property rules.

International legal rules

The depth and density of rules promulgated by inter-governmental organizations is increasing, and these organizations are becoming more assertive vis-à-vis individual sovereign states in rule-making and in implementation.[42] Inequality between member states has become relatively common in inter-governmental organizations: requirements of unanimity in voting, conferring a veto on each, are now rare, despite the frequent use of consensus; systems designed to reflect major interests through weighted voting or specially defined functional majorities have become more common; and a few organizations are able to make intrusive demands on member states. State dominance in rule-making organizations is slowly accommodating increased roles of non-state groups, for example in the International Standards Organization, the Arctic Council, and the influence of industry in the operation of the Montreal Protocol stratospheric ozone system.

There is some evidence of convergence of substantive legal rules across various groups of states, and of increasing cross-recognition by states of each other's national laws and institutional acts. To this body of convergent state norms must be added the norms established and applied by non-state actors *inter se*, whether with or without state involvement—standard terms in particular industries, the UNCITRAL rules, normative practices of lawyers and other professionals in structuring capital market transactions, and the international arrangements of credit card agencies and global franchises. While these might be regarded as informal social norms, they are effective in shaping behaviour, and often constrain the regulatory possibilities effectively open to states and inter-state institutions.[43] In contemporary practice such transnational normative phenomena are important and must not be ignored simply because the sources-based conceptual apparatus of international law struggles to deal with them.[44] It is not realistic or adequate in all cases simply to reformulate such private norms on the basis of some consent or delegation by sovereign will. The net effect of such changes in the making and implementation of norms has been to shift decision-making to powerful states and non-state groups, widening the gulf between law-makers and law-takers.

Transnational civil society

For many proponents of the emergence of a transnational civil society,[45] states should be seen simply as important loci of power and authority within a transnational civil society which permeates their borders.[46] That society finds voice and political expression through states but not only through states—the interests of individuals and groups are also expressed in many other ways, and proposals abound for institutional reform to enhance such representation.[47] International law can be seen as the law of such a transnational society, regulating states but not dependent entirely on states for its existence, content, or implementation. In more ambitious versions of this theory, state sovereignty is in some respects constituted by the law of the transnational civil society, escaping the tendency within the traditional framework for international law to take sovereignty as a pre-legal social fact. Inequalities in access, participation, power, and accountability within this emerging transnational civil society have scarcely been confronted in international law, in part because of liberal commitments to the marketplace of ideas and suspicion of attempts to regulate information.

Democratization

Democratization potentially reinforces sovereignty: democracy legitimizes state institutions, and these institutions rather than international or transnational bodies are the principal organized expression of the popular will or interests whose vindication is sought by democratic theory. Nevertheless, it is sometimes argued that the realization of true democracy in complex polities may have the consequence that the unified sovereignty of states itself disappears, undermining the assumption that unitary sovereign states are the foundation for the international legal system. Authority and power are still identifiable, but the argument is that the concentration of these in any particular location has been so thoroughly checked, balanced, and dispersed that there is no traditional 'sovereignty'. The critiques of unity and centralization directed at the sovereignty model by feminist theorists, radical ecologists, advocates of democratic decentralization, and institutional cosmopolitanists all favour wide vertical dispersion of sovereignty as a means to achieve such ethical goals as peace and security, reduced oppression, global economic justice, and participation.[48] Systems of divided or dispersed sovereignty provide one possible approach to the representation problems that are central to liberal political theory. Movements toward greater power for local communities, land and government rights for indigenous peoples, autonomy for various ethnic or territorial groups, fragmentation of authority to promote identity and difference, and legal recognition of civil society organizations all promote more pluralistic governance arrangements. Thus far, however, such arguments have been met by responses of the sort formulated by Hans Morgenthau:

Democratic constitutions, especially those consisting of a system of checks and balances, have purposely obscured the problem of sovereignty and glossed over the need for a definite location of the sovereign power . . . In their endeavor to make democracy 'a government of laws and not of men' they forgot that in any state, democratic or otherwise, there must be a man or group of men ultimately responsible for the exercise of political authority . . . in a democracy that responsibility lies dormant in normal times . . . Yet in times of crisis and war that ultimate responsibility asserts itself, as it did under the presidencies of Lincoln, Wilson, and the two Roosevelts, and leaves to constitutional theorists the arduous task of arguing it away after the event.[49]

But the reality is that crises of authority in which the pinpoint location of concentrated sovereignty must be established are sufficiently infrequent that more diffuse models are beginning to acquire some legitimacy, especially in the prosperous democracies. The European Union provides the most influential archetype. Nonetheless, the state has proved remarkably enduring as a locus of authority.[50] This is true even in the European Union, the most far-reaching institutional project for divided sovereignty and multiple levels of governance. While there is clearly a possibility of the European Union evolving in ways that displace the sovereignty model of the place of the state and do not simply substitute the EU as a new sovereign,[51] states have so far managed the institutional architecture to preserve major roles for themselves in taking the crucial decisions on forms of governance, and the kinds of roles played by states in international relations are still played within the EU.[52]

The cumulative pressure on the traditional international legal doctrine of sovereignty arising from these empirical and conceptual changes is considerable. Some incidents of state sovereignty—the attributes of membership in the international legal order, such as the capacities to make treaties, join the United Nations, and claim sovereign immunity in other states' courts for certain governmental acts—are deeply embedded as constitutive rules of the game in the international law system.[53] This set of arrangements, established partly on the basis of mutual interest and reciprocity, has become a structural equilibrium.[54] Each actor has incentives to be part of this membership system, both for reasons of efficacy in the conduct of international affairs and because of benefits conferred on leaders in internal politics by international recognition. No significant powerful actors have an incentive to defect from the system. It is self-enforcing, self-perpetuating, and reinforced to some degree by cognitive entrenchment. It is likely to change only incrementally unless it becomes grossly inefficient for its purposes, or suffers a crisis of legitimacy.

The position is more complex, however, in the case of other incidents of sovereignty in international law. *Independence*, in the sense of the freedom to make choices as to economic, political, and social systems, domestic policy, and foreign policy, is routinely infringed. Where such infringement is non-forcible, the rules of general international law do not provide very comprehensive protection for independence, and not all of the rules bearing on this topic are upheld even by strong social pressure. Thus the prohibition of the use of force does not encompass economic coercion,[55] and economic pressure *simpliciter* in the conclusion of a treaty is not a ground for its nullity.[56] *Territorial supremacy* is more fully protected by international law rules, including most fundamentally the prohibition of the acquisition of territory by conquest, and the clear rules against overflight and incursions by foreign law enforcement officials. Even here, however, there are exceptions, including, for example, the stationing of UN guards in Northern Iraq, US air patrols over Iraq, the UN sanctions against Libya tied to the surrender of the Lockerbie bombing suspects,[57] and the relatively weak rules on remote sensing and on extraterritorial jurisdiction based on the effects doctrine. *Personal supremacy* of the state over its nationals has been eroded by human rights law, increasing acceptance of dual nationality with rights of one state of nationality against the other,[58] and increased availability to individuals and corporate bodies of a variety of national courts and international tribunals in which the action of a particular state may be challenged.[59] *Organizational sovereignty* is protected by doctrines limiting jurisdiction of other states and by the principle of non-intervention, but the burgeoning range of inter-state, mixed, and private entities engaged in norm formation and governance is not closely controlled by international law; some European states found it necessary to amend constitutional monopolies on legislative power to accommodate the increasing legislative capacity of the European Community.

In sum, pressures on the traditional sovereignty-based system of international law have resulted in the weakening of the domestic/international split, percolation of commitments to formal isonomy and to some principles of substantive equality from domestic law and politics to international law, promotion internationally of forms of market equality and extra-market inequality associated with economic liberalism, gradual acceptance of international obligations toward non-state groups, the forced enlargement of the minimalist involvement of international law in human rights and in the internal structure of polities, and the clouding of the concept of international law as a pure state-privileging inter-state system. These adaptations in doctrine reflect the practical and normative inadequacies of the traditional conception of international law as the law among sovereign states that have long been recognized in international legal scholarship. Over the past century these adaptations have been accommodated by manipulation of the traditional framework rather than construction of a widely endorsed alternative. The traditional system of sovereignty is under strain, but for the time being is continuing to creak along.[60]

III. IMPLICATIONS FOR INEQUALITY OF DISCARDING TRADITIONAL INTERNATIONAL LAW SOVEREIGNTY

The continuing rapid changes often described as 'globalization' and 'democratization', and the new possibilities and uncertainties opened by the lifting of Cold War rigidities, have spurred intensified criticism of the traditional system of sovereign equality, and the construction of incipient alternatives.

It is all too evident that the high twentieth-century commitment to virtually universal formal equality of states in the sovereignty model has not resolved many of the underlying problems. In terms of their capacity to manage issues of national economic and social policy, their political ability to represent and regulate, their provision of a rule-of-law system and guarantees of property rights and basic civil rights, many putative states have only the trappings but not most of the effective functions of states. The activities of some state institutions appear to make human flourishing and economic activity more rather than less difficult. In some cases, they have neither monopolized the use of force nor achieved the maintenance of basic order; in other cases, there is order, but it is not provided by the institutions of the state. All of this leads to the argument that the traditional sovereignty-based system of international law has in egregious cases proved to be a travesty, in which priorities of good governance and human welfare have been subordinated to a very formal commitment to ineffective structures.

One alternative to the traditional approach, deriving from Western liberal democratic theory, begins with individuals, organized into political groupings to pursue collective interests through the institutions and public politics of civil society, local, state, transnational, and international institutions.[61] Institutions reflect both past decisions and the interests of particular constituencies presently wielding power. The regulatory influence of institutions characteristically reaches beyond those groups who are influential within them, but democratic principles require that all influenced by regulatory decisions have at least the possibility of a voice in the relevant institution. Regulatory competences are allocated among institutions on the basis of principles of constitutional design that vary with the architects but are seldom based purely on efficiency.[62] This approach leads to a view of state institutions not as representatives of sovereign power but simply as functional institutions competing with each other and with other actors in a market to provide cost-effective governance at the requisite standard. Responsiveness to the needs and interests of particular constituencies is a vital element of success in such a market.

What would be the effect of a general rejection of the present commitment to traditional sovereignty, and its replacement by a functionalist liberal view of market-based governance institutions? States would not disappear: they would remain the principal units of order and governance. Legal rules of mutual respect and coordination would continue to be necessary. The crucial change would be normative—the protections and status conferred by the concept of sovereignty would cease to be fundamental norms upon the maintenance of which the stability of the legal system depends, becoming instead overtly contractual, and defeasible. Just as the abolition of elaborate diplomatic orders of precedence, or of aristocratic titles, wrought a change to the normative environment without in itself redistributing material power, states would continue as loci of power and authority; but without the privilege conferred by sovereignty, some might suffer severely, and this suffering would be distributed unevenly. International law would perhaps arrive at a functional conception of sovereignty as a bargaining resource of variable quantity, similar to that described by Robert Keohane:

Sovereignty no longer enables states to exert effective supremacy over what occurs within their territories . . . What sovereignty does confer on states under conditions of complex interdependence is legal authority that can either be exercised to the detriment of other states' interests or be bargained away in return for influence over others' policies and therefore greater gains from exchange.[63]

The normative inhibitions associated with sovereignty moderate existing inequalities of power between states, and provide a shield for weak states and weak institutions. These inequalities would become more pronounced if the universal normative understandings associated with sovereignty were to be discarded, and sovereignty were to become simply a summation of the operations of the market, a bargaining resource to be traded off against other sources of value. Specific rules presently associated with sovereignty would continue to have a basis in contract and reciprocity, but the terms of these revisable bargains would reflect inequalities of power between states rather than the shared social understandings of what is inherent in statehood. Legal sovereignty would become, as the international relations aphorism has it, a variable rather than a parameter. Three more specific implications for inequality among states of a diminution in the normative power of the traditional concept of state sovereignty may be briefly noted. The question whether heightened inequalities amongst states might be justified by a reduction in inequalities and injustices among individuals and groups that an alternative system might achieve will be considered in the conclusion.

Diminished restraints on coercive intervention

The traditional international law concept of sovereignty constitutes an important normative inhibition to military intervention. There have been extraordinarily few cases of recolonization of former colonies once recognized as independent states.[64] Since 1945 not only has the death rate of sovereign states been remarkably low,[65] there have been few military invasions intended to terminate the independent existence of an established state. Direct large-scale unilateral military intervention without an invitation has probably been constrained somewhat by the sovereignty model and the UN Charter norms that give expression to it. Advocacy of displacing sovereignty in favour of a less state-centric, more liberal international legal order undervalues the importance of this achievement. Such advocacy is animated by international political economy and other governance issues rather than issues of military security and the use of force in inter-state wars. This emphasis is defended by proponents on the ground that the absence of international war between liberal states reduces the importance of military security in a liberal 'zone of peace'.[66] But the world is far from being a zone of peace. There is a great risk of weakening hard-won normative arguments against military intervention that have been associated, especially since 1945, with the universal system of sovereign equality.

One of the major historic arguments for intervention, used frequently in the century prior to 1945, has been the unwillingness or ineffectiveness of local authorities in discharging international obligations. This was a principal justification of, for instance, extraterritorial consular jurisdiction imposed by European powers and the US on Turkey, Japan, China, Siam, Morocco, and other entities, and the collective military interventions in Mexico in 1861 (conducted primarily by France, with the support of Britain and Spain), China in 1898–1901 (the suppression of the Boxer uprising by a group of Western powers and Japan), and Venezuela in 1902 (Britain, Germany, and Italy). In Greece, Turkey, Bulgaria, Serbia, China, Argentina, and several other states, one or more foreign states took control of various government revenues to ensure payment of international obligations (principally debts and reparations).[67] The tenor of Western attitudes toward such foreign administration of struggling entities may be gauged from a report on US administration of the customs house in the Dominican Republic after 1905. According to the US author of this 1907 report, in the period since the failure of the movement to annex San Domingo to the USA in 1869–70, the country had experienced 'a miserable sequence of revolution and anarchy, interrupted by ruthless and blood-stained dictatorships'. After 1899, the 'country was laid waste, the people crushed to hopelessness, the treasury left to stew in utter bankruptcy, and a host of creditors, foreign and domestic, after tightening their hold upon the future became more and more insistent in the present'. Administration of the customs house used almost 55 per cent of the net revenues to repay debts, with the remainder going to government expenditure. Once put in place, 'the Dominican Republic enjoyed a civil calm and an economic well-being such as it had not known for two generations'. If continued, 'we shall speedily see a West Indian people who have never had a fair chance, developing into a decent, prosperous peasantry'.[68]

The modern form of this argument holds that states deemed

insufficiently democratic, or with deeply divided societies not truly represented by the state institutions, or unable or unwilling to meet the plethora of international demands for adequate regulation, institutions, and policies, ought to lose their legitimacy. In particular circumstances this may culminate in forcible intervention. The normative case for increased intervention has been made with passion and conviction,[69] but is less convincing as an argument for the uneven patterns of intervention that actually occur.[70] Force may achieve narrowly defined short-term objectives such as the delivery of food aid or the removal of a particular tyrant, but outside powers without fundamental interests directly at stake are ordinarily unwilling to commit forces on a scale or for a duration sufficient to have even a prospect of establishing long-term democracy or bringing peace to bitterly divided societies. Multilateral intervention has notable achievements, but inevitably political calculations and interests in the intervening states weigh heavily in all aspects of military operations, and in the case of conflict are likely to prevail over the liberal principles offered as justification.

Diminution of state functions without effective alternatives

Functionalist arguments for the delegitimation of state institutions in weak states presume that state functions are replaceable. Thus where a state is held to have 'failed', its governance functions may be taken over by external agencies or private entrepreneurs: they may organize settlement of foreign investment disputes, repayment of debts, provision of security for diamond mines or oil pipelines, delivery of food and medical supplies, the conduct of plebiscites, and trials of alleged human rights abusers or narcotraffickers. Or outsiders may be positioned as 'trainers' or 'advisers' to judges, police forces, or government ministries.

Some functions of states are not easily replicated by other institutions, however. In the traditional sovereignty system, even relatively fragile states play a potentially important function as a basis of identity and a focus of loyalty, balancing the pull of identities based on clan or ethnic group or religious solidarity or city. The representativity of the state and the performance of its institutions condition its effectiveness in these functions, but it is almost impossible for externally based institutions to perform these functions.

Some liberals are remarkably sanguine about this issue, proposing that the world will eventually evolve as the West is thought to have done in the account of Dan Deudney and John Ikenberry: 'As civic and capitalist identities have been strengthened, ethnic and national identity has declined. A distinctive solution to the problem of nationalism and ethnicity has evolved in the West.' In their account, markets, a common civic identity, and a distinctive institutional order of international relations have produced in the West 'a complex polity spilling across the juridical borders of states and enveloping state institutions'.[71] But the West remains a region of strong and popular states. Delegitimizing the state by dispensing with its sovereignty—a process likely to be targeted on weak states outside the West—leaves identity and loyalty to be conditioned exclusively by other forces in ways that may disserve the liberal objectives animating this challenge to sovereignty.

Another significant function of sovereignty has been to preserve some autonomy in decision-making, and hence some space for difference, for the community within the state. The liberal functionalist argument is that such autonomy is waning because of economic globalization, that real difference is declining inexorably with cultural, economic, and political convergence, and that differences protected by state sovereignty often comprise such undesirable traits as the subordination of women, the maintenance of corrupt elites, and the suppression of political dissent or religious freedom. Thus it is argued that the economic and cultural basis of the traditional sovereignty system is disappearing, and that the legal order must adjust accordingly.

The processes of colonial expansion and state formation that made the traditional sovereignty system global were themselves highly intrusive, but the system now provides a mild check on further intrusion. The formation of modern states has transformed local political forms; a return to a pre-existing 'culturally authentic' system for the organization of power and decision-making is improbable even in countries where the modern state is least well rooted. Nevertheless, the apparent homology among state institutions for international purposes does not reflect homogenization of local political forms, let alone uniformity in the social and economic patterns to which effective political institutions must be responsive. These patterns are often inegalitarian, but the freedom to seek to exert influence in a polity still open to local concerns is an empowering attraction of the sovereignty system. Governance by outside institutions, and external intervention, may transform local politics into struggles to capture the benefits supplied from outside or to lead resistance. In the long term, state institutions may be discredited from outside without any credible alternative means to achieve particular governance functions. In weak or externally dominated states, and in deeply divided societies or those with systemic social violence, it is not at all clear that liberal functionalist alternatives to the traditional sovereignty system are likely to be realized in practice or to effectuate enduring improvement.

Re-dividing the world into zones

The universalization of the system of formally equal sovereign states—Oppenheim's 'Family of Nations'— has been a remarkable feature of the international legal order of the past century. The quest to fulfil these universalist aspirations, to establish more substantive equality among states in their capacities to influence legal development and to pursue agendas that are not simply those of the powerful, has been a leitmotif for generations of anti-colonial *tiers-mondiste* international lawyers.[72] Emerging liberal thinking about the international legal order argues increasingly that it is possible to divide the world into zones,[73] with a liberal zone of law, constituted by liberal states practising a higher degree of legal civilization, to which other states will be admitted only when they meet the requisite standards.[74] This is in some respects a continuation of recurrent patterns in the history of Western legal thought, traceable, for example, in the sixteenth-century European divisions between Christians and infidels,[75] or in James Lorimer's late-nineteenth-century division of the world into a hierarchy of civilized nations, barbarous humanity, and savage humanity.[76] As in the past, this identification of zones may be defended simply as a description of existing or emerging reality,[77] but its many normative advocates see the liberal West as the vanguard of a transformed global legal order in which many of the limitations of the sovereignty-based legal system can finally be transcended. The theory of liberal and non-liberal zones proposes differential treatment where the boundaries of the liberal zone are crossed, conferring privileges based on membership in the liberal zone, and setting high barriers to entry.

The new standard of civilization is defended normatively as the means to promote the advancement of the backward. It is not clear, however, why human flourishing is better promoted by the construction of an identifiable 'other', an 'us' and 'them' from amongst the myriad ways of understanding and classifying the world. The construction of the zones of law in spatial terms reflects a territorial and state-based view of the world which much of the argument from globalization and the cross-cutting constituencies of liberalism is concerned to reject. The outcome seems likely to be the maintenance of a classificatory system which is itself both an explanation and a justification for those at the margins remaining there for generations.

IV. CONCLUSION

Proposals to move away from the traditional account of international law based on state sovereignty—the account found in Oppenheim and preponderant throughout the twentieth century—have not crystallized as a single coherent alternative. Some advocate a broader view of the range of norms encompassed in the concept of 'international law': norms of interaction for individuals and groups in transnational civil society, many of which are chosen voluntarily by contract even if they often rely on state power for enforcement; rules and decisions promulgated by state institutions in transnational dialogue with other relevant institutions; and the law controlling state action, which will be a mixture of international agreements and national law, and will generally be subject to enforcement in national courts and in supra-national courts, of which the European Court of Justice is a prototype.[78] Others propose to move away from the requirement of explicit consent by each state as the basis for binding obligation, finding universal law in a range of normative pronouncements from inter-governmental conferences, repeated provisions in treaties, the practice of international organizations, and other evidence of a general will of a diverse international community.[79] Modern extensions of natural law approaches, including the policy science and communication approach long advocated by the New Haven School, have an enduring attraction in seeming to base international law on community policies that reflect higher purposes and not simply on the putative will of formal sovereigns.[80] These different approaches all allow greater scope for the substance of international law to be influenced by 'global public policy'. This policy spans managed trade, market liberalism, protection of intellectual property and wildlife, civil rights, public participation, and a range of other values favoured in the political West. It encompasses a commitment to some basic equality among human beings, but it is not at present a strongly egalitarian policy.[81] The commitments of different advocates differ, but the aggregate of forces pushing to shift legal thought from a normative-status view of sovereignty to a functional-contractual view are not at present accompanied by a corresponding impetus to ameliorate and manage problems of inequality.

A decline in the traditional sovereignty system weakens the relationship of mutual containment between sovereignty and inequality. The justification sovereignty provides for the silence of international law as to the management of inequality within national societies—the weakness of international law regimes on landlessness, unemployment, gender inequity, basic education, mental illness—threatens to disappear at a time when inequalities in many societies are rising. Inequalities between many societies are also growing larger, while the weakening of the sovereignty paradigm would remove the segmenting buffer that has been a moral underpinning, however incoherent, for inter-societal inequalities.[82] Inequalities in the structure of transnational activities and the incidence of their legal regulation intensify these inter-societal inequalities. The increasing need for regulation of non-state actors, including actors in the emerging transnational civil society, and for the development of a democratic transnational law, coincides with the weakening of the prerogatives of the institutions of some states, leaving many communities dependent in practice on the regulatory efforts of the strong states or of international institutions.

People experiencing a decline in their ability to shape deleterious or unsettling changes can be expected to resist. Sovereign states open the prospect of some autonomy, the possibility for individuals and groups to make a difference in a structured political space whose institutions and community shape their conscious identities. The suspension of the OECD negotiations on the Multilateral Agreement on Investment in May 1998, which occurred partly through the involvement of citizens' groups in the OECD but, more importantly, through public opposition expressed in the political systems of a number of participating states, illustrates the value many individuals place on autonomous decision-making within the state in the face of the imperatives of globalization. In strong states, the US above all, there is little prospect that the autonomy inherent in the traditional sovereignty system will be compromised, and the politics of the civil society will continue to be channelled through state institutions even as the activities and concerns of the civil society gradually become more transnational. Citizenship and loyalty will continue to have a vital political meaning defined by reference to the state. The 'citizenship' of the European Union, promised but underspecified in the legal texts of the Union, seems likely to take its substance as a gloss on the enduring loyalties and citizenships of individuals attached to the member states.

The imperative for some degree of participation and autonomy has buttressed the traditional sovereignty system. It is often argued that a new liberal global legal order, or indeed a post-modern post-sovereignty international law, will make participation and active citizenship more possible, overturning tyrannies and hierarchies and increasing freedom and community and equality. But there will not soon exist a global community which is capable of sustaining the politics and institutions necessary to realize such ambitious visions. Their realization would require not only the conceptual change which their advocates promote and have begun to achieve, but extraordinary resources which new technology and global economy do not yet provide. In their aspirational but unrealized state, such visions serve in the interim to legitimate an extraordinary range of interventionist or otherwise coercive activities in other countries that reflects struggles and dilemmas in politics in the West: removal of dictators; extraterritorial police operations against narcotics cartels allegedly protected by corrupt regimes; no-fly zones to safeguard threatened ethnic groups; the empowerment of victims of gender discrimination, religious persecution, or gun control laws; protection of the unborn, tropical forests, intellectual property, marine mammals, foreign investors, or telecommunications service providers; promotion of peace processes, free if ethnically divisive elections, and unsafe safe havens. These agendas involve, and are often responsive to, groups outside the West, but they are largely set in the West, with timing suitable to political interests in the West, and with inconsistencies and vagaries driven in many respects by dynamics in the West. To be pursued effectively they require, paradoxically, organized inequality, on a larger scale than presently exists. They also require a system for the management of inequality that international law at present lacks. The traditional sovereignty system is flawed, and will continue to be stretched and strained. But for the time being it remains a more realistic system for the management of enduring inequalities, and of other pathologies of the international system of law and politics, than any of the alternatives on offer.

4

Gender Inequality and International Human Rights Law

Christine Chinkin

In 1995 at the Fourth United Nations (UN) Conference on Women the governments of the 189 states that participated recognized that 'inequalities between women and men have persisted and major obstacles remain'.[1] It is therefore somewhat surprising to read the words of the former Secretary-General of the United Nations, Boutros Boutros-Ghali, when he asserted in the same year that 'Few causes promoted by the United Nations have generated more intense and widespread support than the campaign to promote and protect the equal rights of women.'[2] He explained that the 'organization has helped to create a historic legacy of internationally agreed strategies, standards, programmes and goals to advance the status of women world-wide'. The first section of this chapter will survey the reality of women's global inequality. In the second section it will look at the source of the Secretary-General's assertions, at the international legal standards of equality between men and women, and at the strategies and programmes that have been introduced. In Section III it will examine some of the reasons for the enormous disparity that exists between legal regulation and reality. The explanations appertain to flaws within the legal framework, to defects in the concept of equality used to promote women's advancement, and to the inadequacies of law to amend behaviours that are deeply rooted within tradition and culture and are supported by global economic structures. In light of these, the chapter will conclude by questioning whether legal prescription, and in particular international legal prescription, can ever generate fundamental societal change.

I. GLOBAL GENDER INEQUALITY

Throughout the world women continue to face inequality in all spheres of their life. Some examples will present the picture.[3] In public life women remain under-represented in international and national decision- and policy-making bodies. Politically, adult women have not yet achieved the right to vote in all countries.[4] Only 24 women have ever been elected heads of state, although the 10 women heads of state who were in office at the end of 1994 is the highest in history.[5] Women are under-represented in national decision-making bodies, including legislative and economic bodies,[6] and those agencies responsible for law and justice. Indeed, in Eastern European states that have undergone sweeping economic and political transformation in the 1990s, the participation of women in legislative bodies has decreased.[7] The target endorsed by the Economic and Social Council (ECOSOC) of 30 per cent women in national decision-making levels by 1995 remains far from realized.[8]

The national picture is replicated internationally. The UN does not lead from the front. Article 8 of the Charter provides that no restriction shall be placed on the eligibility of both men and women to participate 'under conditions of equality in its principal and subsidiary organs'. Nevertheless, there has never been a woman Secretary-General and only after some concerted effort do women now occupy a third of professional-category posts within the Secretariat. The goal of 50 per cent women in professional posts by the fiftieth anniversary of the United Nations in 1995 was deferred to the year 2000.[9] Out of 50 Presidents of the General Assembly since 1945 only two have been women; out of 89 executive heads of various organizations within the United Nations system there are no women. There are currently more women heads of major UN programmes than ever before, that is, the United Nations High Commissioner for Refugees (UNHCR), the head of UNICEF, and the Directors of World Food, the United Nations Population Fund, and the United Nations Environment Program. These are the 'soft' programmes of the international arena, comparable to such matters as education or child-care in domestic governments. Women still do not occupy senior positions in the 'hard' areas of international peace and security, peace-keeping, and disarmament and in programmes for trade and investment or economic development.[10] From 1957 to 1993 no women were appointed to decision-making positions within UN peace-keeping headquarters. Only since 1994, following specific requests from the Focal Point for Gender within the UN, have there been a few female appointments to professional military posts in the UN Secretariat.[11]

Accurate data in economic, social, and cultural matters is uncertain, not least because of the frequent concealment of women within the private sphere of the home and family. None the less, the index ranking of 130 countries on gender equality in basic health, education, and income contained in the 1995 *Human Development Report* prepared by the United Nations Development Programme shows that in no country do women fare as well as men.[12] Poverty has emerged as a markedly feminine phenomenon throughout the world. 'Of the more than 1 billion people living in abject poverty, women are an overwhelming majority.'[13] At Beijing it was recognized that international economic development can further disadvantage women. States carrying crippling foreign debt and undergoing internationally prescribed structural adjustment programmes have reduced social expenditures and transferred social responsibilities to individuals, with disproportionately adverse impact upon women.[14] Women earn less for comparable work, are often barred from certain forms of (lucrative) employment, and perform much of their work in the unpaid private sector, including the rural sector. They have no choice but to accept poorly paid, undervalued work in often dangerous working conditions and with no job security. Legal barriers, including those derived from customary law to the ownership of, or access to, land, resources, capital, and technology, restrict women's economic advancement.[15] Women migrate in enormous numbers to seek work and too frequently become exposed to violence and sexual exploitation. The breakdown of political and economic inequality symbolized by the fall of the Berlin Wall has been followed by increased trafficking in women and children.[16] While women are participating in greater numbers in the paid labour force almost everywhere, there 'has not been a parallel lightening of responsibility for unremunerated work in the household and community'.[17]

Literacy rates worldwide are improving, but in all regions illiteracy remains higher for women than for men.[18] Worldwide, women live longer than men. 'However, health and well being elude the majority of women',[19] and the ways they die and the health risks they face are different. Female infanticide and selective abortion of female foetuses have led to the claim that over '100 million women are missing'.[20] Over 80 million women worldwide are subject to female genital surgery that may result in life-long health problems. Death is caused by malnutrition through food preference being given to males.[21] 'A major barrier for women to the achievement of the highest attainable standard of health is inequality, both between men and women and among women in different geographical regions, social classes and indigenous and ethnic groups.'[22]

Eighty per cent of the world's refugees and displaced persons are estimated by UNHCR to be women and children, many fleeing armed conflict in which they were allowed no part in decision-making.[23] As refugees they are subject to further discrimination, violence, and insecurity.[24] The widely publicized 'massive, organised and systematic' use of rape in the former Yugoslavia shamed the Security Council into establishing the War Crimes Tribunal for Former Yugoslavia, with rape located for the first time in an international instrument within the category of crimes against humanity.[25] This comparatively strong institutional response on this occasion obscures the reality that women continue to be subject to rape and sexual violence in armed conflict, as they always have been, and that these atrocities cannot be dismissed, as they so often are, as merely a matter of chance, of women victims being in the wrong place at the wrong time, or as normal incidents of war.[26] Focus on sexual violence and armed conflict screens yet another reality, that women are subjected to other forms of violence in peacetime in all societies, irrespective of religious, political, or economic ideologies, class, or culture. The UN Special Rapporteur on Violence against Women has located this violence in three sites: the home, the community, and the state.[27] She has reiterated that violence at personal, social, and international levels stems from the same roots and that sustainable global peace cannot be achieved without eliminating 'normal' violence against women.[28]

Throughout their entire lives women suffer restrictions in their life choices. They are exposed to discriminatory attitudes and unjust social and economic structures and bear the brunt of inadequate resources.[29] Inequality in all its aspects derives from cultural patterns 'that perpetuate the lower status accorded to women in the family, the workplace, the community and society'.[30] It deprives women of the opportunity of full and equal participation as citizens within their own societies, and within international society.

II. EQUALITY BETWEEN WOMEN AND MEN:
LEGAL REGULATION TO 1979

The negative prohibition of discrimination is the corollary of the positive right to equality. Campaigns for women's equality have therefore demanded recognition of the right of women not to be discriminated against on the basis of their sex. Although such movements were active well before the establishment of the UN in 1945,[31] the Charter was the first international instrument to contain an unequivocal commitment to that principle.[32] The purposes of the UN include a commitment in Article 1(3)

To achieve international co-operation in solving international problems of an economic, social, cultural, or humanitarian character, and in promoting and encouraging respect for human rights and for fundamental freedoms for all without distinction as to race, sex, language or religion . . .

The General Assembly was authorized in Article 13 'to initiate studies and make recommendations' in a number of matters, including 'assisting in the realization of human rights and fundamental freedoms for all without distinction as to race, sex, language or religion'. Articles 8, 55, 56, 60, 62, 68, and 76 also articulated the principle of non-discrimination, including on the grounds of sex, in a number of institutional contexts.

The Commission on Human Rights (CHR), established in 1946, was given the task of elucidating the general principles in Articles 55 and 56 of the Charter. In 1948, with Eleanor Roosevelt as chair, it concluded the Universal Declaration on Human Rights, which embraces in Articles 1 and 2 the concept of non-discrimination, *inter alia* on the grounds of sex.[33] The non-binding Declaration was given legal force through the two UN Human Rights Covenants of 1966 that, together with the Declaration, comprise the so-called International Bill of Rights.[34] Article 2 of the International Covenant on Civil and Political Rights (ICCPR) prohibits discrimination in the exercise of any of the rights enumerated in the Covenant, and Article 3 of the International Covenant on Economic, Social and Cultural Rights (ICESCR) does likewise.

Perhaps most importantly, the ICCPR also has a free-standing non-discrimination clause that affirms equality before the law. Article 26 states that

All persons are equal before the law and are entitled without any discrimination to the equal protection of the law. In this respect the law shall prohibit any discrimination and guarantee to all persons equal and effective protection against discrimination on any ground such as race, colour, sex, language, religion or other political opinion, national or social origin, property, birth or other status.

The general human rights treaties therefore provide an unambiguous legal prohibition of discrimination on the grounds of sex. Indeed, the weaker, aspirational character of the ICESCR is not applicable to Article 3, which is expressed in mandatory terms. Accordingly, discrimination in the provision of a benefit that is not required by other provisions of the Covenant would be contrary to Article 3.[35]

The work of the CHR has been supplemented by that of a number of the specialized agencies, especially the ILO and UNESCO, and the regional human rights organizations. From its inception the ILO had been committed to the principle of equal pay for equal work.[36] It has accordingly produced a number of conventions with respect to women in the paid workforce, including the Convention concerning the Equal Remuneration for Men and Women Workers for Work of Equal Value[37] and the Discrimination (Employment and Occupation) Convention.[38] The ILO has also been instrumental in generating further legal obligation.[39] The 1960 UNESCO Convention on Discrimination in Employment was also an acknowledgement of the importance of access to education in achieving equality.[40] Prohibitions against discrimination on the grounds of sex were formulated at the regional level through Article 14 of the European Convention on Human Rights,[41] Article 1 of the Inter-American Convention on Human Rights, and Article 2 of the African Charter on Human Rights.[42]

The anti-discrimination/equality stance is not always favoured by international policy-makers. Another approach is that of bestowing 'special' protection upon women.[43] For example, in some of its early treaties, the ILO limited women's access to employment, at night or in underground work, for protective purposes.[44] These made gendered assumptions about appropriate paid work for women while protecting 'men's work'. That women's interests were not paramount is shown by the exceptions that were allowed in 1934 when 'in serious emergency the national interest demands it'. Protectiveness is also apparent in Article 27 of the Fourth Geneva Convention, which asserts the obligation to protect women in international armed conflict 'against any attack on their honour, in particular against rape, enforced prostitution, or any form of indecent assault'.[45] The objective of according protection to all civilians during armed conflict is to be applauded, but explicit characterization of these acts as prohibited acts of violence against women would have been preferable to protection of honour. It is perhaps not too cynical to wonder whose honour is paramount. It might also have forestalled subsequent argument as to whether they constitute grave breaches of the laws of war.[46] The ICESCR too states that 'special protection should be accorded to mothers ... before and after childbirth', a provision that again focuses upon women's vulnerability and characterization in terms of motherhood.[47]

III. THE CONVENTION ON THE ELIMINATION OF ALL FORMS OF DISCRIMINATION AGAINST WOMEN, 1979

It was recognized early within the UN that discrimination against women was global, all-pervasive, and persistent. In 1946 a Sub-commission on the Status of Women was formed under the CHR, but this was soon elevated to parallel Commission status.[48] The original mandate of the Commission on the Status of Women (CSW) was to prepare recommendations and reports for the ECOSOC for the promotion of women's rights in 'political, economic, social and educational fields and to make recommendations on urgent problems requiring immediate attention in the field of human rights'. While intended to highlight the magnitude of the task of securing the advancement of women, this institutional separation has had the unfortunate tendency of marginalizing women's rights outside the mainstream human rights work performed by the CHR. The differentiation has been further emphasized by the choice of the Division for the Advancement of Women (rather than the UN Centre for Human Rights) as secretariat for the CSW.[49]

The CSW was responsible for a number of specialized conventions on women's political and personal rights.[50] These, combined with the work described above, began to build up an impressive array of formal obligations with respect to the rights of women. However, such obligations were either of general application (as in the UN Covenants) or subject-specific. Further, neither discrimination nor equality were defined in any of the general instruments.[51] It was therefore unclear whether their objective was limited to the prohibition of legal discrimination to achieve formal equality, or could be extended to equality of opportunity or result, approving positive discriminatory measures to redress past injustices. Nor was any distinction drawn between direct and indirect discrimination, but without inclusion of the latter, culturally and structurally rooted discriminatory behaviour remains unaddressed.

Support therefore grew for comprehensive prohibition of discrimination against those people who most frequently suffer its adverse effects and covering those areas where discrimination was most pervasive. In 1965 the first specialized convention on the elimination of discrimination was completed by the CHR, the Convention on the Elimination of All Forms of Racial Discrimination, the 'Race Convention'.[52] This provided a blueprint for the subsequent work of the CSW in drafting first the 1967 Declaration on the Elimination of All Forms of Discrimination against Women,[53] and subsequently the Convention on the Elimination of All Forms of Discrimination against Women, the 'Women's Convention'.[54]

The First UN Conference on Women, held in Mexico City in 1975, had called for a binding convention on the elimination of discrimination against women. The Women's Convention was prepared rapidly by the CSW to be ready for the Second UN Conference on Women, held in Copenhagen in 1980. The purpose of the Women's Convention is spelled out in its preamble. It is to achieve equality for women based on the recognition that full global development, the welfare of the world, the establishment of a just new international economic order, and the cause of international peace and security require the maximum participation of women on equal terms with men in all fields.[55]

Part I of the Women's Convention imposes general obligations upon states parties. Article 1 defines discrimination against women as any distinction, exclusion or restriction made on the basis of sex which has the effect or purpose of impairing or nullifying the recognition, enjoyment or exercise by women irrespective of their marital status, on a basis of equality of men and women, of human rights and fundamental freedoms in the political, economic, social, cultural, civil or any other field.

This definition draws upon that in the Race Convention.[56] It affirms that it applies only to adverse discrimination and includes direct and indirect discrimination. Intention to discriminate is not required. The definition was noted and approved by the United Nations Human Rights Committee in its General Comment No. 18 on the ICCPR, which provides consistency and cohesion between the Women's Convention and the more general, mainstream human rights treaties.[57]

Article 2 condemns such discrimination and imposes obligations upon states parties to institute with 'all appropriate means and without delay' policies to eliminate it in national laws and constitutions, and to take steps to ensure the practical realization of this principle. Article 3 requires parties to undertake appropriate measures in all fields for the 'full development and advancement of women'. Article 4 recognizes that assertions of formal equality, whether in legislation or national policies, are insufficient to achieve substantive equality, by providing that temporary special measures are acceptable during a transitional phase until 'the objectives of equality of opportunity and treatment have been achieved'. Article 5 also takes account of the inadequacies of legislative measures, by requiring parties to take appropriate measures to modify social and cultural patterns of conduct in order to remove prejudice and to change attitudes with respect to sexist stereotyping. Finally, Part I of the Convention requires that states shall take all appropriate measures to suppress trafficking in women and exploitation of prostitution.

Parts II, III, and IV of the Convention identify areas where gender-based discrimination is most marked. There are provisions on the participation of women in the public life of states (Articles 7 and 8), on equality in acquisition and conferral of nationality (Article 9), in access to, and in all other aspects of, education (Article 10), in matters of paid employment (Article 11), in access to health services (Article 12), in other areas of economic and social life (Article 13), before the law (Article 15), and within the family (Article 16). The specific needs of rural women are asserted in

Article 14. Part V establishes the Committee on the Elimination of Discrimination against Women (CEDAW), comprising 23 independent experts to receive initial and periodic reports from states parties 'on the legislative, judicial, administrative or other measures' taken to implement their obligations under the Convention. Unlike the Human Rights Committee, established under the ICCPR, or the Committee on the Elimination of Racial Discrimination, CEDAW is given no power to receive inter-state or individual or group complaints.[58] In the final Part, Article 28(2) prohibits reservations that are 'incompatible with the objects and purpose' of the Convention although the consequence of such a reservation is not specified.[59]

The Women's Convention does not provide a comprehensive catalogue of women's rights but rather affirms prohibition of discrimination on the basis of sex in specified areas. It has been criticized for its weak language. States retain considerable discretion with respect to performance in that they have only to take 'all appropriate measures' to eliminate discrimination in the various contexts. It provides few specific rights based upon the life experiences of women.[60] For example, women's independent right to reproductive freedom is not affirmed.[61] Where it does affirm specific rights, they are framed primarily in terms of protection and of the special situation of women as childbearers. Examples are found in the context of family education on the 'proper understanding of maternity as a social function',[62] in the 'special protection to women during pregnancy in types of work proved to be harmful to them',[63] and in appropriate measures to be taken in connection with pregnancy and childbirth.[64] Even in a Women's Convention, women are first accorded equality with men and then given further guarantees in accordance with their identification as 'the other'.

However, on the merits side, the Convention does articulate 'an international standard for what was meant by equality between men and women'[65] and goes beyond formal equality by requiring equality of access and opportunity. Importantly, it has inspired and become the framework for national anti-discrimination legislation. It explicitly prohibits discrimination against women and is thus not able to be appropriated by men claiming discrimination, as occurs in litigation under national anti-discrimination legislation and the regional human rights treaties.[66] Unlike the UN Covenants, where the two groups of rights were separated, it covers both civil and political rights and economic and social rights. This recognizes that for women the guarantee of the former category of rights can be meaningless without attention being paid to the economic, social, and cultural context in which they are claimed.[67] The Convention foreshadows the assertion in the Vienna Declaration and Programme of Action of the 'indivisibility and interdependence' of all human rights.[68]

Most significantly, the Convention attempts to break down the public/private divide that has undermined guarantees of women's rights. Feminists, especially those in the West, have argued that one of the reasons for women's lack of participation in public policy- and decision-making is their traditional consignment to the private arena of family and home.[69] Liberal political theory distinguishes between the public domain and the private. The former is properly occupied by men in paid employment who exercise power and authority through the structures of law, economics, politics, and governmental activities. The latter, the private world of the family and the home, is the proper (and natural) domain of women. This distinction is normative as well as descriptive: greater economic and political significance is attached to the public arena than to the private, and the public arena is accordingly subject to legal regulation. This confers primacy upon the male world and supports the global exercise of power, wealth, and legal control by men.[70] The explanatory force of the public/private divide has been questioned, especially in the context of Southern countries, where it has less empirical support, for example in light of women's co-option into the multinational labour force.[71] Nevertheless, although the understanding of public and private arenas varies across different societies, the location of women within a devalued 'private' sphere is general.

The major tenets of international law derive from Western political theory and this is reflected in human rights law. The primacy accorded to civil and political rights is one aspect of this.[72] Another is the continuation of the public/private divide by limiting the reach of human rights guarantees to wrongful state intervention in the public realm and by not extending it to abuse of power in the private.[73] A third is the doctrine of attributability, whereby states are only internationally responsible for the wrongful acts of public officials.[74] By asserting women's equal rights to participation in public decision-making bodies at all levels, the Convention forcefully locates women within the public arena.[75] Even more significantly, it explicitly affirms women's equality within the private arena. The requirement in Article 5 for appropriate measures to modify social and cultural attitudes digs deep into the private realm. Article 16 goes further than other human rights instruments which have designated the family itself as the unit for protection, through its provision for equality in 'all matters relating to marriage and family relations'.[76]

There are advantages in the historic association and textual coherence between the Race Convention and the Women's Convention. Common language is more readily absorbed and similar reporting requirements perhaps encourage efficiency. More fundamentally, matters within the domestic jurisdiction of states are excluded from UN intervention.[77] Human rights law has eroded the area of exclusion, most significantly in the context of race discrimination and apartheid.[78] It is widely accepted that the principle of racial equality constitutes customary international law and probably *jus cogens*.[79] The association between the two Conventions might be thought to facilitate similar assumptions about discrimination on the grounds of sex, or what has been termed 'gender apartheid'.[80] This, however, has not transpired. Despite identical prohibitions against discrimination on the grounds of sex, a state's treatment of its women is still widely claimed as falling within domestic jurisdiction and therefore protected from international scrutiny. Conflicting state practice, asserted justifications, broad reservations to the Women's Convention, and weaker enforcement measures have made protests against gender discrimination infrequent and assertions of customary international law harder to sustain.[81]

IV. THE LIMITATIONS OF EQUALITY

Equality, development, and peace

Despite the significant advances made for the legal guarantee of women's rights by the Women's Convention, it falls squarely within the liberal framework of equality for women with men. The link between women's equality and other primary objectives of the international legal order was made explicit in the Forward-Looking Strategies for the Advancement of Women adopted at Nairobi in 1985.[82] This linkage was continued into the Fourth World Conference at Beijing, where the empowerment of all women was asserted to be the duty of states and it was accepted that the full enjoyment by women of their human rights (including the right not to be discriminated against) is instrumental to the broader objectives of 'equality, development, and peace'. Despite the evident failure of the human rights guarantees to achieve gender equality, this is still asserted as the appropriate standard. Nevertheless, the appropriateness of the standard itself has been challenged. This section examines some feminist arguments on the inadequacies of the standard of equality for the emancipation of women and the following section locates those arguments within the framework of international human rights law.

Feminist challenges to equality

Perhaps the most problematic aspect of equality between men and women within human rights discourse remains that of accommodating difference. The protective labour treaties are based upon notions of difference, but exclude women from possibly desirable employment, deny women the right to choose their own form of paid work from the full range available to men, and maintain male control over the public domain of paid labour. They also suggest women's vulnerability to attack at night without allocating the blame for violations upon those responsible. The Aristotelian principle of equality expounds that like should be treated alike, while those who are different should be accorded unlike treatment in ways that are relevant to the differences.[83] The problem lies in determining what characteristics determine likeness. Equal treatment for women and men assumes commonality based upon human dignity. The standard of equality therefore works best where women are most like men, for example in public fields of employment. But equality also assumes meanings that have been constructed by patriarchy and uses men as the yardstick for comparison (for example, in workforce practices). Women are either the same as men or different from men, and it is men who have determined the standard and who devalue the difference.[84] The most striking difference between men and women as biologically determined is women's capacity to bear children, from which gendered accounts of women as primary carers of young and old have been constructed. Even in the context of paid employment, municipal courts have struggled with the concepts of equality and difference, especially in construing appropriate responses to claims arising out of discrimination on the basis of pregnancy.[85]

Feminists too are divided in their response to difference.[86] Liberal feminists have favoured emphasizing human sameness and minimizing difference in promoting formal equality. Cultural feminists have urged valuing difference,[87] and radical feminists have discounted equality in view of its entrenchment of male standards in the context of structural power imbalance between men and women and the global subordination of women.[88] Even equality of opportunity (as articulated in the Women's Convention) holds out no more than the promise for the same treatment as similarly situated men. It is not adequate where there is no male standard, or where cultural assumptions disguise the realities of gendered oppression. Nicola Lacey, for example, has argued that the liberal guarantee of equality assumes a world of autonomous individuals starting a race, or making free choices, an assumption that has no cutting edge against the fact that men and women are simply running different races.[89] Achievement of equality might offer advancement for individual women competing in the public male-dominated world but it offers no basis for a more fundamental reconceptualization of society. Rather, the promise of equal rights tacitly reinforces the existing political and economic power structures of society and offers women access to a world already defined and controlled by men.[90] It has been argued that in this situation of disempowerment, the discourse of rights that is structured by the power-bearing elites can offer little to transform the position of women.[91]

These labels are themselves constraining and many feminists move easily between them. It is not surprising that claims of difference are not readily reconciled with those of equality in international arenas where there are multiple diversities between men and women of, *inter alia*, race, religion, ethnicity, age, class, and sexuality. These differences apply to women *inter se* and the intersection between gender and other attributes makes still more complex the legal prohibition of discrimination on the basis of sex.

V. EQUALITY UNDER INTERNATIONAL LAW

Equality of peoples

The meaning and desirability of equality between peoples (as opposed to the sovereign equality of states) within the international legal order has also long been the subject of political and legal debate.[92] Equality was first considered in the context of the League of Nations' attempts to protect the position of national minorities in Europe after World War I.[93] By a number of treaties two underlying principles were established for the protection of minorities:

1. the principle of equality or non-discrimination;
2. the principle that persons belonging to minority groups should be guaranteed a number of special rights.[94]

This second principle fuelled the debate about difference at the international level. Does according special obligations to ensure the preservation of minority cultures create equality with the dominant population (who have the preservation of its culture ensured) or inequality through the bestowal of privileges? The Permanent Court of International Justice gave effect to the spirit of the minority clauses and brought the concept of specialized treatment into international jurisprudence.[95] Throughout the inter-war years the concept of legal guarantee of the rights of all individuals, and not just those belonging to an identified minority within a state, began to gain ground and generated the international guarantees of human rights discussed above. Nevertheless, disputes as to the meaning and achievement of equality between peoples have continued, and have resurfaced in the context of rights of minorities and indigenous persons. They have also been intrinsic to the debate as to the meaning of women's human rights and how best to achieve them.

Equality, equivalence, or equity?

The Western derivation of human rights law is highlighted in the assertion of equality between men and women, which is rejected within other cultures that emphasize concepts such as equivalence and equity. Such preferences have been given legal expression through the entering of substantive reservations by states parties to the Women's Convention that are apparently contrary to the terms of Article 28(2).[96] Reservations, and the lack of objections to them, suggest that the treaty obligation to accord equality can be counterbalanced by other considerations, such as those stemming from religious or other traditional behaviours. This is especially true of reservations to Article 2, which contains the fundamental obligation to condemn discrimination. Bangladesh, for example, has entered the following reservation: 'The Government of the People's Republic of Bangladesh does not consider as binding upon itself the provisions of articles 2, 13(a) and 16(1)(c) and (f), as they conflict with Shariah law based on Holy Qur'an and Sunna.'[97] This wording rejects the categorical prohibition of discrimination against women to the extent that it conflicts with Shariah law. However, there are many interpretations of Shariah law, as is evidenced by legal differences between countries that accept its teachings. The reservation therefore uses subjectively determined religious considerations to derogate from an absolute standard of gender equality. The force of the religious argument is such that in 1987 a proposal from CEDAW that ECOSOC should 'promote or undertake studies on the status of women under Islamic laws' in order to be able to appraise more fully the effect of these reservations was rejected at the behest of a number of Islamic states that saw the initiative as hostile to Islam. The General Assembly refused even to enter into discussion of the impact of Islamic law upon the legal articulation of equality.[98]

Reservations do not need to refer to religious or customary norms to make it apparent that there is no commitment at the national level to the international standard of equality.[99] Some reservations reject both the specific requirement in Articles 2(f) and 5(a) to modify or abolish discriminatory laws and the general responsibility under international law to ensure conformity between domestic and international law.[100] One of the most sweeping examples is the final paragraph of the Maldives reservation: 'Furthermore, the Republic of Maldives does not see itself bound by any provision of the Convention which obliges [it] to change its constitution and laws in any manner.'[101] Reservations to the Women's Convention have had a paralysing effect. Very few objections to these reservations have been entered by other states, thereby assuming their validity and consequently undermining the Convention's assertion of universal standards.[102] The Beijing Platform of Action urges governments to limit the extent of any reservations to the Convention, to formulate such reservations as precisely and narrowly as possible, to ensure that reservations are compatible with the object and purpose of the Convention, and to review reservations with a view to their withdrawal.[103] Even as states were accepting this wording, reservations were being made to the Platform of Action itself, including many with respect to the rights of the girl child.[104] The Human Rights Committee in a General Comment has adopted a hard line with respect to the validity of reservations incompatible with the ICCPR.[105] This approach is welcome but states retain the formal competence to enter objections to reservations by other states parties and this institutional competence may be resisted by states.[106]

Although discrimination is defined in the Women's Convention the meaning of equality is not. Its fluidity allows various interpretations, for example that of 'separate but equal' through the notion of equivalence.[107] This can be illustrated by the Egyptian reservation to Article 16, which refers to 'the Islamic Sharia's provisions whereby women are accorded rights *equivalent* to those of their spouses so as to ensure a just balance between them' (emphasis added).[108] The Egyptian government explains that the reason for rejecting formal equality is to ensure substantive equality between man and wife:

one of the most important bases of these rights is an equivalency of rights and duties so as to ensure complementarity which guarantees true equality between the spouses. The provisions of the Sharia lay down that the husband shall pay bridal money to the wife and maintain her fully and shall also make a payment to her upon divorce, whereas the wife retains full rights over her property and is not obliged to spend anything on her keep.

Reliance upon equivalence ignores other factors, such as the economic and personal dependence of a wife upon her spouse and their respective economic and social positions upon divorce. Nor does it consider the comparative valuing of men and women within society. As Rebecca Cook has argued, enhanced economic and social status is enjoyed by men, as indicated by the separate tasks allocated to each during marriage.

The specification of tasks may preserve a patriarchal social model in which men and women are segregated respectively into public and private spheres . . . and provide different opportunities of access to commercial, civic and political paths to personal growth and self realization.[109]

It must also be remembered that confronting the status quo through the assertion of women's right to equality with men is frequently seen as destabilizing, undermining the position of the family within society, and as culturally challenging. Indeed, members of CEDAW questioned the Egyptian representative on whether harmony was being equated with equality.[110] These tensions, and the disadvantaged position in which a wife can find herself upon divorce, are illustrated by the case of *Md Ahmed Khan v. Shah Bano Begum*. An Indian Muslim woman who had been married for over forty years claimed maintenance under the Indian Code of Criminal Procedure while her husband argued that Muslim personal status law was applicable, which limited both the length and basis of payment and left her virtually destitute.[111] The Supreme Court of India upheld her claim to be treated under secular Indian law but the decision aroused considerable opposition from within the Muslim community. After widespread public protests the Indian government undid the court's decision by passing the Muslim Women (Protection of Rights on Divorce) Act 1986.[112] Muslim personal status law provides for some financial settlement after divorce, but does not promote equality with Indian women subject to Hindu law, nor does it place former spouses in either equivalent or equal positions.

Radhika Coomaraswamy (now the UN Special Rapporteur on Violence against Women) elucidates how Shah Bano suffered from three layers of gender-based discrimination: simply as a woman; as a Muslim woman within a predominantly Hindu society; and as a Muslim woman claiming against the injustices of her own social group.[113] In South Asia rights discourse is weak and legal strategy may, as here, fail to empower victims of discrimination. She concludes: 'In the end Shah Bano had no rights. She became a metaphor in the political discourse of communalism which has shaped the violent history of post-colonial South Asia.'

The case also demonstrates that even where the national judiciary are prepared to uphold women's rights, strongly expressed opinions from powerful political forces may prevail. A similar tension between the courts and the government was seen in the case

of *Attorney-General of Botswana* v. *Unity Dow*. Dow, a
Botswanan, who had lived in Botswana all her life apart from brief
visits abroad, married an American citizen. Her children were born
and raised in Botswana. Two of her children were born after 1984,
when the applicable Botswanan nationality law came into effect.
Although the Botswana Constitution guarantees equality between
men and women, the nationality law provides that only illegitimate
children can acquire Botswanan citizenship through their mothers.
Children of Botswanan fathers acquire citizenship wherever they
are born. The law denies married women the right to bestow their
nationality upon their children and assumes the continuation of
identity between father and child.[114] Dow challenged this law,
arguing that it constituted discrimination against women. In legal
argument that drew widely on national and international jurisprudence, she pointed to Botswana's ratification of the African Charter
of Human and People's Rights, which in Article 18 incorporates the
international guarantee of women's rights. The trial court agreed
that the Nationality Law was discriminatory and contrary to the
provisions of the Botswana Constitution. Judge Horowitz in the
High Court cited both the Women's Convention and the African
Charter, surmising that 'it is . . . difficult if not impossible to accept
that Botswana would deliberately discriminate against women
in its legislation whilst at the same time internationally support
non-discrimination against females or a section of them'.[115] In the
Court of Appeal, the Attorney-General argued that the Constitution should be interpreted in the light of a pervasive culture of
discrimination. He urged that a decision in favour of Dow would
greatly disturb customary norms and that if this law was struck
down very little customary law could survive. This, he argued,
could not have been the constitutional intent. The Court of Appeal
reaffirmed the significance of Botswana's adherence to the African
Charter, which created an obligation 'to ensure the elimination of
every discrimination against their women folk'. As in the Shah
Bano case, this ruling was received badly by the government, which
suggested a constitutional amendment to uphold customary inequality. This did not occur, but the aftermath of the case again
shows the great obstacles to domestic acceptance of women's
claims to equality. Like Shah Bano, Dow was criticized for seeking
to uphold her rights through confrontational litigation.

The particular issue of reservations is but one part of the broader debate on the general aptness of the standard of equality in the face of competing claims based on religious or cultural difference. At the United Nations World Conference on Human Rights in 1993 the principles of universality, inalienability, indivisibility, and interdependence of human rights were affirmed.[116] Nevertheless, at Beijing the challenge to universality was again mounted. The wording of paragraph 9 remained unsettled until the concluding Conference session, where it was finally agreed that 'The full realization of all human rights and fundamental freedoms of all women is essential for the empowerment of women.'[117] However, it continued, the 'significance of national and regional particularities and various historical, cultural and religious backgrounds must be borne in mind' and, in what has been described as a 'leap of faith',[118] it was opined that 'full respect for various religious and ethical values ... should contribute to the full enjoyment by women of their human rights'. Such indeterminate language fosters continuation of claims of cultural relativity and detracts from the standard of equality.

Another strategy pursued at Beijing by opponents to equality was to assert equity as an alternative criterion, rather than in conjunction with equality and empowerment as at Cairo.[119] Equity and the use of equitable principles have been promoted by the International Court of Justice as a rationale for boundary delimitation and consequent allocation of resources.[120] While equity has the transformative potential for achieving fairness and justice, its subjectivity permits its appropriation for other ends. For example, at Beijing, Islamic states argued against equal inheritance rights for girls and boys because different adult roles require an 'equitable' distribution of assets in correlation with responsibilities.[121] This argument was rejected but again demonstrates the explicit objections of some states to the standard of gender equality.

Essentialism and elitism

It is not only state and other powerful elites that find the concept of equality problematic. Arguments against essentialism and elitism have been combined to challenge the international agenda for women's equality on the grounds that it is inspired by the experiences of Western women and silences those of women elsewhere.[122] It has been observed that

Women of the ex-colonial world have seen much of the substance of feminist struggles as irrelevant to them. Women struggling to liberate themselves from the burden of oppression by imperialism—a burden that manifests itself in extreme ways through poverty, disease, genocide,— appear to find little point of comparison between their own goals and the concerns of Western women.[123]

Geraldine Heng has argued that three factors inform women's movements in the South in ways that differentiate them from the North.[124] First, the indigenous history of women's movements in the South is entwined with the wider struggle for national liberation from colonial rule.[125] Reasons for the failure of decolonization to deliver equality to women are complex and inform Southern women's understanding of what it is to be female.

Second, the activities of women in developing countries (and indeed developed states) must be mediated through the state. Women are manipulated as a socio-economic resource in the post-colonial state, which is increasingly driven by the imperatives of economic development. Heng argues that at its most benign the state is a fiscal beneficiary of the exploitation of women, through, for example, the sexual division of labour consigning women to undervalued, underpaid positions within the paid labour force and according no economic value to other forms of labour typically pursued by women in the home and the community. At its least benign the state is an active agent structuring that exploitation for its own benefit. In neither instance is the state receptive to claims for women's equality. Another example is the manipulative use of religion and religious codes in defiance of international norms, which has been described as a 'new manifestation of the post colonial state'.[126] Recourse to law is not an option in resisting such legislation as the Hudood Ordinance in Pakistan, for the law has been subverted to the demands of the state. Instead, mobilization of national and international civil society must be attempted. However, state control of national imperatives, of the forms of participation, and of the instrumentalities at the disposal of the state for retention of that control determine the level and effectiveness of political activism.

The third factor that has been identified as affecting feminisms in

Southern states is an ambivalence towards modernity. Even as modernization and economic development are actively pursued to compete with the West, national cultural identity is sought. An antipathy to Western cultural norms is expressed through opposition to modernity for women. Cultural difference and religious conformity are defined in the private sphere of family and stereotyped sexual roles to which both modernizing and traditional politics relegate women, while economic development is pursued in the public sphere.

Western feminism too often fails to take account of these factors and assumes an essentialist female identity and agenda that ignores factors of race, class, history, economic well-being, religion, nationality, ethnic origin, and culture which all identify and construct a person as well as gender.[127] For example, less attention has been paid to the manifestations of inequality endured by those living in extreme poverty, including forced prostitution and trafficking in women and girls. These claims also emphasize that human rights demands for equality are limited to equality between men and women within their own societies, not for equality between all women across borders. In this they are reminiscent of the divide between Northern and Southern states that was expressed in the demands for a New International Economic Order.

Participation

Throughout much of the Beijing Platform there is an assumption that equal participation of women in national and international law- and policy-making bodies would empower women and enhance substantive equality elsewhere.[128] In the context of the UN, the low participation of women runs counter to the principles of equity and fairness upon which the Organization is constructed and that are firmly upheld with respect to geographical distribution. This position is underpinned by state sovereignty in the selection by states of their delegates and representatives. Inadequate gender representation also denies decision-making bodies access to a broader range of voices and experiences, whether or not issues are defined as appertaining to women. Experience suggests that male-dominated delegations do not pursue what are perceived as

women's issues, even when those issues have been extensively prepared in pre-conference documentation.

Increasing women's participation would certainly improve the
appearance of fairness but there is no guarantee that it would lead
to changed decisions, more genuine gender-awareness, or enhanced
transparency and accountability as aspects of global good governance. Women appointed (or elected) to such positions would have
to learn the language and processes of the bureaucracies. Feminists
would have to face the probably inevitable conflict between 'selling
out' or remaining marginalized in a replay of the debates about
'femocrats' within the national bureaucracies.[129] Targets have not
generally been set in the Platform for Action, and the UN experience suggests that compliance even with specified targets is not
easily attained. It is impossible to guess at the consequences for
decision-making of equal, or even improved, participation but unless it is accompanied by gender-awareness education (for men and
women) it is less likely to be greatly effective in achieving change.

VI. RECONCEPTUALIZATION OF RIGHTS: A CASE STUDY OF VIOLENCE AGAINST WOMEN

The campaign conducted by women's NGOs to have gender-
specific violence recognized as a violation of human rights was part
of the broader campaign for the recognition of 'women's rights as
human rights'. The traditional exclusion of such violence from the
discourse of human rights highlights many of the themes raised in
this chapter and will therefore be briefly examined.

First, the global incidence of diverse forms of violence was perceived as an issue around which women could unite despite
situational differences. Second, the high level of violence directed
at women because of their gender constitutes a direct denial of
women's right to equality.[130] Women suffer the same forms of
violence as men, for example torture in official detention, but in
ways that are gender-specific, for example rape and other forms of
sexual violence. They also suffer myriad forms of violence that are
not directed at men.[131] Third, the consequences of and fear of such
violence inhibits women's enjoyment of all other rights contained
within the human rights canon. Fourth, the Women's Convention
had not explicitly addressed gender-specific forms of violence, since

they did not fit within the framework of equality. This highlighted the fact that gender-neutral legal definitions of rights were framed in terms of men's experiences and excluded those abuses that occur most frequently to women. In particular, the limitation of state responsibility for violations of rights to acts of public officials excluded acts of violence committed against women by private agents within the family or community, the main locations of such violence.[132] Inclusion of private acts of violence would require extending the parameters of human rights law,[133] as had been accepted by the Inter-American Court of Human Rights in the case of disappearances,[134] but not in ways of direct benefit to women. Fifth, documentation of the condition of women repeatedly demonstrates that the global prevalence of gender-specific violence is not a private matter but is structural.[135] It is directly related to women's lack of social and economic power and is a 'manifestation of the historically unequal power relations between men and women, which have led to domination over and discrimination against women by men and to the prevention of women's full advancement'.[136]

The omission of violence against women from human rights law has been challenged in the 1990s on a number of fronts and in a variety of arenas. In 1992 CEDAW rectified its absence from the Women's Convention by General Recommendation No. 19, which states that 'the definition of discrimination includes gender-based violence' and that 'gender-based violence is a form of discrimination that seriously inhibits women's ability to enjoy rights and freedoms on a basis of equality with men'.[137] It stipulates that CEDAW will question states on steps taken in national laws and policy to eliminate violence against women.

However, CEDAW was constrained by the language of equality. It can only offer recommended interpretations of the Convention text as agreed by states and cannot articulate new rights. Other arenas did not require the traditional language of equality or non-discrimination. In similar language at Vienna,[138] in the General Assembly,[139] and at Beijing,[140] texts defined violence against women as 'any act of gender-based violence that results in, or is likely to result in, physical, sexual or psychological harm or suffering to women, including threats of such acts, coercion or arbitrary deprivation, whether occurring in public or private life'. They required the elimination of such violence, whether committed by public officials or by private actors, as a human rights obligation upon states. State responsibility is extended for acts of private individuals where there has been failure by the state to exercise due diligence in preventing and eliminating such violence. Perhaps most importantly, gender-specific violence is identified as 'structural' and as a barrier to women's realization of the objectives of equality, development, and peace.[141]

These instruments have placed violence against women firmly on the international agenda. Equality is an inadequate discourse for addressing the issue of gender-specific violence, but changing the discourse to that of power and systemic subordination has both positive and negative implications. On the positive side, it has the potential to effect change by offering a way to address the obstacles to women's social and economic advancement that is not constructed upon exclusively male experience. On the negative side, this transformative language has not been echoed in other areas, especially in those relating to economic and social rights. For example, at Beijing feminization of poverty was conceded, but the long-term benefits of economic development or of global capitalism were not questioned.[142] There has not even been full acceptance of violence against women as a human rights issue. The Vienna Declaration and Programme of Action are not binding instruments and create no formal obligations. At best they are a form of 'soft law' and represent political consensus. Their provisions are not incorporated into the admittedly minimal implementation procedures of the UN treaty bodies.[143] Neither the General Assembly Declaration on the Elimination of Violence nor the Beijing Platform are human rights documents, and therefore neither embodies the understandings of that discourse.

VII. CONCLUSION: EQUALITY, DEVELOPMENT, AND PEACE

Weighing the positive and negative aspects of the campaign for categorization of violence against women as a violation of human rights law encapsulates the dilemma for feminists working in this field. Is international law an appropriate vehicle for enhancing women's equality? The starting point of individual equality does not hold out to women the same promise of human dignity and worth as it does to men in a world where men continue to retain their grip over all forms of economic and political power. Feminists have raised a number of concerns about rights in the context of domestic law: women's concerns do not translate readily into the individualistic, atomist language of rights; rights-talk distorts the complex issues of structural power imbalance; conflicting rights (for example, the rights to privacy, to religious expression, and to free speech may all conflict with guarantees of women's rights) are frequently not resolved in favour of women; rights are readily appropriated and are consistently used to benefit those already advantaged within society.[144] These concerns are perhaps all the greater in the international system, where mechanisms for enforcement of human rights are inadequate and the political will for compliance often lacking. Economic and other imperatives are given priority by states and asserted to justify denials of rights. Where human rights discourse is perceived as out of tune with local mores, it lacks moral legitimacy.

Nevertheless, while the limited outcomes of legal strategies must be conceded, there are some strengths in legal instrumentality. Experience has shown that where people achieve legal recognition of rights, they use them to challenge their denial.[145] Rights discourse provides a familiar and symbolically powerful vocabulary to challenge political and societal wrongs that is not shared by other discourses, for example those cast in terms of needs, development, or justice. Internationally recognized human rights provide a yardstick against which to assess government performance. Recognition of rights is most effective at the national level, and rights instruments equip judges in national courts with a basis for finding against governments that reject their own assertions of equality. Admittedly this stance rests upon the willingness and courage of judges to use international instruments in this way. Even unsuccessful claims can help foster a human rights culture through legal articulation of the issues, and reaffirmation of the legal basis of rights. Legal literacy programmes, human rights education programmes, and gender training aimed at law enforcement officials and policy- and decision-makers at local and national levels are vital accompaniments to claims of rights. This requires generating and supporting programmes for the insertion of women's human rights into the mainstream of all United Nations activities, as was required at Vienna and Beijing, in an attempt to make them central to institutional understandings of human rights. The articulation of rights must themselves be relevant to women and the process of redefining the traditional scope of human rights law must be continued. This requires going beyond thinking in terms of inequality, or even of gender-specific issues such as violence against women. There must also be gendered analysis of global trends, such as democratization, good governance, international economic and trading systems, and international environmental law, to determine their impact upon women. The ability of the international legal system to be relevant to women requires the collapsing of legal conceptual boundaries between, for example, human rights law and international economic law, between state sovereignty and transnational law, so as to identify the interests of women, and to show how taking account of those interests can open the way to re-imagining possibilities for change which may permit the promise of international law for peaceful co-existence and respect for the dignity of all persons to become a reality.

Women appear to have a choice: either to strive to change the parameters of human rights law to incorporate women's experiences, or to move outside those parameters and risk losing its benefits. I believe this must be a false choice. Human rights law is a dynamic and tenacious construct. Women should continue both to seek to extend its reach and to pursue other avenues towards their advancement. Feminist analyses of international law have been attacked for 'being able to criticise international law [and by derivation also human rights law] for its doctrinal failure with regard to the rights of women and then, without missing a beat, criticise states and governments for their failure to apply and implement international law doctrine'.[146] Our defence is to point to the disadvantaged position of women worldwide, a position that is in many ways worsening rather than improving.[147] In these circumstances the existing tools of international law must be utilized, even while we decry their inadequacies for achieving global change.

5

Resources, Environmental Degradation, and Inequality

Michael Redclift and Colin Sage

Before 1987 an edited collection of essays on global inequality might not have considered the environment, particularly if the analysis was confined to international politics. Since the publication of the Brundtland Commission's report *Our Common Future* in 1987, and the Earth Summit (UNCED—UN Conference on Environment and Development) held in Rio de Janeiro in 1992, environmental issues have emerged on the global stage as central concerns, both because of the way they are linked to social and economic aspects of development, and because they appear to set limits on what can be achieved by 'development' itself. Other chapters in this book consider the ways in which inequality relates to, for example, market liberalization and economic globalization, security and military power, distributional justice, sovereignty, and human rights. They also consider the way in which international institutions may work either to exacerbate or to counter growing global inequality. The environment encompasses, in one form or another, most of these efforts, from the evolution of a mix of policies and agreements to correct environmental problems (through regulation, voluntary agreement, and market mechanisms) to the management and implementation of local environmental action, along the lines of Agenda 21.

This chapter identifies four critical dimensions of inequality which are relevant to any consideration of environment and resource degradation:

1. The unequal distribution of historical responsibilities for global environment changes, especially climate change.
2. The fact that global changes have disparate impacts on different regions and peoples in the world. For example, global

climate change is likely to be particularly prejudicial to countries within the tropics, as a result of climate perturbance (increased incidence of cyclones, adverse weather conditions, etc.) increasing the aridity of soils, and food insecurity.

3. The degree to which the international discourse over global changes tends to reflect different environment and development priorities: the industrialized countries showing more anxiety about climate and population, while the developing countries express concern about structural adjustment, the debt, and local-level 'livelihood' concerns, such as safe drinking water and adequate diets.

4. The extent to which distributive problems lie at the heart of the failure to undertake effective and concerted action in the face of global environmental changes. The agreements at the Earth Summit in Rio de Janeiro in 1992 have not led to significant concerted actions, or the release of adequate funding to address global problems.

The chapter begins by exploring the way in which environmental problems are constructed, both through structural processes, like trade and technology transfer, and through attachment to cultural 'models' of development, disseminated on television screens and illustrated by new patterns of consumption.[1] This social construction of environmental problems forms the backcloth against which we consider global inequality and the effects of economic globalization on the environment. Before considering these levels of analysis, however, we need to examine the pivotal links between sustainability and economic growth, on which our analysis of global inequality must depend.

Viewed from the perspective of developing countries, distributive issues lie at the heart of the new policy agenda labelled Global Environmental Change (GEC). In examining the importance of global inequality in the debates surrounding GEC it is useful to rehearse some of the reasons why the perspectives of most developing and industrialized countries vary so widely, as well as the increasing difficulty in categorizing individual countries in this way.

In the first place, for many countries in the South the issues most associated with GEC, notably climate change and biodiversity losses, are not considered among the principal environmental problems which they face. Consequently much of the discourse surrounding GEC is not shared. In the view of many commentators in the South the GEC agenda is essentially a Northern agenda, of little relevance to them. Second, it follows that many people in the South are more immediately affected by other aspects of globalization. For example, it is argued that structural adjustment policies, the liberalization of trade, and the continuing impact of international debt repayments exert more importance on poor peoples' environments than anticipated changes in climate are likely to do. In addition, poverty and insecurity assume importance in peoples' lives, they are socially transmitted, in a way that climate and biodiversity are not. In this chapter we explore these different approaches to globalization, as well as the priority given to 'livelihood concerns' (or poverty ecology) over 'lifestyle concerns' (or wealth ecology) in the South.

However, the matter does not rest there, since the discussion of environmental problems in relation to development has itself been influenced by the debates surrounding climate and biodiversity. Some people argue that, even if we confine ourselves to climate (the 'Northern agenda'), there are still major considerations of global equity to consider. The historical responsibilities for global warming are unequally distributed between the industrialized and the developing countries, current contributions to global warming are markedly different for the North and South and, further, the impacts of global warming are also likely to be highly unequal. The bulk of this chapter is concerned with this line of enquiry, which assumes that the GEC agenda really is a global one, and explores the issues from within a developing-country perspective. Although we explore the background to GEC in terms of cultural definitions, as well as structural policies, we are principally concerned with 'global' environmental policies as constituting the political context for differences over GEC.

Finally, it is important to emphasize that there are significant divisions within the Group of 77 (G77) states themselves that make up the 'developing world', and these differences serve to underline the global tensions and difficulties in reaching binding international agreements. There are differences in levels of economic development, and in dependence on the export or use of fossil fuels (and commitment to policy alternatives to fossil fuels). Finally, of course, inequality within societies in the South is of considerable importance. As Gadgil and Guha have shown, India consists of both 'carnivores' (people who consume resources indirectly, at a distance) and 'ecosystem people' (who are heavily dependent on their immediate, usually rural, environment).[2] Differences between lifestyle and livelihood are apparent not only between North and South, but also within developing countries themselves.[3]

ECONOMIC GROWTH AND SUSTAINABLE RESOURCE USE

There are, broadly speaking, three views of the relationship between economic growth and sustainability. The first and most common view is held by most governments, and most conventional economists. This is that sustainability and economic growth are more or less compatible, provided that we recognize the need for minimal international regulation, and make efforts to protect endangered ecosystems and species. The second view is that they are totally incompatible. As Herman Daly has expressed it: 'sustainable growth is an oxymoron'.[4] On this reading, the pursuit of economic growth implies increased throughput of energy and materials in an economy, and this in turn serves to undermine the sustainability of the environment.

The third perspective is somewhat different. It asserts that whether or not economic growth is compatible with sustainability depends on prior definition of a number of concepts, notably 'wealth', the interests of 'future generations', and the nature of 'economic efficiency'. In the view of its protagonists this third view requires giving priority to sustainability, as a goal rather than a set of *ex post* management tools. Given a political commitment to considering sustainability as a goal of international politics, economic growth would itself become redefined, the reduction of waste and pollution would constitute an objective of policy, together with the eradication of world poverty. It is a measure of the cynicism that pervades many international policy fora that such sentiments should appear utopian, rather than practical and necessary. But before considering ways of grounding these objectives in practical policy measures, it is worth stepping back and considering the global balance sheet of environmental and resource degradation.

The discussion of climate change has concentrated our attention on shifts in the climate system which are difficult to understand and predict, but severe problems of pollution lie near at hand. 'Indoor' pollution, from burning wood and poor ventilation, harms over 400 million people worldwide, and contributes to acute respiratory infections, from which four million children die annually. Household sewage is another 'global' problem which starts in the family. Sewage is the major cause of water contamination, and poor sanitation for over one and a half billion people worldwide contributes to even larger numbers of infant deaths. In the developing world, almost 95 per cent of sewage is untreated. The provision of clean drinking water would enable two million fewer children to die from diarrhoea each year; currently thirteen and a half million children die as the result of the combined effects of poor diet and poor domestic sanitation.[5]

Perhaps more alarmingly, there is evidence that the numbers of people without adequate sanitation actually increased during the 1980s, and measures to mount preventative campaigns are jeopardized by growing water scarcity in many parts of the world. Forty per cent of the global population experiences periodic droughts but, at the same time, rising per capita water consumption (by 50 per cent since 1950) has largely been for irrigated agriculture, and at the expense of domestic water provision. In the world's cities, the problem is frequently the quality of the air, as well as the water. Today almost one and a half billion people live in cities with air quality below minimum standards set by the World Health Organization (WHO), producing respiratory and other ailments from which half a million people die prematurely every year.[6]

Even the environmental problems that we usually regard as remote from these problems of primary health and livelihoods, such as the production of industrial wastes and the extinction of species, are inextricably linked not only to levels of consumption ('ecological footprints') but also of resource degradation. The losses to our global environment through the pursuit of unsustainable economic growth, in the form of increased pollution and resource degradation, put individual livelihoods at risk throughout the developing world. They are survival issues for the poor, as well as the subject of informed speculation for policy analysis.

CULTURAL CONSTRUCTIONS OF ENVIRONMENTAL PROBLEMS

Before discussing the structural processes which have contributed to environmental vulnerability in the South, it is important to emphasize that environmental 'problems' (including GEC) are not defined within a cultural vacuum. The way that environmental issues are represented reflects social and cultural perspectives. Although most of the mass media is devoid of explicit environmental messages, it clearly communicates a great deal *about* the environment.

Cinema and television depict environmental values in the form of buried messages about consumption, nature, and the world of goods. The values associated with media messages may not be readily assimilated into existing cultural categories. The tension between 'Western' (primarily Northern) values, and those of traditional Hinduism, or Islam, serve to underline the difficulties posed by 'globalization'. If clean drinking water is the principal environmental issue for millions of people in the South (and its absence contributes to the premature death of thirteen and a half million children each year) it is hardly surprising that global climate predictions appear even more remote than they do in the developed world.

The underlying social commitments, and practices, of everyday life constitute the 'filter' through which people, and their governments, perceive 'global' environmental problems. In the poorest countries, the 'environment' consists of problems associated with health, shelter, and food availability. In the newly industrializing countries, the 'environment' is bound up with the short- and medium-term costs of pursuing very rapid economic growth, such as high levels of air pollution in cities. In the privileged, developed world, the 'environment' increasingly involves exposure to largely invisible, and unforeseen, risks, such as levels of radon, or beef contaminated by BSE. Issues of equity appear less important, in dealing with these problems, than freedom of information, or civil rights.

However, from a sociological perspective equity is important for GEC not only because of measurable differences in the flow of energy and materials, levels of personal consumption, or the difficulty in arriving at international agreements, but also for ideological reasons. Ideology shapes the discussion of GEC in several important ways. First, as we have seen, the perceptions of environmental issues are subject to ideology, and vary markedly in different societies and cultures. Second, ideological assumptions govern the trust that can be placed in the behaviour of others toward the environment. One of the most persistent debates within the GEC literature concerns the so-called 'free rider' question: the extent to which countries that do not sign up to global environmental agreements will be able to benefit from them. Similarly, the loss of 'sovereignty' means quite different things in different contexts. Sovereignty itself is an ideological construct which needs to be investigated in order to establish how rights and responsibilities to the environment vary.

Many of the structural processes at work in the international economic system also have ideological components which we should not ignore: for example, the view taken of environmental regulation (or deregulation), and the value of trade liberalization and the market economy, rather than command economies or economic protection. The political economy of the environment is governed by opposing ideological precepts, as well as disparate economic strengths and weaknesses. Perhaps the best example of ideological factors influencing the debate is the discussion of 'sustainable development' or 'green development' itself, which is often polarized between the respective value of technological trans-formations (ecological modernization) and more thoroughgoing cultural changes ('deep green' solutions).

Some writers claim sustainability for small-scale societies, or earlier civilizations. Others argue that sustainable development needs to totally embrace global technology and global means of communications—the Internet, satellites, and the media. There are thus two dimensions to international equity: intra-generational and inter-generational. The concern of most commentators in the North has been with future generations of 'our people', although this is usually implicit, while that of those in the South has been with the current generation. The importance of intra-generational equity, however, is such that unless we can successfully resolve differences between North and South, the prospects for future generations in the developed world (too) are bleak. Consequently, in the conclusion to this chapter we examine the kind of international policies, and mechanisms, which might persuade the developing countries to participate in a global contract to combat GEC.

THE DEVELOPMENT PROCESS AND
GLOBAL INEQUALITY

International development policy has long been a source of contention between countries of the North and the South, even during the Golden Age of 1945–73. This was a period of sustained economic growth in which Keynesian principles guided the Bretton Woods institutions and trade developed along the lines of comparative advantage, but within a framework of rules, tariffs, and controls. During the 1950s and 1960s all countries—even the poorest—registered rates of economic growth that were sufficient to produce improvements in per capita income. While some countries sought to pursue a strategy of import-substituting industrialization, the majority were largely dependent upon the extraction and export of primary commodities, and capital flows naturally encouraged this international division of labour. Between 1956 and 1970, for example, over half of the private foreign direct investment originating from OECD countries was invested in raw material production.[7] The exploitation of farmland, forests, minerals, and marine resources was thus seen as a necessary route to economic development, and a degraded, polluted environment an inevitable consequence—a strategy that remains current despite the rhetoric of sustainability, as we shall see.

Yet flows of development aid and private investment could not disguise the lack of progress that the South was making in 'catching up' on living standards and levels of material consumption that were increasingly universally enjoyed by citizens in the North. Indeed, the persistence of absolute impoverishment and deprivation and increasing inequality within the South led to demands in the early 1970s for a New International Economic Order (NIEO) which, it was hoped, would deliver a more equitable share of global resources. One of the central pillars of the NIEO was the establishment of a series of commodity agreements, under the auspices of UNCTAD, in which (Southern) producers would effectively enjoy the benefits of a cartel to achieve higher prices and repeat the success of OPEC. Unsurprisingly, the proposals for the NIEO were given a hostile response by the North, whose strategy of foot-dragging and referral ultimately led to their being overtaken by other developments. Thus, even while it enjoyed a period of unprecedented political unanimity which saw the foundation of the Group of 77 and the strengthening of the Non-aligned

Movement, the South could not secure meaningful economic concessions from the North. This bears out Zartman's words, that 'there is neither equality of present status nor equality of opportunity for the future and the inequality of condition is mirrored and magnified by the inequality of capability to change it'.[8]

Since the early 1970s the Golden Age has, of course, given way to an era of global restructuring and a reconfiguration of the international division of labour. The collapse of the fixed exchangerate system and the fourfold increase in oil prices marked the onset of a period of much greater economic uncertainty and indebtedness. The reliance of the middle-income, oil-importing countries on borrowing from the international banks to finance higher energy costs seemed economically rational as their share of manufactured exports rose. However, once the monetarist experiment got under way in the UK and USA from 1979, and interest rates became the principal tool for controlling domestic inflation, rates rose across the financial markets and the world economy moved into deep recession. This placed strong downward pressure on prices of raw materials, so that they fell to their lowest level since 1945, severely hitting the poorest economies. Meanwhile the high interest rates on heavy borrowings put many of the middle-income countries under intense financial pressure.[9]

Following Mexico's announcement in August 1982 that it could no longer meet its debt-service commitments, short-term rescue packages for indebted countries have gradually given way to the development of programmes of structural adjustment.[10] These have been designed, *inter alia*, to reorient most developing economies away from domestic concerns with employment generation and poverty alleviation and towards the needs of the world market and the dictates of market prices. Above all, structural adjustment has served to ensure that countries continue to meet debt-service obligations. According to Khor, debt servicing by capital-importing developing countries rose from $90 billion in 1980 to $158 billion in 1992, so that the total flow from South to North over the period 1980–92 was $1,662 billion, of which $771 billion was interest payment and $891 billion repayment of principal.[11] Debt servicing is draining about $160 billion annually from developing countries, yet the overall stock of debt in the South is rising by about $100 billion per year and the debt-to-export ratios remain extremely high (e.g. 29 of the 32 severely indebted low-income countries still have debt-to-export ratios of more than 200 per cent despite bilateral relief measures[12]). As Khor notes, this overhang of huge debt stocks poses a major constraint on prospects for financing sustainable development in most countries of the South. The imperative of meeting their international financial obligations, together with the deregulation and liberalization of world trade, has certainly encouraged governments in the South to reposition themselves within the new global order wherever possible. Increasing competition between states in attracting new rounds of international investment as the basis for economic development has led to strict controls over labour and the tendency to sell cheaply their environmental resources and ecosystem service functions. The exploitation and sale of tropical hardwoods and other rare plant and animal species, as well as non-renewable mineral resources, constitute examples of natural resource depletion through trade and attest to the dominant development paradigm in which nature provides the raw materials for economic growth. Yet given the vital importance of ecosystem service functions, which include the provision of sinks for the sequestration of CO_2, the maintenance of crop genetic diversity through *in situ* conservation, and the existence of species for their intrinsic worth apart from any possible future commercial value, it is unsurprising that international capital has come to embrace sustainable development, a point to which we return later.

Nevertheless, international capital still favours concentration rather than dispersal. According to figures examined by Broad and Melhorn-Landi, between 1989 and 1992 72 per cent of all foreign direct investment (FDI) went to ten countries, while around fifty of the world's poorest countries received just 2 per cent of FDI. This polarization has strong regional patterns, such that in 1993 East Asia and the Pacific received 55 per cent of all FDI and Latin America and the Caribbean 24 per cent, while Sub-Saharan Africa accounted for 3 per cent and South Asia just 1 per cent. The authors conclude from their analysis that the ten to twelve countries which appear to be the prime beneficiaries of FDI are likely either to join the ranks of the North, or at least move closer to levels of Northern economic performance over the next generation. For the remaining 140-plus countries, prospects are less attractive and they may slip further behind levels of economic growth in the North, especially if they remain largely dependent upon the export of primary commodities.

While methods of calculating the deterioration in terms of trade may vary, there is agreement that the real value of non-oil primary products has been falling: by an estimated 5.7 per cent per year during 1974–80, 3 per cent per year during 1981–6, and 1.8 per cent per year from 1987 to 1993.[13] Consequently, the real concern is with the way the World Bank and IMF prescriptions for raising export earnings under structural adjustment have placed emphasis on primary commodities, especially given the criticisms of the environmental lobby. Yet increasing the volume of exports of agricultural and forest products, minerals, and marine resources has consequences beyond the maintenance of the long-term integrity of those resources.

The widespread development of plantations, livestock ranching, and large-volume trawling has had dramatic consequences for the livelihoods of small farmers and fisherfolk, especially during the imposition of other forms of conditionality under structural adjustment. The removal of import quotas and tariff barriers, for example, has allowed Northern goods to flood small national markets and undermine domestic production through a combination of price, quality, and fashion. More importantly, directions to slash spending on social welfare, including health and education, and to eliminate subsidies, for example on public transport and basic food staples, in order to remove price 'distortions' on local goods and services, have severely hit the poor. During the 1980s real wages fell sharply in Latin America and throughout Africa, and by the mid-1990s incomes had barely recovered in either region for the majority of the population.

Although it is difficult to establish direct causal connections between structural adjustment policies and environmental degradation, it is apparent that such policies have set in motion processes whereby increased demands on resources are made by desperate people in order to meet their livelihood needs.[14] As a recent UNRISD publication outlines, removing subsidies, reducing wages, and increasing market competition forces people to diversify their livelihood activities in order to survive.[15] In urban areas this means a second job or participation in the informal sector—as well as the opportunity to challenge the economic reforms (witness the frequent incidence of 'IMF bread riots' during the 1980s). In scattered, often highly differentiated rural communities, on the other hand, the increased cost of agricultural inputs and declining incomes forces farmers to seek other survival measures: to squeeze residual fertility from exhausted fields; to plant adventitious crops on marginal land; and to make use of common-property resources for the extraction of timber, wood fuel, and other forest products. Such short-term activities may all have long-term consequences for local sustainability, and together with wage-labour migration can result in declining food security.

GLOBALIZATION, THE ENVIRONMENT, AND THE POOR

The notion of globalization, as a means of social and economic ordering within a highly integrated capitalist world economy, has a vital bearing on our understanding of change within the global environment. Taking Giddens's definition of globalization as 'the intensification of worldwide social relations which link distant localities in such a way that local happenings are shaped by events occurring many miles away and vice versa',[16] it follows that the site of environmental degradation may be far removed from its agent of causation. It is apparent that such situations result from interdependent patterns of development involving the mobility of capital and the relocation of industrial processes that deepen the international division of labour while reflecting comparative advantage and regional patterns of specialization. Globalization simply provides an interpretive device in which environmental change arising from the use and transformation of sources, sinks, and resources can be traced and attributed to a set of structured practices and processes guided by the underlying dynamic of material accumulation. This dynamic, argues Saurin, concentrates wealth in certain locales and amongst certain social groups largely by extracting from and dispossessing other locales and social groups.[17] The environmental consequences thus arise from employing the biophysical system as a source of materials and as a sink to assimilate wastes and pollution.

Central to our understanding of globalization, however, is that the location of these material sources, the sites where these materials are transformed and where they are consumed, and the location of the waste sinks need not—and increasingly do not—coincide. As the penetration of the market displaces the production of use values by exchange values, the coevolutionary basis by which local environmental resources and ecological processes provide for rural people is undermined.[18] Incorporation into the world economy effectively diminishes the capacity of local producers to exercise control over their choice of production systems and the way resources are to be managed. Instead, a web of decisions made many miles away, that might involve the imposition of externally derived macro-economic goals and market incentives, can exert greater influence over production systems and the local environment.

One sector which perfectly illustrates this development is the food industry, which exercises an extraordinary level of influence over land use in the South. The Netherlands, for example, appropriates the production capabilities of 24 million hectares of land, ten times its own area of cropland, pasture, and forest.[19] Part of these 'ghost acres' support cassava production in Thailand and Indonesia which enters the feed industry for intensive pig farming in the Netherlands. Indonesia has been anxious to maintain or even increase its share of the European Union's cassava quota and its vigorous promotion of exports has seen domestic prices rise.

In response, farmers are switching from more sustainable and less erosive mixed-cropping and perennial crop-farming systems to monocropping cassava. They are even removing terracing and other soil and water conservation structures to increase the area of cassava cultivation. ... the on-site productivity costs and off-site erosion impacts of the recent price distortions may have already impaired the prospects for secure livelihoods for many upland farmers, and for the sustainable management of upper watersheds as a whole.[20]

The above example of the 'cassava connection' shows how a distortionary trading structure, combined with short-term policy objectives, can lead to economically and environmentally unsustainable outcomes, with the costs borne in Indonesia, principally by small farmers whose livelihoods are undermined. While many observers might attribute such unsustainable outcomes to local agents who may be thought to be acting out of ignorance or wilful self-interest, a structural analysis informed by the principles of political ecology serves to challenge the received wisdom based on simplified and inherently localized models of linear causation.[21] Such challenges are vital, not least to counter tendencies toward global environmental management which would strengthen the hand of transnational and multilateral institutions in the name of the common good.

Buttel and Taylor have argued that packaging multiple environmental problems and concerns within a common rubric conveys a scientific legitimacy and the political rationale for responding urgently.[22] Such a basis for global environmental management can provide the opportunity for the powerful to exert control over the resources of others in the name of planetary health and sustainability.[23] The emergence of a paradigm of global environmental management, with its curative rather than preventative approach to environmental problems, rests upon the rise to dominance during the past twenty-five years of a discourse in which the metaphor of 'Spaceship/Planet Earth' has played an important role. Arturo Escobar argues that the visualization of Earth as a 'fragile ball' offers a narrative for managerialism best exemplified by *Scientific American*'s September 1989 special issue on 'Managing Planet Earth', which asked: 'What kind of planet do we want? What kind of planet can we get?'[24] While Escobar in turn enquires as to the identity of this 'we' who knows what is best for the world as a whole, the answer to his question is self-evident. The existing international political economy is managed by a small number of multilateral institutions (principally the World Bank, the International Monetary Fund, and the World Trade Organization), with policy determined by the richest industrialized countries (the Group of Seven—G7), who control over 60 per cent of world economic output and over 75 per cent of world trade.

Indeed, it is important to be clear about the central role of the Bretton Woods institutions, and the World Bank in particular, in providing a global management function. Critics of the Bank have observed how, since the late 1970s, it has changed from an institution largely dispensing funds through individual project loans to one increasingly targeting its operations at broad structural changes within developing economies.[25] Although the Bank has sought to manipulate its public image in order to improve its standing in the South, its policy-making and voting procedures remain heavily weighted in favour of the richest countries. During the McNamara era the Bank set a new moral tone in defence of 'basic human needs', and substantially increased the proportion of loans destined for agricultural and rural development. In Central America, however, 57 per cent of the total loan funds allocated by the Bank to this sector between 1960 and 1983 supported the production of beef for export, creating massive social displacement and devastating environmental impacts.[26]

Just as the Bank had been able to disguise the greater part of its lending programmes under the mask of basic needs and poverty alleviation during the McNamara years, so it sought to offset criticism of the environmental impacts of its policies through the introduction of a series of environmental reforms in 1987. The creation of a new Environment Department and regional units responsible for reviewing projects in their different parts of the world, and the introduction of new environmental programmes with new lines of credit, were developments initially greeted with optimism. However, by the early 1990s, as Bruce Rich notes, 'it became clear that many new as well as ongoing projects were causing senseless environmental and social destruction'. As Rich goes on to argue,

Beneath its long, self-proclaimed mission of banker to the poor, and behind the new green facade, the Bank continued to do what it had always done: move larger and larger amounts of money to developing country government agencies for capital-intensive, export-oriented projects.[27]

Unsurprisingly, the Bank has now added the language of participation to its existing remit of poverty alleviation and sustainable development. First, 'the Bank's overall strategy to reduce poverty is centred on participation by the poor', and secondly, 'there is an increasing trend towards participation in formulating Bank policies by listening to a broader range of perspectives'.[28] Putting to one side arguments about whether 'listening' constitutes participation, this would undoubtedly make interesting reading for the 90,000 oustees displaced by the Sardar Sarovar dam in India, or the 40,000 people displaced by the Itaparica dam in Brazil, amongst many others who have suffered directly and indirectly as a result of World Bank funding of socially and environmentally destructive development projects.

Alongside the World Bank the International Monetary Fund has also imposed its own programmes of regressive social engineering under the banner of economic stabilization and structural adjustment, designed to ensure that countries continue to meet their debt obligations and deepen their integration into world markets. The World Trade Organization, established under the Uruguay Round of GATT, is meanwhile charged with responsibility for ensuring the continuing liberalization of trade through the elimination of subsidies and import controls. Together these three organizations— the World Bank, the IMF, and the WTO—provide a level of global economic management that has led to the wholesale reorganization of economies and societies in the South.

In this respect globalization has not only resulted in a narrowing of policy options for developing countries, but a diminution of their national sovereignty. This is most especially apparent in relation to the emergence of global environmental management and its application to resolving social-ecological problems in the South, in which the moral imperative to ensure biospheric integrity justifies the creation of a new global regulatory order. Initiatives such as the 'Pilot Programme for the Amazon', a proposal approved by the Group of Seven industrialized countries at their summit in Houston in 1991, provides one example of this approach. The programme contains elements of environmental education, the transfer of science and technology, and environmental zoning in order to reduce levels of deforestation in Brazilian Amazonia. There is little room, however, for participation either by state agencies or local groups.[29] In these circumstances it is perhaps fortunate that donors have so far demonstrated even greater reluctance to fund the programme than to accord people affected by the project a say in shaping their own destiny.

For the vast majority of developing countries, the current strategy for maximizing economic growth is strongly associated with activities that result in high levels of pollution and resource depletion. This is because under contemporary processes of global restructuring and flexible specialization governments are in strong competition to enhance their perceived comparative advantage to attract foreign investment and stimulate growth. This often means relaxing environmental standards and working conditions while maintaining strong downward pressure on wages. Latin America, for example, depends heavily on exports of non-renewable resources, goods manufactured by polluting industries, and the production of agricultural commodities using unsustainable farming systems.[30] The exploitation of Chile's native old-growth forests, the massive expansion of shrimp aquaculture in Honduras with the resulting destruction of mangrove ecosystems, and mineral extraction on the scale of Brazil's Carajas scheme are all examples of renewable and non-renewable resource exploitation to generate export earnings. Yet, arguably, it is with the expansion of the industrial sector that Latin America's environmental crisis most clearly demonstrates the logic of globalization under the dominance of transnational capital with the benefits ultimately reaped in the rich industrialized countries.

The adoption of capital- and energy-intensive technological processes of mass production during the last thirty to forty years has ensured Latin America's full incorporation into the global economy. However, it has a small share of world markets for services (e.g. banking and insurance), high-tech industries (e.g. biotechnology) and other high value-added/low environmental impact activities, and a proportionally greater share of the polluting industries (oil refineries, chemical plants, iron and steel foundries, etc.), with a predictable choice of associated energy paths, including nuclear power.[31] Indeed, given the imperative of economic growth—especially to make up ground lost during the debt crisis and the 'lost decade' of the 1980s—Latin America has become something of a pollution haven, attracting corporations and their production processes driven out of the United States, Canada, or Western Europe by more stringent environmental regulations. The US–Mexican border industrialization programme best illustrates the nature of this case.

Although the programme began in 1965, the number of maquiladoras (manufacturing plants) increased rapidly during the 1980s as wages fell, and is now more than 2,000 units. Each plant operates by importing components free of duty for assembly, for re-export to the United States. More than half of the largest US companies have established operations in the border zone,[32] attracted by the combination of relaxed environmental standards and low labour costs. More than half of the maquiladora plants produce hazardous waste which is supposed to be shipped back to the US: in 1987 only 20 of the 1,000 plants did so. Moreover, Mexico's Secretariat of Urban Planning and Ecology announced in 1990 that it had no plans to enforce the registration and reporting provisions for toxic wastes required by law.[33]

The public health consequences of unregulated toxic waste disposal, for example in drainage ditches, are appalling: 'The incidence of anencephalic [brainless] baby births in towns like Matamoros is 30 times the Mexican average'.[34] This is in addition to the 206 million litres of raw sewage dumped daily into the local rivers, which has made the region 'a virtual cesspool and breeding ground for infectious diseases',[35] with hepatitis and tuberculosis rife on both sides of the border.[36] The parlous state of living standards in the region, together with work which is repetitive, stressful, insecure, and low paid, forcefully demonstrates the sheer depth of poverty in Mexico, where such jobs represent social and material improvement. It is this which ultimately underpins the dynamic of globalization.

In an era of globalized production systems the corporate agenda remains dominant and national governments, especially in the South, are severely compromised in their capacity to ensure the social welfare of their populations. The multilateral institutions oversee the doctrine of trade liberalization and deregulation to ensure a suitable climate for investment and enhanced profits. Northern governments, meanwhile, proceed cautiously in their domestic policy, aware that raising environmental standards and levels of social provision can lead to capital flight and an investment gap in their own programmes for continued economic development. However, they vigorously promote programmes of environmental management overseas, not least because it represents a new source of earnings in an area where the North retains a scientific and technological advantage in pollution control and in the development of environmentally safer products and processes.

For example, up to the end of 1995 the Inter-American Development Bank had loaned almost $300 million to the five Central American countries for environmental projects, much of which, together with bilateral funding, is being used to finance private-sector environmental projects and involve the business community in 'sustainable development'. There are rapidly growing business opportunities in the environmental sector, according to one source, with the market for environmental products and services in Latin America reaching $7 billion in 1995 and expected to double by the end of the decade. This same source reports the following:

'Trade liberalization, infrastructure development, privatization and strengthened environmental legislation and awareness are combining to create terrific opportunities for US environmental firms in Latin America' read a recent report by the US Department of Commerce. . . . In fact, the US Agency for International Development has announced a new program to help US environmental technology companies with credits and data on potential opportunities in Latin America.[37]

Globalization is partly an underlying dynamic of global environmental change, yet is being seen to offer new commercial opportunities for the corporate sector to resolve pressing ecological problems. As Buttel and Taylor note, the lack of corporate opposition to global warming policy can be explained by the business opportunities that the likelihood of carbon taxes will create, including the possible revitalization of the civilian nuclear power industry. It is not surprising that the apparent consensus linking multilateral agencies, Northern governments, transnational business, and parts of the 'green lobby' has brought forth developing-country opposition to a global climate treaty as an example of environmental colonialism.[38]

CONTRIBUTIONS TO GLOBAL ENVIRONMENTAL CHANGE: POINTS OF DEPARTURE

As Bhaskar argues, the emission of greenhouse gases is a classic international case of market failure, since the costs of an individual nation's economic activity are incurred worldwide, while the benefits of these economic activities are appropriated nationally.[39] The problem of addressing global warming is then posed at the level of international relations. How can countries be induced to take measures which may only benefit them indirectly?

Looked at from the perspective of the developing countries, there are serious difficulties in agreeing to take measures to reduce atmospheric emissions of greenhouse gases. In part, their objections reflect the history of their development during the last half century, as we saw earlier. The effect of structural adjustment, the burden represented by their external debt, and the liberalization of trade policies have all drawn attention to the inequitable basis of the global economic system.

The discussions surrounding climate change have added to this distrust of Northern intentions. As Figure 5.1 shows, carbon dioxide emissions per capita are very much lower in the South than in the North. At the same time, anticipated increases in population, together with improvements in living standards, are likely to increase the aggregate contribution of the developing countries. Clearly, continuing economic growth in the South will exacerbate the problem of global climate change within the next thirty years, particularly through increased energy generation.

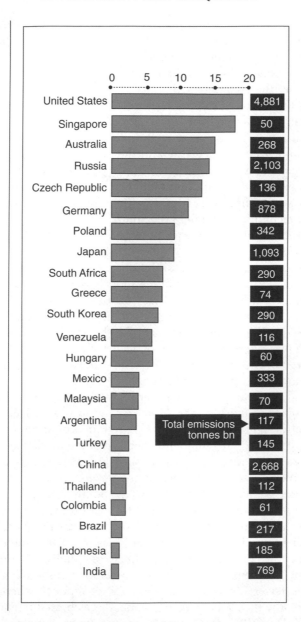

F ig. 5.1. Carbon dioxide emissions per person, 1992 (tonnes)
Source: based on The Economist, 17 Aug. 1996, using data from the World
Resources Institute.

From the viewpoint of a dispassionate observer, greenhouse gas emissions are so much lower in the South, on a per capita basis, that developing countries should have more room to increase their emissions, while developed countries reduce theirs. At the same time, the technological transition to lower energy intensity (the amount required to produce a corresponding increase in Gross Domestic Product) is not as advanced in the South. Thus the potential for economic growth through energy saving and technological improvements is greatest in the developing countries. Logically speaking, and from a 'global' perspective, the industrialized countries could therefore optimize their financial assistance to the South by providing incentives for the adoption of cleaner, more efficient technology, and help the South to effectively 'leapfrog' the stage of dirty, labour-intensive industrialization where it is not yet fully under way.

Unfortunately, this dispassionate analysis has several serious difficulties. First, calculations of atmospheric emissions based on per capita contributions spell disaster for the global situation, since the knowledge that they are not the main contributors to 'the problem' provides little inducement for the developing countries to pursue more efficient use of energy. Developing countries have little incentive to endorse global objectives above meeting the more immediate needs of their own people.

Second, the transition to cleaner technology in the South is not encouraged by most of the Northern, industrialized economies, whose efforts (in so far as they are geared to 'ecological modernization') are focused on gaining for themselves the market advantages conferred by higher environmental standards in tradeable products. They have an interest, in other words, in *not* transferring cleaner, more energy-efficient technologies to the South. Acting in the global environmental interest is secondary, for most transnational companies, to their pursuit of profit, until such time as profits reflect the internalization of environmental variables in trading standards.

Third, the labour-displacing effect of 'high-tech' industries recommends them to countries where labour costs are high, but provides fewer obvious advantages for economies where labour costs are low (hence Lawrence Summers's celebrated remark, prior to UNCED in 1992, that it was more efficient to direct pollution to poorer countries). For most developing countries, the incentives to achieve lower energy intensities pale into insignificance beside the economic benefits of providing dirty (and frequently unsafe, and unhealthy) employment. In addition, the need to reduce levels of some greenhouse gas emissions, such as methane, is confused by the fact that goods traded in the world economy take no account of emission levels.[40]

From the perspective of a developing country, then, the real costs of reducing emission levels, in the 'global' interest, are very high. It is by no means clear that 'sustainable development' should be given precedence over achieving increased economic growth. Environmental gains can even be measured in terms of economic growth foregone, and jobs that would have been created. Posed as a conflict between intra-generational equity and inter-generational equity, most developing countries are more likely to choose to reduce the inequalities in the present global economic system, rather than make sacrifices to achieve gains for future affluent generations in the North.

Much of the discussion of climate change policy has followed a completely different trajectory. Taking the idea of 'carbon budgets', for example, it has sought to identify principles for allocating reduced emissions among countries. It begins, then, with what is assumed to be a shared problem, and proceeds to allocate national reductions in emissions as measures for resolving it.[41]

Within the international relations community, and especially among environmental economists, attention has been given to mechanisms which might ease the differentials (or inequalities) between countries that currently make them unwilling to act for the 'greater good'. International environmental taxes, tradeable permits, and joint implementation are all methods for seeking to overcome current opposition to collective action. Nevertheless, there has been a marked reluctance, even on the part of most of the industrialized countries, to agree to implement these environmental policy measures. This is largely because they place their own short-term economic advantages above longer-term, global benefits. In practical terms, most developed countries are unwilling to endorse the precautionary principle as a guide to resolving the contradictions between equity and efficiency at the international level, or to face the severe political problems which would be likely to accompany a new world economic order.

The international picture is also obscured by another factor—the anticipated impacts of climate change—which is likely to affect developed and developing countries rather differently. The evidence from the Inter-governmental Panel for Climate Change (IPCC), and other bodies, is quite clear: global warming is likely to lead to more unpredictable weather in the tropical zones. The increased incidence in tropical regions of hurricanes, typhoons, and drought poses problems for countries whose physical environments are already vulnerable, and whose populations are poorly equipped to cope with 'natural' disasters on this scale.

As Martin Parry observes,

although we know little, at present, about how the frequencies of extreme events may alter as a result of climatic change, the potential impact of concurrent drought or heat stress in the major food-exporting regions of the world could be severe.[42]

The major food-producing regions will only be able to maintain present production at considerable economic cost as

relatively small decreases in rainfall, changes in rainfall distribution or increases in evapo-transpiration could markedly increase the probability, intensity and duration of drought in currently drought-prone (and often food-deficient) regions.[43]

Moreover, the adverse impacts of global climate change are unlikely to affect developing countries equally. In many cases the principal impact will not be sea-level rise, or even marginal increases in temperature, but rather the impact of drier growing seasons for crops on already vulnerable systems of production. Changes in agricultural productivity might be expected in situations where small farmers are unable to compensate for shifts in natural climatic conditions. The importance of climate change is to exacerbate existing problems, both environmental and socio-economic, producing an additional burden on the capacities of resource systems and small farmers.

Climate impacts are likely to have their most uneven effects not at the farm level, but at another remove—that of international food policy. Indeed, 'the impact of climate change on crop yields is only one part of the picture of how changing climate will impact [upon] the welfare of countries'.[44] Climate impacts will exacerbate existing differences within countries but, at the same time, will increasingly serve to differentiate between countries, a legacy to which the global economy will inevitably have to respond. Perhaps of most importance are the likely impacts of climate change on international food security—with the biggest impacts on developing countries that are net importers of staple food crops, especially as prices rise.[45] The effect of major shifts in agricultural trade will not be confined to any one region of the globe, and the combined impacts of contracting production, and increased environmental and social vulnerability in resource-poor regions, are likely to be serious.

Some of the countries most likely to be adversely affected by global warming, such as those of South Asia, are already heavily dependent on advanced technology (such as the supercomputer) to help anticipate 'normal' events, such as the annual monsoon. There is less capacity, and less urgency, to calculate the effects of global warming. Global Circulation Models (GCMs) are relatively poor at predicting levels of precipitation, and rainfall is the key factor for most of Asia's population dependent on paddy rice cultivation. Technological capacity for climate modelling lies overwhelmingly in the North, while the countries most likely to be adversely affected by global warming lie in the South. This is one, small example of the way global economic imbalances affect both our ability to mount a global response to environmental problems, and our understanding of the issues themselves.

Distributive problems lie at the heart of the failure to take global action, as Grubb and others have observed.[46] First, there are differences over the extent to which historical contributions to climate change should be considered. The problem of anthropogenic global warming is essentially one which the industrialized countries have induced through their own industrialization. Since developed countries have a larger responsibility for current greenhouse gas concentrations than for current emissions, the question arises as to whether they have a responsibility for their earlier contribution to the problem. Before energy intensities began to decline in the North emissions were linked to unbridled pollution, for which we are all paying the costs.

Second, aggregating emissions is not the same as equating them. Some commentators, such as Anil Agarwal, have argued that methane emissions from the cultivation of rice paddies, or ruminant animals, are essentially 'livelihood emissions', rather than 'lifestyle emissions' like those of the North, which are based on high levels of personal consumption.[47] In addition, methane emissions are extremely difficult to quantify and assess, and the data very unreliable. Similarly, CFCs, which are overwhelmingly produced in the North, have no known sinks, and should not, therefore, be equated with carbon dioxide or methane, gases for which sinks exist.

Third, it is not clear that we all share an equal stake in the 'global commons', whether it is common property or open-access resources that are being considered. The global 'commons' are being privatized through the patenting of nature itself. The inconclusive deliberations over the Biodiversity Agreement at UNCED demonstrated that, for most countries in the North, the wish to preserve tropical forests was linked to the preservation of patent rights in nature. The resources of developing countries needed to be preserved, so that they could be 'discovered', or utilized as a 'laboratory' for commercial ends on a 'first come, first served' basis.

The key question, as Martinez-Alier has suggested, is the economic value we place on the functions of natural ecosystems. At present the forests and oceans are global sinks, but they do not attract payments to developing countries, even those containing large amounts of forested land, for their global conservation value.[48] Acknowledging this principle would immediately upset the existing consensus surrounding GEC, and serve to undermine the current basis for global environmental management.

It is clear that we cannot begin by agreeing to share 'emission reserves', on an equitable basis, without undermining the very nature of the global economic system on which they ultimately depend. If we are all allocated pollution quotas, or carbon budgets, the problems posed by GEC are not resolved, they are merely deepened. Would such quotas still be available if the poor became richer? What would be their price? Which international institutions would collect the receipts on quotas, and to what ends would they then be applied? It is clear that the use of the concept of 'stakeholder', to imply that everybody has a 'stake' in the global environment, is ambiguous. If the countries of the South are disadvantaged through being unequal stakeholders in the global environmental problem, how can they benefit from being stakeholders in global environmental solutions?

CONCLUSION

The scale of environmental degradation, and the difficulty in mounting policies to reverse current trends, can lead to a sense of foreboding. The magnitude of the problems, the absence of political will, and the complexity of some of the proposed solutions rarely promote optimism. Prior to UNCED, however, there was one point on which a measure of hope still prevailed. This was the assumption that 'the potential environmental implications of Southern development [would] at last give the South some leverage in global politics: if the North wanted them to change their future behaviour and development paths, they would have to meet Southern demands'.[49]

In the final analysis such vestigial hopes were dashed, for a number of reasons. First, as Grubb and colleagues argue, the economic forces that have thwarted development in much of the South remain operative: adverse terms of trade, structural adjustment and, increasingly, the penetration of transnational capital. They note that

the interminable references to the special circumstances of developing countries [in the UNCED documentation] are nothing to do with restructuring international economic relationships, and little to do with enhanced aid: they are simply protective clauses which assert that developing countries are not committed to anything unless additional money is made available.[50]

In this chapter we have shown that such a stalemate was inevitable, given the failure to address the underlying inequalities and lack of mutual confidence between North and South so reminiscent of the 'New International Economic Order' discussions of the 1970s, and beyond. It remains apparent that the North still largely regards the underlying problems of poverty and inequality in the South as of marginal concern to its interests, while solutions to the problems of poverty, and resource degradation, appear to rest on the achievement of higher rates of economic growth. Moreover, it is unclear whether the North is sufficiently concerned about future projections of climate change, and the threat posed by rapidly growing emissions in a number of large developing economies, for the countries of the South to be able to exert leverage in international negotiations. At the time of the Earth Summit in Rio de Janeiro in 1992 this seemed a more plausible outcome.

It is also unclear what international mechanisms would ensure that distributive policies to effect improvements in commodity prices, better terms of trade, and increased investment will work to the advantage of those populations whose livelihoods are most vulnerable. At the very least, a concern with sustainability as a policy goal, rather than with environmental management as a necessary corrective to growth, implies a radically different role for the Bretton Woods institutions, such as the World Bank and the International Monetary Fund. No such changes are currently contemplated, and even divesting the World Bank of control over the Global Environment Facility has proved difficult.

There are other obstacles to a major transfer of funds, and technology, from North to South. Political constraints to such a transfer exist in both regions, and they are constraints largely unrecognized by the other party. Governments in the North do not get elected on promises to increase overseas aid and pay developing countries more for their products. Any concessions to increasing welfare in the South are viewed by Northern electorates as unwarranted acts of charity. For their part, most governments in the South are under domestic political threat if they fail to reward powerful economic interests at home, and the exigencies of the market make it difficult to act decisively to conserve natural resources. Moreover, it is difficult to see how capital transfers could be undertaken without political conditions being set by the North. To many governments in the South such conditions, which amount to forms of 'green conditionality', would be unacceptable.

Finally, is there any evidence that other pressures will be brought to bear—for example, by international non-governmental organizations—to counter the trends toward greater global inequality, and the increasing vulnerability of the environment and livelihoods in the South? At the local level environmental movements are often depicted as a response to externalities, a form of resistance to the costs of environmental degradation being met by the poor. At the global level, however, it is difficult to see how such resistance could be mounted. Most international NGOs are, quite properly, mainly concerned with issues of poverty and civil rights at the national or sub-national level. The meaning of citizenship and environmental security at the international and global level is more difficult to communicate, and more elusive. As one group campaigning on these issues expresses it:

Currently the [World Bank] seeks to award environmental rights by income. Perpetuating the right to pollute and exploit in the direction of those who can 'afford' to is a pseudo-efficiency argument, won at people's expense, and will only result in further emiseration . . .[51]

Perhaps the best hope for a way out of the impasse lies in more measures to reduce consumption in the North, by recovering our power over the underlying social commitments which we take for granted in everyday life, and which leave 'ecological footsteps' throughout the globe.[52] Inequality in world politics is not merely an outcome of the way the nation state, or the transnational corporation, has developed: it is bound up with inequalities in the distribution of resources, and the means to exploit them, which are the legacy of colonialism and the history of industrialization itself.

6

Globalization, Liberalization, and Inequality: Expectations and Experience

Frances Stewart and Albert Berry

INTRODUCTION

The last two decades have seen major changes in economic and social policy in both developed and developing countries—which may well be regarded as a sea change by future economic historians—with a swing back towards the non-interventionist stance of governments in both economic and social arenas that was dominant before the Second World War. The changes are broadly defined as 'liberalization', or yet more broadly as 'globalization'. They have had important effects on world inequality.

The aim of this chapter is to explore the effects of liberalization on income distribution within countries, and also to consider briefly its impact on inter-country inequality. The emphasis is on inequality *within* countries because this is where world inequalities have been most exacerbated over the past two decades. In itself this represents an important change in inequality in world politics. The gap between rich and poor countries has long been the major source of inequality among people in the world. Yet this gap has, if anything, closed slightly over the past couple of decades. Indeed, as we argue later in this chapter, had intra-country distribution remained the same over the 1980s, world distribution would have improved considerably. However, intra-country distribution did change and this has had a deleterious effect in many parts of the world.

The policy changes described as 'liberalization' commenced at the end of the 1970s, with a move from Keynesian towards monetarist macro-economic policies in most developed countries and a shift from state-provided welfare 'from cradle to grave' towards pay-as-you-go social services. At the same time the public provision of basic services, such as water and electricity, at frequently subsidized prices, has been replaced by privatized provision at 'economic' prices; industrial interventionism and labour protection have given way to laissez-faire; and from tax systems whose major purpose was to correct inequalities have been transformed into systems mainly intended to promote incentives and economic efficiency. In many respects, the changes in policy, and in the prevalent economic and social paradigms which underlay them, amounted to a retreat to pre-Second World War philosophy and policies.

There were parallel changes in developing countries, where policy was subject to the same paradigmatic shifts largely as a result of the influence of the developed countries, most directly through conditionalities of the International Monetary Fund and the World Bank, and more subtly and effectively through the dominance of their educational systems, particularly those of the USA, which produced cohorts of so-called Third World 'technocrats', ready to advocate and 'own' the new policies. The resulting policy changes have been well documented.[1] The principal change among developing countries was a move away from state intervention in trade, industrial, and social policy towards a laissez-faire market; from 'dirigisme', as the interventionist policy was deridingly named, to 'liberalism'.

A third major area of liberalization has been in the ex-communist countries. In 'countries in transition' similar changes away from state intervention and towards the market have occurred, but on a much more heroic scale.

'Liberalization' encompasses all these moves towards reduced state intervention. It has both a domestic and an international component. The international component comprises reduced restrictions on trade, capital flows, and technology movements (but not, significantly, labour). These changes are responsible, along with new communications technologies and reduced transport costs, for the 'globalization' phenomenon. Both conceptually and empirically it is impossible to differentiate globalization and liberalization completely, and here we make no attempt to do so.

The policy changes associated with liberalization potentially have pervasive effects on many aspects of economic and social performance. The central concern of this chapter is not with the effects of liberalization on growth and efficiency, about which much has been written,[2] nor the direct implications for poverty.[3] We aim to assess the impact of liberalization on *income distribution* within and among countries.

There are strong reasons to be concerned with the impact of liberalization on income distribution. Income distribution is important in itself as people's well-being depends on their relative as well as their absolute standards of income. It is also important for its implications for social and political stability, poverty, and growth. This has been underlined by recent evidence indicating that more equal income distribution tends to be associated with higher growth rates.[4] From a welfare perspective, it can be argued that the changing incidence of poverty is more important than what happens to income distribution, especially in very poor countries. The impact on income distribution is important from this perspective, since changes in poverty levels are the combined outcome of changes in income distribution and economic growth. Moreover, there is a relative component to absolute poverty—the same absolute level of income provides less in terms of meeting basic needs in richer societies, as the availability of simple goods diminishes and processing, packaging, and transport costs become more important.[5]

It is extremely difficult to assess the impact of liberalization on income distribution. One reason is that the changes described as constituting liberalization were introduced with varying combinations and rigour and at varying dates in different countries. Another reason is that other changes were occurring simultaneously, some associated with liberalization, some independently—for example, changes in technology, the terms of trade, the geopolitical situation, even the weather—and it is often impossible to disentangle the effects. Thirdly, there are many data deficiencies and lacunae in the area of income distribution, as well as complex problems of what measures to use. To cut through these difficulties, we adopt a dual methodology. First, drawing on economic theory, we try to predict the changes one would expect to follow from liberalization. Secondly, we review actual changes in income distribution over the years when liberalization accelerated (i.e. mainly the years from the early 1980s). Although other changes may have caused the changes in distribution observed, to the extent that there is a coincidence of theoretical expectations about the effects of liberalization and actual developments it is plausible to conclude that the changes observed were due to liberalization.

The next section of the chapter provides a brief overview of some of the distributional impacts one might expect as a result of market liberalization, from a theoretical perspective. After that we present some empirical evidence: for developed countries; for different regions of the developing world; and for countries in transition. Developments at world level are briefly reviewed before the conclusions are presented.

EXPECTATIONS: ECONOMIC THEORY, LIBERALIZATION, AND INEQUALITY

Existing studies demonstrate that inter-country income differences are a more important source of world income inequality than are differences in incomes within countries.[6] Changes in inter-country income distribution depend on relative growth rates across countries and changing terms of trade between them. Growth rates are affected by liberalization but they also depend on other factors, such as savings and investment rates and, education policy.[7] In examining inequalities within countries, a further set of theoretical considerations is crucial. In particular, in looking at distributional outcomes it is vital to distinguish *primary incomes* from *secondary incomes*. Primary incomes are those generated by the economic system (e.g. wages or dividends) and these are affected by the impact of changes in the structure of the market on the incomes people earn. Secondary incomes, on the other hand, consist of deductions from individuals' primary incomes (e.g. through taxes), or additions to income such as through pensions provided by the state, or remittances from other family members, or public goods, provided mainly by the state, but also by non-governmental organizations (NGOs) and families. Secondary incomes are thus affected by changes in government taxation and expenditure policies and by access to publicly provided goods and services.

The policy changes undertaken during the 1980s have affected both types of income. However, it must be noted that the effects of liberalization differ according to how the policy changes are undertaken.[8] In particular, it is reasonable to expect variation according to how quickly the liberalization is carried out, the sequencing of the steps taken, and the policies adopted to facilitate the adjustments of firms and of groups of workers and families.[9] Hence, liberalization produces a great variety of results. This variation is highlighted when we examine more closely the theoretical impact of liberalization on primary and secondary incomes respectively.

Primary incomes

In the world as a whole and within particular countries, the upper-income groups and upper-income countries (shorthand for the 'rich') have disproportionately more capital, land, and skills, while lower-income groups and lower-income countries (the 'poor') have disproportionately more labour. It follows that changes which lead to a rise in returns to land, capital, and skills, or which increase the concentration of these assets among families, are likely to make income distribution more unequal, while changes which lead to a rise in returns to labour, or decrease the concentration of the assets, are likely to make income distribution more equal.[10]

Economic policies affect income distribution in the following ways. Interventionist government policies, such as those which affect exchange rates and import restrictions, wage rates, interest rates, and factor movements, tend to prevent factor rewards from reflecting factor endowments in the way they would in a 'free' market environment. Liberalization relaxes these restrictions and hence brings about a situation closer to what one would expect with a free-market equilibrium.

In *developed countries* the restrictions have generally depressed returns to the well off (profits, the returns from skilled labour) and improved returns to those whose main asset is labour. Hence removal of the restrictions would tend to worsen (i.e. make more unequal) income distribution, as profits and skilled wages rise and unskilled wages fall. In developed countries restrictions on capital movements have tended to lower interest/profit rates on capital, since international opportunities are more limited than they would be in the absence of those restraints. Restrictions on movements of goods and labour have raised rewards to unskilled labour, by protecting it from competition from developing countries. Restrictions on trade in skill-intensive products have tended to lower returns to skills in developed countries by reducing their share of developing-country markets and hence the demand for skilled labour.[11] Finally, restrictions on intellectual property have tended to raise returns to research and development (R&D) and innovation (mainly a Northern monopoly).

In *developing countries*, the expected effects of liberalization on income distribution vary with the type of economy, making any general prediction implausible.[12] It is helpful to divide developing countries into four types:

1. *Manufacturing-goods export producers* (MEP): those which have the ability to penetrate world markets in the production of labour-intensive manufactured products on a major scale, i.e. with manufacturing export potential; many of the Asian countries are examples, like Thailand.
2. *Primary-goods export producers* (PEP): relatively unindustrialized countries whose economies specialize in primary products produced by peasant farmers, such as coffee or cotton; some African economies, such as Ghana and Uganda, are examples.
3. *Mineral exporters* (MINEX): relatively unindustrialized countries which specialize in mineral exports produced by large companies; Zambia and Nigeria are cases.
4. *Import-substitution industrializing countries* (IS): countries with large import-substituting industrial sectors, whose main exports are primary products of either kind; many Latin American economies were in this category in the late 1970s.

The first two groups of countries are most likely to experience an improvement in income distribution from liberalization: the first as labour-intensive manufactures expand and employment rises; the second as the incomes of small peasant primary exporters increase. However, as will be seen below there are some factors which may worsen income distribution even in these first two categories. In both the last two categories of developing country, income distribution is likely to worsen with liberalization. In the case of mineral exporters, it is the large companies and the relatively few skilled workers they employ that are likely to benefit from increased trade opportunities. In the case of the big import-substituters, where urban employment predominates, liberalization is likely to reduce wages and employment in the import substitution sector, with knock-on negative effects on urban employment and income-earning opportunities. Consequently, deterioration in urban income distribution is unavoidable, and this will be likely to outweigh improvements, if any, in the rural sector.

In addition, there are some general effects applicable to all of the four types of country. Mostly, these work towards worsening income distribution. First, as international markets evolve for managers, the professions, and skilled labour, salaries of such people are likely to increase in developing countries, worsening salary/wage differentials. An offsetting factor would be the tendency for the demand for skilled labour to fall, and consequently their wages, because trade liberalization gives a comparative advantage to developed countries in these products.[13] Secondly, the development of private enterprise on a significant scale, in countries which previously had a relatively limited private sector, opens up opportunities for people to make large incomes. Thirdly, some of the preliberalization domestic interventions, such as those holding down interest rates or supporting minimum wages, had tended to reduce the share of profits.

The move towards market liberalization has not been uniform across all categories. Most of the restrictions that have been maintained or even enhanced tend to harm the developing countries as a whole, and those without assets within them. For example, restrictions on intellectual property have not been removed but rather reinforced by the recent policy changes. This will tend to maintain income of developed countries. Restrictions on the movement of unskilled labour have also been increased, albeit rather ineffectively. Some of the restrictions on the import of goods from developing countries (e.g. with the maintenance of the Multi-fibre Agreement and the controls on trade in agricultural products) have been maintained, though there are plans to relax them. These restrictions will tend to depress incomes of unskilled labour in developing countries and raise them in developed countries, compared with an unrestricted situation.

In *countries in transition*, worsening income distribution is to be expected. This is not so much because of the trade effects, which dominate the situation in developing countries, but because of the changed domestic policy situation. First, legal changes have given individuals the right to accumulate private assets, whereas previously private asset ownership had been severely restricted. Possibilities of massive accumulation for a few were made possible by the extensive privatization of state assets and the continued restrictions on competition, access to raw materials, and markets, thereby offering a limited number of people considerable potential to exploit monopolies. Secondly, skilled people were enabled to enter international markets and skill differentials would therefore be likely to increase. Thirdly, there was relaxation of prior constraints on internal wage and salary differentials, which included minimum wages and restrictions on worker mobility. Fourthly, the communist system had put a floor on poverty by providing full employment. This has disappeared, leading to a dive in primary incomes for the newly unemployed.

Secondary incomes

Policy changes associated with liberalization have included changes in tax policy and in the provision of social services, affecting secondary income distribution. On the macro side, reforms tend to reduce the total share of taxation and expenditure in GNP. Most tax systems taken as a whole are neutral with respect to income distribution, while most expenditure systems are mildly progressive. Where this is the case, a reduction in the tax and expenditure share would have a small regressive effect on secondary income distribution.

On the tax side, emphasis on efficiency has led to reduced marginal income tax rates and a change in the distribution of taxes away from direct towards indirect taxation. Indirect taxation has been made more uniform across goods. On balance, these tax changes would tend to decrease the progressiveness of the tax system (i.e. exacerbate inequality).

On the expenditure side, the reforms involve a shift from free provision of social services towards charges with means-tested exemptions. In principle, this might improve the distribution of benefits, especially if free provision was previously limited, covering only a small proportion of the poor and a larger proportion of the rest of the population.[14] In practice, the relative distribution of benefits in the reformed system compared with the previous situation depends on the efficiency of targeting of the new system, and the evidence on this is still quite partial.[15]

In summary, in so far as the reforms lead to reduced taxation and expenditure they can normally be expected to worsen the distribution of secondary incomes; the tax reforms also tend in this direction; the expenditure/charges switch could improve distribution, but this will vary according to the particular situation and reforms.

Families are also a source of secondary incomes: families can help individuals to survive during crises, through a variety of changes in behaviour and support, including cash transfers. But this would only affect the distribution of income if members of the (extended) family come from different income strata. Sometimes this is the case, but more often it is a matter of sharing poverty. The impact of changes in family transfers on secondary income distribution is usually small, although it may help moderate poverty. Families may, however, have a more marked effect on *primary* income distribution, especially in economies with a large subsistence sector, by retreating into subsistence if the terms of the cash economy become too harsh. Consequently, in such economies—notably in Africa—measured changes in income distribution will tend to exaggerate any worsening because they often fail to capture rising subsistence production.

Non-governmental organizations (NGOs) may also affect secondary distribution, but, although important at a micro level, their effects are generally negligible in aggregate terms.

EXPERIENCE: THE EVIDENCE OF CHANGES IN INCOME DISTRIBUTION

Changes in developed-country income distribution

Most advanced countries saw a worsening of both primary and secondary income distribution from around the mid-1970s. This reverses the previous apparent trend for income distribution to become more equal in developed countries, after worsening in the initial stages of development.[16]

Primary income distribution in developed countries became more unequal as a result of several factors. A major one was an increased variance of wage and salary earnings. According to Corry and Glyn, 'The 1980s saw a general increase in earnings inequality'.[17]

They find that the largest increase occurred in the US; Sweden saw a reversal of strong earlier declines in inequality and in the UK a century of near-stability in earnings dispersion gave way to a sharp increase; Germany was an exception to this pattern. Among men, the ratio of upper- to lower-decile wages rose in three-quarters of OECD countries from the mid-1970s/early 1980s to the late 1980s or early 1990s, with the sharpest rise in the UK and the US.[18] Other factors contributing to the worsening trend of distribution were a tendency for a rising share of profits and a falling share of wages (Table 6.1); rising unemployment, affecting every OECD country; and the changing age-profile of the population, with a rising share of households having heads above retirement age.

The net effect of these changes was a worsening of household income distribution by most measures in almost every country (Table 6.1). For example, the Gini coefficient rose in every country for which there is evidence, except France, while the ratio of the income share of the top to the bottom decile rose in Finland, the Netherlands, Norway, Sweden, the UK, and the US, remained broadly unchanged in Australia, Belgium, France, and Canada, and fell slightly in New Zealand.[19] In Sweden, the ratio of household incomes of the top 20 per cent to the bottom 20 per cent rose from 4.5 to 5.5 between 1980 and 1988. In the US the top quintile of the population received ten times the average income of the bottom quintile in 1989 compared with a ratio of seven in 1967. In the UK this ratio rose from four at the beginning of the decade to nearly six in 1991.[20]

In a number of countries the secondary distribution of income was affected by a fall in welfare expenditure as a per cent of GDP— by 1 per cent of GDP in the UK, Germany, and the Netherlands, by somewhat more in Belgium and probably in Sweden, Australia, and New Zealand also. But at least six countries showed a continued upward trend in social expenditure. There was a general move towards means-tested provision of benefits. Taxes continued to increase as a proportion of GDP in most countries. Between 1980 and 1991 large declines in the ratio of direct to all taxes were recorded in New Zealand, Belgium, the US, Norway, and Sweden; large increases occurred in Spain and Australia. Most direct tax systems became less progressive, with cuts in the top rate of tax in every OECD country except Switzerland (the OECD average was a cut of 17 percentage points). Boltho concluded a survey by noting:

TABLE 6.1 *Change in income distribution, industrialized countries, 1980s*

Country	Change in profit share manufacturing, 1979–89 (%)	Unemployment (%)		Change in share of top 20%, late 1970s to mid-1980s	Change in % of population with less than 50% of median income, 1979–85	Change in Gini coefficient	
		1973–9	1980–9			early 1980s	late 1980s
Australia	+11.0	5.0	7.5	n.a.	n.a.	0.287	0.295
Belgium	+14.1	6.3	10.8	n.a.	-0.7	0.228	0.235
Canada	+2.3	7.2	9.3	n.a.	n.a.	0.286	0.289
France	+3.1	4.5	9.0	-0.2	+0.6	0.297	0.296
Germany	+3.4	3.2	5.9	-0.8	+1.7	n.a.	n.a.
Italy	+3.1	6.6	9.5	+2.3	+1.8	n.a.	n.a.
Japan	-0.5	1.9	2.5	+0.6	n.a.	n.a.	n.a.
Netherlands	+2.5	4.9	9.7	+1.3	+0.8	0.247	0.268
Norway	-0.5	1.8	2.8	n.a.	n.a.	0.222	0.22
Sweden	+11.1	1.9	2.4	+0.9	n.a.	0.199	0.304
UK	+10.8	5.0	10.0	+2.8	+3.0	0.27	0.341
USA	+1.8	6.7	7.2	+1.2	+1.3	0.309	0.341
OECD	**+5.6**	**4.2**	**7.4**	**+1.2**	**+1.3**	**n.a.**	**n.a.**

n.a. = not available.

Sources: Andrew Glyn, 'Stability, Inegalitarianism and Stagnation: An Overview of the Advanced Capitalist Countries in the 1980s', prepared for WIDER (Helsinki, 1992); A. B. Atkinson, Lee Rainwater, and Timothy Smeeding, 'Income Distribution in European Countries', Department of Applied Economics Working Papers Amalgamated Series No. 9535 (Cambridge, 1995).

In summary, despite continual increases in public expenditure, the combined effects of shifts in spending away from major social programmes and in tax policy toward a broadly regressive position meant that in the 1980s most OECD countries spurned or severely moderated the concept of the generous welfare state that had been current during the 1960s.[21]

Distributional changes in developing countries

The extent of policy changes in developing countries, and the effects of liberalization, have differed across regions because of differences in economic situation and structure among them. The foreign exchange and debt crisis that hit the developing world in the 1980s was mainly concentrated on Africa and Latin America. With obvious exceptions—e.g. the Philippines—Asia was less badly affected. IMF and World Bank conditionalities were therefore focused on Latin America and Africa. Many Asian economies adopted similar policy liberalization, even without the assistance of the IMF or World Bank, but because their economies were less affected by acute crisis, the changes were generally less deflationary. In much of Africa and Latin America adjustment was combined with deflationary stabilization.

For these reasons, the impact of liberalization in developing countries has depended upon a range of factors which are best brought to light by examining the experience of specific regions and economies. While the data are poor, it is difficult to ascertain changes in income distribution in Africa, as there were forces working in both directions. However, most of the evidence shows worsening distribution. A clearer correlation between liberalization and growing inequality emerges from the Latin American data, although comparisons among different Latin American countries also reveal the differential impact of different policy packages, depending upon the timing, nature, and abruptness of liberalization. Finally, Indonesia and China provide important contrasting cases of the impact of liberalization on inequality in Asia. We examine each region in turn.

Africa

As we have seen, theoretically the impact of liberalization on primary incomes will be influenced by the production profile of a country: what they produce and what they export. This is very clearly the case in African economies, where the impact on income distribution has been mixed (Table 6.2), although the very poor data in this part of the world make it difficult to find reliable evidence.

African economies are almost all primary exporters, specializing in peasant crops (PEP) or in minerals (MINEX). Mauritius is the one exception, having successfully penetrated world textile markets. Following this success, Mauritius had a steady and large improvement in its income distribution, which is attributable to the expansion of employment opportunities as textile exports grew.

The other categories of country show divergent performance. Mostly, the peasant primary producers (PEP) experienced a worsening in income distribution, rather against expectations. This was true of Ethiopia, Kenya, Tanzania, and Uganda,[22] whose recovery was peasant-based, but the improved earnings failed to reach the very poor in rural and urban areas and income distribution worsened. However, the data in Table 6.2 suggest a small improvement in distribution in Ghana, where liberalization led to a revival of peasant-produced cocoa; but other measures of income distribution for Ghana show a worsening income distribution.[23]

The performance of the two mineral-based economies, shown in Table 6.2, differed. There was a severe worsening of income distri-

TABLE 6.2 *Income distribution in Africa during adjustment*

Country	early date		most recent date	
	Year	Gini coefficient	Year	Gini coefficient
Ghana	1987/8	0.359	1992	0.339
Kenya	1981/2	0.40	1992	0.49
Lesotho	1986/7	0.57	1993	0.57
Mauritius	1980/1	0.48	1991/2	0.37
Nigeria	1985	0.387	1992	0.449
Uganda	1989	0.377	1992	0.409
Zambia	1974/5	0.59	1993	0.46

Source: World Bank data from *Poverty Assessments* and *World Development Reports* (various years).

bution in oil-producing Nigeria, but an improvement in Zambia's copper economy. However, there was a collapse of world copper prices over this period, and Zambia turned to agriculture in the 1980s, which may explain the improvement.

For other African countries, where there is no direct evidence on income distribution, some useful leads can be deduced from the structure of the economies.

As argued earlier, improved rural–urban terms of trade are likely to have benefited the rural poor[24] in countries where peasants dominate agricultural and export production. The available data do suggest that the domestic agriculture–industry terms of trade improved in the majority of cases (12 out of 19) during the 1980s (see Table 6.3). But rising prices of agricultural inputs partially offset the effects of improved terms of trade on farmer incomes. For instance, in Malawi the weighted average price of the three main types of fertilizer used by smallholders increased by 87 per cent between 1983–4 and 1987–8.[25]

In many countries, although the poor do participate, export production tends to be concentrated among the richer farmers,[26] while subsistence farmers and net food purchasers with little or no land were less favourably affected. Each of these groups contains a high concentration of those below the poverty line. Subsistence producers were broadly unaffected by the adjustment programmes. Net food purchasers, who account for some of the poorest households in Zambia, for example, faced rising prices of purchases.[27] Food producers, who are also among the poorest rural dwellers according to the detailed data available for Ghana and Côte d'Ivoire, benefited less than producers of export crops, or experienced a loss in income.[28] A study of price liberalization of rice in Madagascar showed that there were substantial welfare losses among poor rice farmers and gains were concentrated among a minority of relatively large landholdings.[29]

There is evidence of significant deterioration in the position of formal sector urban workers, especially those in the public sector. An average wage earner in the non-agricultural sector earned three times the country's average per capita income in the mid-1980s compared to more than four times the average in 1975. During the 1980s, average real wages declined in 26 out of 28 African countries, while the real minimum wage fell in 22 out of the 29 countries for which figures are available.[30] In some cases, the fall was very

TABLE 6.3 *Domestic terms of trade in adjusting countries in Africa, late 1980s*

Countries	Real exchange rate, 1988 (1980 = 100)	Share of agricultural exports in total, 1989 (%)	Agriculture/ Industry terms of trade, 1989 (1980 = 100)
Intensively adjusting countries[a]			
Côte d'Ivoire	91.1	91	100.1
Ghana	22.4	63	59.5
Guinea Bissau	n.a.	n.a.	83.3
Kenya	72.7	85	100.7
Madagascar	51.3	85	100.8
Malawi	85.6	94	100.0
Mauritania	87.0	54	164.3
Mauritius	79.5	38	125.3
Nigeria	28.6	5	122.4
Senegal	99.8	72	142.5
Tanzania	54.7	84	123.9
Togo	81.6	38	83.1
Zambia	66.3	3	78.1
Other adjusting countries[a]			
Benin	n.a.	71	102.8
Burkina Faso	80.0[b]	88	115.9
Burundi	97.4[b]	93	84.1
Cameroon	112.5[b]	49	134.2
Central African Republic	98.8[b]	47	138.1
Congo	99.3[b]	15	163.9
Gabon	80.7[b]	21	169.3
Gambia	80.0[b]	n.a.	97.5
Mali	77.4[b]	90	93.6
Niger	64.3[b]	n.a.	61.8
Sierra Leone	121.8[b]	21	114.5
Somalia	65.1[b]	96	56.9
Sudan	119.7[b]	95	100.0
Zaire	30.3[b]	6	106.8
Zimbabwe	72.7	40	81.8

n.a. = not available.

[a] As defined by World Bank, *Adjustment Lending and Mobilization of Private and Public Resources for Growth (RAL III)* (Washington, DC, 1992).
[b] 1978–80 = 100, index for 1988–89.

Sources: World Bank, *Report on Adjustment Lending II* (Washington, DC, 1990); World Bank, *World Development Report 1991* (Washington, DC, 1991); World Bank, *World Tables 1992* (Washington, DC, 1992); David E. Sahn, *Fiscal and Exchange Rate Reforms in Africa: Considering the Impact upon the Poor* (Ithaca, NY, 1990).

large. For example, in Tanzania the real minimum wage in 1987 was only 36 per cent of its 1980 value. A rising proportion of employment in the urban informal sector,[31] together with the decline in real average and minimum wages in the formal sector, depressed real incomes in the urban areas. It seems probable that in most countries urban income distribution worsened over these years, with a decline in the share of wages in output and increased wage differentials, especially in countries where the reforms widened differentials in public sector pay.

Other potentially distribution-improving effects of the typical policy package were rarely manifest in African countries. Agricultural goods continued to be the primary source of employment and exports in most African countries, with little diversification. Textiles and clothing exports give an indication of the extent of the labour-intensive manufacturing sector. There was no significant increase in the share of exports from this sector except for Mauritius (Table 6.4).[32]

Optimism that adjustment policies would benefit the small-scale sector as a result of reduced financial repression and the removal of other artificial favours enjoyed by large firms also awaits confirmation. Employment expansion in Ghanaian small-scale enterprises exceeded that of the large-scale formal sector, but output expansion did less well.[33] Surveys in Niger in 1982 and 1987 showed a rising level of activity and wage rates in the informal sector.[34] Evidence from Zimbabwe, Zambia, and Malawi on micro-enterprises suggests faster employment expansion than in the larger-scale sector, but evidence is not available on output or incomes, and these could well have shown less growth (as in Ghana), since informal sector employment growth is as often a sign of lack of productive options as of the health of the sector itself. In Zambia, the foreign exchange auction is reported to have had a more severe adverse effect on small firms than on large ones.[35]

In summary, of the predicted structural changes that might have improved income distribution in African economies, there is evidence of improved rural–urban terms of trade, but very little diversification into labour-intensive industrial products, and although the share of the small-scale sector in employment expanded, there is no evidence of a rising share of output.

Although general conclusions about income distribution in African countries are inevitably speculative given the lack of data, we

TABLE 6.4 *Textiles and clothing as a percentage of exports in some African countries, 1980 and 1992*

Country	1980	1992	Change (%)
Intensive adjusting countries[a]			
Côte d'Ivoire	3	2	−1
Ghana	0	0	0
Kenya	1	3	+2
Madagascar	2	10	+8
Malawi	5	3	−2
Mauritius	19	54	+35
Nigeria	0	0	0
Senegal	1	1	0
Tanzania	8	7	−1
Togo	4	3	−1
Other adjusting countries[a]			
Benin	0	1	+1
Burkina Faso	2	2	0
Burundi	0	1	0
Cameroon	1	0	+1
Central African Republic	0	0	0
Congo	0	0	0
Mali	1	7	+6
Niger	1	1	0
Sudan	1	1	0
Zimbabwe	0	6	+5

[a] As defined by the World Bank, *Adjustment Lending and Mobilization of Private and Public Resources for Growth (RAL III)* (Washington, DC, 1992).

Source: World Bank, *World Development Report* (Washington, DC, various years).

would conclude that income distribution within both urban and rural sectors probably worsened but this was offset in some cases by the improved agriculture–industry terms of trade.

A further set of effects of liberalization on inequality has resulted from policies affecting secondary incomes. A falling share of direct taxes, a fall in the ratio of government expenditure to GNP, and a fall in the share of health and education in government expenditure in the majority of countries implied a worsening in secondary distribution. The introduction of user charges further hurt some of the poor in absolute terms, though the distributional incidence may have been progressive.

A general fall in the share of direct taxes in total public sector revenue which occurred in the 1980s, which was more marked among adjusting than non-adjusting countries, is likely to have implied a more regressive incidence of taxation. The ratio of total government expenditure to GNP declined in about two-thirds of the African countries for which data are available. This declining ratio, combined with falling GNP per capita, implied severe cuts in total government expenditure per head over the 1980s. The worst cuts were in Tanzania (nearly 50 per cent), Zambia (60 per cent), Sierra Leone, and Zaire (around 70 per cent) among adjusting countries and Liberia (about 50 per cent) among non-adjusting ones. The expenditure cuts followed a significant rise in government expenditure per head in the 1970s.

Between 1981 and 1990, the ratio of social expenditure—defined here to include expenditure on education and health[36]—to total government expenditure fell in 12 out of 17 countries for which data are available, with little difference between those undergoing adjustment programmes and others. Public expenditure on education and health as a proportion of GNP declined during the 1980s in 13 out of 17 countries, including most of the adjusting countries. The average budget share going to education fell from 15.4 to 12.8 per cent, while that destined to health fell only slightly from 5.5 to 5.3 per cent. There was no marked trend in the share of primary schooling in total expenditure (we assume that lower-income households receive a larger proportion of the benefits of primary education). Data are lacking on trends in priority ratios in the health sector, although there is evidence of attempts to shift expenditure towards primary health care in at least nine countries.[37] Internationally supported immunization efforts permitted a big improvement in immunization coverage; for example, regional coverage of measles vaccination increased from 29 to 61 per cent between 1981 and 1989.[38]

One particular element of many adjustment packages has been user charges for social services, including school fees and health care charges. Such charges were introduced and/or increased in many countries, including Ghana, Guinea-Bissau, Niger, Nigeria, Swaziland, Tanzania, Zaire, Zambia, and Zimbabwe. In principle, low-income users are often intended to be exempt, or eligible to receive refunds. But in practice the exemption systems appear to work haphazardly, requiring complex procedures, while refunds cover only a proportion of those who should qualify. For example, in Zimbabwe only about 10 per cent of the schoolchildren who should have qualified for refunds in fact received them.[39] School fees appear to have had a direct negative effect in Tanzania, where attendance at primary school fell sharply, simultaneous with the introduction of 'voluntary' fees. In Zimbabwe, where 40 per cent of a sample of textile workers revealed that they had reduced their children's schooling after school fees were introduced for primary and secondary education, and there was also a sharp reduction in O-level candidates as the examinations fees rose.

Use of health services was adversely affected by the combined effect of reduced resources (including drugs), reduced incomes, and rising charges. Rising charges appeared to have negative effects on attendance in Zaire, Lesotho, Ghana, Swaziland, and Zimbabwe.[40]

In summary, the declining proportion of GNP going to the social sectors is likely to have cut the secondary incomes of lower-income groups more than of upper-income groups. The introduction of user charges and the reduction of food subsidies may have improved the distribution of secondary benefits, but clearly worsened the absolute position of the poor. Changes in the tax system appear broadly to have been in a regressive direction, though detailed investigation of tax incidence in particular countries is needed to support this conclusion.

Latin America

In Latin America a deterioration in income distribution was most marked and extensive over the liberalization period. Typically, prior to liberalization Latin American economies were import-substitution industrializing, with exports dominated by primary products, a large and quite sophisticated industrial sector under heavy protection, an agricultural sector with an agricultural class that was landless (or had very small holdings), and a particularly high number of lower-income people in the large urban informal sector. In the wake of liberalization in these economies, inequality of both primary and secondary income seems to have been exacerbated.

Secondary incomes have been affected by tax and expenditure reforms. The shift from income tax to general sales taxes[41] has resulted in systems which are in theory less progressive, although the poor administration and loopholes of the old systems may in fact mean they are not markedly less so. Public expenditure has decreased in areas such as education,[42] although not in health, where expenditure has slightly increased.[43] At the same time, targeting has become increasingly popular, in spite of its obvious problems.[44]

In terms of primary income, although the precise extent and explanation of changes in income distribution is still uncertain, the record shows a clear preponderance of negative shifts in distribution around the time of the introduction of policy reforms, an impact not readily explicable by other obvious candidates like the stage of the cycle, the rate of inflation, and so forth. The evidence from Argentina, Colombia, the Dominican Republic, Ecuador, Mexico, and Uruguay, taken together, points strongly at the policy package as a possible source of increasing inequality. In no case with data of satisfactory quality do we have clear evidence of the opposite pattern, though Costa Rica appears to be the one possible exception.

The discussion below deals first with the earliest liberalizers—the Southern Cone countries (Chile, Argentina, and Uruguay), who altered policy in the early or mid-1970s. The second wave of liberalizers, Mexico and the Dominican Republic, are then discussed, and then the latest liberalizers, Colombia and Ecuador. The section ends with a brief look at Costa Rica, the one Latin American case where liberalization does not seem to have been accompanied by a widening of income differentials. Overall, these Latin American cases demonstrate the extent to which the nature and timing of policy reform has affected its impact on inequality.

The first wave of liberalization: the 1970s

In *Chile* some of the most radical policy 'reforms' of any nation in the region were undertaken in the period after 1973.[45] Over the same period a major change in distribution could be observed. Data on the distribution of consumption among Greater Santiago house-holds show one of the largest deteriorations ever recorded statistically in a developing country, occurring primarily between 1969 and 1978 but also over the decade which followed (Table 6.5). If the national trend in consumption distribution were like that of Santiago, the consumption decline in the bottom quintile of households over 1969–78 would have been over 40 per cent. A further aspect of income inequality was an increase in the relative income of persons with university education vis-à-vis those with less education.

In *Argentina* liberalization was undertaken in the late 1970s and led to a fall of 11 per cent in manufacturing output between 1976 and 1982, and a reduction in employment of 37 per cent accompanied by a large rise in labour productivity.[46] However, although the Gini coefficient among income earners in Greater Buenos Aires rose from about 0.36 over 1974–6 to 0.44 in 1978, since then income concentration has fluctuated without a clear trend, seemingly affected both by the real exchange rate[47] and by the structural changes wrought by the change in trade policy.

In *Uruguay* liberalization was undertaken after a military coup in 1973[48] but labour reforms were reversed when Uruguay returned to democracy in 1985. The evidence points to a substantial increase in inequality during the 1970s, when most of the important policy

TABLE 6.5 *Quintile distribution of consumption among households in Greater Santiago, 1969, 1978, and 1988*

Quintile	Per cent of total consumption		
	1969	1978	1988
1	7.6	5.2	4.4
2	11.8	9.3	8.2
3	15.6	13.6	12.6
4	20.6	21.0	20.0
5	44.5	51.0	54.9

Source: Ricardo Ffrench-Davis, 'Economic Development and Equity in Chile: Legacies and Challenges in the Return to Democracy', Institute of Development Studies Discussion Paper No. 316 (Brighton, 1993), 16.

changes were introduced.[49] At this time there was a sharp fall in wages and a widening in the earnings differentials across educational levels. Favaro and Bension suggest that the opening of the economy, the reduction in relative size of the government, and the prohibition of labour union activity all contributed to increasing inequality.[50]

Hence, in all three countries of the Southern Cone, liberalization has coincided with greater inequality in income distribution. This picture is repeated in countries who liberalized later—in the 1980s, after the debt crisis hit Latin America.

The second wave of liberalization: the 1980s

Mexico undertook reforms in the 1980s,[51] liberalizing trade, finance, and investment, and in the early 1990s crowned these measures by signing the North American Free Trade Agree-ment (NAFTA). In the period after the reforms, Alarcon and McKinley[52] report that the Gini coefficient of total household income rose from 0.43 in 1984 to 0.475 in 1992, most of the increase having occurred by 1989.[53] Yet more dramatically, the Gini coefficient of wage and salary earners rose moderately from 0.419 in 1984 to 0.443 in 1989, then leapt to 0.519 in 1992.[54]

Probably contributing to the changes in income distribution in Mexico was the large inflow of capital in the late 1980s,[55] as negotiations on NAFTA moved towards completion. This interpretation bears out the view that a movement of capital from an industrial to a developing country (in this case the US and Mexico respectively) lowers the relative wages of unskilled workers in both countries, creating a similar relative wage movement on both sides of the border.[56]

In the *Dominican Republic* an adjustment programme was undertaken in the early 1980s. Inequality increased sharply at the end of the 1980s, with the Gini leaping to 0.51 in 1989 (in contrast with a fall in the period 1976–84 from 0.45 to 0.43). The timing of the increase in inequality suggests that the growing trade ratios may have played a role, along with inflation.[57]

The final wave of liberalization: the 1990s

Yet further evidence of rising inequality in the wake of liberalization is provided by Latin America's most recent liberalizers—

Colombia and Ecuador—who pushed through market-friendly policy packages only in the early 1990s.

Colombia embarked on liberalization in the 1990s.[58] While the post-implementation period has been too short to provide definitive answers about the effects of reforms, there appears to have been a sharp reversal of a previous (and perhaps unique) equalizing trend in the urban distribution of income.[59] The 1990–3 period saw significant declines in the income share of the first six deciles of earners (30.8 per cent to 27.4 per cent), while the only major gainer was the top decile (36.2 per cent to 40.4 per cent). In percentage terms the biggest losers were the lowest deciles: the first decile saw its share fall by 23 per cent from 1.93 per cent to 1.48 per cent, about the level of the late 1970s. The dearth of data on rural incomes makes it impossible to know for sure whether the trends observed in urban areas hold for the nation as a whole. A best guess is that there was not much change between 1988 and 1992, years for which surveys are available.

Ecuador implemented structural adjustment policies from 1981 onwards in a gradual, slow, selective, highly conflictive, and still incomplete way. Over this period the evolution of functional income distribution points strongly toward increases in inequality over 1980–4 and 1987–91. Urban household survey data available since 1987 point to a sharp increase in income concentration around 1990. The Gini coefficient among earners jumped from an average of 0.431 in 1988–90 to 0.483 in 1992–3. Household income distribution followed a similar ascending path. The evolution of real income by income stratum discloses a severe deterioration for the poorest half of the population, exceeding 25 per cent for the bottom quintile, an unstable or slightly declining situation for the next 45 per cent, and a sharp improvement (of 25 per cent) for the richest 5 per cent; the income of the top decile relative to the bottom one rose from 24-fold to 30-fold using unadjusted data. The incidence of urban poverty is estimated to have risen from 66.3 per cent in 1988 to a peak of 73.8 per cent in 1992, after which a decline occurred in 1993.[60] The timing of this recent accentuation of inequality suggests that both trade liberalization and the reduction of public employment played a role.

Costa Rica: an exception

Costa Rica appears to be the only Latin American country to have undertaken significant market-friendly reforms without suffering a large widening of income differentials.[61] Liberalization was undertaken in the 1980s in a more gradual and less erratic way than in Chile. The government increased tax, weakened the power of unions, privatized, and offered new incentives for exports. However, wage indexation was left in place, and unemployment fairly quickly returned to its low average of 5 per cent. Over this time, Trejos and Sauma[62] report that measured inequality among households fell during the crisis and again during the adjustment period (which they date as 1982–6), then rose sharply over 1985–7 and tended to fall after that.[63] The increase between 1985 and 1987 could reflect the first effects of the liberalization, but it may be due to a change in survey methodology. The best guess at this time is that there was no significant, lasting negative impact of the post-1986 reforms on the level of inequality in Costa Rica.

One broad interpretation of the Costa Rican experience is that reforms differed in degree, timing, and abruptness from other Latin American countries. For example, while the earnings differentials by skills did stop falling, they did not increase sharply at the time of economic liberalization. And though the variance of salary incomes rose for a couple of years after liberalization began, it then continued its downward movement. It is possible that when changes are made more gradually, as in Costa Rica, they do not produce as great a negative impact on distribution as when the same degree of policy change takes place more quickly.

Paraguay and export-led growth

Finally a note about Paraguay, which has not liberalized in the way discussed in this chapter, but which has pursued a strategy of outward-oriented, agriculture-based, export-led growth strategy since the 1950s.[64] This is a strategy which might theoretically be supposed to have distributional merits. Yet Paraguay's experience provides no positive evidence of this. Rather, in this country there were sharp increases in inequality across the three census years, the Gini coefficient rising from 0.531 in 1972 to 0.564 in 1982 to 0.596 in 1988.[65]

Asia

In Asia, the varied structures of the economies make it difficult to generalize about the probable impact of liberalization on income distribution. Many of the economies are in the 'manufacturing exporters' category, which suggests a capacity to respond to policy change by raising employment and incomes of unskilled workers. On the other hand, the rural sector is more differentiated than in Africa.

Below, the discussion focuses on two economies showing contrasting performances: China, where distribution has worsened, and Indonesia, where it has improved, at least since the late 1970s. Data for a wider sample of countries (Table 6.6) suggest that in most cases (eight out of the nine) income distribution improved between the mid-1970s and the end of the 1980s, although the improvement came to an end and showed signs of reversal in several countries at the end of the period.[66] We have not attempted to relate movements in distribution to degree of liberalization in any detailed way, and it must be emphasized that these data are derived from international sources and may not be comparable over time. However, in Asia, the rapid rise in total exports in almost every case, with an increasing share of manufactures (typically relatively labour-intensive), lends support to the standard trade model suggesting that expansion in labour-intensive exports associated with liberalization would improve income distribution, which would be consistent with the earlier findings for Taiwan.[67]

A superficial overview of factors affecting secondary incomes (Table 6.8) shows a mixed, but on balance negative, picture of changes in secondary distribution. Direct taxes fell as a proportion of the total in two-thirds of the cases and social expenditure as a proportion of GNP fell in the majority of countries. However, the rapid growth meant that in real terms there were significant increases in social expenditure per capita in most cases over this period. The two detailed studies below illustrate the varying performance.

Indonesia is an interesting case where liberalization appears to have been accompanied by improvements in both primary and secondary income distribution. Adjustment started in 1983, when

TABLE 6.6 *Income distribution of households in some Asian countries, 1976–1992*

Country	Year	Share of bottom 20%	Share of bottom 40%	Share of top 20%	Gini coefficient
Bangladesh	1976–7	6.2	17.1	46.9	
	1981–2	9.3	22.4	39.0	
	1985–6	10.0	23.7	37.2	
	1988–9	9.5	22.9	38.6	
	1992	9.4	22.9	37.9	
India[a]	1975–6	7.0	16.2	49.4	
	1983	8.1	20.4	41.4	
	1989–90	8.8	21.3	41.3	
	1990–1 (rural)	9.58	23.35	37.15	
	1992 (rural)	9.38	22.60	38.99	
	1990–1 (urban)	8.24	20.16	41.96	
	1992 (urban)	7.88	19.33	43.91	
Indonesia	1976	6.6	14.4	49.4	
	1984	8.1	20.4	n.a.	0.33
	1987	8.8	21.2	41.3	0.32
	1990	8.7	20.8	n.a.	
	1993[a]	8.7	21.0	40.7	0.32
Korea	1976	5.7	16.9	45.3	
	1980	5.1	16.1	45.4	0.39
	1988	7.4	19.7	42.2	0.34
Malaysia	1973	3.5	11.2	56.1	
	1987	4.6	13.9	51.2	
	1989	4.6	12.9	53.7	

TABLE 6.6 Continued

Country	Year	Share of bottom 20%	Share of bottom 40%	Share of top 20%	Gini coefficient
Pakistan[a]	1984–5	7.8	19.0	45.6	0.49
	1991	8.4	21.3	39.7	
Philippines	1971	3.6	11.7	67.0	0.447
	1985	5.2	14.3	52.1	0.445
	1988	5.2	14.3	51.8	0.474
	1991	4.7	13.0	54.6	
Sri Lanka[a]	1969–70[b]	5.5	19.2	43.4	0.35[b]
	1973[b]		19.3[b]		0.46[b]
	1978–9[b]		16.1[b]		0.29[c]
	1985–6	4.8[b]	13.3[b]	56.1[b]	0.49[b]
	1986–7[b]				
	1990–1[d]	8.9	22.0	39.3	0.27
Thailand[a]	1975	5.6	15.2	49.8	0.48
	1988	6.1	15.5	50.7	
	1992	5.6	14.3	52.7	0.46

[a] Expenditure shares by persons.
[b] Derived from Consumer Finance Survey.
[c] From Labor Force and Social Survey.
[d] From Household Income and Employment Survey.

Sources: F. Johansen, 'Poverty Reduction in East Asia: The Silent Revolution', World Bank Discussion Papers No. 203 (Washington, DC, 1993); World Bank, Report on Adjustment Lending II (RAL II) (Washington, DC, 1990); World Bank, World Development Report (Washington, DC, various years); L. Cornista and M. Bravo, Review and Assessment of Rural Development Programs and Projects in the Philippines: The Comprehensive Agrarian Reform Program (CARP) Component (Los Banos, 1994); B. Hewavitharana, Economic Consequences of the Devolution Package and an Evaluation of Decentralization (Colombo, 1997).

TABLE 6.7 *Exports in Asian economies, 1980–1994*

Country	Textiles and clothing exports as a percentage of total exports		Manufacturing exports as a percentage of total exports		Growth of exports (% per annum)	
	1981	1992	1980	1993	1980–90	1990–4
Bangladesh	56	72	69	83	6.6	11.7
China	21	30	48	81	11.5	16.0
India	23	25	59	75	5.9	13.6
Indonesia	1	18	2	53	2.9	10.8
Korea	30	20	90	93	12.0	10.6
Malaysia	3	6	19	70	10.9	12.9
Pakistan	41	69	49	85	8.1	11.3
Philippines	7	10	37	76	3.5	8.0
Sri Lanka	16	52	16	74	3.7	10.7
Thailand	10	17	28	73	14.0	14.6

Source: World Bank, *World Development Report* (Washington, DC, various years).

the price of oil fell. Unlike many countries, growth remained positive (albeit slowed down) during the adjustment period.[68] Inequality remained stable over the period 1984–90, the reported Gini coefficient falling from 0.33 to 0.32.[69] According to official estimates, the incidence of poverty continued to decline, from 21.6 per cent (1984) to 17.4 per cent (1987), with a greater fall in the rural than the urban areas, largely due to rising incomes of self-employed farmers; there was little further change in poverty over 1987–91.[70]

On the whole, Indonesia's record shows considerable success in combining adjustment, growth, and equity. How was this achieved? First, maintaining a significantly positive growth of GDP per capita was important. This success was partly due to the balance of macro-policies adopted, with considerable emphasis on switching as against disabsorption (associated with the big depreciation and the rising budget deficit from 1983–5), and partly to the very favourable supply response—both in terms of expansion of cash crop exports (estate crops grew by 9 per cent per annum over

TABLE 6.8 *Taxation and government expenditure in some Asian economies, 1980–1993*

Country	Taxes as a percentage of GNP		Direct taxes as a percentage of total		Education and health as a percentage of GNP	
	1980	1993	1980	1993	1980	1993
Bangladesh	10.0	n.a.	10.1	8.6^a	1.8	2.4^a
India	13.2	16.9	18.3	18.7	0.5	0.7
Indonesia	23.1	18.9	78.0	49.3	2.5	2.4
Korea	17.6	17.1	22.3	31.4	3.3	3.0
Malaysia	29.6	26.7	37.5	34.5	n.a.	6.9
Pakistan	17.7	24.0	13.8	13.9	0.7	0.4
Philippines	13.4	18.1	21.1	29.1	2.3	3.4
Sri Lanka	41.6	26.9	15.5	13.9	4.8	4.2
Thailand	19.0	16.3	17.7	27.9	4.6	4.8

n.a. = not available.
^{a} 1991.
Source: World Bank, *World Development Reports* (Washington, DC, various years).

1984–8, farm non-food crops by 4.3 per cent per annum—this was not greatly at the expense of other agricultural products, which continued to expand albeit at a lower rate) and of labour-intensive manufactured exports (manufactures had risen to 29 per cent of the value of exports in 1988 from 8 per cent in 1983). The favourable supply response was in turn due to earlier developments, which had provided Indonesia with reasonably developed rural infrastructure, improved human capital, and some industrial and entrepreneurial experience. Secondly, growth was relatively egalitarian. Relatively equal land distribution meant that the rural poor participated in the increased output; while not proportionately represented in cash crops, they did participate in those activities and also in the sustained expansion of food crops, while non-agricultural rural opportunities expanded. Within the urban sector, the focus on labour-intensive manufacturing led to growth in manufacturing employment, which is estimated to have expanded by nearly 10 per cent per annum from 1985–8 in enterprises with more than 15 employees. In both rural and urban areas there was a slight rise in real wages.

Finally, while government expenditure was curtailed (the expenditure ratio fell from 26.4 per cent in 1981 to 20.9 per cent in 1990), the services benefiting the poor were broadly protected over the period of severest cuts (1983–6). Three measures stand out. First, while central government development expenditure fell by 43 per cent over 1982–3 to 1986, routine expenditure grew by over 7 per cent. Second, transfers to the provinces were protected, growing despite the aggregate cuts. Third, development expenditures were reallocated to priority areas—thus development expenditure on human resources rose from 16 per cent of the total (1982–3) to 24 per cent (1986–7). The social allocation ratio remained constant over the 1980s, while the priority ratio improved, as measured by the proportion of educational expenditure going to primary and secondary schools and the proportion of health expenditure going to basic health care. In summary, macro-policies led to labour-intensive growth while meso-policies improved the distributional incidence of government expenditures.

China undertook quite far-reaching market reforms from around 1978. The starting point was, of course, quite different from that of most other countries considered here—a socialist economy, with mainly public ownership and strong interventions in prices and incomes that kept inequality to a very low level. The Gini coefficient was estimated to be around 0.25 in 1978, somewhat greater in the rural than the urban areas. When the reforms were initiated, rising inequality was expected: according to Deng,

We must expect some regions, some enterprises, and some workers and peasants to have a greater income first and better lives first, as a result of their hard work and achievements . . . the entire national economy will move forward like a series of waves and the peoples of every nationality in China will then become rich.[71]

As predicted, the reforms led to rising inequality within and between rural and urban areas, especially after 1984. In the first phase (1978–84) there is some dispute about whether rural inequality rose or not, but from 1985 there was a major deterioration, the Gini rising from 0.244 to 0.335 in 1991.[72] Howes and Hussain conclude that the dominant factor in this income concentration was the rapid growth of non-agricultural activities—more than ten times as fast as agricultural output.[73] Income from non-agricultural activities was always more unequally distributed than that from agriculture (Gini 0.55, compared with 0.21 for agriculture). There was also a small increase in inequality within both sectors, but the main source of growing inequality was the increasing role of non-agricultural activities in the total.

In the urban areas, inequality prior to the reforms was remarkably low, with a Gini of 0.185 in 1977. The reforms removed price controls and permitted more private enterprise and greater wage differentials. Griffin et al. estimate the urban Gini to be 0.233 for 1988. In the first phase of the reforms, the rural–urban gap narrowed as terms of trade for the rural areas improved with price reforms. But from 1984, the emphasis shifted to urban reform; the sector grew rapidly, as did worker remuneration and enterprise surpluses. By 1988, it is estimated that the rural Gini had risen to 0.338 and the urban to 0.233,[74] with an overall Gini at 0.382, higher than either of the others because of inequality between the sectors.[75]

Although the reforms were accompanied by a significant rise in inequality, average incomes also rose very fast, reflecting the 10 per cent average rate of GDP growth from 1978. Consequently, the incidence of poverty fell dramatically, according to World Bank estimates, from 28 per cent in 1978 to 8.6 per cent in 1990,[76] being now virtually confined to remote resource-constrained areas. By contrast, using a Chinese Academy survey, Riskin identified a poverty incidence of 12 per cent, of which only 40 per cent were in the World-Bank-designated poor areas.[77] However, there is agreement that poverty fell—the issue is by how much and where it is currently located.

COUNTRIES IN TRANSITION

Countries in transition have, of course, experienced the most dramatic form of liberalization, as they were furthest from a laissez-faire market initially. As restrictions were removed—some of which were intended to reduce inequality—one would expect rising inequality. Reforms most likely to raise inequality of primary incomes were the privatization of state assets and liberalization of labour markets; secondary distribution would be likely to worsen with tax reforms and downward pressure on state social-support payments.

There was, indeed, a marked increase in primary and after-tax income distribution in every country between 1989 and 1994, starting from a very equal distribution, as illustrated in Table 6.9. In some countries, notably Russia and Moldovia, the increase was very sharp and by 1994 the estimated inequality was comparable to, or even greater than, that in most developed market economies. Cornia's analysis of the sources of change in income distribution in these countries shows that:

TABLE 6.9 *Inequality in countries in transition, 1989–1994 (Gini coefficients)*

	Net per capita household income		Gross earnings	
	1989	1994	1989	1994
Bulgaria	0.250^c	0.353	0.21^c	0.28^b
Czech Republic	0.185	0.210^a	0.198	0.24^b
Estonia	0.277^d	0.386	n.a.	n.a.
Hungary	0.214	0.232^b	0.268	0.308^b
Lithuania	0.275	0.370	0.26	0.35
Moldova	0.267^e	0.40^e	0.264	0.385
Poland	0.269	0.304	0.206	0.298
Romania	0.223^c	0.252	0.166	0.298
Russia	0.257	0.409	0.273	0.464^b
Slovakia	0.187	0.225	n.a.	n.a.
Slovenia	0.237	0.250^b	0.22	0.28

n.a. = not available.
[a] 1992.
[b] 1993.
[c] 1990.
[d] Not directly comparable to subsequent data because of changes in sampling frame.
[e] Estimate.

Source: Giovanni A. Cornea and UNICEF, *Ugly Facts and Fancy Theories: Children and Youth during the Transition* (Florence, 1995).

- wages and salaries fell sharply as a source of incomes: for example, in Russia wages accounted for three-quarters of personal income in 1990 and this had fallen to 40 per cent by 1995;
- the distribution of earnings became more sharply unequal in every country (Table 6.9), partly because of a relative decline in the minimum wage;
- entrepreneurial income, which is far more concentrated than wage and salary income, rose from about 13 per cent in Russia (1990) to nearly 40 per cent (1995);
- there was a rise in the concentration of property income for countries where evidence is available.

While all the changes in primary incomes made for increasing inequality, against expectations the changes in secondary transfers did not move systematically in this direction. In the first place, secondary transfers, i.e. pensions, family allowances, etc., were maintained as a proportion of income; secondly, in some countries the distribution of these transfers actually became more equal (e.g. in Hungary).

WORLD TRENDS IN INEQUALITY

Trends in the distribution of world income depend on the evolution both of inter-country income differences and intra-country differences, or the distribution of income within countries. Most analyses suggest that inter-country income differences are the main contributor to the inequality which exists among the people of the world.[78]

Changes in world distribution are likely to be much more subject to changes in inter-country income gaps than to changes in intra-country inequality, because the former are so large and because they appear to change more quickly than do the intra-country gaps. Berry et al. concluded that there was little change in the standard indicators of income inequality over the period 1950–77.[79] An important aspect of the evolution of world distribution over this period was the fast growth of the largest low-income country, China; estimates of distribution of income within the non-socialist world show increases in inequality (especially of consumption, whose Gini rose from 0.64 to 0.66); in this part of the world, the bottom deciles lost out together with the middle ones.

The estimates just cited indicate that world inequality (as measured by the standard indicators) fell during the 1950s, rose during the 1960s, and then showed no clear trend during most of the 1970s. Where the lowest decile suffered relative losses (i.e. in the non-socialist world, and especially for consumption) that loss took place in the 1960s.[80] During the period 1950 to the late 1970s, the main single factor working for world equality was the fast growth of China and the main factor working in the opposite direction was the slow growth of the Indian subcontinent. Slow growth in the USA contributed to equality, and slow growth in a group of poor countries other than the subcontinent (including a number in Africa) was a small factor making for greater inequality. Since the mid-1970s both the weak economic performance of Africa and its fast population growth have come to be important contributors towards world inequality and poverty, at the same time that the performance of the Indian subcontinent has been reversed.

Table 6.10 summarizes regional patterns of the 1980s. Over this period, the low-income countries break down into two very clear groups, the Asian and the African countries; in the former category, China recorded average growth of per capita GNP of 7.8 per cent, India of 3.2 per cent, Indonesia of 3.9 per cent, and Pakistan of 3.2 per cent.[81] The African countries, mostly among the low-income category and with a few in the lower-middle-income group, saw GNP per capita fall by 1.2 per cent per year. As a result, the share of world poverty located in Sub-Saharan countries rose rapidly during this period, both because per capita income performed so poorly and because population growth was faster than in South Asia and much faster than in East Asia (especially China). The other two lagging regions of the world economy during the 1980s were Latin America/the Caribbean and the Middle East/North Africa. Since each of these has a per capita income above the world median, their slow growth does not have the impact of raising world inequality.

Unlike the earlier part of the post-war period, during which intra-country trends in distribution do not appear to have been strong enough to have a measurable impact on the world

TABLE 6.10 *Economic performance and population growth, by region, 1980–1990 (growth rates per annum, %)*

Region	Total GDP (1)	Population (2)	GDP per capita (3)	Terms of trade (4)	GNP per capita (5)
Low- and middle-income countries	3.2	2.0	1.2	−3.0	1.2
Sub-Saharan Africa	2.1	3.1	−1.0	−4.8	−0.9
East Asia and Pacific	7.8	1.6	6.2	−1.1	6.3
South Asia	5.2	2.2	3.0	0.4	3.1
Europe	2.1	0.1	2.0	−4.3	0.9
Middle East and North Africa	0.5	3.1	−2.6		−2.5
Latin America and Caribbean	1.6	2.1	−0.5	−1.8	−0.5
High-income Countries	3.1	0.6	2.5	0.2	2.4
World	3.2	1.7	1.5	−0.4	1.4

Sources: Column (1), World Bank, *World Development Report 1992* (Washington, DC, 1992), 220; column (2), ibid. 269; column (4), World Bank, *World Development Report 1991* (Washington, DC, 1991), 189, 231, and *World Development Report 1992*, 245; column (5), World Bank, *World Development Report 1992*, 32.

distribution (thus Berry *et al.*, after undertaking simulation exercises, disregarded them in their calculations[82]), the 1980s were a decade in which a rather general pattern of worsening seems to have appeared, ranging from China, where its scope is open to question but its presence seems incontrovertible, to the former Soviet-bloc countries, most of the industrialized Western countries, and most countries in Latin America. Countries where improvements occurred appear to be few. Had there been no intra-country variation of distribution the world distribution would have improved considerably over the decade, the Gini falling according to our estimate from 0.645 to 0.611 (Table 6.11). A rough attempt to take account of worsening within countries suggests that a mild improvement may have occurred, the Gini falling to perhaps 0.64. In either case, however, it is noteworthy that the bottom two deciles of the world distribution appear to have gained share.

TABLE 6.11 *Decile distribution and Gini coefficient, world average, 1980 and 1990*

DECILE	1980 UNADJUSTED		1990 UNADJUSTED		1980 ADJUSTED (for intra-country variations)	
	CUM	D	CUM	D	CUM*	D*
1	0.69	0.69	0.82	0.82	0.95	0.95
2	1.84	1.15	2.24	1.42	2.24	1.29
3	3.42	1.58	4.18	1.94	3.87	1.63
4	5.58	2.16	6.39	2.21	6.00	2.13
5	8.51	2.93	10.37	3.98	8.98	2.98
6	12.84	4.33	15.55	5.18	13.06	4.08
7	19.5	6.66	23.26	7.71	19.65	6.59
8	30.52	11.02	33.62	10.36	30.93	11.28
9	50.43	19.91	53.28	19.66	50.94	20.01
10	100.00	49.57	100.00	46.72	100.00	49.06
	Gini = 0.6452		Gini = 0.6106		Gini = 0.6383	

CUM = cumulative total

D = share of decile

Sources: World Bank, *World Development Reports*, 1989–92 (Washington, DC, 1989–92); World Bank, *World Tables 1992* (Washington, DC, 1992).

CONCLUSIONS

Despite serious data gaps, the evidence reviewed in this chapter has broadly confirmed the theoretical expectation that liberalization affects income distribution differently according to countries' initial conditions (factor endowments, institutions) and their policy set-ups. Countries with abundant labour, sufficiently educated (and with other necessary conditions present) to take advantage of international markets to expand labour-intensive manufactured exports, showed some tendency to improve income distribution. By contrast, middle-income countries, with comparative advantage in more skill-intensive products, and upper-income countries, with comparative advantage in capital and skill-intensive areas, showed a definite tendency for a worsening in income distribution.

African economies whose comparative advantage lay in peasant production were expected to show an improvement in income distribution, but where there are data there appears to have been a worsening in income distribution in most of these economies. Transition economies universally showed a sharp worsening in income distribution, mainly because of the institutional changes that took place.

Relevant institutional arrangements include the nature of property rights and their distribution. The liberalization moves were associated with reinforced private ownership in both agriculture and industry, liable to lead to growing inequality in the distribution of assets. In the longer run, this will form a new source of income inequality.

Other types of institution forming a sort of filter which can accentuate or modify the impact of changes on distribution include labour legislation, the strength of unions, and a variety of government safety-net provisions. Liberalization policies often involve modifying or eliminating these institutions. Where they do, this adds to inequality—as in Chile, Argentina, and the UK—but where they remain in place, they can help offset some inegalitarian tendencies, as noted in Costa Rica. For the most part, changes in secondary incomes associated with liberalization tend to be inegalitarian, but in practice this is an area where governments exercise considerable choice and exhibit a variety of behaviour.

On balance, the swing away from government intervention and towards the market has tended to increase inequality *within countries*. However, the acceleration in growth of large poor countries—notably China—has worked in the opposite direction, so that world income distribution appears to have improved. This acceleration of growth is partly due to the opportunities offered by liberalization and globalization.

In this review we have compiled evidence on what happened to income distribution during liberalization. It is easier to do this (though difficult enough, given data limitations) than to explain why the changes we observed occur. Counterfactual reasoning remains problematic and our account of causality is inevitably speculative. However, the common tendencies observed among similar economies are, tendencies which do not seem to be simply continuations of historic trends. Rather they suggest that the changes observed were, in part at least, due to policy changes.

7

Justice and Global Inequality

David Miller

It is evident even to the most casual observer that inequalities in today's world are very severe. Inequality can be measured along many dimensions, but the inequalities that seem to be of most direct ethical concern are inequalities in people's life chances: in life expectancy, education, access to medical care, income, and wealth. Tables of world development indicators, such as those issued by the World Bank, quickly reveal the huge gulf that divides poor countries such as Tanzania, where average life expectancy is 51 years, less than 6 per cent of children receive secondary education, and per capita GNP is about $140 per annum, from rich countries such as Germany, where average life expectancy is 76 years, 100 per cent of children receive secondary education, and per capita GNP is about $25,000 per annum.[1] Even after the necessary corrections are made to these figures, in particular to take into account differences in the purchasing power of a dollar in the two countries, the inequality in life prospects between a baby born in Tanzania and one born in Germany remains vast.

For many people, observations such as these—admittedly drawn from two ends of a spectrum with many intermediate cases—effectively settle the issue of justice and global inequality. If Tanzania were a province of Germany instead of an independent state, we would regard such disparities as a flagrant violation of social justice. And why should the political separation of the two societies make a moral, as opposed to a psychological, difference to the case? The only issue, it would seem, is finding the most effective way to transfer resources from countries like Germany to countries like Tanzania, in the face of the practical and political obstacles to doing so.

I want to argue in this chapter that such a response, although understandable and in some ways morally praiseworthy, overlooks several issues of principle that need to be addressed if we are going to talk about global justice. My aim is not to defend the global status quo. There are many respects in which the present world order is unjust. But the bare facts of inequality, stark as they are, are not sufficient to prove this. We need to interrogate the facts, asking why, for example, the Germans are on average relatively rich and the Tanzanians relatively poor, and we need to get clear about the reasons we have for condemning such inequalities as unjust. Let me make a start on the second issue by asking, in quite general terms, why we may find inequalities in people's material situation ethically repugnant.

PRINCIPLES OF EQUALITY

Political philosophers who have thought about this question often now begin by drawing a distinction between inequality and deprivation.[2] Suppose that I have £1,000 and you have £10. Why might this be objectionable? One reason is simply that inequality is wrong. In the absence of countervailing reasons, it is unfair for you to have more than me, so we ought to have £505 each. A quite different reason is that you have too little to meet some basic standard—for instance with your £10 you can't afford a bed for the night. The fact that I have £1,000 matters because it shows that there are resources available which could raise you above this threshold. Suppose that if I gave you an additional £15 you could then find a room to rent. If all we are concerned about is avoiding deprivation, and not with reducing inequality as such, then a £985/£25 division is as good as a £505/£505 one. There is no reason to go further in the direction of equality once everyone has crossed the relevant threshold.

We can apply this distinction to the Tanzania/Germany case. Is what concerns us about the figures revealed above the *inequality* between people living in the two countries, or is it the low absolute living standard of the average Tanzanian? When we look at the GNP figures, for instance, is what concerns us the *difference* between $140 and $25,000, or is it our sense of how few basic goods—food, clothing, and so forth—$140 per annum can buy (even when corrected for purchasing power differences, which raises the figure to $620 per annum)? I suggest that we are primarily concerned about the absolute deprivation of the Tanzanians: about the fact that their average life expectancy is well below what we think of as the natural life-span of a human being, that so few have secondary education, with almost one-third of adults remaining illiterate, that barely half have access to safe drinking water, and so on. To back up this suggestion, compare Germany with a country nearer to the top of the range, for instance Spain, whose per capita GNP is $13,000 per annum, not much more than half that of Germany. Do we find the inequality between German incomes and Spanish incomes objectionable or unjust? On the face of it we don't, because we know that most Spaniards live lives that are reasonably satisfactory, albeit less affluent than those led by most Germans. In the absence of real deprivation, international inequality seems not to matter, morally speaking.

But perhaps this conclusion is too hasty. Is there really nothing wrong about people's opportunities, material advantages, life chances being unequal once we have separated inequality from material deprivation? Isn't it just unfair that your prospects in life should depend on arbitrary factors like the country in which you are raised? To answer these questions we have to know when justice requires (substantive) equality and when it does not.

I shall explore two sets of circumstances in which what is due to people as a matter of justice is a kind of material equality.[3] One arises from membership of various communities and associations, among which the community of citizens in a nation-state is arguably the most important. When people belong to groups of this kind, it becomes a matter of justice that they should be afforded equal treatment with respect to those rights and other advantages that the group has been instituted to provide. To treat people unequally would amount to a failure of recognition and respect; it would be to declare that those who receive a smaller quota of advantages are not members in full standing but mere adjuncts. Thus suppose a nation-state were to give unequal voting rights to different classes of citizens, or were to create two tiers in its public health service, with those on the lower tier receiving a reduced level of care: this would inevitably be experienced as humiliating by those placed in the category of second-class citizens. Although it is not a universal truth that people must win recognition for themselves by associating with others on the basis of equal respect, it is a contingent truth about modern societies. And this in turn grounds the claim that justice here must take the form of an equal assignment of legal rights and the other benefits that attach to membership.

Clearly, however, this argument only applies within the relevant communities and associations. For me to experience discrimination as unfair, I must already be conscious of belonging to the group concerned. I protest when I discover that the standard of medical treatment offered to me is markedly inferior to that enjoyed by my compatriots in the next city, but I make no such complaint when told that French citizens enjoy certain rights that British citizens do not. (I might think that the French system is a better one and that we ought to introduce it in Britain, but this is a different argument: it is not a complaint that the *inequality* between the two countries is unfair to the citizens of one of them.) Can we argue on this basis that there is a world community whose members are all entitled to certain kinds of equal treatment? This is a difficult and contentious issue, but the short answer I shall give is that we cannot.[4] A community of the kind that supports egalitarian principles of justice must, I think, have at least the following three features. Members must have a shared identity, an awareness that there is something distinctive about them that holds them together in a single unit; there must be common understandings or common purposes that give the community its ethos; and there must be an institutional structure that acts on behalf of the community, in particular overseeing the allocation of resources among the members. Now although in the contemporary world there are clearly forms of interaction and cooperation occurring at the global level—the international economy provides the most obvious examples, but there are also many forms of political cooperation, ranging from defence treaties through to environmental protection agreements—these are not sufficient to constitute a global community. They do not by themselves create either a shared sense of identity or a common ethos. And above all there is no common institutional structure that would justify us in describing unequal outcomes as forms of unequal treatment. When I protest at the injustice of people in the next city receiving better medical care than I receive, this is against the background of a single public health service which ought as a matter of justice to ensure equal treatment for all citizens. The inequality of treatment is probably not deliberate, but there is nonetheless an agency—in this case a public bureaucracy—

which can be held responsible for allowing it to continue. In contrast, the common institutions that exist at global level, such as the UN and its various offshoots, are still essentially collaborative undertakings set up by independent states. Now clearly this is a matter of degree, and it may be that we shall move slowly towards a condition in which consciousness of belonging to a single world community exists alongside political institutions with genuinely global functions. At that point membership-based arguments for equal treatment would have real force. But until that point is reached we cannot condemn global inequalities in the way that inequalities of citizenship within nation-states are condemned.

There is also, however, an argument for the justice of equality that makes no reference to common membership. This is simply the claim that where there are no relevant grounds for thinking that one person has a better claim than another to any given benefit or resource, that benefit or resource should be shared between them equally. Two people out walking in the desert happen upon a palm tree with ripe fruit. Unless one of them can establish a special claim to the fruit—he took pains to discover the tree, or needs more fruit to sustain himself than the other, or something of that sort—they should divide the fruit between them equally. Since people usually do have special claims, this is only a residual argument for equality, but it has been thought by some to apply to the distribution of natural resources—land, minerals, wild fruits, and all those things that are useful to human beings but are not produced by them. Since no one has a special claim to these resources, they ought to be shared equally between the world's inhabitants, each person being entitled to resources of equal value.[5] This principle would license transfers from rich to poor countries in so far as it could be shown that the current inequality in living standards arose from an unequal original endowment of natural resources.

But the principle faces some serious difficulties that we must confront before concluding that it helps us in thinking about why present-day global inequality is unjust. To begin with, what would it mean for a distribution of resources among a number of people to be an equal distribution? In the palm tree case the answer is relatively straightforward: assuming that the fruit are of roughly uniform size, each person takes the same number. But clearly, natural resources are very heterogeneous in nature, and we should expect different people and different societies to value them differently. So what would equality mean here? The most ingenious answer to this question that I know of is that proposed by Ronald Dworkin, who invites us to imagine a Walrasian auction in which a group of people bid for a set of heterogeneous items using a token currency—clamshells in Dworkin's story—distributed equally at the outset, and rerun the auction until each person is convinced that she has made the best possible set of bids given the number of clamshells at her disposal. At this point each person will typically have bid for a different set of items, but nobody will envy anybody else's set, and this, Dworkin argues, makes the distribution of resources an equal distribution.[6]

Dworkin is not suggesting that the whole population of any country, let alone the world, should actually sit down and auction off their natural resources in the way that he describes; his purpose is simply to show that it is possible to talk meaningfully of an equal distribution of (heterogeneous) resources. Within certain limits I believe that he succeeds in this aim. But the limits are important, especially when we think about the issue at global level.

One limit is that before anybody can make sensible bids for the items that are being auctioned, he or she needs to know what rules are going to be applied to the use of items post-auction. Before bidding for a potential vineyard, for example, I need to know whether I will be able to sell the wine that I hope to make, or whether alcoholic drinks are going to be prohibited. In later refinements to his model, Dworkin has tried to indicate the kind of rules that he thinks are optimal here—rules broadly of the kind that would support a free market.[7] But if we are thinking about the issue globally, it becomes problematic to define equality by applying Dworkin's favoured rules. Suppose one country has land which, if used for the production of wine, would yield a rich harvest; but suppose also that the inhabitants of that country have for religious reasons prohibited the making and sale of wine. Should we count the country as resource-rich on the grounds that, if it adopted Dworkinian rules to govern property rights and market exchange, its inhabitants would together be in possession of a valuable asset? This would be controversial, because it seems to require that the value of resources should be measured by the market, and this is not a neutral yardstick as between, for instance, religious and secular cultures. The population of the country in question would argue that they should not be credited with 'resources' that only have a value if you already presuppose the legitimacy of certain ways of using them. A related difficulty is that the value of a natural resource depends upon the technical skills and knowledge of the people who intend to use it. Uranium-bearing rock had no value until very recently: no one knew how to extract the uranium, and no one would have been able to think of a use for it even if they had. Now it is a valuable resource. So the bids that people would make in a Dworkinian auction would reflect their own talents and skills because these would fix, for them, the value of each item. Now it might be said that this way of putting the point is misleading. I might bid for a patch of land that I lacked the skill to cultivate myself, on the grounds that I could later rent it or sell it to someone who *could* make direct use of it: its value depends not on my particular skills and talents but on the whole pool of available talents, on the complete range of uses to which a particular item might be put. However, this again emphasizes that we cannot fix the value of a resource until the whole of the background has been filled in. Suppose that a country at a low level of development has uranium deposits, but lacks the technology to mine or use the uranium. Should we say that it has a valuable resource because it could invite a Western mining company to come in and extract the uranium on certain terms? But it is not difficult to think of good reasons that its inhabitants might have for rejecting this option. So the value of the resource remains indeterminate, and it follows that we cannot say whether the citizens of this country have more, or less, than their equal share of natural resources.

Finally here I want to develop a different objection to global equality of resources, one which arises once we apply the principle dynamically rather than statically. Suppose that we were able to circumvent the difficulties just laid out in deciding when the inhabitants of different countries could be said to enjoy an equal per capita share of natural resources, and imagine two neighbouring countries starting out with just such an equal endowment. The citizens of one country, call it Affluenza, share an ethos of consumerism, and their democratically elected government allows oil deposits to be used up to make petrol for private cars, permits the cutting down of forests for timber and paper, and so forth. Next door in Ecologia, by contrast, there is a strict policy of sustainable development, with a heavy carbon tax on the use of fuel, higher prices for wood products to cover the costs of replanting trees, etc. As will be immediately apparent, if we look at natural resource levels one generation into the future, Ecologia will turn out to have a higher per capita share than Affluenza. Or, for a variation on what is essentially the same theme, compare Procreatia, which allows its population to grow by, say, 5 per cent per annum, with Condominium, whose strictly enforced family planning policy achieves a stable population: if our principle is per capita equality of natural resources, then, other things being equal, it is plain that per capita shares in Procreatia will become progressively smaller than those in Condominium unless there is a programme of resource transfers from the second to the first.

What are the arguments against enforcing global equality over time by redistributing from Ecologia to Affluenza and from Condominium to Procreatia? One is that there would be little incentive for any state to behave in the responsible way that the citizens of Ecologia and Condominium have decided to behave if the result is that the resources that have been conserved are then transferred away to states that follow no such policy. In my simple example Ecologia and Condominium could expect to lose only half of their savings; but if a global equalization policy was applied in a world of many states, any one state that tried to conserve per capita resources, either through environmental or through population policy, would find that it lost almost everything that it had saved— so no state would make the attempt. Another argument is that the equalization policy is simply unfair to the citizens of Ecologia and Condominium. They have made sacrifices—they have consumed fewer natural resources, and raised fewer children than they would ideally have liked—in order to achieve policies that they see as either in their own long-term interests or as in the interests of their successors. It is wrong to frustrate this achievement by transferring resources to people who have made no such sacrifices.

But, it may be said, these arguments fail to consider the position of individuals who are born into resource-poor countries. Suppose someone is born in Affluenza after several generations of consumerism, and as a result faces the prospect of a much lower standard of living than his contemporary in Ecologia. How is this fair to him, since after all he wasn't responsible for the policies that have led to this state of affairs? While we may want to hold people responsible for having diminished resources as a result of the choices they have made personally, we cannot simply treat individual persons as parts of collectivities like states, and therefore as liable to bear the consequences of the decisions that these collectivities have made in the past.

This riposte has some force, but not enough, I shall try to show, to resurrect global equality of resources in the face of the previous criticisms. To begin with, political cultures typically exhibit a high degree of continuity from one generation to the next, so it is very likely that our new-born Affluenzian will be brought up to acquire and identify with those consumerist values that have guided his society in the past. To the extent that he does embrace those values, he has no good grounds for complaining about the low per capita level of natural resources available to him in Affluenza, since that level is a product of policies that reflect the values he shares with his fellow citizens. But what if he rebels and adopts principles closer to those prevailing in Ecologia? His position is then essentially no different from that of anyone who holds a minority view among his contemporaries: he will find it frustrating that the majority does not share his ideals, but, provided certain safeguards are put in place to protect people such as him against the bare assertion of majority will, no injustice is done. In other words, he can demand a mini-mum set of rights and benefits, but he cannot reasonably expect his political community to promote the values that he favours rather than those of the majority. Likewise, I am suggesting, the dissident Affluenzian can fairly demand some minimal access to natural resources—I shall return to this point shortly—but he cannot fairly demand the per capita share which would have been available if Affluenza had conducted itself in the past like Ecologia. If he holds his new-found ideals sincerely, his position is in some respects an unfortunate one, but he does not have a just claim to resource transfers from Ecologia.

My argument has been that global equality of resources, even if it can be coherently defined in the abstract, must be defeated over time by the different policies followed by autonomous political communities, which give rise to fair inequalities in per capita shares of natural resources. In making it I have made one assumption that needs underlining: the policies in question are ones that express a local political culture which at least the majority of citizens endorse. In other words, I have been taking it for granted that the states we are considering are democratic to the extent that their policies reflect the popular will, whether or not they have open elections or other formal mechanisms of accountability. To the extent that this assumption is false, the argument looks weaker. Someone in Russia today, for instance, might claim that their relatively poor access to resources was the result of political decisions taken under the communist regime, which in no sense reflected the values even of earlier generations of Russians. Or a Tanzanian might argue that the forced villageization of peasants and the other quasi-socialist policies followed by the ruling TANU party in the 1960s and 1970s, whose effects on the Tanzanian economy were so disastrous, were never endorsed by the people themselves. For these claims to be convincing, proponents would need to show that earlier generations had not colluded with the regimes in question, that they would have overthrown them if not held down by coercion and fear. Inevitably this will be a controversial issue.[8] But it might be possible in certain cases to make a convincing argument to this effect.

Even here, I think, a global equalization policy would be hard to justify. We may be persuaded that Russians or Tanzanians are suffering from resource deficits which cannot be explained in terms of the values held and decisions made by an autonomous political community. But it will be impossible to specify what per capita level of resources they are entitled to without engaging in hypothetical speculation about what an 'authentic' Russian or Tanzanian path of economic development would have looked like: we cannot simply assume that without communism Russia would have used its natural resources in the same way as Germany or that without Nyerere's philosophy of *ujamaa* socialism the Tanzanian economy would have grown as fast as Botswana's. So unless we are willing to wipe the slate clean and say that people everywhere are entitled to equal quantities of resources regardless of the impact of their own and their political community's past decisions—and I have argued strongly against saying this—we must jettison equality of resources as a guiding principle of global justice.

Where does this leave us? I have been looking critically at two attempts to show that present-day global inequalities are unjust. One involves claiming that people across the globe have equal rights in the same way as citizens of a political community have equal rights. This attempt, I suggested, founders because there does not yet exist a world community of the kind that would be needed to sustain such a claim to equal treatment. The second attempt involves arguing that each person has an equal right to natural resources, independently of their membership in any particular community. I have argued that there are severe difficulties with this claim, some having to do with the definition of equal shares in a culturally plural world, others having to do with the application of the equality principle over time, in a world where resource levels are crucially affected by the practices of different political communities. The conclusion is that global justice is not egalitarian, if by equality we mean that rights or resources must be distributed equally among all the world's inhabitants.

Does it follow that there are no principles of justice at all that apply cross-nationally, that our ethical response to poverty in Tanzania and elsewhere is simply a humanitarian response to deprivation which has nothing essentially to do with justice?[9] If we accept this picture—that global inequalities are merely a matter of humanitarian concern—then it would be left up to each of us to decide how to show our concern, through charitable giving or similar forms of voluntary aid. Compulsory redistribution—for instance an international scheme whereby rich states agreed to transfer a certain percentage of their GNP to developing countries, funding this through taxation—would be ruled out as illegitimate. So it is a vital political question to decide whether there are principles of global justice that can avoid the objections I have levelled against global principles of equality.

To show that there are indeed such principles, I shall make use of two ideas: one is the idea of *basic rights*; the other is the idea of *exploitation*. To put the argument in its simplest terms, a just international order would be one in which basic rights were universally protected, and in which actors in the international arena, corporations as well as states, conducted themselves so as to avoid exploiting either individuals or other collectivities. Conversely, global inequalities are unjust *either* when they entail that some people's basic rights are being violated *or* when they result from exploitative transactions between the relatively powerful and the relatively powerless; otherwise they are not. I shall try to show that these conditions can be made precise enough to give us a firm critical perspective on the present international regime.

BASIC RIGHTS

The idea of basic rights will be familiar to most readers, and I shall spend less time on the idea itself than on its implications for the question of global inequality. It involves the claim that there are certain conditions that are universally necessary for human beings to lead minimally adequate lives, and the list of basic rights corresponds to the set of these conditions. Thus men and women need to be able to use their bodily capacities to achieve whatever aims they set themselves and so there is a basic right to bodily integrity (which also entails sub-rights such as the right not to be tortured or subject to medical experimentation against your will). They need to enjoy certain liberties—freedoms of thought and expression, for instance—if they are to give their lives a coherent shape and a meaning, hence they have rights to these kinds of freedom. There are also material requirements that must be met in all human lives—people need access to sufficient food to avoid starvation or malnourishment, and they need access to resources that can serve as means of production—which give rise to rights to subsistence. Other rights are generated in the same way.

The resulting list, it should be stressed, is a minimal list. Someone who enjoys his or her basic rights but nothing beyond this will not live a rich or happy life, because there are many other ingredients that must be supplied to achieve the higher forms of human good. But these other ingredients tend to vary quite widely from one society to the next, depending on the particular culture that each embodies. The basic rights are intended to be universal conditions, forming a low-level plateau on which fuller systems of social rights can be erected.[10] For this reason I prefer the language of basic rights to that of human rights, which has frequently been extended to embrace claims and demands which make good sense as elements of social citizenship, but which lack the universality I am requiring.[11] The right to education, for instance, is an extremely important citizenship right in all technologically advanced societies, but, considered as a candidate for basic-rights status, it has to be drained of so much content as to become virtually meaningless.

Let me deal quickly with two criticisms of the doctrine of basic rights that I have just sketched. The first is that, if the purpose of the doctrine is to establish a minimum standard of justice which all societies are obliged to respect, it lacks the requisite universality. According to this line of criticism, not only the claim that there are universal basic rights, but the very concept of individual rights itself, is a specific product of the Western liberal tradition and it is therefore unreasonable to expect people in societies with different traditions to accept it.[12] My answer is that although the *formulation* of the doctrine may be culturally specific, its *substance* is not. In other words, so long as the list of basic rights reflects the conditions that are universally necessary for human beings to lead minimally adequate lives, its content will be captured in each society's system of ethics, even though the form in which these demands are expressed is likely to vary. Here I follow Michael Walzer in assuming that we can discover a cross-cultural moral minimum that 'consists in principles and rules that are reiterated in different times and places and that are seen to be similar even though they are expressed in different idioms and reflect different histories and different versions of the world'.[13] I go a little beyond Walzer, however, in assuming that this moral minimum includes not merely prohibitions on damaging behaviour—rules forbidding murder, torture, rape, and so forth—but also certain positive injunctions to supply life-preserving resources to those who lack them when it is in your power to do so.

The second criticism I wish to consider is that the basic rights doctrine is simply global egalitarianism under another name. After all, if we say that each person possesses a set of basic rights that must be respected, we appear to imply that these are *equal* rights. But I argued earlier that justice demands equality of rights only within the boundaries of specific communities. So how can basic rights be defended at the global level?

This criticism rests on a confusion which can best be brought out by considering a specific example, the right to food. If we say that every human being has a basic right to food, our meaning is that each person is entitled to that minimum quantity of food which enables his or her body to function satisfactorily. It does not require equality in the distribution of food except in the singular case where only an equal distribution can ensure that everyone's basic right is met. There is nothing wrong in Anne having more food than Bill, from the basic-rights perspective, so long as Bill has access to sufficient food to satisfy the minimum requirement. The appearance that the basic rights doctrine involves a principle of equality is delusive: to say that each person has *equal* basic rights is to say no more than that each has basic rights.

Why is the protection of basic rights a principle of global justice? To show this, we require two basic premises. The first, which is ethical, is that my recognition of others as human beings like myself implies that I have a duty to safeguard them against conditions which would unavoidably blight their lives. I am not required to help an unknown X build a temple in which to worship his god, since I may think that this is a fundamentally misguided undertaking, but I am bound to refrain from disabling X or to feed X when he is starving, because I must recognize disablement and starvation as conditions that impair any human life I can conceive of.[14] This is a basic premise in the sense that the duty in question cannot be grounded on anything beyond itself, though I think it would be difficult to recognize a set of practical beliefs that did not include it as ethical at all.[15] The second is that the protection of basic rights cannot be guaranteed by the rights holders themselves, either individually or acting in concert: people are deprived of them by forces that are outside of their control, often involving chains of causation that may extend worldwide. In consequence, it makes sense to say that we all to some degree share in the responsibility of ensuring that such rights are protected. It makes sense, therefore, to talk of rights violations as violations of global justice.

It would be wrong to infer, however, that the obligations corresponding to these rights are equally distributed in the first instance. The members of each political community bear a special responsibility to ensure that rights are secured within that community. This does not merely amount to a convenient division of labour, but reflects the fact that the strength of interpersonal obligations generally depends on the ties that bind the two parties concerned.[16] There is nothing mysterious in the idea that rights which are universally held should generate obligations that fall in the first instance on particular people: every child has a right to a secure home, but it is the child's parents that bear primary responsibility for securing this right. Only when the parents are unable to meet their obligation are third parties required to step in to fill the breach.

Can this account of basic rights help us to assess global inequalities? If we take countries like Tanzania which stand close to the bottom end of the inequality spectrum, there seems little doubt that many of their citizens suffer deprivations of basic rights: available per capita resources are simply not sufficient to secure a minimally adequate standard of living, as, for instance, the life expectancy figures reveal, as well as indicators such as the proportion of the population with access to safe drinking water. Since there is little question that the missing resources could be supplied externally, should we conclude that this failure to secure the basic rights of Tanzanians and others who are similarly placed in many African and Asian countries is proof of global injustice?

To get this question into sharper focus, let me outline four ideal-typical cases in which rights deprivations might occur in a poor country, and then ask what obligations would fall on external actors such as rich states. (The cases are ideal-typical in the sense that when we look at real-world examples we may well find a combination of elements from two or more of my categories.) The first case is one in which there is no effective rights-enforcement mechanism in the country in question, because the government has collapsed and/or because the country is in the throes of civil war. Here the absence of an effective political community internally shifts the obligation directly onto the shoulders of outsiders, and there is a clear case for military intervention by an international force to halt the systematic violations of rights—murder, torture, rape—that invariably accompany political breakdown and civil war, together with an emergency aid programme to provide for basic medical and food needs. Although there are many difficult political issues that arise in these circumstances, the ethical argument at least is relatively clear-cut: it is a serious injustice if rich nations simply stand by and allow the rights violations to continue.

The second case is one where rights violations stem from the failures of a political regime which nonetheless continues to hold power and may indeed have considerable popular support. These failures might arise either from corruption in the office-holders, who are syphoning off a considerable part of the society's wealth to their own advantage, or from misguided ideological doctrines such as a commitment to the forced collectivization of agriculture. Here it is assumed that the technological and other capacities of the society are such that if it were well governed it could protect its citizens' basic rights adequately if not easily.

In this case the obligations of outsiders are harder to determine, since what is involved is essentially a failure of domestic social justice. We can certainly say that foreign states and other outside institutions such as banks are obliged not to collude with the injustice by, for instance, providing a safe haven for the resources that are being extracted by the ruling elite. If economic co-operation is offered, it should be made conditional on internal policy reforms which promise to protect basic rights more effectively. In other words, rich countries here should offer incentives to the regime to change the direction of its policy, and above all avoid profiting themselves from the injustice that is being perpetrated internally. Direct intervention is ruled out not only on the grounds that it is very unlikely to succeed, but also on the grounds that primary responsibility for putting right the injustice lies with the people themselves.

The third case I wish to distinguish is one where a political community is pursuing prudent and reasonably just policies internally but is facing a hostile external environment, for instance an international market in which the prices of key commodities fluctuate wildly, making it very difficult for the country in question to maintain economic stability. As the result, perhaps, of rising levels of international debt, living standards inside this country fall below the basic-rights threshold for many people.

I believe that when we think of rights violations in particular countries as manifestations of global injustice, it is most often this case that we have in mind. The injustice consists in the fact that the costs of maintaining basic rights are being distributed in an unreasonable way between rich and poor countries. It would require only small sacrifices on the part of rich countries—perhaps paying a slightly higher price for their coffee beans or other raw materials—to create an environment in which poor countries could achieve stable growth. Primary responsibility for rights protection would remain where it should lie, with the political community in question, but international actors would agree to bear part of the cost—small for them but very much greater for the society that is now at the receiving end of market instability.

Finally, we should consider cases where a political community simply lacks the resources to secure its members' basic rights, no matter how well it is governed, and no matter how friendly the external economic environment. Although there is a common perception that much deprivation in today's world falls into this category, I think in fact that such cases will turn out to be relatively rare. Suggestive evidence is provided by Amartya Sen's study of famines—the most extreme form of resource deprivation—which shows that the cause of famine is not the physical unavailability of food in the famine area, but a failure of entitlement: many people lack the purchasing power to buy the food that is nonetheless available.[17] If sufficient food can be shown to be available even within societies that are experiencing famine conditions, this strongly suggests that we should be looking at failures either of domestic policy or of international policy if we want to explain why so much of the world's population remains malnourished, rather than at a straightforward lack of resources in a particular state. Nevertheless, we may still want to ask what global justice would require if there are states which simply cannot command the resources to be economically viable without outside intervention.

The answer, a fairly obvious one, is development aid of the traditional sort, that is, long-term investment by outside agencies and technology transfers to build up the resource base of the society to the point where it can secure basic rights. Indeed, this is the only case in which development aid is required by justice rather than as a humanitarian or prudential policy. At the same time, the aid, since it is given for a particular purpose, can be made conditional on the domestic government following appropriate policies. It is becoming increasingly common now to see the aid relationship as involving a contract between donor and receiver whereby the donor undertakes to provide aid on a regular and long-term basis and the recipient undertakes to ensure that the investment capital provided gets down to local economies, and is not simply used for prestigious government projects.[18] The aim would be an aid programme that tapered off as the resource base rose, while at the same time a fairly stable international trade regime of the kind described in relation to the third case above gave the society in question the opportunity to make further advances.

To sum up here, looking at the issue of global inequality through the lens of basic rights does reveal a number of ways in which rights violations, whether these take the active form of killings and woundings, or the passive form of failures to provide food, medicine, and other basic needs, involve injustice at the global level. But the corresponding obligations will depend very much on the nature of the case. Sometimes direct intervention by outside agencies is called for, but in other cases the obligation is less direct: to help create an environment in which there is less reason or less incentive for the rights violations to continue.

EXPLOITATION

Global inequalities, I have argued, are unjust when they entail that some people's basic rights are being violated. They are also unjust, I shall now try to show, when they are the results of exploitation. Exploitation is a notoriously slippery idea, far harder to pin down than that of basic rights. My attention here will be focused on economic exploitation, on what makes an economic transaction between two parties (either of which might be an individual, a company, a state, or some other actor) exploitative. Once we have grasped the general concept, it will be fairly easy to see how international transactions (investments and trade, for example) can exploit poor individuals and poor countries.[19]

Exploitation in the sense that concerns me involves three main elements.[20] First, it is a property of transactions between at least two parties, in which each party has some freedom of manoeuvre: in particular, it must have been open to the exploiter to engage in an alternative transaction which would have left the exploited party better off in some respect. We cannot infer exploitation from a distribution of resources as such: the fact that I have £10 and you have £1 does not by itself entail that I have exploited you. At most it might lead us to enquire into the process whereby the inequality has come about, to see whether it displays the other features of exploitation. It follows from this that the facts of global inequality do not by themselves prove that the international system is exploitative: we need to investigate the mechanisms by which the present distribution of resources has come about.

Second, an exploitative transaction must be unfair when it is measured against a suitable benchmark. The exploiter must have gained more from it, and the exploited gained less from it, than would have happened in the benchmark situation. This is not to say that the exploited party has gained nothing. A worker who is exploited by her employer may still be better off than if she had no job at all; the point is that she is worse off than she would be if she had been given a fair price for her labour. The problem then is to decide on the proper benchmark, and this may be controversial.

Third, there must be a power inequality between the two parties which explains why the exploiter is able to conduct the transaction on terms that are comparatively favourable to him. Often this means that the exploited party is vulnerable, either in the absolute sense of being in a desperate situation (a starving man who must get a job to stay alive) or in the sense that relative to the potential exploiter he has little bargaining power (if I have something that you very badly want, and all you can offer in exchange is something that I don't care much about, then I am well placed to drive a hard bargain).[21]

An exploitative transaction, therefore, is one that is actively entered into by the parties concerned, one whose terms are unfair when measured by the appropriate benchmark, and one whose unfairness results from an inequality of power between exploiter and exploited. It is these three factors in combination that explain what is particularly objectionable about exploitation: it involves actively taking advantage of another agent's relative weakness when it is open to you to make a fair exchange instead. It offends against the ethical norm that we must deal fairly with those who are vulnerable to our actions. Even if the consequences of exploitation do not involve infringements of basic rights, there is still a peculiar kind of wrong involved in engaging in exploitative transactions.[22]

How can we apply this concept to inequalities between rich and poor countries? Many theories of international exploitation have been inspired by the Marxist belief that economic transactions are exploitative whenever they result in workers receiving less than the full value of their product, measured according to the labour theory of value. Thus it has been argued that foreign investment in Third World countries is exploitative simply because the investing companies make substantial profits after paying their workforce that they are then able to repatriate; alternatively, it has been claimed that international trade is exploitative because the prices at which the traded commodities exchange reflect large differences in wage levels between rich and poor countries.[23] These arguments, however, rely on a theory of value, and thereby implicitly on a theory of fair exchange, which few people would now regard as defensible.[24] They move too quickly from the facts of global inequality—in particular the relatively low wages paid to workers in developing countries by comparison to those paid in industrial countries—

to the conclusion that an economic system which sustains those inequalities must be exploitative.

In contrast to this *a priori* argument, I think we can get a better grip on international exploitation by considering examples of transactions that we instinctively feel to be exploitative and then asking what it is about these transactions that produces this reaction. Let me give two of these which will be familiar to students of international political economy. One is the case where an international corporation sets up an operation in a developing country which exposes its employees in that country to working conditions which would be seen as hazardous or in some other way unacceptable in an industrialized society, and which would there be outlawed or at the very least strictly regulated by government. A concrete example of this would be a nuclear reprocessing plant to handle nuclear waste generated in a developed country which because of stringent safeguards it would be very costly to process domestically. Why do we see such an operation as potentially exploitative of the foreign workers and the communities they belong to? First, given the levels of unemployment prevalent in many poor countries, those who sign up with the corporation are likely to be desperate to earn wages, and therefore willing to take on these jobs despite the health and other risks that they may pose. Second, they are also likely to lack the technical knowledge to evaluate these risks properly. In both respects there is a very large power inequality between the corporation and its prospective employees, and therefore a high degree of vulnerability on the part of the latter. Attempts to counter this imbalance by, for instance, forming trade unions may be met with a variety of threats—to hire blackleg workers, to shift the operation elsewhere, etc. Exploitation of this kind might in theory be practised domestically within an industrialized nation, but it is easy to see why the opportunities are far greater internationally given (1) the far weaker bargaining position of workers in poor countries and (2) the absence of an agreed regulatory framework which could constrain the corporation's activities.

For a second case, consider the position of producers of cash crops like coffee or bananas in circumstances where the export of these crops is handled by a single large purchaser, or a small group of purchasers who can easily form an informal cartel. The growers are dispersed and uncoordinated, and they depend on selling their crop in a short space of time to keep themselves above the breadline; it is also likely to be difficult for them to switch to a different crop. The purchasers, by contrast, are not dependent on any one grower, or any particular set of growers. If Colombian coffee farmers try to improve their terms of trade, the coffee companies can simply start buying more of their coffee from Kenya or Brazil. In these circumstances, it is easy to predict that the price of commodities will be set at a level that is far more favourable to the purchasers than to the producers. Although in one sense there is a market in coffee or bananas—the beans and fruit are voluntarily sold by the growers to the purchasing companies—the conditions for a classically free market—many buyers, many sellers, no one obliged by physical necessity to make any particular exchange—are absent. So the argument that the price obtained for goods or services in a free market is a fair price does not apply here. Rather, we should ask what price coffee or bananas *would* sell for in a free market in order to give us a benchmark for judging how far the producers are exploited by the bargaining process in the real world.

These examples are intended to illustrate the kind of power inequalities in today's world society that are likely to lead to exploitation of men and women in poor countries.[25] I do not think one can arrive at a simple general theory of international exploitation along the lines of the Marxist theories referred to earlier. I would say instead that if one begins from a state of affairs in which there are very large inequalities both in income and in wealth and in organizational capacity between rich and poor countries, and where many of those in poor countries are in a condition of absolute vulnerability, it is inevitable that opportunities for exploitation will arise, though the exact mechanism will vary from case to case. If exploitative transactions then occur, the effect is that the inequalities will widen still further, even if there is no absolute deterioration in the position of the poor countries.

It also follows that many existing inequalities are likely to be the result of past exploitation of the poor countries by rich countries, or organizations based in rich countries. So they will be unjust. The problem, however, is how to form even a rough estimate of the extent of the injustice, since that involves us in counterfactual claims about the resources that might now be available to the relevant individuals or groups if a different (fair) set of transactions had occurred.[26] It seems to me more fruitful to look forward and ask how an international economic order can be created in which opportunities for exploitation are minimized.

There are broadly three ways to prevent an exploitative relationship from occurring or continuing. One is simply to sever the relationship. If A no longer engages in any transactions with B, then clearly, according to the analysis given above, he cannot be exploiting B. The second way is to secure B's position so that she is no longer vulnerable to A's power: if she chooses to transact with A, it will be on terms that are fair to both parties. The third way is to constrain A's freedom of action so that he can no longer impose exploitative terms in transacting with B: for instance to require A to exchange with B only at a fair price.

Applying this to relationships between rich and poor countries, the first path seems distinctly unpromising. It would involve a complete severance of trade and investment links between the two groups of countries. Leaving aside the huge definitional and practical problems involved in making this work, it overlooks the salient fact that poor countries are likely to make net gains from their relationships with rich countries even while they are being exploited, in the same way that an exploited worker is better off for having some job than no job at all. The only escape route from absolute poverty is to gain access to the capital and consumption goods currently held by the rich countries.

The second route looks more promising, but it would require resource transfers from rich to poor countries on a scale that is so massive as to be politically unfeasible. Opportunities for exploitation are created not just by the absolute vulnerability of one party but by relative inequalities in bargaining power. So even policies that would raise all countries above the threshold that bodies such as the UN use in defining world poverty would not guarantee an end to exploitative investment and trade on the part of the rich countries. The only remaining option, therefore, is to create an international regime that constrains the actions of potential exploiters.

It is beyond my competence to give a detailed set of prescriptions for such a regime, but very broadly it would involve, on the one hand, creating a more genuinely free international commodity market by breaking up trading monopolies and dismantling tariff barriers which often now discriminate against imports from poor to rich countries; on the other hand, trying to reach international agreement on a set of common standards for working conditions and workers' safety. This requires concerted action from governments who may well have particular interests in allowing exploitative practices to continue (such as the tax revenues they generate), so there is no point in pretending that creating such a regime will be easy. However, given the compelling practical objections to the first two alternatives canvassed above, it represents the most hopeful way forward to a world without exploitation.

CONCLUSION

I have argued that present-day international inequalities are unjust, but they are not unjust merely by virtue of being inequalities. Although comparisons such as that between Germany and Tanzania, with which I began the chapter, are important because they demonstrate the scale and seriousness of the issue that confronts us, they can also mislead us into adopting a facile kind of global egalitarianism. One important first step is to keep the distinction between inequality and deprivation firmly in mind. The next is to see when justice requires material equality and when it does not.

My argument has been that international justice is not rightly understood in terms of principles of equality. There are indeed contexts in which such principles are valid, but the circumstances of international society are such that neither principles of equal treatment nor principles of equal initial resource distribution can be applied to it. International inequalities *are* ethically challengeable, on the other hand, when they constitute infringements of people's basic rights or when they arise through exploitative economic processes. From this perspective, snapshots of comparative socioeconomic indicators such as per capita GNP or life expectancy are less important than an understanding of the mechanisms which create meagre life prospects for many people in poor countries. What should concern us is how these mechanisms—domestic and international—can be changed; the issues we should be addressing are those of power and responsibility, not resource distribution as such.

It might be said in response that the key to the problem does finally lie in resource distribution. If we could equalize individuals' access to material resources, then on the one hand we would go a long way to ensure that everyone had the means to protect their basic rights, while on the other hand the power imbalances between states and economic organizations that give rise to exploitation would disappear. So haven't I arrived at the case for global equality by a different route? Well, I concede that if global equality of resources were feasible, and not open to the objections that I laid out earlier in the chapter, principally deriving from the justifiable autonomy of each political community, it would have these desirable results. But I believe that global equality cannot even be properly defined unless we suppose that the peoples of the world come to form a single political unit with common rules governing the holding and use of resources. If that is true, the quest for equality of this kind becomes a distraction, diverting our attention away from feasible changes in the international regime which would strengthen the machinery for protecting basic rights and reduce opportunities for exploiting the powerless.

8

Social Policy in a Global Context

Bob Deacon

In this chapter it is argued that the concerns of social policy, traditionally the prerogative of sovereign states, have become supranational and global in scope. The management of economic activity such that it also serves the purpose of social justice both within and among states is now high on the agenda of global fora such as the G7 and international organizations such as the World Bank and the World Trade Organization (WTO). This chapter begins by further elaborating this proposition. The new terrain of global social policy analysis is conceptualized more precisely. In the third section, the implicit and explicit social policies of major international organizations (particularly in the sphere of income maintenance and the management of inequality) are reviewed. Finally, the global governance reform agenda is reviewed in terms of its relevance to the task of securing more global social justice.

I. GLOBALIZING SOCIAL POLICY AND SOCIALIZING GLOBAL POLITICS

In the present phase of world economic development social policy activities traditionally analysed and undertaken within one country have taken on a supranational and transnational character. This is so for several reasons. Economic competition between countries may lead to the economic costs of social protection being shed in order to be more competitive ('social dumping') unless there are supranational or global regulations in place that discourage this.[1] International migratory pressures generate the political logic that there could be income transfers between nations to stave off the political consequences of mass migration.[2] Similarly, common markets in capital and labour between countries give rise to the possibility of supranational authority providing at a supranational level social citizenship rights denied or threatened at national level.[3]

The implications for national, supranational, and transnational social policy of this present phase of globalization is an undertheorized and under-researched topic within the subject of social policy. Whereas globalism has received considerable attention recently from scholars working within the disciplines of political science,[4] sociology,[5] economics,[6] and international relations,[7] this has not been the case for social policy. Supranationalism in the context of Europeanization is, of course, an exception. Kleinman and Piachaud[8] and Liebfried[9] among others have usefully reviewed work in this sub-global context. Huber and Stephens[10] have speculated on the future for Scandinavian social democracy in the light of increased global economic competition and Europeanization. Esping-Andersen[11] has similarly reviewed comparative welfare trends in a global context. Abram de Swaan has advanced furthest the case for social policy analysis to shift gear to the global and transnational.[12]

The relative decline of the power of national governments in the face of globally mobile capital challenges the traditional frameworks of social policy analysis in a number of ways. First, it suggests that the supranational and global actors need to be given more attention in explanations of changing social policy. Because social policy's analytical frameworks have derived from work on economically privileged Northern and Western welfare states they have tended to downplay the importance of background institutions like the International Monetary Fund (IMF) and the World Bank. Now that social policy analysis is encompassing less economically privileged Southern and Eastern welfare states,[13] and because the sustainability of the welfare states of Europe is questioned by global economic competition, the relative neglect of these institutions is no longer justified. In Section II below the implicit and explicit social policies of the major international organizations are analysed.

A second challenge to traditional social policy analysis is posed by the introduction of a new field of enquiry into the subject. This field encompasses what I shall call the *supranationalization* or *globalization of social policy instruments, policy, and provision*. This supranationalization of social policy takes (at least) three forms. These are supranational regulation, supranational redistribution, and supranational provision or empowerment. This typology is elaborated at the end of this section.

The other side of the coin of the globalization of social policy is the socialization of global politics. In other words, the major issues on the agenda at intergovernmental meetings are now in essence social (and environmental) questions. The G7 summit in June 1996, with the presidents of the IMF, World Bank, and World Trade Organization and the UN Secretary-General in attendance, resolved, for example, to discuss the relationship between free trade and the 'internationally recognized core labour standards' at their Singapore meeting in the autumn of 1996. In the example of UN preventative intervention in Macedonia,[14] a focus of concern is to find social policy mechanisms that increase cooperation across ethnic divides. Figure 8.1 captures this shift in the content of global politics.

With the collapse of the Cold War, the rise of international migratory pressures, the human suffering arising from social instability in many parts of the globe, world leaders today face a problem of social security. Today's top agenda items include: the cancellation of debts arising from structural adjustment; transnational humanitarian aid to create global political security; and the 'threat' to economic competitiveness posed by the 'social protectionism' of European welfare states. The 1995 UN Summit on Social Development merely echoed this growing concern with issues of social policy.

In sum, I suggest here and argue at greater length elsewhere[15] that globalization:

- sets welfare states in competition with each other and creates the danger of a race to the bottom of the welfare league table;
- therefore raises social policy concerns to a supranational level;
- generates a global discourse about the best way to regulate global capitalism in the interests of social welfare in East, West, North, and South;
- brings in a new era of international relations dominated by the social (and human) rights agenda, which presents challenges to the existing institutions of global governance;
- brings new actors into the field of a globalized social policy in terms of international non-governmental organizations (NGOs), individuals, and groups with rights at a supranational level, and transnational communities of interest.

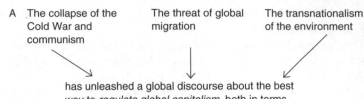

A The collapse of the   The threat of global   The transnationalism
   Cold War and   migration   of the environment
   communism

has unleashed a global discourse about the best
way to *regulate global capitalism*, both in terms
of the defence of Northern welfare states and
the export of welfare capitalism to the South,
and the most effective way to engage in *transnational
redistribution and provision*

B   Foreign policy and diplomacy are shifting from

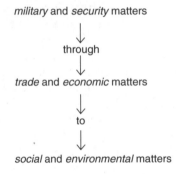

military and *security* matters

through

trade and *economic* matters

to

social and *environmental* matters

FIG. 8.1. The globalization of social policy and the socialization of global
politics

The typology of global social policy responses and mechanisms
noted earlier that might enable us to conceptualize these changes
would include, first, global intervention into national policy and
secondly, three forms of global social policy, namely transnational
redistribution, supranational regulation, and global or supranational provision or empowerment. All three types of supranational
activity already take place but they are often confined within one
regional economic trading bloc such as the European Union. Elements of all three are, however, to be found at a global level.
Redistribution can be seen in the economic assistance from the
West to the East, which, even though it may fall short of a Marshall
Plan, is motivated in part by the wish to secure social stability in the

former Soviet Union by securing social safety nets. Regulation can be seen in the emergence of concerns to prevent 'social dumping' by multinational capital which are now on the WTO's agenda. Provision and empowerment are taking place in the elementary system of global citizenship entitlements for stateless persons operated by the United Nations High Commission for Refugees (UNHCR), and in the Council of Europe, which empowers citizens to take their government to court when they have been refused their human rights.

Within this intellectual map the scholarly work presently being undertaken on the emerging social policy of the European Union could be a special case and exemplar of a future global social policy analysis and practice. Recent work by Kleinman and Piachaud[16] discussing the issues of subsidiarity, citizenship rights, and democracy in the emerging supranational European social policy can be transposed onto a global terrain, where similar concerns apply: at what level can policy best be formulated?; how can national citizenship be reconciled with supranational mobility?; and how can national democratic constituencies be recast to ensure meaningful accountability at supranational level?

Fleshing out this initial conceptualization requires us to analyse which supranational and global agencies are actors in the emerging processes of influencing national policy and engaging in transnational redistribution, supranational regulation, and supranational and global provision. Coupled with this we need an analysis of the instruments with which agencies and organizations acting above the level of the state can redistribute resources, influence and regulate national social policy and international competition, and contribute to supranational and global policy and provision. There are a very large number of agencies using a variety of instruments to push and pull national social policy and practice often in very different directions and which are seeking to impose very different degrees of regulation on international competition.

Table 8.1, which focuses on global intervention in national policy, captures the idea of the web of interconnectedness that, say, an East European country wishing to join the European Union (EU) finds itself within in the sphere of income maintenance policy. This clearly demonstrates the contending influences of, for example, the IMF, concerned to balance the state budget, and the International Labour Organization (ILO), concerned to seek the adoption

TABLE 8.1 *Some contending influences on national income maintenance policy in the European region*

	Agency	Type of influence
All countries		
	International Monetary Fund	Public expenditure limitations as loan conditions affect income maintenance budget
	World Bank	Advice on social 'safety net' policy and social security expenditure
		Loans on condition of social reform
	International Labour organization	Conventions on social security systems
		Advice on tripartite forms of government
Countries within the Council of Europe	Council of Europe	Obligatory Charter of Human Rights
		Subject to Strasbourg Court of Human Rights
		Optional Social Charter
		Subject to independent expert judgements
		Optional conventions on social security
Countries within the EU	EU	Obligatory Social Chapter (except UK)
		Subject to Luxembourg Court of Justice
		Participation in Social Exclusion Project
		Net loser/winner in redistribution of structural funds

of decent social security conventions. The tension between the budget-balancing requirements of the IMF and the expenditure requirements of the Social Charter of the Council of Europe is another example.

Table 8.2 focuses on the global social policy mechanisms of redistribution and regulation and provides an initial indication of the most important global and regional agencies engaged in those aspects of supranational policy and the instruments with which they either facilitate redistribution or seek to regulate activity. An important contrast is shown up here between the EU, where between-country redistribution accompanies free trade, and the North American Free Trade Association which, while freeing trade, does not engage in compensatory social redistribution (or even significant social regulation).[17] Of note also in this table is the lack of power the WTO has in the social redistribution and social regulation fields. The comments in the table indicate where current international debate and discussion on the issue of developing global social regulatory mechanisms now stands.

An important complexity arises if we turn to the social provision afforded by supranational and global authorities and agencies. Little direct provision of services operates yet at supranational level although the work of the UNHCR is an exception. We can, however, speak of the empowerment of citizens that some supranational bodies facilitate. One of the supranational in struments identified in Figure 8.2 operates through the rights conferred on individual citizens by legal authorities existing at supranational level. Government policy and practice within the European region, for example, in the spheres of social security, the right to social assistance, and the equal treatment of men and women as well as human rights generally now has to take account of the legal judgments of both the European Court of Justice in Luxembourg and the Council of Europe's Court of Human Rights in Strasbourg. Elizabeth Meehan[18] has documented the impact of the Luxembourg Court on aspects of the social rights of citizens of the European Union. Davidson[19] has recently reviewed some of the judgments with human rights implications of the Strasbourg Court. As yet, individual citizens globally do not have recourse to the UN International Court of Justice in The Hague. This is reserved for disputes between states or for war crime tribunals. In principle, however, and not just as a utopian vision, such a court could in due course adjudicate on aspects of the human and social rights of global citizens. Figure 8.2 captures this evolving situation.

TABLE 8.2 *Supranational and global redistribution and regulation*

Agency	Instrument					
	Raises revenue from citizens or business	Raises revenue from states[a]	Expends money on some basis of social need	Lends money on non-market terms	Has capacity to influence national social policy	Social regulation of trade
UN[b]	x (not yet)	√	√	x	√	x (not yet)
World Bank	x	√	√	√	√	x (not yet)
IMF	x	√	x	x	√	x
OECD	x	x	x	x	√	x
WTO	x	x	x	x	x (not yet)	x (not yet)
EU	x	√	√	?	√	√
NAFTA	x	x	x	x	x	x
ILO	x	x	x	x	√	√ (aspires to)

[a] Revenue over and above that needed just to fund the running of the organization.
[b] At this stage 'UN' is an umbrella term for all its social and other agencies, unless indicated separately. The most important agencies through which the UN redistributes resources for social welfare purposes are UNICEF, UNDP, UNFAO, the World Food Programme, and the UNHCR.

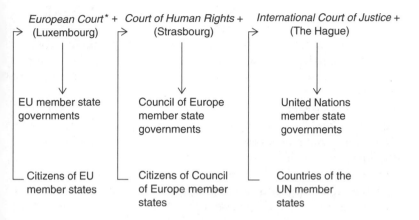

Competencies in the social rights sphere
+ *Competencies in the human rights sphere*

FIG. 8.2. The emergence of supranational citizenship in the sphere of human and social rights

Supranational and global agencies already contribute to the shaping of national policy and the terms of international competition by laying down social policy conditions on governments for the receipt of financial assistance, or by redistributing resources between governments, or by establishing conventions and offering technical advice and assistance as a step towards legal social regulation. Furthermore, because individual citizens are empowered to appeal to an authority above the state, a world within which universal human and social rights are recognized and reinforced is in principle already possible.

II. THE SOCIAL POLICY OF INTERNATIONAL ORGANIZATIONS

In this section the focus is on the implicit and explicit views of the major international organizations, with regard primarily to their prescriptions for national social policies. Issues of transnational social redistribution, social regulation, and social provision and

empowerment are also touched on. In focusing on the social policies of the international organizations as partially autonomous
with respect to the states that give them authority I am not arguing
entirely against those who, to the contrary, see the policy of international organizations as derived from the interests of major state
players. I am, however, asserting that the international organizations themselves and particularly their human resource specialists
have a degree of autonomy to fashion an implicit global dialogue
about the social policies of the future that goes beyond the political
thinking or political capacity of the underpinning states. The
approach is to regard these organizations, in the words of de
Senarclens, as 'depositories of principles and norms which confer
on their secretariats a degree of political autonomy . . . [and which]
are involved in their own right in conflicts of interest and power
struggles between actors on the international stage'.[20]

The International Monetary Fund: Unrepentant liberalism?

The IMF still has to be regarded as the proponent of unrepentant
liberalism in the competition of ideas about the best way to manage
global capitalism. Even so, it has been forced by events to make
more explicit what this means for the social policies of those
countries to which it lends its money. Finally, some attempt at
being publicly accountable to professional colleagues is being made
by the fiscal affairs/human resource technical specialities inside
the IMF, as is emerging through the work of Koppits,[21] Tanzi,[22]
Ahmad,[23] Chand and Shome,[24] Bruno,[25] Hardy,[26] and others. At the
World Summit on Social Development the Fund even produced
a glossy brochure on the social dimensions of the IMF's policy
dialogue.[27]

The impact of the IMF and World Bank structural adjustment
programmes in developing countries has of course generated a vast
and critical development studies literature. Requiring governments
who need to access loans to open their countries to free trade, to
reduce their public expenditures, and to ensure a non-inflationary
monetary policy has been argued by many to be the cause of
impoverishment, the further indebtedness of many countries, and
the political exhaustion of potential opposition forces.[28] The policies of the Bretton Woods institutions have generated calls for 'the

end of the tyranny' of the Bank and the Fund over developing and transition countries.

Killick and Malick[29] usefully summarized the social impact of IMF-inspired structural adjustment policies in the developing world as:

1. having appreciable effects on the distribution of incomes but that these effects are apt to be complex and vary from one situation to another,
2. meaning that groups of the poor can indeed be among the losers, with the urban working class particularly at risk,
3. ensuring that governments adopting Fund programmes are nonetheless free to adopt measures to protect vulnerable groups, although there may be hard negotiations with the Fund over measures which are liable to create large claims on public revenues.

As early as 1992 the Fund did acknowledge the shortcomings of some of the structural adjustment programmes it had influenced. 'Mistakes have been made. . . . One of the results, as is well known, is a greater emphasis on social aspects of adjustment and the explicit incorporation of affordable safety nets in an increasing number of instances.'[30] However, the IMF defends structural adjustment policies that are acknowledged to have a negative impact in the short term on some citizens, on the grounds that 'social development requires a strategy of high quality economic growth'.[31] Such a strategy requires macroeconomic stability, a market-based environment for trade and investment, good governance 'through accountable institutions and a transparent legal framework, and participatory development through active involvement of all groups in society', and, most relevant to this chapter, 'sound social policies, including social safety nets to protect the poor during the period of economic reform, cost effective social expenditures, and employment generating labour market policies'.[32]

The thrust of publicly stated IMF social policy in the short term is the safety net. These can 'comprise targeted subsidies, cash compensation in lieu of subsidies, improved distribution of essentials such as medicine, temporary price controls for essential commodities, severance pay and retraining for retrenched public sector employees, employment through public works, and adaptation of permanent social security arrangements to protect the poorest'.[33] In the longer term, the stated aim is 'to achieve significant real growth in social expenditures including primary education and health ... [while in some cases] ... shifting resources away from university education or advanced medical care'.[34] Kopits, when head of the Fiscal Operations Division of the IMF, did explicitly address the issue of a longer-term strategy for social security, as distinct from safety net short-termism.[35] He suggests that the perceived crisis of the typical European Bismarckian social security system is seen to result from 'generous eligibility for benefits granted for political expediency rather than on the basis of either past contributions or genuine need',[36] together with 'excessive claims for sick pay, partial disability pensions, early retirement pensions, length of service pensions, and health care benefits'.[37] Cost-effective reform, the argument continues, is required: 'Social security can no longer be viewed simply in terms of magnitude and coverage of benefits, but must be assessed also in terms of fiscal and allocative costs.'[38]

Since 1989 the IMF has provided assistance to more than a dozen countries in the design of new social security schemes. These include Algeria, Bolivia, Brazil, Greece, Hungary, Indonesia, and most former Soviet republics. In proposing reforms Kopits suggests the following considerations.[39] First, the cultural and historical context must be considered. In some societies the extended family or village structure 'operates relatively well as an informal social security scheme, obviating the need for the urgent introduction of large scale public pensions'. At the other end of the spectrum, where 'households have been atomised ... there is an immediate need for provision of an extended safety net, as in much of the former Soviet Union'. Secondly, social security schemes should not 'interfere with the efficient allocation of resources and not act as a disincentive to save or to work'. Thirdly, the link between benefits and contributions should be strengthened but also contributions should be kept relatively low. Fourthly, they should discourage waste by, for example, introducing user fees in health and education provision. Fifthly, clear distinctions should be drawn institutionally between elements of the scheme, such as pensions, sick pay, etc. Lastly, the schemes should be 'financially self sustaining over a long period of time'.

The above kinds of proposals point in the direction of greater individual investment funds with individually earned benefits. They create the possibility for a greater role for Chilean-style mandated private pension funds. They suggest an overall retrenchment in contributions and benefits levels in the public sector of the scheme. In terms of public poverty relief of pensioners in some countries, it suggests a greater role for means-tested assistance. In a manner which we will find recurring in the World Bank work on pensions, Australia and New Zealand crop up in a footnote as the only countries that have 'faced up to' the limits of the Bismarckian strategy by means-testing all benefits.[40]

In summary, the IMF continues its normative role of 'fostering economic policies that have traditionally been labelled liberal internationalist',[41] but it has come to acknowledge (as has the World Bank) the social impact on the vulnerable of some of its structural adjustment programmes. The Annual Report of the IMF in 1994 noted that 'the Board reaffirmed its recognition that some policy measures may have important distributional implications, that such distributional effects can undermine public support for the reforms, and that the design of Fund-supported reform programmes should evaluate and seek to mitigate the short term adverse effects of policy measures on vulnerable groups'.[42] It is to the role of the Bank in this task of poverty alleviation in the context of structural adjustment that we now turn.

The World Bank: A safety net for the poor?

As a development bank the World Bank is far less cautious than the IMF about proclaiming in public its mission to foster social development to eradicate poverty. 'It is intolerable that, as the world approaches the twenty-first century, hundreds of millions of people still lack minimally acceptable levels of education, health and nutrition. Investing in people must therefore be the highest priority for developing countries—until human capital limitations no longer restrain growth or keep people in absolute poverty. Investing in people is the core of the World Bank's work', asserts Armeane Choksi, its Vice-President for Human Resources.[43]

The World Bank has clearly responded to the earlier criticisms of its policy and practice in developing countries by adopting an anti-poverty strategy.[44] Several World Bank publications followed up this concern in the early 1990s,[45] and the focus on poverty in developing countries had already led to some softening of the earlier structural adjustment policies in Africa and Latin America. More socially sensitive adjustment policies were being conceived and implemented. The criticism by, for example, UNICEF, in its report *Adjustment with a Human Face*,[46] had already begun to tell a little. By 1993 the Bank was able to claim that 'the share of adjustment lending that addresses social issues climbed from 5% in fiscal year 1984–86 to 50% in 1990–92. In the fiscal year 1992, eighteen out of thirty-two adjustment loans included an explicit poverty focus, and fourteen of these adjustment loans had tranche release conditions.'[47]

Interestingly, the events in Eastern Europe of 1989 overtook this new 1992 Anti-Poverty Initiative and, in a development that had not been foreseen, the Bank's work on poverty alleviation became focused on the countries of the Confederation of Independent States (CIS) and Eastern Europe. This meant that the Bank was having to deal with and make recommendations for developed industrial economies on the mainland of continental Europe. It was ill-equipped to do this, and in order to undertake the task it needed to recruit a significant number of new officials and engage a new tranche of consultants more familiar with the income maintenance systems of developed economies and more sensitive to the social guarantees of the earlier regimes. The Human Resources Sector of the Europe and Central Asia Division of the Bank expanded rapidly.

The dominant tradition and practice in the Human Resources Sectors of the Bank had been one influenced by US liberalism at home and South American models of private welfare development abroad, combined with anti-poverty thinking appropriate to developing countries. The new influx of talent were engaged in a different discourse. They brought an understanding of and commitment to the 'European' tradition of wage-related social security systems and a sensitivity to the guarantees of 'communism'. It is within this context that it can be argued that it is not simply that the World Bank is an important actor in shaping post-communist social policy but that the pre-existing social guarantees of 'communism' continue to influence the Bank and reshape its understanding and thinking about appropriate social policy. Of course the factors leading to what has become a significant internal Bank dispute are more complex than this. Also shaping Bank thinking are the 'little miracles' of South-East Asia that have demonstrated the case for state infrastructure expenditure on education and health, thus denting the case for liberal 'fundamentalism'.[48] The Bank does not speak with one voice on social policy.

The dominant public-face view of the Education and Social Policy Department of the Bank, which owns the Bank's Anti-Poverty Strategy, combines labour-intensive growth with investment in health and education, backed up by an ill-defined safety net for the poor. This embraces a number of ideas, through food for work (although the Bank favours this less than the IMF), partial subsidy, and unresolved ideas on social assistance. A technical head-count of the poor combined with some mechanisms of income transfer, if informal systems are not working, characterizes this approach. Where this department addresses public social security schemes, it tends to do so in terms of flat-rate and means-tested provision. The heretics in the social policy 'Thematic Team of the Environment Department' prefer a more anthropologic and social assessment of the social relations involved in the generation of poverty. In a further contrast within the Human Resource Operations Division in Eastern Europe and between these operations people and their small team of specialist advisers, controversy exists about the desirability of wage-related pay-as-you-go state social security systems versus fully funded and privately managed individual accounting schemes. Proponents of the former are also to be found in the Policy Research Department, proponents of the latter in the Education and Social Policy Department and the Development Economics Department.

As a consequence of these internal divisions, on pensions policy the Bank is in the unusual position of publishing two differently orientated texts at the same time by staff and consultants working in different parts of the Bank. One of these, published by the Development Economics Vice-Presidency and edited by Estelle James, is the focus of much controversy with the ILO and ISSA.[49] The text proposes severely reducing public pension provision in transition economies to either a mere subsistence-level universal flat rate or even a means-tested flat-rate system funded by payroll tax or general revenue. It argues that there should be a wage-related pension scheme, ideally individually accounted and privately managed, as a second tier, in addition to a third, voluntary private pillar. The other World Bank text on pensions, produced from within the Operations Division for Eastern Europe, puts forward a set of policy options much more in keeping with existing practice in mainstream European systems.[50] Both texts argue that there is a need to raise pension age, and to protect minimum benefits. The key differences lie in the scope for state wage-related pensions and their private alternatives and the degree of solidaristic redistribution embodied in the scheme.

Policy on means-tested safety nets remains unresolved and experimental. The Chair of the joint Development Committee of the Bank and the IMF concluded that 'there is no general consensus on the correct approach to these [safety net] problems or the detailed solutions appropriate in each case'.[51] The joint World Bank–IMF paper prepared for this committee, however, comments in its discussion of the administrative obstacles to means-tested safety nets that 'public works programmes paying low wages may provide a cost effective, if more limited, alternative with admin costs reduced through self selection'.[52] This clearly reflects the influence of IMF thinking mentioned earlier. The Education and Social Policy Department of the Bank has been commissioned to produce a report on *The Effectiveness of Social Safety Nets* which will focus on best practice. Similar research is to be undertaken by the Operations and Policy Research Department!

While internal Bank discussion is evident, it is none the less possible to discern a dominant approach which is powerful in its logic and derived ideologically from the broader Bank consensus on the need for free trade and deregulation. This is the social safety net approach, or, as I will coin it, social liberalism—liberalism with a human face. Nelson captures the political logic of this dominant approach sharply when addressing the twin equity issues that exist in the structural adjustment process,[53] One issue is what to do with the very poor, often rural, who 'can be helped without jeopardising the economic requirements and constraints of adjustment'. The other issue is how to buffer the 'urban formal sector workers and middle strata from the social costs of adjustment without undercutting the adjustment effort itself'. Faced with these twin problems 'the World Bank, the IMF and other external donors encourage governments to protect the poor [but] often urge them to stand firm against the demands of labour unions and urban popular classes'. Carol Graham, a one-time visiting fellow in the Vice-

Presidency for Human Resources at the World Bank, describes with clarity the political logic of the dominant Bank policy on the dust jacket of her volume on *Safety Nets, Politics and the Poor*. An extract reads:

> Countries world-wide are attempting difficult transitions from state-planned to market economies. Most of these countries have fragile democratic regimes that are threatened by the high social and political costs of reform. Governments—and ultimately societies—have to make hard choices about allocating scarce public resources as they undergo these transitions. A central, often controversial, and poignant question is how to protect vulnerable groups and the poor. What compensation, what safety net, will be provided for them? In this book, Carol Graham argues that safety nets can provide an environment in which economic reform is more politically sustainable and poverty can be permanently reduced ... Rather than focus their efforts on organised interest groups—such as public sector unions—which have a great deal to lose in the process of reform, governments might better concentrate their efforts on poor groups that have rarely, if ever, received benefits from the state. The poor, meanwhile, may gain a new stake in the ongoing process of economic and public sector reform through organising to solicit the state for safety net benefits.[54]

The dominant anti-poverty thinking within the Bank would seem to be against organized labour and against European corporatist social security structures for the very poor. The new alliance the World Bank is making with NGOs in order to reach the poorest more effectively is part of this strategy.[55] By being seen as defenders of the poor in the South (interestingly, the World Bank and Oxfam recently joined forces to lobby the US Congress to continue to release funds to the Bank) and co-opting a section of the international NGOs into this project the Bank's strategy is to out-manoeuvre the attempts by the ILO (described below) and the EU (also below) to maintain patterns of state wage-related social security systems that serve the narrow interests of the regularly employed in the globalized economy. The dispute between the Bank and the ILO on good governance, for example, is an echo of this. While, as we shall see, the ILO believes the best defence for social security is tripartism,[56] the Bank believes this excludes the poor from effective participation in poverty policy-making.

The OECD: From welfare as a burden to welfare as investment?

Whereas since the founding Bretton Woods Conference of 1944 the IMF has had the self-appointed role of making the world safe for free trade with a minimum of impediments to the 'allocative efficiencies' of the market and the World Bank has increasingly assumed the enormous task of facilitating economic development globally while protecting the poor and the environment, the Organization for Economic Cooperation and Development (the OECD), founded in 1961, has the relatively modest aims of helping to achieve the highest sustainable economic growth, employment, and living standards among its member countries. Nonetheless, the OECD does have secondary aims of contributing to economic expansion in non-member countries and to the expansion of world trade (Article 1 of the OECD Convention). Unlike the IMF and the World Bank, the OECD does not provide loans on economic or social or political conditions. Its influence is limited to sharing the experience of member states among others and, through its strings-free technical assistance, and encouraging societal learning of best practice.

The Directorate of Education, Labour and Social Affairs was established in 1974 and brought social policy into the spotlight at a conference convened in 1980 on the welfare state in crisis in OECD countries. Although this brought social welfare and policy to the fore, the conference concluded that 'social policy in many countries creates obstacles to growth'.[57] The association of the OECD with the 'welfare as burden' approach stems from that publication. Further work on social expenditures in OECD countries followed from this initiative. The interest in this and the enthusiasm of Ron Gass as Director of the 'Social Affairs' Directorate led to the first meeting of social affairs ministers in 1988. OECD work in this field continued and became widely used among scholars. Publications followed on pensions,[58] on health expenditure and policy,[59] and on unemployment.[60]

In 1991 the concern of the Council of the OECD, concerned about the burden of taxes on employment to sustain welfare expenditure, gave rise to further work on social policy by the Directorate, under the new Director, Tom Alexander. Attempts were made to avoid simply repeating the 'welfare as burden' litany and to learn perhaps from parallel work of the OECD Development Centre which, in its review of the dynamic South-East Asian economies, concluded that 'limited but effective action by the state . . . [has led to] . . . rapid return to growth'.[61] The social affairs official responsible for the draft of a recent Ministerial Conference fashioned the *New Orientations for Social Policy* document, which asserted that 'non inflationary growth of output and jobs, and political and social stability are enhanced by the role of social expenditures as investments in society'.[62] This and other sentiments, such as 'restrictions on social expenditure could be counter productive if the objectives of social policy are sacrificed. Jeopardising the quality of life . . . may be the most costly route of all',[63] were adopted with minimal change as they progressed from the office in the Social Affairs Directorate, through middle- and high-ranking meetings of government ministers, to the 1992 Ministerial Conference itself.

It is worth reproducing the five new orientations of the Ministerial Conference's document in full:

1. Contributing to social and economic welfare: non-inflationary growth of output and jobs, and political and social stability, are enhanced by the role of social expenditures as investments in society.
2. Reconciling social policy objectives and budget limitations: there is a need to reconcile social programme costs with overall limits on public budgets, but at the same time to ensure that economic measures are consistent with programme effectiveness and social objectives.
3. Managing the mix of public and private responsibilities: the optimal balance should be sought between public and private sector responsibility in providing for the variety of needs of society, and in light of the comparative advantage of each sector.
4. Encouraging and facilitating the development of human potential: high priority should be given to active measures which relate to employment, rather than to reliance on income maintenance alone; in general, the emphasis should be on the encouragement of human potential as an end in itself, as well as a contribution to market efficiency. Consistent with this objective, income transfer programmes should be structured to foster self-sufficiency through earnings, without sacrificing the goals of systems of social protection.

5. Achieving greater policy coherence: greater policy coherence should be achieved by a renewed focus on the means by which the strands of policy, from setting goals, formulating policies, implementing them, and thereafter administering programmes, may be pulled together across social, labour market, education, and economic policies and across levels of government.

Taken together, the new orientations reflect the fact that, in contrast to the USA-influenced IMF and World Bank, the economic and social policy of the OECD represents a much more balanced set of economic and social considerations typical of mainstream European social and economic policy. The Head of the Social Affairs Section of the Directorate of Education, Labour and Social Affairs explained that the OECD preferred to work from the political realities of countries and attempt to balance economic and social considerations and work out the budgetary implications, whereas the IMF approached this as a top-down budget-balancing exercise.

The Annual Report of the OECD for 1992 reports on its work on social policy and goes even further, articulating that 'the role of social policy . . . is to provide a framework which enables the fullest participation in all aspects of society for its citizens . . . to achieve this goal social expenditure should be regarded as underpinning the quality of life for all citizens'.[64] This comes close to privileging social over economic policy, and is not unlike the vision of social development reflected in the work of some of the UN agencies I examine below.

The ILO: The setting and keeping of global labour and social standards

In refreshing contrast to the neo-liberal preoccupations and orientation of the IMF and the World Bank and to a lesser extent the OECD, the International Labour Organization (ILO) derives its brief to set and keep common international labour and social standards from the social democratic climate of the initial post-First World War days. In the context of the Bolshevik unrest sweeping Europe, the Treaty of Versailles included an important reference to labour conditions. In a phrase which has resonance today in the context of the drive to free trade and the consequent perceived danger of the 'race to the welfare bottom' the Treaty noted that 'the failure of any nation to adopt humane conditions of labour is an obstacle in the way of other nations which desire to improve the conditions in their own countries'.[65] Part XIII of the Treaty was concerned with international efforts to establish common provision for: the right of association, wages for a reasonable standard of living, an eight-hour day and 48-hour week, no child labour, and equal remuneration for men and women with equal rights for migrant workers. These provisions were not, however, linked to any sanction, nor linked to trade law. The attempt to link increased trade with common labour and social standards continues today, as we shall see in the next section. The strategy, via the adoption of ILO conventions, the first of which date from its founding year in 1919, was to persuade governments by peer and moral pressure to sign up and ratify conventions of good practice. Only when governments ratify conventions has the ILO any power to seek an enforcement of them.

Over the three decades after the Second World War, the ILO established a large number of conventions which, if ratified, provided for a well-functioning system of social insurance, social support, and social assistance. Some two hundred conventions cover employment policy, human resource development, social security, social policy, wage-fixing machinery, conditions of work, industrial relations, labour administration, and the protection of women, children, and indigenous peoples. An important emphasis in the internal workings of the ILO and in its policy prescriptions is tripartism: that good governance to secure social security requires the consensus of industry, workers, and government.

The ILO can claim some success over the years of its existence. The ratification of its conventions is by no means universal. However, by 1994 the average number of ratifications per country had reached 41.[66] More conventions are ratified by developed countries (an average of 52 in Europe, 42 in the Americas, 27 in Africa, and 21 in Asia), although this does not mean ILO influence in developing countries is minimal. However, one analyst has concluded that 'the ILO's most concrete contributions to policy are seen in the laggard welfare states of the industrialised world . . . where welfare is politically viable but contested, international standards most usefully amplify, legitimate and depoliticlize policy options'.[67] In such cases reform elites use external standard setting ('our international obligations') to further labour and social reform. The ILO, then, 'celebrates the enlightened social and labour policy of Western Europe' and is involved in 'a difficult bootstrapping operation, using the existing prestige of the Western welfare model to promote its further realisation'.[68]

It comes as no surprise that this European welfare policy orientation of the ILO should have come under challenge in the 1980s with the ascendancy of neo-liberal thinking and the increased influence of the IMF and World Bank in shaping structural adjustment policies in many developing countries. How has the ILO held up to this challenge? What are the prospects for the continued influence of the ILO? Reviewing the impact of the 'decade of structural adjustment' (1980s) on ILO policy and practice and the maintenance of standards, Plant concluded that as more flexible forms of working contract were being encouraged in more developing countries in the context of the globalization of production there was a real danger that 'the relevance of the ILO's standard setting framework will be necessarily limited as a reference point for addressing practical problems experienced by a growing proportion of the workforce in most developing countries'.[69] At a conference on the informal sector in 1991, the Director-General of the ILO asked: 'Have we been too ambitious and unrealistic in standard setting activities, and thus contributed to the widening gap between the protected workers of the modern sector and the large number of people in the informal sector deprived of any form of social protection?'[70] He answered that standards should not be lowered in this context but an appropriate strategic response might be 'to concentrate in the first instance on the promotion of core standards'. These would cover the basic human rights of association, equality of opportunity, and abolition of child labour. However, as Plant comments, the real issues in structural adjustment are not these but 'how adjustment can take place without undue sacrifice for employment and social protection and how enough of the state budget can be set aside for unemployment compensation, retraining of redeployed workers, etc.'[71].

In the context of the globalized restructuring of work, and the particular struggle between international agencies to influence social policy, the following dilemmas appear to exist for the ILO.

First, can it hold the line in favour of state social security against a mixed state/private system? Here the new dominant tendency articulated by Cichon[72] and others is to accommodate some mix of provision in order to defend the basic Bismarckian structure. It has, however, fought long and hard to expose the flaws in the dominant World Bank thinking on pensions,[73] by arguing that there is no demographic imperative leading to privatization, that the European-type schemes are sustainable, and that the privatization strategy is merely a cover to increase the share of private capital savings. A second question is whether the ILO can hold the line for wage-related social security when such policy increasingly reflects the interests of a reducing number of citizens. G. E. Standing has articulated from inside the ILO the alternative case for a basic citizens' social security policy.[74] A third question arises in the face of the power of the Bretton Woods institutions to limit the agenda to social liberalism at best: how can the ILO maintain a broader commitment to social security and social protection? Here two kinds of response are forthcoming. One way forward is to work to create the political and social conditions to enable citizens to resist the fiscalization of welfare: Cichon and Samuel argue that to make social protection work there is a paramount need for forms of governance, including tripartism, that bring the views and interests of those to be socially secured into the decision-making process.[75] The other way forward is to attempt to secure a greater role at the international level for the ILO when structural adjustment is on the agenda. Plant has proposed, following a 1993 ILO Conference resolution to this effect, that procedural guarantees should exist that ensure that no proposal for labour law reform, in the context of World Bank-facilitated structural adjustment, should be submitted to governments without prior ILO consultation.[76]

The other way in which the ILO might secure a greater role for itself in the emerging global governance reform agenda is through the insertion of a labour or social clause into trade agreements policed by the World Trade Organization. The prospects for this are discussed in the next section. Finally, the ILO is concerned about the World Bank's separation of the issue of protecting the poor in the context of structural adjustment (by a safety net) from the social security of established workers (secured by 'unaffordable and inflexible' social insurance schemes). In contributing to the World Summit on Social Development, the ILO stressed that its labour standards strategy was not incompatible with policies to eradicate poverty in developing countries. It noted the importance of 'alliance building, involving in particular a search for the common interests of the trade unions, the employers, and other groups in civil society. New groups entering the labour market need to be organized and represented, dialogue needs to be established with the associations, action groups, and local communities which often represent substantial segments of the poor'.[77] However, it also seemed to recognize the writing on the wall in terms of the threat of flexible employment and globalism to labour standards by concluding that 'It is imperative to promote universal coverage of at least a minimum set of protections, such as . . . those ILO conventions that relate to primary legislation in the area of child labour, discrimination, and occupational safety. In the context of poverty eradication a clear focus must emerge on what and how to regulate'.[78] This leads to the link between standards and free trade.

The WTO: Can social and labour standards and free trade co-exist?

Nowhere is the historic role of the ILO to prevent competitive free trade undercutting labour and social standards put more sharply to the test than in the context of the ongoing global debate about whether and how to insert a social clause (guarding against social cost-cutting) into free trade agreements and in particular into the remit of the World Trade Organization (WTO). A compelling historic counterpoint to the contemporary global irresolution on this issue is the view taken by President Roosevelt in the context of the 1937 New Deal legislation. He asserted then that 'goods produced under conditions which do not meet rudimentary standards of decency should be regarded as contraband and ought not to be allowed to pollute the channels of interstate commerce'.[79]

The completion of negotiations on the General Agreement on Trade and Tariffs (GATT) in 1994 ushered in an era of greater free trade which has prompted concerns that this will undermine social protection measures, labour and social regulations, and standards that have been secured at least in parts of the developed capitalist world. We have reached the bizarre moment in history when calls to conserve social protection measures in Europe by exporting them to other countries via, for example, social clauses in trade agreements is labelled 'protectionism' by an alliance of free market liberals and some Southern governments.

Developing and middle-income countries were almost universally opposed to the insertion of social clauses. The strongest defender of the idea of inclusion apart from France was, interestingly, the USA.[80] Historically it has operated a kind of social clause unilaterally in the context of its 1984 Trade and Tariff Act. In determining with whom it trades preferentially the US excludes those countries that do not recognize its interpretation of workers' rights. This includes the right of association, the right to organize, the prohibition of forced labour, a minimum age for child labour, and acceptable conditions of work. These are different and generally weaker provisions than those in ILO conventions—which the USA does not ratify. Peer pressure combined with a loss of preferential trade terms has, over the years, led to changes in labour standards of some countries with which the USA trades. The European Union has very recently introduced a bilateral clause which offers additional trade preferences for countries which meet the ILO convention on forced labour, freedom of association and collective bargaining, and the minimum age of employment. Only the forced labour part is currently operational. The remainder took effect from 1998.[81]

The GATT and now WTO rules would outlaw this kind of preferential trade based on a unilateral social clause. In 1953, for example, Belgium attempted to trade preferentially with those countries that had a universal family allowance scheme.[82] This was outlawed under the GATT because the general agreement does not cover the general economic, labour, and social context within which manufacturing takes place. The WTO meeting of ministers in Singapore late in 1996 seemed to confirm that the WTO would continue in this tradition. While it noted that it was desirable to raise labour and social standards, it rejected the idea that there should be a social clause in trade agreements that could be used as a sanction against countries which had unacceptable standards. Progress has not been smooth outside the WTO. The ILO, for example, agreed in 1994 at its 75th Conference to establish a working party on the implications of free trade for social standards. However, such is the politically charged nature of the issue, and such is the potential for a North–South split, that the ILO governing body would only agree to consider the issue should the entire 56-person governing body itself be the working party. Woolcock reports that 'the main proponents of a social clause (the US administration, the French government and the trade unions) faced the main opponents (India, China, Brazil and the employers)'.[83] By the second meeting in April 1995 it became clear that little progress was possible and it was agreed that the issue of a sanction-based social clause should be set aside for the time being.

The impasse on the issue of social standards illustrates sharply the complexity of the contending interests converging to shape a post-Cold War global social policy that might be concerned to achieve at one and the same time the increased prosperity of the South (via free trade), the greater redistribution of resources from North to South, and the regulation of the global economy in ways that preserve and enhance in sustainable ways the social achievements of developed welfare states. I will return to this issue later in this chapter when the current global governance reform agenda is reviewed.

The UN agencies (UNICEF, UNDP, UNRISD): The global social reformists?

Casting around for the opposition to the free market position of the IMF and (at best) safety-net social liberalism of the World Bank, we encounter, along with the ILO, other elements of the UN system. The United Nations is a complex and divided organization. Even its work in the social sphere is divided among a number of agencies. In overall charge of these activities is the Economic and Social Committee of the UN (ECOSOC). This committee, through its Social Development Commission, was responsible for the UN Summit on Social Development that took place in 1995. This, however, is not the place to describe systematically the diverse agencies of the UN, nor to track policy proposals and resolutions through the labyrinthine committee structure. Other books do the former,[84] and much more work on the latter is required. Rather, what is important for our purposes is to pick out for particular attention those elements of the UN system which, largely through the entrepreneurial and visionary drive of its key professional cadre, have stood out as the counterweight to the otherwise laissez-faire, free trade orientation of the World Bank and the IMF. The key voices engaging in debate with the institutions we have already discussed are UNICEF and the United Nations Development Project (UNDP) or, more particularly, the publications of the annual Human Development Report section of the UNDP Offices, and the work of the semi-autonomous United Nations Research Institute for Social Development (UNRISD).

Long before the Bank invented its poverty programme, in the decades of stringent structural adjustment, it was dedicated professionals such as James Grant, as Head of UNICEF until his recent death, Richard Jolly, Frances Stewart, and Andrea Cornia, as UNICEF economists, and others inside UNICEF who did so much to (1) monitor the impact on children of the global economic conditions of the 1980s, (2) articulate an alternative strategy of adjustment with a human face,[85] and (3) engage not only in public polemic but directly with the Bank and Fund professionals to attempt to shift thinking. Jolly reports that as early as 1982 James Grant was in discussion with leading Bank and Fund personnel on the impact of adjustment policy.[86] As a consequence, a joint Bank/UNICEF meeting took place in 1994 at which the UNICEF paper entitled 'IMF Adjustment Policies and Approaches and the Needs of Children' was presented. To cut a long story short (detailed by Jolly), the influence that began then and continued through, for example, the annual UNICEF publication on the *State of the World's Children* led to the reform of World Bank policy and the adoption of lending strategies that aimed to protect the poorest, as I described earlier. By 1995, UNICEF was able to make the following claim: 'In 1990 the World Summit for Children set goals for reducing deaths, malnutrition, disease and disability among the children of the developing world. Four years later, a majority of nations are on track to achieve a majority of these goals.'[87]

Towards the end of this period, the work of UNICEF was reinforced by the work of the Report Office of the UNDP. In 1990 it began its series of annual publications entitled *Human Development Report*.[88] It fashioned out of the earlier debate among development analysts a new measure of social progress: the Human Development Index, which combines longevity with educational attainment and a modified measure of income to rank countries on a scale somewhat differently from the rank order that would pertain if GNP alone were used. This measure further reinforced the paradigm shift from market liberalism towards some kind of socially orientated adjustment and development policies that have come to be articulated even by IMF and World Bank economists.

The 1992 *Human Development Report* joined the emerging debate on the reform of global governance and argued that 'human society is increasingly taking on a global dimension. Sooner or later it will have to develop global institutions to match . . . a system of progressive income tax [from rich to poor nations] . . . a strengthened UN'.[89] Interestingly, Richard Jolly moved to author the 1996 UNDP report, which has drawn attention to the widening economic inequality that is developing both within and between countries. Working rather more in the background but coming to prominence in the context of the global debate at the World Summit on Social Development, UNRISD had been commissioning a series of working papers from leading scholars on the impact of globalization on societies. Its publication *States of Disarray: The Social Effects of Globalisation*, after analysing the array of socially disintegrative effects of globalization such as identity crisis, war and conflict, the internationalization of crime, the uncertainties of changing work and changing family life, makes an imaginative call for the concept of citizenship to be reformulated above the level of the state, not only at a regional (e.g. EU) level, but on the global scale.[90]

The UNRISD report reminds us that citizenship has three central propositions: individual and human rights; political participation; and socio-economic welfare.

In practice, these three propositions of citizenship developed in sequence: acceptance of individual and human rights led to social mobilisation for political participation, which then implied progression to socio-economic welfare . . . Many of the issues that were central to the long debate on national citizenship are at the forefront of current attempts to channel global forces of socio-economic development in a more constructive direction. Perhaps the time has come, therefore, to focus attention explicitly on global citizenship.[91]

The concrete institutional reforms that might follow from the adoption of this global social reformist perspective are discussed next.

III. THE GLOBAL GOVERNANCE REFORM AGENDA

A casual review of the relevant political science, international relations, and political economy periodicals will reveal a number of parallel themes within what this chapter calls the 'global governance reform agenda'. All these themes are directed at containing the threat of a post-Cold War global disorder and seeking to establish a more humane and socially just new world order. All are partial responses to the globalization of social policy issues. These themes are:

1. Regulating global competition.
2. Making the Bretton Woods institutions more accountable.
3. Reforming the United Nations.
4. Strengthening global political, legal, and social rights.
5. Empowering international civil society.

These themes are reflected in the conclusions of the Commission on Global Governance,[92] the thinking of the United Nations *Human Development Reports*, the contributions of the United Nations Research Institute for Social Development,[93] the reflections upon these themes by Held,[94] the valuable contributions in edited volumes by Griesgraber and Gunter,[95] and many other sources.

Regulating global competition

The core contemporary problem is that 'global integration can destroy hard won social gains in many countries—driving them down to the lowest common denominator in a competitive market—or, on the contrary, integration can begin to raise social standards towards levels attained in the most successful cases'.[96] The future of welfare states will depend partly on how they compete in this global market place and partly on the rules of the game that regulate this competition, and the political decisions made about this.

A recent articulation of the conflicting global interests bound up with the issue of free trade and social standards was provided by the French president in the context of the G7 summit in Lille on 2 April 1996. He argued that public opinion in the West could accept that lower wages, less extensive social security, and different labour laws enabled developing countries to compete successfully for export markets. But other aspects of labour markets in developing countries would not be tolerated. 'Can it be accepted that fundamental rules of social democracy be so grievously stretched in this great world-wide market? Can more or less disguised forms of adult or child slavery be tolerated? The citizens of our countries are becoming better and better informed about such forms of abuse and rightly judge them to be intolerable.'[97] Apparently, the festering row among the West's leading industrial nations over linking free trade to human rights burst into the open at this G7 summit. The European Commission's call for minimum global labour standards threatened to split the G7 down the middle. Padraig Flynn argued for the Commission that 'free collective bargaining, free association, and the abolition of child labour are fundamental rights'. Britain and Japan claimed to the contrary that the move was an attempt to defend the high-cost economies of the West from international competition and represented protectionism by the back door.

The issue of labour standards surfaced again at the G7 summit in Lyons in June 1996. This summit involved not only the G7 nations (France, Germany, the US, the UK, Japan, Canada, and Italy), who represent only 12 per cent of the world's population, but also, for the first time, the heads of the World Bank, IMF, WTO, and UN. The summit concluded that there was a need, in the context of freer trade, to combat social exclusion.[98] Chirac concluded that 'globalisation holds out advantages in terms of growth but also carries dangers of exclusion for nations and individuals. Certain safety barriers have to be introduced.' The conference recognized 'that there is a will to address the relationship between trade and internationally recognised core labour standards'.[99] These relationships were discussed in Singapore in autumn 1996, as reported earlier, but with little positive outcome.

Making the Bretton Woods institutions more accountable

This chapter has demonstrated the importance of the IMF and World Bank in shaping the character of the social policy of countries in transition. It is often proposed in critical discussions of the Bretton Woods institutions that they should be made more accountable for policies they effect and promulgate (see also the discussion in Chapter 1 of this volume). At present they are accountable to the governments that fund them in proportion to the capital provided. The Commission on Global Governance modestly suggests that voting strength should reflect gross domestic product based on purchasing power parity.[100] More radically, it argues that 'the time is now ripe for a global forum that can provide leadership in economic, social and environmental fields. It would be more broadly based than the G7 or the Bretton Woods institutions, and more effective than the present UN system.'[101] A proposal is made for an Economic Security Council (ESC) which would be more broadly representative of all large economies (measured in purchasing power parity terms) and of regional associations, and of smaller states via representatives. It would provide a policy framework within which the Bank, IMF, and WTO would work. Others, more enamoured of the effectiveness of the existing UN's ECOSOC, and wanting a greater voice for the South, have proposed the accountability of Bretton Woods to ECOSOC.[102]

Singer argues that it is not a matter of either making the Bretton Woods institutions more accountable to the countries that fund them according to a measure of the size of their population, or subjecting them to a reformed UN Economic Security Council. Rather, he proposes that reforms in voting systems for both Bretton Woods and the UN are needed and that, once this is undertaken, the two could work more closely alongside each other, with the Bank and IMF focusing on harder finance issues and the UN focusing on 'softer' social policy issues: 'The system of decision making in the Bank and Fund could be democratised and moved in the direction of the present UN system, while the UN system could be made more realistic and moved in the direction of the Bretton Woods system.'[103] Majorities of both donor countries (Bank and Fund) and all countries (UN) might be needed for policy agreement.

At stake is not only the question of accountability but also the role of the Bretton Woods institutions. While there is general agreement among the rich capitalist countries that the IMF role of credit of last resort is important, there is more debate about the role of the Bank. Regardless of the populist politics of the USA which might want to curtail the Bank, most opinion is concerned with the scope of the Bank's brief. Put simply, it is perhaps time that the Bank as a development agency continued to expand its brief to encompass not only the environment and poverty alleviation, as described in this chapter, but also responsibilities for refugees and humanitarian disasters, presently shouldered by the UNHCR and the UN's Bureau for Humanitarian Assistance. The question is whether the UN social agencies should be given greater resources and responsibility for shaping national and transnational social (and other) policies or whether the Bank should replace them.

In the context of the G7 Summit in June 1995, and the fiftieth anniversary of the founding of the UN in March 1996, calls were made for the United Nations Conference on Trade and Development (UNCTAD) to be abolished and even for the ILO's role to be reconsidered. Subsequently, at the G7 meeting in June 1996, the ILO issue appears to have been dropped and indeed the communiqué thanked the ILO for the quality of its work. The IMF, World Bank, WTO, and UN Secretary-General, however, were invited to the meeting to discuss, among other things, concrete proposals to abolish UNCTAD and United Nations Industrial Development Organization (UNIDO). The Bank and the World Trade Organization between them could end up being, not partners with the UN, as Singer wants, but Global Ministries for Education, Health, Environment, Welfare, Trade, and Labour, leaving the IMF as Global Ministry of Finance, as Susan Strange has suggested.[104]

Reforming the United Nations

It is impossible to do justice to the volumes written on the need for reform of the UN. The importance of the topic for the future of the ILO, WHO, UNESCO, UNICEF, UNDP, UNHCR, and the other global social reformists identified as having a distinctive voice in world social affairs, however, cannot be under-estimated. As a bulwark against Bretton Woods, the ILO stands out in my analysis. There could be little confidence that the WTO could perform the same job, even if, as it has been argued above, the WTO were to uphold labour and social standards in its regulatory work. UNICEF and UNDP stand out as critics of existing global policy and practice, and their disappearance would be a severe blow to progressive opinion.

The horns of the dilemma appear to be that, as presently constituted and managed, some of the G7 nations will continue to give little credence to the UN work in the social field, but, if reformed in the way some of the Northern industrial nations are suggesting, it will become an institution less open to the influence of the smaller nations of the South. The price that might have to be paid for a UN that is taken more seriously by the developed and large economies is that it becomes more subject to the interests of these developed nations. To put it differently, to ensure that it is a UN Economic Security Council that contributes to the regulation of global trade with a view to protecting labour and social standards, it might have to be a UN reconstructed to better reflect the interests of developed nations.

The crisis of the UN is also one of financing, brought about by the continued reluctance of the USA to contribute its required share of resources and by overlapping and ill-coordinated divisions among specialized agencies. It is possibly also a crisis of internal management styles. Amidst many calls for reform or reshaping of the UN, the draft communiqué of the G7 Summit in June 1995 (which was eventually watered down) called for: (1) consolidation and streamlining of organizations in the economic and social fields; (2) examination of the role of bodies such as UNCTAD in the light of the establishment of the WTO; (3) arranging for high-level sessions of the Economic and Social Committee to take more responsibility for issues of public concern; and (4) the reduction of costs.

Over recent decades the periodic financial crisis of the UN has generated proposals for forms of global taxation that are not dependent upon the political whim of national governments. The Brandt Report of 1980 first raised the issue, and more recently the UNDP has pressed for forms of global taxation. At the UN Summit on Social Development in 1995, the Tobin tax, first proposed in 1972, became a serious candidate for discussion. This would be a small tax levied on currency transactions (0.5 per cent). The target would be international financial speculators, which has a ring of justice about it given that it has been the free movement of finance capital that has contributed to the competitive challenge to welfare states. The UN Secretary General has proposed a tax on international air travel. A recent review of options concluded that 'the airport tax surcharge seems the simplest and least controversial idea, if political pressure for global revenue were to develop. The Tobin tax remains the scheme on which most work has been done . . . but there is little political pressure to translate it into action.'[105]

Strengthening global political, legal, and social rights

The Commission on Global Governance has argued for a global civic ethic: 'We further believe humanity as a whole will be best served by recognition of a set of common rights and responsibilities. It should encompass the right of all people to: a secure life, equitable treatment, the definition and preservation of their differences through peaceful means, participation in governance at all levels . . . [and] equal access to the global commons'.[106] Dharam Ghai has argued too that 'in a fragmented and somewhat inconsistent way, the world seems therefore to be moving towards a debate on global citizenship similar to that which marked the affirmation of certain inalienable rights within advanced industrial societies'.[107] Baubock has elaborated the case for and obstacles to the establishment of transnational citizenship rights.[108] Held has called for the creation of a new International Human Rights Court[109] reflecting on a global level the work already done on the European continent by the Council of Europe's Strasbourg Court of Human Rights.

These increasingly frequent calls for global citizenship rights of the political, legal, and socio-economic kind are, of course, a subject of heated dispute. Are these ethical concerns of the emerging global civil society, whose spokespeople are usually international NGOs, on the side of the 'guardian angels' in their concern to humanize global capital, or are they merely providing a new legitimization for Western imperialist forces to claim global hegemony under post-war conditions—are they actually working for the 'global gangsters'?[110]

In practical terms at present there are three instruments which have been formally adopted by the UN. The 1948 Universal Declaration of Human Rights was adopted without dissent. In 1966 the International Covenant on Civil and Political Rights and the International Covenant on Economic, Social, and Cultural Rights were tabled and came into force in 1976 after they had been ratified by 35 countries. Humana has documented the extent to which these rights are adhered to and has reported 'an improvement over a 5 year period which is unparalleled in history'.[111] In compiling the guide, he is dismissive of those who would argue the relativist case that some Muslim or other countries governed by religious laws do not, in practice, wish to be bound by these conventions: 'If the indicators have to bear the label of being Western liberal ... then the guide will have to live with such criticism.'[112]

In terms of socio-economic rights and, for example, the right to social assistance, these global conventions are silent although the right to work is acknowledged. On the European level, of course, the Council of Europe's Social Charter is more explicit about this. The real issue is whether any practical meaning backed up by judicial force could be given to the idea of the right to social assistance. It is not fanciful to suggest that in some decades' time the right either to social assistance or to a minimum income could be enshrined as one of the global citizenship entitlements that the reformed UN system would expect its member states to uphold.

Empowering international civil society

Within the context of making the Bretton Woods institutions and/ or the UN agencies more accountable, a greater role is being argued for and given to international NGOs. 'Global governance ... now involves not only governments and intergovernmental organisations but also non-governmental organisations, citizens' movements, transnational corporations, academia, and the mass media.'[113] The critical appraisal of the role of NGOs in Rwanda suggests that this is not an unproblematic development.[114] The assumption that NGOs are representative of international civil society raises questions about which elements of civil society are being 'represented' and which other ones effectively disempowered. The extent to which NGOs are increasingly dependent for their existence upon the funds of official intergovernmental organizations raises questions about their independence and autonomy. This challenges the simplistic view that NGOs are the conscience of the world.[115] The trend, however, to more NGO involvement is clear. In financial year 1994, 50 per cent of World Bank projects had provision for NGO involvement.[116] A principal element in the Bank's poverty strategy is to conduct poverty assessments and these increasingly involve participatory research projects with local

NGOs. In the context of targeting resources on the poorest, the Bank is stepping around the potentially corrupting obstacles of state agencies and delivering resources to localities.

The World Summit on Social Development and the previous and subsequent summits have been characterized by active NGO involvement in agenda-setting. In the wake of the Summit UNRISD has analysed four approaches to Summit follow-up within the international NGO community: developing alternative thinking, defining specific targets for implementation, establishing a non-governmental monitoring system, and lobbying for United Nations reform.[117] The report cautions, however, against exaggerated claims that NGOs represent the poor at the grassroots: 'It is widely agreed that NGOs are often less accountable to the intended beneficiaries of their support than to their financial donors.'[118] Among some of the most determined defenders of ECOSOC are NGOs who have won recognition rights from the Council. This NGO involvement has of course complicated the process of negotiation, agenda-setting, and decision-making in ECOSOC. In 1994, 980 NGOs were accredited to ECOSOC. This could be one of the reasons why those impatient with the existing work of the UN in the economic field are calling for a streamlined Economic Security Council, and propose hiving off NGO involvement to the proposed annual NGO assembly.

In this context Hirst and Thompson have argued that the emerging form of global governance should be understood as one whereby states, even though they have ceded some powers to international organizations, continue to be important actors in both influencing international organization policy and implementing such agreed supranational policy.[119] Because of this, the empowerment of global civil society in relation to global governance takes place partly through the traditional forms of national democratic accountability. International NGOs are here ascribed the role of informing such traditional electorates:

Such representation is very indirect, but it is the closest to democracy and accountability that international governance is likely to get. The key publics in advanced democracies have some influence on their states and these states can affect international politics. Such influence is the more likely if populations of several major states are informed and aroused on an issue by the world 'Civil Society' of transnational non-governmental organisations.[120]

This approach differs sharply from the more visionary picture painted by Held of a future cosmopolitan democracy whereby a global parliament, with revenue-raising capacity, shares global governance with an International Court which empowers global citizens to take their 'local' national governments to court if they deny them their basic citizenship rights, which would include a 'guaranteed basic income for all adults'.[121]

None of the reforms listed above are guaranteed. Obstacles to such global social reformist ideas are legion. They include the drift towards regional trading blocs and associated cost-cutting competition between them, the perceived national self-interest of Northern electorates, the difficulties of agreeing on global standards in a culturally diverse world, and the problem of ecological sustainability. The course of making a global social policy in the twenty-first century will be as fraught as the course of making national social policies in the twentieth.

9

Security and Inequality

Andrew Hurrell

This collection is concerned with the changing ways in which various forms of inequality affect the practices of world politics. The relationship between inequality and security captures one of the most important arguments for change. On the one hand, inequality of power amongst major states was widely viewed as the most fundamental issue on the traditional agenda of international security. On the other hand, increasing inequality of condition amongst individuals, groups, and communities is seen as central to the new and expanded agenda of security studies. The relationship between inequality and security also helps us grapple with one of the most difficult issues in international relations: under what conditions may unequal power serve as a necessary and legitimate instrument of social order? This concluding chapter addresses three questions:

1. What was the relationship between inequality and security within the classical state system that developed in Europe and became global in the course of the twentieth century?
2. In what ways does inequality affect the generation of contemporary security challenges?
3. What is the role of unequal power and the distribution of military capabilities in the management of contemporary international security?

CLASSICAL CONCEPTIONS

The classical state system was a system that was both marked by inequality and structured around inequality. The combination of rapid industrial development, the emergence of more efficient administrative and organizational state structures, the consolidation of national states, and changes in military technology and organization—all of these factors led to the emergence of a small number of major powers that dominated the international political landscape. Moreover, if inequality marked the core of the state system, the relations between the European core and the periphery were still more unequal. The industrial revolution and technological innovations in armaments provided the base for unparalleled dominance of the European powers over the rest of the world. The European colonial order was built around formally subordinate territories which played no role in international relations; institutionalized controls over colonies and semi-colonies involving unequal treaties, imposed export regimes, enforced concessions, and 'temporary occupations'; an economic system marked by the enforced opening of peripheral economies and by demographic openness; a series of cultural assumptions that stressed the superiority of Western and white culture and a natural belief that progress entailed the replication of European models; and finally, European control over the criteria by which non-European political communities could be admitted to membership of international society.[1]

In addition to these disparities in material power and resources, inequality was entrenched in the norms, institutions, and shared understandings that shaped and gave meaning to the system. Of particular importance was the special role and status of Great Powers as the managers of international security; the dominant role of major states in establishing, by their practice or agreement, the rules of international law; and the extent to which that law reflected the interests of the powerful, imposing few restrictions on the use of force and resort to war, upholding the validity of treaties signed under duress, and providing no place for notions of self-determination or of human rights.[1] These shared norms also shaped the ways in which the very notion of security was conceived and understood. It was only around the middle of the eighteenth century that the terms of the modern debate on war and peace became established.[2] From this time security came to be understood primarily (but never exclusively) in terms of the security of states, and increasingly of nation-states, confronted by threats emanating from outside their borders and to which governments responded with military power and alliances.[3] In addition, the legal conventions on war began to be codified and institutionalized in the practices of governments and of armies, giving war a special status distinct from other forms of social violence.

The relationship between inequality and security within the classical state system was paradoxical. On one side, inequality was widely viewed as central to the *generation* of insecurity, in two main ways. In the first place, the 'natural' inequalities among states were seen as the driving force behind power-political competition and as fuelling the security dilemma that inevitably resulted.

Internally, inequality is an important part of the political story, though far from being the whole of it. Internal politics is also the realm of authority and law, of established institutions, of socially settled and established ways of doing things. Internationally, inequality is more nearly the whole of the political story. Differences of national strength and power and of national capability and competence are what the study and practice of international politics are almost entirely about. This is so not only because international politics lacks the effective laws and institutions found within nations but also because inequalities across nations are greater than inequalities within them.[4]

On this realist logic, states within an anarchic international order must provide for their own security. Unequal power and the material capabilities of opponents create threats to national security. If a state is much more powerful than its neighbours, then that power is highly likely to be seen as dangerous and to inspire fear: 'By fear we mean not an unreasoning emotion, but a rational apprehension of future evil.'[5] It is precisely this logic of security competition that drives the balance of power as the central mechanism of the system. As von Gentz put it in 1806: 'The state which is not prevented by any external consideration from oppressing a weaker, is always, however weak it may be, *too strong* for the interests of the whole.'[6]

Excessive power, then, comes to be understood as a potential problem for international security. But so too does excessive weakness. Small and weak states may invite an attack that greater power would have deterred. They may also become the focus for geopolitical competition amongst the major powers. The existence of weak and insecure states whose conflicts and instability would draw in outside power has been a consistent source of concern for traditional security analysts, especially in respect of the new and often weak states created in each of the four great waves of decolonization and imperial break-up. But it is crucial to emphasize that, on this reading, the problems of the weak have no intrinsic importance either politically or morally, except in so far as they complicate relations among the major powers and become subordinate to their rivalries and conflicts. It was in this sense, for example, that the Third World was deemed to 'matter' to the US and its Western allies during the Cold War. The weak, the poor, and the dispossessed only enter the story of international security in so far as they cause problems for the powerful, or themselves come to acquire some form of power. It is only by entering into the cult and calculus of power that they make some difference to the patterns of inter-state politics that are 'naturally' dominated by the powerful.

This hard realist view is of course wrong in its claim that this logic of unequal power applies at all times and under all conditions. It neglects the extent to which these power-political understandings and the states to which they referred were the product of particular historical and, very importantly, regional circumstances. It is still more misleading in its neglect of the norms and institutions that shaped how states understood their interests and structured their power relations. Conflict and war took place within a highly institutionalized set of normative structures. But this view does correctly point to a central issue whose relevance still has to be addressed in the post-Cold War world: if coercive power is not harnessed to some collective authority or tied within stable structures of inter-state or inter-societal cooperation, then the security implications of unequal power cannot be ignored.

The hard realist view is also wrong in its assumption that states are driven only by concerns of power and security and that all claims for justice can be reduced to self-interest.[7] Amongst the politically most powerful of these other values has been the striving towards greater equality. This is the second way in which inequality has been classically related to insecurity. Running against the brute realities of unequal power and the inequalities of the international legal order was a powerful counter-tradition that stressed the importance of equality. In terms of the classical state system this tradition developed only gradually and was only applied in particular and limited ways. The idea of equality of states had first to be asserted against the surviving universalist and strongly hierarchical conceptions of political life inherited from Western Christendom. This was a long process. The replacement of older formal hierarchies by a hierarchy of power only occurred with Napoleon's abolition of the Holy Roman Empire in 1800 and with the new forms of diplomatic precedence introduced at Vienna in 1815.

Gradually, however, the concept of equality emerged as a corollary to the mutual recognition of sovereignty and drew on the application of state-of-nature analogies to international life—analogies which, for all the changes in the world, still retain immense resonance. In addition, from the early nineteenth century the idea developed that equality was not just a matter for states but should also apply to nations and to peoples under alien rule, opening the door to doctrines of national self-determination, of anti-colonialism and national liberation. By the First World War the scope of claims for equality had widened still further with Japanese demands that the norms of international society should acknowledge the importance of equality among races. Finally, the emergence and consolidation of the international human rights regime in the post-1945 period carried with it the claim that equality among individual persons should have a legitimate place in international politics and that the equal protection of the core rights of all individuals as individuals should be a matter of international concern.

Equality as a political idea is hard to fit into the categories of political scientists and its impact is difficult to assess with any precision.[8] But a very great deal of the international history of this century has involved demands made by states, by peoples and other groups, and by individuals for greater equality—of power, of conditions, of rights, and of status. Sometimes this has involved calls for the equal application of existing laws or norms, for example the demand that all states be entitled to equal sovereignty or all peoples to self-determination. Sometimes it has involved a demand for equality of substantive rights, as in the call of small states not simply for the equal application of existing laws but for reform of the way in which international law is made. And sometimes this has involved calls for material equality in the distribution of wealth and resources, as in the calls of the Third World for a New International Economic Order in the 1970s.

Clearly not all of the responses to perceived or actual inequality led to conflict and insecurity. But many did and often dramatically so. Think, for example, of the role of national self-determination in the wars and conflicts of this century. It is also important to note that the political tensions and the insecurity that resulted from the drive towards greater equality rarely involved the weakest of the weak. It was far more likely to stem from those states or peoples with the capacity and political organization to demand a revision of the established order and of its dominant norms in ways that reflected their own interests and values. Thus a central theme of twentieth-century international history has been the struggle of revisionist states for the redistribution of territory or for equality of status and *Gleichberechtigung*: Germany for an equal place under the imperial sun before 1914; Germany and Japan in the inter-war period; China and the major Third World states in the post-1945 period. Indeed, central to so many of the tensions of the Cold War lay Soviet demands for equality of status and for acknowledgement by the US of its equal rights as a super-power— demands that the United States was reluctant to grant even at the high point of détente.

Yet if inequality was implicated in the generation of security problems, it was also viewed as central to the *management* of international security and to the pluralist conceptions of international order that dominated the classical state system.

In the first place, it was precisely the inequality of states that, for the classical theorists of the state system, differentiated international life from the state of nature amongst individuals. For Hobbes, it was the equality of fear resulting from the equal ability to kill possessed by everyone that persuaded men in the state of nature to bind themselves into a commonwealth. As Hobbes famously put it: 'From Equality proceeds Diffidence. From Diffidence Warre.'[9] And yet the very differences between states and individuals and the disparities of power amongst states opened up the possibility of international society as a distinct form of political association.[10]

Second, inequality was tied to order to the extent that war was central to both foreign policy and to the system as a whole. War involves the rational exercise of coercion and the imposition of the will of one political community over another. It is thus the most direct and brutal test of strength and weakness. Military force represented a legitimate instrument that could be resorted to, controlled, and used with at least the expectation of effectiveness to promote state objectives and for the self-enforcement of basic rights, above all the right of self-defence. Politically, it was, in Clausewitz's famous phrase, 'a real political instrument'; legally, it was, as one leading nineteenth-century international lawyer put it, a 'permitted mode of giving effect to decisions'. It also represented an institution of international society, to use Hedley Bull's terms, to the extent that it was necessary for the operation of the balance of power and as a means of effecting change in the structure of the system.[11]

Third, these elements came together in the institutionalized forms of hierarchy that were central to classical understandings of international order. Although the logic of the balance of power might indeed operate automatically, its dangers and inevitable frictions could be minimized by the recognized managerial role of the Great Powers. As exemplified by the concert system, Great Powers could promote order not only by managing relations between themselves (through diplomacy, conferences, missions, joint interventions), but also by exploiting their own unequal power over subordinate states within their spheres of influence and alliance systems. This conception of security management has remained extraordinarily powerful and influential throughout the twentieth century. As John Dunbabin has argued,

the League of Nations did not represent a total departure from the previous international system. Symbolically, its Covenant was not a separate compact, but formed part of the Paris peace treaties, which in turn stemmed from a conference dominated by the five principal victors. . . . Even after the signature of the peace treaties, many consequential problems continued to be settled by the Supreme Council of the Allied and Associated Powers or its deputy, the Conference of Ambassadors in Paris, and its offshoot the Reparations Commission.[12]

Such ideas were even more central to the management of international security between the US and the USSR as the tensions and uncertainties of the early Cold War years gradually stabilized. Indeed, the Cold War 'order' and the long peace of 1945–89 were constructed in very traditional fashion around the regulation of relations between the super-powers (through arms control agreements, summits, and mechanisms of crisis management) and through the exploitation of hierarchy (through the mutual, if tacit, recognition of spheres of influence and the creation of a highly discriminatory and oligarchical non-proliferation system designed to limit access to the nuclear club). Finally, even as the idea of sovereign equality gained ground and as international institutions expanded so dramatically in both number and scope, the argument that major powers should enjoy a special status and that inequality promotes effectiveness remained prominent throughout the post-1945 period: as in the special rights and duties of the permanent members of the UN Security Council or the practice of ad hoc groupings and contact groups to deal with particular crises. Whilst inequality was increasingly difficult to reconcile with post-1945 conceptions of an international legal order, in terms of political order it remained fundamental both in theory and in practice.

INEQUALITY AND THE GENERATION OF INSECURITY

To what extent do these classical conceptions still hold given all the changes that have followed the end of the Cold War and the impact of globalization? To what extent has this old security agenda become obsolescent? If so, what is the nature of the new security agenda that has replaced it and what is the role of inequality within that agenda?

The obsolescence of the old agenda?

The centrality of power politics and of an inescapable and ineluctable security dilemma driven by unequal power among states is difficult to reconcile with many features of contemporary international society. In the first place, despite the urgings of neo-realist theorists, emerging 'Great Powers' such as Germany and Japan do not seem very keen to take on the military trappings of their traditional forebears. In both cases the balance between welfare and security goals has shifted and both see all sorts of other ways to promote their interests and objectives. Profound domestic changes and altered external circumstances have led to very different definitions of interest and, more fundamentally, of identity.

A second argument in this direction suggests that major war itself has become obsolete. On this view, military capacity is unnecessary given the declining role of territorial control and conquest in the definition of state power. It is irrelevant to the success and prosperity of individual states (cf. the 'lessons' of Germany and Japan) and to the management of the economic, social, and environmental problems that are characteristic of globalization. The nuclear revolution and the increased totality of total war have undermined the rationality and controllability of force that was central to the Clausewitzian world. The unthinkability of major modern conflict means that war must be seen as the breakdown of policy and politics, rather than as its servant. The costs of major conflict and political tolerance of those costs have increased exponentially— because of the high levels of economic interdependence and the impact of globalization; because of the rise in Third World nationalism and social mobilization, which has rendered old-style imperial or neo-imperial control unviable (cf. the lessons of Vietnam and Afghanistan); and, finally, because of the increasingly accepted illegality and illegitimacy of the use of force and the increased unwillingness on the part of citizens in developed countries to bear the economic and human costs of war.

On the one hand, then, the classical imperatives, whether of material gain, of security and fear, or of doctrine and ideology, that produced the major wars of the nineteenth and twentieth century and the need for military power appear to have receded. Mercantilist impulses may well persist but these are not readily susceptible to the use of military power, nor do they obviously threaten to create military conflict. On the other, modern developed societies have been able to learn that major war is 'rationally unthinkable'.[13] This view draws on the deep-rooted belief in liberal thought that 'physical force is a constantly diminishing factor in human affairs', as Norman Angell put it in 1910.[14]

Given these liberal premisses the creation of many more small states is not necessarily a problem. The number of states has grown from 74 in 1946 to 193 in 1998, with a particularly striking expansion in the number of small states: 87 countries have populations of under 5 million, 58 have fewer than 2.5 million, and 35 have fewer than 500,000. Yet in a liberal globalized world, inequality in terms of the classic indices of national power that dominated nineteenth-century political understandings is unproblematic and irrelevant. Indeed, in today's globalized economy small size may be positively advantageous.[15] On this view, then, power and relative gains amongst the major powers no longer drives competition and insecurity, whilst, for the weak, small size is no longer dangerous.

Third, and perhaps most convincingly, the force of these changes is acknowledged but placed within their regional context. One of the most important developments of the post-1989 period has been the regionalization of security. In contrast both with the era of European colonialism and with the Cold War years, the pressures on Great Powers to develop a global role and for regional conflicts to be subordinated as part of some broader power-political competition have declined very significantly. The tight centralization of the past has been replaced by a more pluralist world characterized by a number of loosely connected regional security systems, each with its own local dynamics. In a number of regions (Western Europe, Scandinavia, North America, parts of South America), international relations can be characterized in terms of a reasonably well-established security community—a group of states in which 'there is real assurance that the members of that community will not fight each other physically, but will settle their disputes in some other way'.[16] Within such a community there are dependable expectations of peaceful change, with military force gradually disappearing as a conceivable instrument of statecraft. Inequality of power takes on a very different character. Indeed, security communities may be built around a powerful core to which outside states no longer respond by balancing behaviour, but rather view it as a zone of peace and security in which membership is valued.[17]

Even within and among these zones of relative regional pacification, liberal optimism has led to an exaggerated sense of ease that forgets its own precariousness, for example regarding the potential political impact of severe economic dislocation; the crises of identity provoked by globalization and interdependence; and the co-existence of inter-state peace with domestic violence or civil war. Indeed, the often close juxtaposition of high levels of economic prosperity and successful democratic consolidation with civil war, social violence, marginality, and human rights abuses make a nonsense of the view that the post-Cold War world can be neatly divided into zones of peace and zones of conflict.[18] Moreover, the degree to which power politics has been tamed varies from region to region. US hegemony has always been one (but not the only) factor in explaining the North American security community. Shifts within South America are real but partial, geographically limited, and not necessarily irreversible. Even in Europe the possibility of a return to its conflictual past continues to shape discussions of national policy and argument about European integration.[19] And yet, for all these caveats, the link between inequality and security at the level of the major powers and within several major regions has been profoundly altered.

In many other regions, however, a much more traditional picture persists, made worse by the weaknesses and instabilities of many of the states involved. In South Asia and the Middle East power and the dynamics of unequal power continue to play a powerful role in regional security—for example between India and Pakistan, Iraq and its neighbours, and Israel and Syria. Even discounting the alleged inevitability of geopolitical rivalry in East Asia, inequalities of power and of status (central to China's international concerns) remain all too visible. Finally, military force is still viewed as relevant to many traditional categories of conflict: border conflicts (e.g. Peru–Ecuador); securing economic advantage (e.g. the Gulf War or China and the Sprately Islands); the promotion of ideological values, whether religious (as in Iran) or secular (as with Western attempts to promote human rights and democracy); securing regime change (e.g. Angola in Zaire/Congo, or the US in Haiti); or, finally, in the widespread use of military power to reinforce diplomacy.

The emergence of a new security agenda?

With the end of the Cold War and the reduced salience of conflict amongst the major powers, attention has increasingly shifted to civil wars, domestic social conflict, ethnic strife, and the ensuing humanitarian disasters. In many parts of the world the traditional contrast between domestic order and international anarchy appears wrongheaded and there is a great deal more 'law and order' internationally than on the streets of an increasing number of states, unable to secure even the most minimal conditions of social order. Moreover, where peace exists domestically it appears to depend 'not so much on the authority of a central power, or the law or a sense of community, but rather on an unstable balance of power between groups prepared to use force'.[20]

Against this background there have been increasingly common and increasingly strident arguments that security should be broadened to include migration and refugees, environmental degradation, drug trafficking and drug-related violence, transnational criminality, and worsening public order in the face of different forms of internal violence. These new security threats derive not from state strength, military power, and geopolitical ambition, but rather from state weakness and the absence of political legitimacy; from the failure of states to provide minimal conditions of public order within their borders; from the way in which domestic instability and internal violence can spill into the international arena; and from the incapacity of weak states to form viable building blocks of a stable regional order and to contribute towards the resolution of broader common purposes.

. This is not a new development.[21] But the pattern has been strengthened in the post-Cold War period. In the period from 1989 to 1994, according to one analysis, there were a total of 94 armed conflicts occurring in 64 different locations. But of these only four could be viewed as 'classical' inter-state conflicts. The overwhelming picture is of large-scale social violence taking the form of internal conflicts, ethnic and non-ethnic civil wars, and wars of state formation. Of the 232 parties to these conflicts, 68 were states whilst 164 were non-governmental actors.[22] The majority of violent conflict is therefore within states, often involving irregular forces, low-technology weapons, and the erosion of the classical conventions of war. Given the weakness of many states, the distinction between public and private war and the state's monopoly over legitimate violence—both of which marked the emergence of the classical state system—have been eroded with the empowering of other war-making groups and the widespread privatization of both violence and security.

Inequality enters decisively into the new agenda of security studies in answer to three central questions: whose security? against what kinds of threats? and how protected? Perhaps the most prevalent theme of recent writing is that the agenda of security studies needs to be broadened and expanded away from the traditionalist emphasis on military power and national security—security understood fundamentally in terms of external military threats to the security of the state. For the expansionists, the critical question 'whose security?' can no longer be adequately answered exclusively, or even predominantly, in terms of the state. In other words, the referent object of security should include, below the state, individuals and other collectivities that face threats to their well-being or existence; and, above the state, humanity at large—people in general rather than the citizens of a particular state.[23] Of particular importance to this chapter is the argument that traditional approaches to security have ignored the security of the marginal, the poor, the voiceless.[24] The security of these groups has been marginalized because of the narrowness and ethnocentrism of the definition as to what constitutes security.

This leads to the second question, namely what kinds of threats are to be secured against? For most developing countries and state elites, the security threats that matter most are internal and are rooted in their lack of development and the uncertain and often conflictual processes of state building.[25] Inequality enters here as part of the broader problems of underdevelopment and North–South relations. But, inequality should be seen much more directly as a central cause of the growth of social violence, ethnic conflict, and civil wars. Poverty and immiseration, over-population, resource scarcity, and environmental degradation foster social conflict and are thereby deeply implicated in discussions of collapsing states and the generation of refugee flows. Inequality (especially understood in terms of aggregate levels of deprivation) does not cause conflict in any straightforward sense. Social conflict can take many forms and cannot be reduced to any simple set of causal explanations. And there is little academic consensus on exactly how inequality is related to social violence.[26] Nevertheless, most conflict studies have viewed inequality as a important factor, especially when taken together with the destabilizing effects of globalization and the increased openness of societies and communities to external pressures.

Third, inequality enters in answer to the question 'how protected?', within what kinds of institutional arrangements? Perhaps the most politically salient form of inequality concerns the relative strength and capacity of states. As the model of the state became universal, so the differences between strong and weak states increased dramatically. In many areas the multiple weaknesses of states and of state institutions are both a symptom and a cause of conflict.

The state has received a very bad press, especially at the hands of the self-styled critical security studies community.[27] Reflecting this perspective, John Keane argues that 'states are positively dangerous instruments of pacification'.[28] It is certainly the case that the state can all too easily become a threat to the security of its citizens and concentrations of unaccountable state power have often been responsible for large-scale political violence. Conceptions of social order that focus solely on the state are unlikely to represent promising solutions to the problem of social violence. Such a point is, of course, easily stated but very hard to achieve in practice. As Claus Offe argues:

These three partial components of social order [state, market, and community] stand in a precarious relation to each other: on the one hand, they rely on each other, as each of the components depends on the functioning of the two others. On the other hand, their relationship is antagonistic, as the predominance of any one of them risks to undermine the viability of the two others.[29]

Nevertheless, there is very little to suggest that politics without the state (certainly in the absence of alternative external suppliers of public order) represents a sustainable road to the containing or curtailing of social violence. Rather, the declining capacity of the state to enforce legitimate order has led in many parts of the world to the privatization of violence as diverse social groups are increasingly able to mobilize armed force; and to the privatization of security as social groups seek to protect themselves, whether through the growth of vigilantism, the formation of para-military groups, or the purchase of security within an expanding commercial marketplace. Where privatized security has been most visible (as in Russia or Colombia), it is the weak and the poor who are the most vulnerable. In this case, as in others, the state can certainly be a major part of the problem but remains an unavoidable part of the solution.

Such arguments about the new security agenda and about the role of inequality within that agenda have become commonplace in academic writing, in political statements, and in the rhetoric of various international bodies. But their foundations often remain unclear or obscure. Why, after all, should these clearly serious and pressing problems be considered as problems of *international security*? There are three sorts of answers.

The first is normative. As a simple matter of morality, it is argued, security is fundamentally about the promotion of human security in the face of all kinds of existential threats. Human security should include safety from hunger and disease as well as from all forms of violence. Moreover, if we seek some measure of the numbers of people suffering, then it is on these forms of insecurity that we must focus. The dismal litany of statistics of those killed in civil wars or by disease and starvation provide the most trenchant answer to the modern-day Panglosses who talk glibly of the myth of the post-Cold War chaos and of the 'innovative', 'durable', and 'hugely successful' international order.[30] Even the thinnest conception of duties beyond borders should provide justification enough for international attention and action.

There are, however, difficulties with the argument that all existential threats to human security should be treated together. Large-scale group violence cannot be analysed in terms of the sum of individual insecurities. It is precisely the existence of group conflict that makes most contemporary manifestations of civil violence so deadly.

Hobbes's war of all against all in the context of extreme individualism is a mild form of social conflict compared to what can ensue from clashes between several social groups, each of whose members display high levels of social trust internally, and no trust or active distrust towards outsiders. Conflict becomes more devastating where the possibility for coordinated action exists.[31]

The use of coercive force and social violence between states or other social groups needs to be understood according to its own distinctive logic and, as such, to remain at the heart of security analysis. It is this, rather than the problem of conceptual fuzziness, that represents the most serious problem with expanded notions of security.[32]

Nevertheless, the monstrous numbers of those suffering as a result of internal conflict should still direct our moral attention. For example, in the twenty years from 1970 to 1990 (i.e. before the end of the Cold War) there were 63 civil wars in the developing world claiming around 8 million lives.[33] But whilst the normative argument is compelling, it does not tell us anything very useful about the *politics* of security. It does not explain why only certain issues come to be viewed as security problems and what the consequences of those choices may be.

A second answer also seeks objectivity, but of a material rather than a moral variety. On this view, these kinds of insecurities are politically important because of the ways in which they have or will come to affect those living in other parts of the world. The insecurity of the weak 'matters' to those living both in neighbouring states and in more distant regions because of the direct spill-overs and externalities that it generates.[34] The new security agenda is important to international security but only where drugs, social upheaval, political violence, or environmental destruction directly affects outsiders. Globalization, mass communications, and the liberalization of economic exchanges are problematic for this new security agenda because of the way in which they facilitate illicit flows of drugs, weapons, or mass migration.

There are, however, also serious problems with this approach. For example, external actors, whether states, NGOs, or international organizations, do not engage with domestic conflict only, or indeed primarily, because of measurably important externalities. But it does capture the spirit of much recent writing on security, both liberal (intended to show how 'our' security is bound up with the security of the poor) and realist (intent on arguing that the new security goals are unlikely to achieve their ends and that they distract us from the management of more important security issues). It also helps to focus attention on the critical role of unequal power in the politics of security. This is the third way of making sense of the new security agenda.

Although embodied in institutions and material forces that acquire a high degree of concreteness and reality, definitions of security and the process by which issues come to be understood as security problems ('securitization', to use Ole Weaver's rather inelegant but useful phrase) cannot be understood in purely objectivist or materialist terms. The meaning of security will always depend on inter-subjective understandings that are socially constructed, that change through time, and that inevitably reflect inequalities in social power.[35] To understand what is meant by 'new security challenges' we have therefore to open up the politics of security: to analyse the political process by which issues come to be defined in terms of threats; identify the actors that are involved in the process of securitization and their relative power; and be especially alert to whose interests are being served by treating issues as security issues. A problem becomes a security issue because a particular group (whether a state, an international organization, an NGO, or the media) has successfully forced it onto the security agenda, not because it is in some objective sense important or threatening. The process of threat creation (the 'how') is therefore a central part of the explanation (the 'why').

Take, for example, the case of drugs and drug-related violence. There is no 'objective' reason why this should be treated as a transnational security problem rather than as a problem rooted in the failure of domestic public policy in the US, or indeed as a problem of economic development in the producing countries. But the ability to define it as a security problem and to give precedence to militarized responses reflects the power of the United States and has important political consequences. Equally, being able to decide *what kind of security* also matters. The security challenges caused by drugs can mean many different things: first, a very traditional challenge to *state security* because of the size of the illicit drug economy or because of the violence to which the drug trade gives rise; second, an equally traditional challenge to *regime security* because of the corrosive impact of the drug trade and drug economy on traditional political structures; third, a challenge to *societal security* because of the erosion of trust and cooperation both within political institutions and civil society; and fourth, a challenge to *human security* because of the worsening conditions of social order and, all too commonly, because of the erosion of human rights by governments and militaries intent on suppressing drug production and the drug trade. The nature of the responses and the political interests served by those responses will vary greatly according to the particular kind of security that is being emphasized.

A further example concerns our understanding of the role of inequality in explaining social conflict, or, more accurately, the kinds of inequality that are deemed relevant. Thomas Homer-Dixon, for example, has produced a series of influential studies on the role of environmental scarcity in driving the poverty, refugee flows, ethnic tensions, and weak state institutions that are widely seen as the cause of so much social conflict in the developing world.[36] Such a view downplays the extent to which civil wars are often fuelled by the existence of natural resources rather than environmental degradation.[37] More importantly, Homer-Dixon's natural-sounding category of 'environmental scarcity' conflates resource scarcity, population growth, and the *unequal social distribution of resources*.[38] In other words, it is politics as much as nature that lies at the heart of allegedly environmentally induced conflicts. Finally, the most relevant inequalities in Homer-Dixon's work, or in the more populist writings of Robert Kaplan, are understood as

local to the communities concerned and there is little attention
to the ways in which the environmental causes of conflict might
be related to international political and economic forces and to
global inequalities—a move that would of course open up very different notions of responsibility and very different kinds of policy
responses.[39]

INEQUALITY AND THE MANAGEMENT OF INTERNATIONAL SECURITY

The previous section pointed to the expanding range of connections
between inequality and security. First, although unequal power and
the resulting dynamics of the security dilemma have receded in
relations among the major centres of power, old power-political
logics remain firmly established within several important and
volatile regions. Second, classic understandings of security have
been supplemented by a new security agenda in which inequality
plays a central role. And third, inequalities of power determine why
certain issues come to be treated as security issues and whose
security needs are to be protected.

To what extent is unequal power relevant to the management of
these security problems? Can old hierarchical forms of security
management be used to address this new agenda? The 1990s saw
the revival of two classic variants of the idea of order via inequality:
collective security and US hegemony.

Collective security offers the purest solution to the dilemma of
preponderance. Inequality of power is not to be feared, opposed,
or balanced against, but is instead to be harnessed to the legitimate
collective purposes of international society. Although the 1990s has
witnessed a remarkable expansion in the role of the United Nations
in the management of international security, the old obstacles
to a full-blown collective security system remain all too visible.[40]
Moreover, as in the past, where collective action has been possible
(as in the Gulf, Bosnia, Haiti, and Somalia), it has depended to an
uncomfortable extent on the political interests of the United States
and its allies and on the military capabilities built up in the course
of the Cold War. An effective *system* of collective security has
therefore remained out of reach, although the collective *element*
in security management has expanded (as in the role of regional

alliances or coalitions, international peacekeeping forces, and UN authorizations of the use of force).

Discussion of the potential role of hegemony in the management of international security also revived dramatically in the 1990s. The end of the Cold War had, it was argued, ushered in a new era of United States hegemony, and, at least in terms of military power, a 'unipolar moment'. In this situation, only the US was seen to have the power to 'be a decisive player in any conflict in whatever part of the world it chooses to involve itself'.[41] Although the notion of revitalized US hegemony rests on broader arguments,[42] the 'recentralization of military power' around the US and its core allies has been a central underlying theme. It is, moreover, an idea that contrasts sharply with previous expectations. In the 1960s and 1970s it had become common to argue that the viability of an international order created and imposed by the Great Powers (the so-called Kissinger model) was eroding and that one of the most important reasons for this was the declining utility of military power and the diffusion of effective military capabilities. From a high point at the turn of the twentieth century, symbolized for many by the suppression of the Boxer Revolt, the capacity of the core Western powers to deploy effective military power was seen to be declining.

What arguments explain the change? To begin with, there are two general factors that have resulted in a marked increase in disparities of power amongst states. On the one hand, the end of the Cold War reduced the geopolitical constraints on Western military force that flowed from the operation of the bipolar balance of power. On the other, the recentralization of power reflects the highly differentiated impact of globalization. Whilst globalization erodes the power and viability of many states, it also increases the power of those states that are best able to adapt and to exploit its new opportunities. Globalization, then, involves not only a shift in power from states to markets, but also from weak states to strong states.[43]

In addition, there are a number of more specific arguments. First, that the US and Western states have moved towards a significant tightening of non-proliferation regimes and towards a greater ability to use United Nations authority to enforce arms control measures, thereby controlling the diffusion of military technologies, especially those relevant to weapons of mass destruction. Second, that the US and its NATO allies have been able to dominate the UN Security Council and to exploit the collective authorization of the use of force for their own purposes. Finally, and most importantly, that the technological superiority evidenced by US and Western armies in the Gulf War demonstrated both that electorates would back the deployment of military power and that high technology opened up new possibilities for successful coercion in ways that maximized Western advantages and minimized the potential for casualties. This was soon buttressed by much more far-reaching claims about the impact of the so-called revolution in military affairs on the nature of war and the deployment of coercive power. This revolution refers to a number of overlapping technological developments: the increased accuracy, range, and lethality of weapons systems, the expanded resolving power of satellites to penetrate the 'fog of war', and, above all, vastly increased capabilities in information processing and communications. The result is to place the United States in a class of its own in terms of military power and, just as important, to offer technological solutions to the political problems inherent in the past deployment of US military forces (especially sensitivity to high casualties).

Whether these trends are viewed as a precondition for world order or as ushering in a new era of Western imperialism, the notion of a recentralization of power is deeply misleading. In the first place, arms control and anti-proliferation regimes remain leaky and both the ability of international institutions and the will of major states to police them highly questionable. The case of Iraq points to the enormous difficulties of locating and controlling weapons of mass destruction even in a country that was defeated in battle, that has been subject to an extremely intrusive verification regime that most would-be proliferators would reject as unacceptable, and where there has been firm political commitment on the part of the US and the UN.

Second, not only have weapons technologies tended to diffuse (with chemical and biological weapons being especially difficult to control) but the long-term trend of the twentieth century has been towards the greater social and national mobilization of groups and peoples formerly under the dominance of the European empires. Here it should be remembered that *both* successful modernization and development *and* the emergence of social movements protesting or reacting against globalization work to reduce the possibilities of control by one or a small group of powerful states.

Third, US military power cannot be considered in the abstract. The very first lesson of social power analysis is that power is quite literally meaningless unless placed within a particular context and set against a given set of purposes or objectives. Hegemony requires both power and purpose. Understandings of interest in the US (and still more in Europe and Japan) do not point in the direction of consistent global (or even regional) engagement or international activism. Interventions in recent cases of domestic conflict have involved both material and moral interests but have clearly lacked the strongly felt geopolitical imperatives of the past. In addition, whilst the domestic political constraints on the use of force are not insuperable, they continue to underpin a deep reluctance to engage in military operations that carry a heavy risk of casualties. To overcome this problem, involvement in even small conflicts has tended to lead to large and complex interventions, again limiting the number of cases in which the US is likely to become involved. Yet, precisely because interventions are selective and limited, there is great scope for political division and conflict over how necessarily limited goals should be reconciled with the costs involved.

Finally, the claims made for the revolution in military affairs often miss the point. On the one hand, potential opponents are likely to do everything possible to avoid fighting on terms or in ways that suit the US and its allies.[44] On the other, the major constraint on the utility of military force has never been about 'winning' but rather how victory can be translated into political outcomes that are both favourable and sustainable. Whether we are dealing with the war against drug cartels in the Andes or the use of military power to help solve civil strife, that translation remains as problematic as ever.

The implications for the management of international security are both mixed and messy. To a much greater extent than realists acknowledge, states need multilateral security institutions both to share the material and political burdens of security management and to gain the authority and legitimacy that the possession of crude power can never secure on its own. As a result, international norms affect the purposes for which force can be used and the manner of its use. And yet, at the same time, a fully worked-out and consistent system of collective security remains as far away as ever, and the effectiveness of collective action continues to depend on restricting decision-making and action to a small number of powerful states that have both capability and willingness. Equally, the tremendous military resources of the United States open up the possibility of unilateral action in pursuit of a wide range of security objectives. And yet the difficulties of translating abstract power into politically sustainable solutions and of meshing the unilateral interests of one state with the broader interests of the international society remain daunting.

As a result, in many regions and on many issues inequality enters into the picture in very traditional guise. Discrimination, hierarchy, and selective enforcement continue to characterize most attempts at controlling weapons of mass destruction. Spheres of influence continue to play a significant role in how regional security management is conceived—for example, the US and the Caribbean; Russia and the Near Abroad; Syria and the Lebanon; India and the neighbouring small states of South Asia. And where inequality of power is viewed as potentially destabilizing (as in South Asia, East Asia, or the Middle East), the balance of power remains central to under-standing regional security and to its management.

CONCLUSION

In terms of security—as with so many other issues—our understandings of what is legitimate, indeed perhaps necessary, to expect from the international political system have grown enormously. These expectations lead inevitably away from a pluralist security order built around minimalist norms of co-existence and in which the balance of power played a central role, and towards a security order that both seeks much tighter control over the use of force in states' relations with each other and reaches deep into the ways in which domestic societies are organized. The normative ambitions of international society in relation to security have therefore come to include: progressively tighter limits on legitimate justifications for the use of force by states; more effective control over the development and proliferation of weapons of mass destruction; and increased concern for the security of an expanded range of social groups against an expanded range of threats.

This hugely increased normative ambition has been driven by

moral concerns. However uneven and inconsistent the concerns may have been, major states have been unable to define their security interests solely in narrow instrumental or power-political terms. But it has also been driven by pragmatic pressures. For those affected by state breakdown or large-scale social violence, security and the provision of public order remain a precondition for sustained and equitable development.[45] For those in the developed world, the dangers of diffusion and spill-over remain very real. However difficult it may be to measure and assess particular linkages, it is highly implausible to believe that, over the medium term, the 15 per cent of the world's population living in the OECD world can insulate itself from the instability and insecurity of the rest. Nor can the countries of the North do without the political support of major developing countries if collective and cooperative solutions are to be found to global problems.

Clearly many contemporary security problems, especially the problems of civil violence, migration, and environmental degradation, are not readily susceptible to military responses. There is a widely shared sense that new security issues need to be tackled within the context of economic development because of 'the resistance of new security challenges to resolution via traditional security instruments'.[46] The interpenetration of security and development issues is illustrated by the way in which regional and international financial institutions have increasingly had to grapple with political and security issues, adding 'peace conditionalities' to the ever-growing list of non-economic factors that influence their lending policies.

But in many cases of civil war and complex emergencies, effective military power remains crucial both to provide the preconditions for political settlement and to implement humanitarian relief. It is certainly true that responsibility for the provision of security has expanded away from the state to include groups within civil society (especially humanitarian NGOs) and international organizations. And it is also true that both have come to play important roles in promoting security in complex emergencies. Yet it is states and states alone that command the legitimate coercive power to promote both individual state interest and also the common goals (such as collective security or humanitarian intervention) that may require coercive capacity.

A good deal of recent writing on post-Cold War conflict has

evoked Hobbesian images of unfettered anarchy, of universal fear of physical assault and violent death, and of violence taking on a powerful life and terrifying logic of its own. Violence, on this view, is no longer part of politics and can no longer be usefully conceived of in terms of political interests.[47] Such claims are misleading. On the one hand, although the horrors are real enough, most internal conflicts involve a high degree of social organization and economic and political rationality. On the other, both state interests and the broader purposes of international society continue to require the capacity to deploy coercive power. Hierarchy and inequality of power remain one (but only one) element of international order, even though the difficulties of harnessing military power to political purposes have become more serious and the tensions inherent in the Clausewitzian logic have grown less manageable.

But whilst it is not difficult to construct moral and practical arguments as to why and how the security agenda ought to be expanded, consistent and coherent international responses are another matter. This chapter has sought to highlight and explain the vast gulf that continues to exist between the normative ambitions of international society and the power-political structures on which effective responses will continue to depend; between the increased demands for security from a growing range of subjects against a growing range of threats and the degree of protection or control that is available. The old foundations for the management of security, in which inequality and hierarchy played such a central role, have been weakened but not replaced by anything more secure or reliable.

NOTES

NOTES TO INTRODUCTION

1. An historical precedent for this is detailed in Jeffrey Williamson, 'Globalization and Inequality Then and Now: The Late 19th and Late 20th Centuries Compared', NBER Working Paper No. 5491 (Cambridge, Mass., 1996).
2. Indeed, the communiqué of the Lyons Summit of the Group of Seven (June 1996) reflected these concerns under the heading 'Making a Success of Globalization for the Benefit of All'. See also Dani Rodrik, *Has Globalization Gone Too Far?* (Washington, DC, 1997); Ethan Kapstein, 'Workers and the World Economy', *Foreign Affairs*, 75:3 (1996), 16–37; UNDP, *Human Development Report 1997* and *Human Development Report 1998* (New York, 1997 and 1998 respectively); Matthew J. Slaughter, Phillip Swagel, and IMF, *Does Globalization Lower Wages and Export Jobs?* (Washington, DC, 1997).
3. In 1998 the IMF held a 'Conference on Economic Policy and Equity' at the IMF headquarters in Washington, DC (8–9 June). For increased concern by the Bank for International Settlements, see *BIS Review* (4 Sept. 1998). See also 'Mr Greenspan's Remarks on Income Inequality', remarks by the Chairman of the Board of Governors of the US Federal Reserve System, symposium sponsored by the Federal Reserve Bank of Kansas, Jackson Hole, Wyo., 28 Aug. 1998.
4. See Chap. 1 of this volume.

NOTES TO CHAPTER 1

1. Stanley Hoffmann (ed.), *Conditions of World Order* (New York, 1968).
2. Raymond Aron, chairing the meeting, argued that world order could mean any one of five things: an arrangement of reality; relations among the parts of world politics; the minimum conditions for existence; the minimum conditions for *co*existence; or the conditions for the good life. Yet Stanley Hoffmann notes that the fifth meaning was instantly ruled out on the grounds that it could lead members only 'to platitudes or to an acrimonious reproduction of the conflicts of values that exist in the world' (ibid. 2). Instead, the Conference chose

to focus on the fourth definition, defining order as the 'conditions under which men might live together relatively well in one planet' (ibid.).

3. Although one might equally quote a plethora of other non-European systems—Asian, African, and pre-Columbian American—each of which were also ordered by hierarchically structured suzerain systems of considerable longevity.

4. Hedley Bull, *The Anarchical Society: A Study of Order in World Politics*, 2nd edn. (London, 1995); Martin Wight, *Power Politics*, 2nd edn., ed. Hedley Bull and Carsten Holbraad (London, 1986); Hans J. Morgenthau, *Politics among Nations: The Struggle for Power and Peace* (New York, 1985).

5. Kenneth N. Waltz, *Theory of International Politics* (New York, 1979); and see the critiques by Robert Cox and Richard Ashley in Robert O. Keohane (ed.), *Neorealism and its Critics* (New York, 1986).

6. Barry Buzan, Charles Jones, and Richard Little, *The Logic of Anarchy: Neorealism to Structural Realism* (New York, 1993); David A. Baldwin, *Neorealism and Neoliberalism: The Contemporary Debate* (New York, 1993).

7. Joseph M. Grieco, *Cooperation among Nations: Europe, America, and Non-tariff Barriers to Trade* (Ithaca, NY, 1990).

8. Robert O. Keohane, *After Hegemony: Cooperation and Discord in the World Political Economy* (Princeton, 1984).

9. Robert Keohane, Joseph Nye, and Stanley Hoffmann, *After the Cold War: International Institutions and State Strategies in Europe, 1989–1991* (Cambridge, Mass., 1993).

10. Raymond Aron in Hoffmann, *Conditions of World Order*; Robert W. Tucker, *The Inequality of Nations* (New York, 1977).

11. Many realists cite Thucydides' account of the Peloponnesian Wars, in which we find that when the 'mighty' make any concessions to what is 'right', alas they lose: Thucydides, *History of the Peloponnesian War*, the Mytilenian Debate (Bk. III) and the Melian Dialogue (Bk. V).

12. Tucker, *The Inequality of Nations*.

13. John Mearsheimer, 'The False Promise of International Institutions', *International Security* 19 (1995), 5–49; Stephen Van Evera, 'Primed for Peace: Europe after the Cold War', *International Studies*, 15 (1990), 5–57.

14. George Bush, 'New World Order', *Public Papers of the Presidents, Administration of George Bush*, vol. ii (1990), 1218–22.

15. B. Grosh and S. Orvis, 'Democracy, Confusion, or Chaos: Political Conditionality in Kenya', *Studies in Comparative International*

Development, 31(4) (1997), 46–65; Luiz Carlos Bresser Pereira, Adam Przeworski, and José María Maravall, *Economic Reforms in New Democracies: A Social-Democratic Approach* (Cambridge, 1993); Stephan Haggard and Robert R. Kaufman, *The Political Economy of Democratic Transitions* (Princeton, 1995); Laurence Whitehead, *Economic Liberalization and Democratization: Explorations of the Linkages* (London, 1993); Adam Przeworski, *Democracy and the Market: Political and Economic Reforms in Eastern Europe and Latin America* (Cambridge, 1991).

16. Michael Ignatieff, *Blood and Belonging: Journeys into the New Nationalism* (London, 1994).

17. Bengt Broms, *The Doctrine of Equality of States as Applied in International Organizations* (Helsinki, 1959).

18. Hedley Bull and Adam Watson, *The Expansion of International Society* (Oxford, 1984).

19. Michla Pomerance, *Self-determination in Law and Practice: The New Doctrine in the United Nations* (The Hague, 1982).

20. Robert Cox, 'Ideologies and the NIEO', *International Organization*, 33 (1979), 257–302; Stephen Krasner, *Structural Conflict: The Third World against Global Liberalism* (Berkeley, 1985).

21. See Charles Beitz, *Political Theory and International Relations* (Princeton, 1979); Thomas Pogge, *Realizing Rawls* (Ithaca, NY, 1989); and Janna Thompson, *Justice and World Order: A Philosophical Inquiry* (London, 1992).

22. Robert A. Mortimer, *The Third World Coalition in International Politics* (Boulder, Colo., 1984); Jagdish N. Bhagwati and John Gerard Ruggie, *Power, Passions, and Purpose: Prospects for North–South Negotiations* (Cambridge, 1984).

23. Karl P. Sauvant, *The Group of 77: Evolution, Structure, Organization* (New York, 1981).

24. Roger D. Hansen, *Beyond the North–South Stalemate* (New York, 1979).

25. J. S. Singh, *A New International Economic Order* (New York, 1977); Mahbub Ul Haq, *The Poverty Curtain* (New York, 1976); Edwin Reuben (ed.), *The Challenge of the New International Economic Order* (Boulder, Colo., 1981); Independent (Brandt) Commission, *North–South: A Programme for Survival* (Cambridge, 1980).

26. James B. Morell, *The Law of the Sea: An Historical Analysis of the 1982 Treaty and its Rejection by the United States* (New York, 1992).

27. Kwame Nkrumah, *Neo-colonialism: The Last Stage of Imperialism* (London, 1968).

28. James D. Cockcroft and André Gunder Frank, *Dependence and*

Underdevelopment: Latin America's Political Economy (New York, 1972); Fernando Henrique Cardoso and Enzo Faletto, *Dependency and Development in Latin America* (Los Angeles, 1979); Raúl Prebisch and UNCTAD, *Towards a New Trade Policy for Development: Report by the Secretary-General of the United Nations Conference on Trade and Development* (New York, 1964).

29. John Rawls, *A Theory of Justice* (Oxford, 1973).

30. Beitz, *Political Theory*.

31. Onora O'Neill, *Faces of Hunger: An Essay on Poverty, Justice, and Development* (London, 1986); Pogge, *Realizing Rawls*; Thompson, *Justice and World Order*.

32. Independent Commission, *North–South*.

33. Such arguments were put very bluntly in Peter Bauer, *Reality and Rhetoric: Studies in the Economics of Development* (London, 1984). More philosophical justifications of fair process drew on Robert Nozick, *Anarchy, State and Utopia* (Oxford, 1974).

34. J. Bhagwati and J. Ruggie, *Power, Passions, and Purpose*; Krasner, *Structural Conflict*.

35. John Williamson (ed.), *Latin American Adjustment: How Much Has Happened?* (Washington, DC, 1990).

36. The official 'market-friendly' view is expressed in World Bank, *The East Asian Miracle: Economic Growth and Public Policy* (Oxford, 1993). Critiques and alternative views are offered in Albert Fishlow *et al.*, *Miracle or Design? Lessons from the East Asian Experience* (Washington, DC, 1994); Paul Krugman, 'The Myth of Asian Success', *Foreign Affairs*, 73:2 (1994), 62–78.

37. John Rawls, 'The Law of Peoples', in Stephen Shute and Susan Hurley (eds.), *On Human Rights: The Oxford Amnesty Lectures 1993* (New York, 1993). An excellent critique is Stanley Hoffmann, 'Dreams of a Just World', *The New York Review* (2 Nov. 1995), 52–6.

38. Although poverty is in fact always a relative measure. See UNDP, *Human Development Report* (New York, 1996).

39. See discussion in World Bank, *World Debt Tables 1991–1992* (Washington, DC, 1992), although in practice, it has been argued, increasing amounts of aid are going to the middle- and higher-income developing countries: Roger Riddell, 'Aid in the 21st Century', UNDP Discussion Paper No. 6 (New York, 1996).

40. IMF, *Debt Initiative for the Heavily Indebted Poor Countries (HIPCs)* (Washington, DC, 1998).

41. World Bank, *Governance: The World Bank's Experience* (Washington, DC, 1994); IMF, *Good Governance: The IMF's Role* (Washington, DC, 1997).

42. UNDP, *Human Development Report* (New York, 1997), 86.
43. Ibid.
44. Ibid.
45. Ibid.; Brian Hindley and Patrick Messerlin, *Antidumping Industrial Policy: Legalized Protectionism in the WTO and What to Do about it* (Washington, DC, 1996).
46. See OECD, *Multilateral Agreement on Investment: Consolidated Text and Commentary* (Paris, 1998).
47. Thomas Franck, *Fairness in International Law and Institutions* (Oxford, 1995).
48. Frederick Abbott and David Gerber, *Public Policy and Global Technological Integration* (The Hague, 1997); Michael Blakeney, *Trade-Related Aspects of Intellectual Property Rights: A Concise Guide to the TRIPs Agreement* (London, 1996); Carlos Correa, *Intellectual Property Rights and Foreign Direct Investment* (New York, 1993).
49. UNDP, *Human Development Report* takes 17 countries for which there are data and shows that exports as a share of GDP in 1913 were 12.9% compared to 14.5% in 1993.
50. Indeed, the least developed countries, which account for 10% of the world's people, have seen their share of world trade drop to 0.3%— half of what it was two decades ago: UNDP, *Human Development Report*, 84.
51. See also Adrian Wood, *North–South Trade: Employment and Inequality* (Oxford, 1994); Patrick Minford, Jonathan Riley, and Eric Newell, 'The Elixir of Growth: Trade, Non-trade Goods and Development', CEPR Discussion Paper No. 1165 (London, 1995).
52. See Diana Tussie, 'From Multilateralism to Regionalism', in *Oxford Development Studies Special Issue on Globalization* (Oxford, 1998).
53. Vincent Cable (ed.), *Trade Blocs? The Future of Regional Integration* (London, 1994); Till Geiger, *Regional Trade Blocs, Multilateralism and the GATT: Complementary Paths to Free Trade?* (London, 1996); Andrew Gamble and Anthony Payne, *Regionalism and World Order* (London, 1996).
54. John Whalley, *Why do Countries Seek Regional Trade Agreements?* (Cambridge, 1996); Haggard and Kaufman, *The Political Economy*; Joan Nelson (ed.), *Economic Crisis and Policy Choice: The Politics of Adjustment in the Third World* (Princeton, 1990).
55. Robert Z. Lawrence and Charles Oman, *Scenarios for the World Trading System and their Implications for Developing Countries* (Paris, 1991). For a more general statement about international institutions, see Krasner, *Structural Conflict*.
56. Eric Helleiner, *States and the Reemergence of Global Finance: From Bretton Woods to the 1990s* (Ithaca, NY, 1994).

57. Ricardo Ffrench-Davis, 'The Tequila Effect: Its Origins and its Widespread impact', *Desarrollo Económico: Revista de Ciencias Sociales*, 37 (1997), 195–214.

58. G. Corsetti and N. Roubini, 'Political Biases in Fiscal Policy', in Barry Eichengreen, Jeffrey Frieden, and J. von Hagen (eds.), *Monetary and Fiscal Policy in an Integrated Europe* (New York, 1995).

59. Geoffrey Garrett, 'Shrinking States? Globalization and National Autonomy in the OECD', in *Oxford Development Studies Special Issue on Globalization*; G. Corsetti and N. Roubini, 'Fiscal Deficits, Public Debt and Government Insolvency', *Journal of Japanese and International Economies*, 5 (1991), 354–80.

60. Ffrench-Davis, 'The Tequila Effect'.

61. Williamson, *Latin American Adjustment*.

62. See Chap. 6 in this volume, and A. B. Atkinson and John Micklewright, *Economic Transformation in Eastern Europe and the Distribution of Income* (Cambridge, 1992).

63. World Bank, *Governance*, IMF, *Good Governance*.

64. Ngaire Woods, 'Governance in International Organizations: The Case for Reform in the Bretton Woods Institutions', in UNCTAD (ed.), *International Monetary and Financial Issues for the 1990s*, vol. ix (New York, 1998), 81–106.

65. For critiques of this agenda, see: P. Blunt, 'Cultural Relativism, Good Governance, and Sustainable Human Development', *Public Administration and Development*, 15 (1995), 1–9; A. Goetz and D. O'Brien, 'Governing for the Common Wealth: The World Bank's Approach to Poverty and Governance', *IDS Bulletin*, 26 (1995), 17–26.

66. Thomas J. Biersteker and Cynthia Weber, *State Sovereignty as Social Construct* (Cambridge, 1996); Joseph Camilleri and Jim Falk, *The End of Sovereignty? The Politics of a Shrinking and Fragmenting World* (Aldershot, 1992).

67. Kenichi, Ohmae, *The Borderless World: Power and Strategy in the Interlinked Economy* (London, 1994).

68. Adrian Guelke, *The Age of Terrorism and the International Political System* (London, 1995).

69. Thomas George Weiss and Leon Gordenker, *NGOs, the UN and Global Governance* (Boulder, Colo., 1996).

70. Franck, *Fairness in International Law*, 4.

71. Michael Shapiro and Hayward Alker (eds.), *Challenging Boundaries: Global Flows and Territorial Identities* (Minneapolis, 1996).

72. L. MacDonald, 'Globalizing Civil Society: Interpreting International NGOs in Central America', *Millenium*, 23(2) (1994), 267–85; Thomas Princen, *Environmental NGOs in World Politics: Linking the Local and the Global* (London, 1994).

73. Weiss and Gordenker, *NGOs, the UN and Global Governance*; Nick Wheeler, 'Guardian Angel or Global Gangster: A Review of the Ethical Claims of International Society', *Political Studies*, 44 (1996), 123–35.

74. John Meyer, David Frank, Ann Hironaka, Evan Schoefer, and Nancy Tuma, 'The Structuring of a World Environmental Regime 1870–1990', *International Organization*, 51 (1997), 623–52.

75. R. Bisell, 'Recent Practice of the Inspection Panel of the World Bank', *American Journal of International Law*, 91 (1997), 741–4; Ibrahim Shihata, *The World Bank Inspection Panel* (Oxford, 1994).

76. See the views expressed by IMF Executive Directors as to the non-accountability of NGOs, reported in Anne Bichsel, 'The World Bank and the International Monetary Fund from the Perspective of the Executive Directors from Developing Countries', *Journal of World Trade*, 28 (1994), 141–67; and M. Edwards and D. Hulme, 'Too Close for Comfort: The Impact of Official Aid on Non-governmental Organizations', *World Development*, 24 (1996), 961–73.

77. This point is not new to the 1990s. See: Richard N. Cooper, *The Economics of Interdependence: Economic Policy in the Atlantic Community* (New York, 1968); Robert O. Keohane and Joseph S. Nye, *Power and Interdependence*, 2nd edn. (London, 1989); Joseph Nye, *Bound to Lead: The Changing Nature of American Power* (New York, 1990); James N. Rosenau and Ernst-Otto Czempiel (eds.), *Governance without Government: Order and Change in World Politics* (Cambridge, 1992).

78. Edward H. Carr, *The Twenty Years' Crisis, 1919–1939: An Introduction to the Study of International Relations*, rev. edn. (London, 1995), which can be contrasted with the opposing account of Alfred Zimmern, *The League of Nations and the Rule of Law, 1918–1935* (London, 1939).

79. Mearsheimer, 'The False Promise'; Charles Glaser, 'Realists as Optimists: Cooperation as Self-help', *International Security*, 19 (1995), 50–93.

80. Robert Keohane, *International Institutions and State Power* (Boulder, Colo., 1989); Kenneth Oye (ed.), *Cooperation under Anarchy* (Princeton, 1986); Volcker Rittberger (ed.), *Regime Theory and International Relations* (Oxford, 1993).

81. Early post-war writings include: Ernst Haas, *Beyond the Nation-State: Functionalism and International Organization* (Stanford, 1964); David Mitrany, *The Functional Theory of Politics* (London, 1975).

82. Robert Keohane, *After Hegemony: Cooperation and Discord in the World Political Economy* (Princeton, 1984). Of course, the claim

that hegemony had declined became hotly contested: see Nye, *Bound to Lead*. Cf. the realist view: Hans Morgenthau, *Politics Among Nations: The Struggle for Power and Peace* (New York, 1967) and Robert Gilpin, *The Political Economy of International Relations* (Princeton, 1987).

83. See Oran Young, 'The Effectiveness of International Institutions: Hard Cases and Critical Variables', in Rosenau and Cziempel, *Governance without Government*; and Woods, 'Governance in International Organizations'.

84. Ian D. Clark, 'Should the IMF Become More Adaptive?', IMF Working Paper WP/96/17 (Washington, DC, 1996).

85. Kenneth Abbott and Duncan Snidal, 'Why States Act through Formal International Organizations', *Journal of Conflict Resolution*, 42 (1998), 3–32.

86. Young, 'The Effectiveness of International Institutions'.

87. Bush, 'New World Order'; Boutros Boutros-Ghali, *An Agenda for Peace* (New York, 1992); Commission on Global Governance, *Our Global Neighbourhood* (Oxford, 1995).

88. From a draft of the *Defense Planning Guidance for the Fiscal Years 1994–1999* which was leaked to the press, cited in John Gerard Ruggie, *Winning the Peace: America and World Order in the New Era* (New York, 1996), 162.

89. William Schneider, 'The New Isolationism', in Robert Lieber (ed.), *Eagle Adrift: American Foreign Policy at the End of the Century* (New York, 1997). For background, see Margaret Karns and Karen Mingst (eds.), *The United States and Multilateral Institutions* (Boston, 1990); Charles William Maynes and Richard S. Williamson, *US Foreign Policy and the United Nations System* (New York, 1996).

90. See Cable, *Trade Blocs?*; Geiger, *Regional Trade Blocs*; Gamble and Payne, *Regionalism*; Whalley, *Why Do Countries Seek Regional Trade Agreements?*

91. The GATT was originally a temporary measure and little provision was made for procedures, voting structure, and decision-making rules. These arose subsequently by evolution—the Council, for example, was created by a resolution of GATT contracting parties in 1960.

92. Vincent Cable, 'The New Trade Agenda: Universal Rules amid Cultural Diversity', *International Affairs*, 72 (1996), 227–46, at 232.

93. Jeffrey Schott and John Buurman, *The Uruguay Round: An Assessment* (Washington, DC, 1994); Carl Hamilton and John Whalley, 'Evaluation of the Uruguay Round Results on Developing

Countries', *World Economy*, 18 (1995), 31–49; World Bank, *The Uruguay Round: Winners and Winners* (Washington, DC, 1995).

94. John Odell and Barry Eichengreen, 'The United States, the ITO, and the WTO: Exit Options, Agent Slack and Presidential Leadership', in Anne Krueger (ed.), *The WTO as an International Organization* (Chicago, 1998), 181–209, at 206.

95. On the background to this, see John Jackson, *Restructuring the GATT System* (London, 1990).

96. Information from the WTO Legal Office.

97. Robert Hudec, *Enforcing International Trade Law: The Evolution of the Modern GATT Legal System* (Salem, Mass., 1993).

98. Anne Krueger, 'Introduction', in Krueger, *The WTO as an International Organization*.

99. John Jackson, 'The Great 1994 Sovereignty Debate: US Acceptance and Implementation of the Uruguay Round Results', *Columbia Journal of Transnational Law*, 36 (1997), 157–88.

100. Odell and Eichengreen, 'The United States, the ITO, and the WTO'.

101. Benjamin Cohen, *In Whose Interest? International Banking and American Foreign Policy* (New Haven, 1986); Andrew Walter, *World Power and World Money: The Role of Hegemony and International Monetary Order* (New York, 1993); Helleiner, *States and the Reemergence of Global Finance*.

102. C. Randall Henning, 'The Group of Twenty-Four: Two Decades of Monetary and Financial Cooperation among Developing Countries', in UNCTAD (ed.), *International Monetary and Financial Issues for the 1990s*, vol. i (New York, 1992), 137–54.

103. A Supplemental Reserve Facility has been created.

104. IMF, *The IMF's Response to the Asian Crisis* (Washington, DC, 1998).

105. Marty Feldstein, 'Refocusing the IMF', *Foreign Affairs*, 77 (1998), 20–33; Nigel Gould—Danes & Ngaire Woods 'Russia and the IMF', International Affair's, 75 (January 1999), 23–42.

106. See Woods, 'Governance in International Organizations'.

107. 'Next AMU? Asia Seeks Stable Currencies', *The Economist*, 342 (8 Mar. 1997).

108. James Mayall (ed.), *The New Interventionism 1991–1994: United Nations Experience in Cambodia, Former Yugoslavia and Somalia* (Cambridge, 1996).

109. Articles 17(1) and 18(2) of the UN Charter require that the UN budget be approved by a two-thirds majority of the General Assembly. US demands for a change in this requirement led to a compromise whereby critical budget decisions would be

adopted by consensus at the stage of the Committee for Programme and Coordination—hence giving the United States a de facto veto over the UN budget: Gene M. Lyons, 'Competing Visions: Proposals for UN Reform', in Chadwick Alger *et al.* (eds.), *The United Nations System: The Policies of Member States* (Tokyo, 1995).

110. Michael Wood, 'Security Council: Procedural Developments', *International and Comparative Law Quarterly*, 45 (1996), 150–61.

111. Bruce Russett, Barry O'Neill, and James Sutterlin, 'Breaking the Security Council Restructuring Logjam', *Global Governance*, 2 (1996), 65–80. Note that among the developing countries' regions there are competing contenders for a permanent seat: India vs. Pakistan or Indonesia; Brazil vs. Mexico or Argentina; Nigeria vs South Africa or Egypt.

112. Benjamin Rivlin, 'UN Reform from the Standpoint of the United States', *UN University Lectures: 11* (Tokyo, 1996).

113. Ed Gillespie and Bob Schellhas (eds.), *Contract with America* (New York, 1994).

114. Ruggie, *Winning the Peace*, 172.

115. Joseph Gold, *Voting and Decisions in the International Monetary Fund* (Washington, DC, 1972), 18; and William N. Gianaris, 'Weighted Voting in the International Monetary Fund and the World Bank', *Fordham International Law Journal*, 14 (1990–1), 910–45, 919.

116. Friedrich Kratochwil and John Gerard Ruggie, 'International Organization: A State of the Art on an Art of the State', *International Organization*, 40 (1986), 753–5.

NOTES TO CHAPTER 2

1. Cf. OECD, *The OECD Jobs Study* (Paris, 1994).

2. They range from a 'free' or preferential trade agreement, in which participants do not have a common external trade policy, or a customs union, in which they do, to deeper forms of integration, such as the tying of currencies, the harmonization of some domestic policies, and mutual recognition of standards and regulations; in the extreme it can involve full economic, monetary, and political unification.

3. See, for example, A. Fishlow and S. Haggard, *The United States and the Regionalization of the World Economy* (Paris, 1992).

4. On the one hand, compared to the large number of participants in multilateral trade negotiations (over 120 countries, of which only the 15 countries of the European Union 'speak with one voice'), a small

number of blocs engaging in inter-bloc negotiations would tend to make cooperative solutions more likely; this supports the hypothesis that regional groupings work in favour of a more open world trading system. But it is equally true that the ability of players within blocs to fare well if inter-bloc bargaining fails tends to make cooperative solutions less likely, which supports the hypothesis that regional groupings tend to work against a more open world trading system. Both effects are at work.

5. See Mancur Olson, *The Rise and Decline of Nations: Economic Growth, Stagflation, and Social Rigidities* (New Haven, 1982). See also Charles Oman, *Globalization and Regionalization: The Challenge for Developing Countries* (Paris, 1994).

6. It makes sense, in other words, to speak of a globalization of inter-firm competition, of a globalization of many markets, and of a globalization of many of the things firms do—investment, finance, networking, the management of information systems—all of which have benefited from the new technologies (as well as from deregulation). But when it comes to actual production, i.e. to the sourcing of physical goods, the trend is more towards an intra-regional growth of international sourcing—towards a regionalization, not a globalization, of production.

7. As Robert Solow is reputed to have remarked, 'We see computers everywhere except in the [productivity] figures'.

8. See R. Z. Lawrence, *Scenarios for the World Trading System and their Implications for Developing Countries*, Technical Paper No. 47, OECD Development Centre (Paris, 1991).

9. See J. Womack *et al.*, *The Machine that Changed the World* (New York, 1990); M. Piore and C. Sabel, *The Second Industrial Divide* (New York, 1994); Oman, *Globalization and Regionalization*.

10. See P. Cerny, 'The Dynamics of Financial Globalization: Technology, Market Structure, and Policy Response', *Policy Sciences*, no. 27 (1994), 319–42.

11. See B. Eichengreen, J. Tobin, and C. Wyplosz, 'Two Cases for Sand in the Wheels of International Finance', Working Paper No. C94-45, University of California, Berkeley, Centre for International Development Economics Research (Berkeley, 1994). See also M. ul Haq, I. Kaul, and I. Grunberg, *The Tobin Tax: Coping with Financial Volatility* (Oxford, 1996).

12. See C. Oman, *New Focus of International Investment in Developing Countries* (Paris, 1984); and C. Oman *et al.*, *New Forms of Investment in Developing Country Industries* (Paris, 1989).

13. Average annual rates of growth of import penetration in OECD countries (the share of imports in domestic consumption) by manu-

factures from the Asian NIEs fell from the 1970s to the 1980s, according to OECD data, as follows (average annual percentage rates of growth):

	1970s	1980s		1970s	1980s
United States	14.5	10.7	United Kingdom	3.6	2.7
Germany	14.5	6.5	Netherlands	12.3	8.4
France	22.6	10.0	Japan	14.2	4.4

Import penetration by manufactures from other non-OECD countries decelerated even more markedly, and in some countries—Germany, the United Kingdom, the Netherlands, Japan—actually declined.

14. Reasons for this decline in the share of variable low-skilled labour costs in firms' total costs include a significant rise in the share of fixed costs due, notably, to rapid growth in Research and Development (R&D) costs and in expenditures on the establishment of global brand-names and on global marketing, as well as to some labour-displacing technological change and a shift towards more high-skill requirements in some cases.

15. The resistance to change often starts with top managers who have built highly successful careers putting Taylorist principles into practice, and for whom it is often difficult to perceive problems, much less solutions, other than through 'Taylorist eyes'. Resistance by middle managers tends to be very strong, and is perhaps more understandable, because their jobs are likely to disappear, or to be changed beyond recognition, in any transition from Taylorist to flexible production. Many skilled workers are also threatened, because their skills—often accumulated through years of experience—may be too narrowly specialized for the needs of flexible production. And unskilled workers are threatened because flexible organizations have little use for workers who lack strong basic literacy, numeracy, social, and inter-personal communications skills, and especially 'trainability'.

The resistance to change can easily be exacerbated by an 'unholy alliance' between the actions of entrenched special-interest groups and voters' understandable resistance to change when they see it mainly as a threat, leading, for example, to protectionist pressures and rigidifying regulatory policies that do little to protect the more vulnerable segments of the population. (Indeed, a further reason for such rigidities may be that governments themselves are often plagued by the internal rigidities and compartmentalization characteristic of Taylorist organizations.) This resistance to change in the face of corporate downsizing, growing wage disparities, high unemployment, and widespread perceptions of increased economic insecurity often leads to a search for scapegoats—notably 'globalization', immigration, and imports from developing countries.

16. For a good discussion of industrial clusters in developing countries, see J. Humphrey and H. Schmitz, 'The Triple C Approach to Local Industrial Policy', *World Development*, Dec. 1996, 1859–77; for an early discussion of 'lean production' in large firms in the automobile industry, see Womack *et al.*, *The Machine that Changed the World.*

17. See Oman, *Globalization and Regionalization*, and 'The Policy Challenges of Globalization and Regionalization', Policy Brief No. 11, OECD Development Centre (Paris, 1996). See also M. Best, *The New Competition* (Cambridge, Mass., 1990); and R. Cooper, *When Lean Enterprises Collide* (Boston, 1995).

18. Evidence of lower minimum-efficient scales of production and smaller average production runs, often accompanied by smaller minimum-efficient plant size, has been reported in electronics, machinery, steel, auto parts, and chemicals, for example. See, for instance, R. Kaplinsky, 'Is Flexible Production Relevant for LDCs?', OECD Development Centre Working Paper (Paris, 1993); B. Carlsson, 'The Evolution of Manufacturing Technology and its Impact on Industrial Structure', *Small Business Economics*, 1:1 (1989); OECD, *Technology and the Economy: The Key Relationships* (Paris, 1992); and J. Humphrey *et al.*, *Industrial Organization and Manufacturing Competitiveness in Developing Countries*, special issue of *World Development* (Jan. 1995).

19. 'Natural monopolies' occur, strictly, when the ratio of minimum-efficient scale of output to total domestic market size is greater than 0.5, since there is room for only one efficient supplier. The more general point of course is that even when a reduction in the minimum-efficient scale of production increases the maximum number of efficient suppliers that can operate in the market from, say, 3 to 7, competition is likely to benefit.

20. Cf. Kaplinsky, 'Is Flexible Production Relevant for LDCs?'

21. Cf. Kaplinsky, 'Is Flexible Production Relevant for LDCs?', and Humphrey and Schmitz, 'The Triple C Approach'.

22. See also Fishlow and Haggard, *The United States and the Regionalization of the World Economy.*

23. Cf. J. Stopford, 'Offensive and Defensive Responses by European Multinationals to a World of Trade Blocs', Technical Paper No. 64, OECD Development Centre (Paris, 1992).

24. See Lawrence, *Scenarios for the World Trading System*, and also R. Lawrence, A. Bressand, and T. Ito, *A Vision for the World Economy* (Washington, DC, 1996).

25. Examples include a number of 'growth triangles' in Asia, as well as

several dynamic growth poles that straddle national borders in Europe, and along the US–Mexican and US–Canadian borders.

26. P. da Motta Veiga demonstrates this point in considerable detail for Brazil: cf. *L'industrie brésilienne dans la transition: vers un nouveau modèle productif?* (Paris, 1997). Others have pointed out that while Chinese enterprises, in Taiwan, Hong Kong, South East Asia, or elsewhere (i.e. the 'overseas' Chinese business community) and in China as well, tend to have a number of Taylorist-like traits—e.g. all important decisions are taken at the top, they tend to specialize in one product, and labour relations tend to be marked by paternalism and low workforce loyalty—Chinese firms also tend to be integrated into a dense network of inter-firm relations based on extended kinship ties that provide through external economies what Taylorist firms are forced to organize at considerable cost. What is important for determining the competitive strength of a Chinese firm tends less to be the size of the firm than the size of the network to which it belongs; this provides flexibility, and what grows is the network. Chinese firms, in other words, often combine elements of Taylorist production with elements of flexible production, especially of the network enterprise (see, for example, J. Meyer-Stamer, 'Micro-level Innovations and Competitiveness', in Humphrey *et al.*, *Industrial Organization*.

27. Cf. J. Stopford and S. Strange, *Rival States, Rival Firms* (New York, 1992).

NOTES TO CHAPTER 3

1. The sovereignty of state governments is defined in what has been perhaps the most influential and certainly the most enduring English-language treatise of the twentieth century, Oppenheim's *International Law*, 1st edn., vol. i (Harlow, 1905), 101, as having three features: independence, and authority in the form of supremacy over territory and supremacy over persons. As 'supreme authority, an authority which is independent of any other earthly authority . . . [it] includes, therefore, independence all round, within and without the borders of the country' (ibid. 171). 'As comprising the power of a State to exercise supreme authority over all persons and things within its territory, sovereignty is *territorial* supremacy. As comprising the power of a State to exercise supreme authority over its citizens at home and abroad, sovereignty is *personal* supremacy' (ibid.). Although Oppenheim does not take this approach, sovereignty may also be understood by reference to capabilities attaching uniquely to the supreme authority. The modern bureaucratic welfarist state has

in many polities been understood as having unique capabilities in the organization of public power, public services, 'official' status, etc.— a capability of *organizational* supremacy. See e.g. Charles Rousseau, *Droit international public*, vol. iii (Paris, 1977), para. 106.

2. This applies to state-oriented attempts to change the terms of the international economic order, efforts to recast international law in the spirit of post-1945 European social democracy, various pre-1990s projects to build an international law of development, and ongoing efforts to develop economic and social rights. For illustrative works, see Kamal Hossain (ed.), *Legal Aspects of the New International Economic Order* (London and New York, 1980); Ronald St J. Macdonald (ed.), *The International Law and Policy of Human Welfare* (Alphen aan Zenkijn, The Netherlands, 1978); Anthony Carty (ed.), *Law and Development* (Aldershot, 1992); and Matthew Craven, *The International Covenant on Economic, Social, and Cultural Rights: A Perspective on its Development* (Oxford, 1995).

3. For illustrative works from the vast literature on unmet problems of social and economic inequality, see e.g. United Nations Development Programme, *Human Development Report* (New York and Oxford, annual); Lance Taylor and Ute Pieper, *Reconciling Economic Reform and Sustainable Human Development: Social Consequences of Neoliberalism* (New York, 1996); Hongyi Li, Lyn Squire, and Heng-fu Zou, 'Explaining International and Intertemporal Variations in Income Inequality', *Economic Journal*, 108 (Jan. 1998), 26; Amartya Sen, 'Mortality as an Indicator of Economic Success and Failure', *Economic Journal*, 108 (Jan. 1998), 1; Amy Chua, 'The Privatization–Nationalization Cycle: The Link between Markets and Ethnicity in Developing Countries', *Columbia Law Review*, 95 (1995), 223; Martha Nussbaum and Amartya Sen (eds.), *The Quality of Life* (Oxford, 1993); Amartya Sen, *Inequality Reexamined* (New York and Oxford, 1992).

4. Oppenheim acknowledged that the term 'is used without any well-recognised meaning except that of supreme authority', and showed some sympathy with the notion that it might usefully be eliminated from the list of necessary characteristics of statehood, and from the science of politics altogether: *International Law*, i. 108. Among contemporary writers, Louis Henkin, for example, argues: 'Sovereignty, strictly, is the locus of ultimate legitimate authority in a political society, once the Prince or "the Crown", later parliament or the people. It is an internal concept and does not have, need not have, any implications for relations between one state and another . . . For international relations, surely for international law, it is a term largely unnecessary and better avoided': Henkin, *International Law:*

Politics and Values (Dordrecht and Boston, 1995), 9–10. See also Harold Laski, *A Grammar of Politics*, 4th edn. (New Haven and London, 1938), 44–5.

5. Sketching a similar argument, David Kennedy suggests that sovereignty has been associated by members of each generation positively with its aspirations and negatively with the excessive formalism of its predecessor. In his characterization, sovereignty in 19th-century international jurisprudence enabled separation of public and private, law and morals. After World War I it represented the aspirational liberalism of universality, defining familiar standardized interchangeable units, providing a basis for a strong process-based but non-substantive legal order, from which were eventually teased out substantive principles such as non-intervention. Sovereignty became not a unity but a bundle of rights, 'demystified, available to be parcelled out, rearranged by law, managed by lawyers, technocrats, social engineers': 'Some Reflections on "The Role of Sovereignty in the New International Order"', in *State Sovereignty: The Challenge of a Changing World*, Proceedings of the 1992 Conference of the Canadian Council of International Law (1992), 237, 241.

6. Oppenheim, *International Law*, i. 160 and 161. Of course, 'Legal equality must not be confounded with political equality' (ibid. 162).

7. Julius Goebel, *The Equality of States* (New York, 1920).

8. Emerich de Vattel, *Le droit des gens*, trans. Charles Fenwick (Oxford, 1916), introduction, sects. 18–21.

9. Cf. P. H. Kooijmans, *The Doctrine of the Legal Equality of States* (Leyden, 1964).

10. For a sweeping critique of 'the anthropomorphic fallacy in international relations discourse', applied to Vattel among others, see Carlos Escudé, *Foreign Policy Theory in Menem's Argentina* (Gainesville, Fla., 1997), 30–31.

11. E. D. Dickinson, *The Equality of States in International Law* (Cambridge, 1920). See also Robert Redslob, *Histoire des grandes principes du droit des gens* (Paris, 1923), 34–40.

12. Realists adopting these premises have consequently had some difficulty explaining non-conforming phenomena, such as relations between a dominant state and a client state whose leaders are simply an extension of the dominant state. On this point, see Stephen Krasner, 'Compromising Westphalia', *International Security*, 20 (1995–6), 115.

13. For example, Thomas J. Lawrence, *Essays on Some Disputed Questions in Modern International Law*, 2nd edn. (London, 1885): 'It is not merely that the stronger states have influence proportionate to their strength; but that custom has given them what can hardly be distinguished from a legal right to settle certain questions as they

please, the smaller states being obliged to acquiesce in their decisions.' The same view was maintained long after the 1907 Hague Conference—see e.g. T. J. Lawrence, *The Society of Nations: Its Past, Present and Possible Future* (New York, 1919). Identifying what he believed was a fissure that must be crossed to build an international law for the future, James Brown Scott observed: 'The "Primacy of the Great Powers" was a fixed idea with Dr. Lawrence, just as the juridical equality of nations is an obsession of the present writer': 'In Memoriam—Thomas Joseph Lawrence 1849–1920', *American Journal of International Law*, 13 (1920), 223, 225.

14. P. J. Baker, 'The Doctrine of Legal Equality of States', *British Year Book of International Law*, 4 (1923–4), 1.

15. Oppenheim, *International Law*, i. 161–4.

16. *Luther* v. *Sagor* [1921] 3 KB 532 (English Court of Appeal); *Petrogradsky Mejdunarodny Kommerchesky Bank* v. *National City Bank*, 253 NY 23 (New York Court of Appeals, 1930).

17. This is a major preoccupation of Dickinson, *The Equality of States in International Law*.

18. Hans Kelsen, *Das Problem der Souveränität und die Theorie des Völkerrechts* (Tübingen, 1920); Léon Duguit, *Traité de droit constitutionnel*, 2nd edn. (Paris, 1921); Jackson H. Ralston, *Democracy's International Law* (Washington, DC, 1922); F. P. Walters, *History of the League of Nations* (London, 1961); David Hunter Miller, *The Drafting of the Covenant* (New York, 1928).

19. E.g. Francisco Suarez, *Tractatus de legibus ac Deo legislatore* (Coimbre, 1612); Christian Wolff, *Jus gentium methodo scientifica pertractatum* (1764, repr. Oxford and London, 1934).

20. J. J. Moser, *Gruudsätze des Europäischen Völcker-Rechts in Kriegs-Zeiten* (Tubingen 1752); G. F. von Martens, *Précis du droit des gens modernes de l'Europe*, 3rd edn. (Paris, 1821); K. G. Günther, *Europäisches Völkerrecht in Friedenszeiten* (Alteuburg, 1787–92).

21. Oppenheim, *International Law*, i. 31.

22. For a comparable if slightly more nuanced scheme, see John Westlake, *International Law: Part 1, Peace* (Cambridge, 1904), 44–8. The practice of interactions was so much more textured as to make every element of Oppenheim's schematic summary contestable. Useful reviews include Gerrit Gong, *The Standard of 'Civilization' in International Society* (Oxford, 1984); Hedley Bull and Adam Watson (eds.), *The Expansion of International Society* (Oxford, 1984); Hugh McKinnon Wood, 'The Treaty of Paris and Turkey's Status in International Law', *American Journal of International Law*, 37 (1943), 262; Yongjin Zhang, *China in the International System, 1918–1920* (Basingstoke, 1991).

23. Oppenheim, *International Law*, i. 154–7. In the case of non-Christian states such as China, Korea, Siam, and Persia, and the Christian state of Abyssinia, 'Their civilisation is essentially so different from that of the Christian States that international intercourse with them of the same kind as between Christian States has been hitherto impossible . . . This condition of things will, however, not last very long. It may be expected that with the progress of civilisation these States will become sooner or later International Persons in the full sense of the term' (ibid. 148 and 149). Lorimer in 1883 offered a similar list to that of Oppenheim, although he regarded Turkey and Japan as deserving of only partial political recognition. In the case of Turkey he accepted the good qualities of the peasantry, but was unconvinced about any possibilities for progress amongst the upper classes. In the case of the Japanese, if they continued 'their present rate of progress for another twenty years' they might well become entitled to plenary political recognition: *Institutes of the Law of Nations*, vol. i (Edinburgh and London, 1883), 101–3.

24. Oppenheim, *International Law*, i. 34; see also 346–7.

25. R. J. Vincent, 'Racial Equality', in Bull and Watson, *The Expansion of International Society*, 239–54.

26. See e.g. Benedict Anderson, *Imagined Communities*, 2nd edn. (London, 1991).

27. For criticism, see Anne-Marie Burley, 'Law among Liberal States: Liberal Internationalism and the Act of State Doctrine', *Columbia Law Review*, 92 (1992), 1907, 1923–6.

28. 'Military and Paramilitary Activities' (*Nicaragua* v. *USA*) 1986 ICJ 14.

29. *Oppenheim's International Law*, 4th edn., vol. i, ed. Arnold McNair (London 1928), 100–1.

30. *Proceedings*, vol. i, 76.

31. Ibid.

32. E. H. Carr, *The Twenty Years' Crisis*, 2nd edn. (London, 1946), 167.

33. Thoughtful reviews of the evolution of international law and the tensions within it, stimulated by the publication in 1992 of the ninth edition of Oppenheim's volume on the law of peace, include W. M. Reisman, 'Lassa Oppenheim's Nine Lives', *Yale Journal of International Law*, 19 (1993), 255; D. W. Grieg, 'Oppenheim Revisited: An Australian Perspective', *Australian Year Book of International Law*, 14 (1993), 227; and M. W. Janis, 'The New *Oppenheim* and its Theory of International Law', *Oxford Journal of Legal Studies*, 16 (1996), 329.

34. This approach is defended in Westlake, *International Law: Part 1*

16–17. It is adopted by the ICJ in the North Sea Continental Shelf cases (*Den. v. Ger., Ger. v. Neth.*), 1969 ICJ 3.

35. Jonathan Charney, 'The Persistent Objector Rule and the Development of Customary International Law', *British Year Book of International Law*, 56 (1985), 1; Ted Stein, 'The Approach of the Different Drummer: The Principle of the Persistent Objector in International Law', *Harvard International Law Journal*, 26 (1985), 457.

36. Cf. E. H. Carr's argument at the beginning of *The Twenty Years' Crisis* that international politics is still in its infancy—a position which indicates Carr's distance from political realists, for whom basic political insights are almost timeless.

37. Cf., however, Guy Ladreit de Lacharrière, *La Politique juridique extérieure* (Paris, 1983). For a thoughtful response, see Alain Pellet, 'Le Sage, le prince et le savant', *Journal de droit international*, 112 (1985), 407.

38. See e.g. Marek St Korowicz, 'Modern Doctrines of the Sovereignty of States—II', *Nederlands Tijdschrift voor Internationaal Recht*, 5 (1958), 150, dividing publicists into three camps: those for whom sovereignty is 'a foundation of the whole system' of international law; those who emphasize 'the necessity of increasing limitations of State sovereignty for the benefit of the international community'; and those 'who do not consider sovereignty to be a basic criterion of the State as subject of international law'.

39. See, generally, Chaps. 2 and 6 in this volume.

40. See e.g. Gunther Teubner (ed.), *Global Law without a State* (Aldershot, 1997); and Chap. 8 below.

41. Anne-Marie Slaughter, 'The Real New World Order', *Foreign Affairs*, 76:5 (1997), 189.

42. See Chaps. 1 and 9 in this volume.

43. See e.g. Alfred Verdross, *Völkerrecht*, 5th edn. (Vienna, 1964); Alfred Verdross, 'On the Concept of International Law', *American Journal of International Law*, 43 (1949), 453; Philip C. Jessup, *Transnational Law* (New Haven and London, 1956); Harold Koh, 'Transnational Legal Process', *Nebraska Law Review*, 75 (1996), 181.

44. Anne-Marie Slaughter, 'International Law in a World of Liberal States', *European Journal of International Law*, 6 (1995), 503, 516–34.

45. See Chap. 5 below.

46. Richard Falk, 'The World Order between Inter-state Law and the Law of Humanity: The Role of Civil Society Institutions', in Daniele Archibugi and David Held (eds.), *Cosmopolitan Democracy* (Cambridge, 1995), 163.

47. See e.g. Thomas Franck, *Fairness in International Law* (Oxford, 1995), on the addition of a popular assembly in the United Nations.

48. On the moral cosmopolitanist idea that every human being has a global stature as an ultimate unit of moral concern, see e.g. Thomas W. Pogge, 'Cosmopolitanism and Sovereignty', *Ethics*, 103 (1992), 48–75, p. 49. See also Pogge, *Realizing Rawls* (Ithaca, NY, 1989); and Charles Beitz, *Political Theory and International Relations* (Princeton, 1979). Pogge proposes division of sovereignty, not the creation of numerous autarkic sovereign units or Rousseau's advocacy of return to the city-state. For a more legally oriented cosmopolitanist perspective, see Fernando Tesón, 'The Kantian Theory of International Law', *Columbia Law Review*, 92 (1992), 53.

49. Hans Morgenthau, *Politics among Nations*, 2nd edn. (New York, 1958), 305–6.

50. Applying this insight, Stephen Krasner astutely noted in 1988: 'The Soviet effort to base relations in Eastern Europe on transnational functional agencies rather than state-to-state agreements has eroded over time, despite the continued material domination of the Soviet Union': 'Sovereignty: An Institutional Perspective', *Comparative Political Studies*, 21 (1988), 66, 89–90.

51. See e.g. Joseph Weiler, 'The Transformation of Europe', *Yale Law Journal*, 100 (1991), 2403.

52. See e.g. Alan Milward, *The European Rescue of the Nation-State* (London, 1992); and Andrew Moravcsik, 'Preferences and Power in the European Community: A Liberal Intergovernmentalist Approach', *Journal of Common Market Studies*, 31 (1993), 473–524. This point is emphasized in the 1993 decision of the German Bundesverfassungsgericht (Federal Constitutional Court) on the compatibility of the Maastricht Treaty with the German Basic Law, 33 ILM 388, 424–5 (1994). The Court found that even after the Maastricht Treaty, the Federal Republic of Germany remains a member of an inter-governmental community, the authority of which is derived from the member states and has binding effect in German sovereign territory only if a German order governing application of law is issued. Germany may terminate membership in the European Union by passage of an appropriate act. Germany thus maintains its status as a sovereign state in its own right as well as the sovereign equality with other states referred to in Article 2 of the UN Charter. Some subsequent German actions, including actions of German courts in the controversy concerning the EU bananas regime, substantiate the impact of this view.

53. For fuller discussion, see Benedict Kingsbury, 'Judicial Determination

of Foreign "Government" Status', *Law Quarterly Review*, 109 (1993), 377. A sovereignty of membership is emphasized in Abram Chayes and Antonia Handler Chayes, *The New Sovereignty: Compliance with International Regulatory Agreements* (Cambridge, Mass. and London, 1995).

54. The issues treated here are acutely analysed by Stephen Krasner in a series of articles: 'Sovereignty: An Institutional Perspective'; 'Westphalia and All That', in Judith Goldstein and Robert Keohane (eds.), *Ideas and Foreign Policy* (Ithaca, NY and London, 1993), 235–64; 'Compromising Westphalia', *International Security*, 20 (1995–6), 115; 'Power Politics, Institutions, and Transnational Relations', in Thomas Risse-Kappen (ed.), *Bringing Transnational Relations Back In: Non-state Actors, Domestic Structures and International Institutions* (Cambridge, 1995), 257.

55. See also *Nicaragua v. USA* (1986), where the ICJ showed little disposition to rule against the US under general international law on the abrupt and coercive denial of sugar import quotas to Nicaragua. On non-forcible counter-measures, see Laurence Boisson de Chazournes, *Les Contre-mesures dans les relations internationales économiques* (Paris, 1992).

56. The formulation in Article 52 of the 1969 Vienna Convention on the Law of Treaties provides that a treaty is void where the agreement was secured by the threat or use of force, but a proposal by a group of developing states to define force so as to include economic or political pressure was rejected. This represented, at the time, a diplomatic and legal victory for a group of Western states. For the perspective of US negotiators, see Kearney and Dalton, 'The Treaty on Treaties', *American Journal of International Law*, 64 (1970), 495, 532–5.

57. For criticism of various actions of the UN Security Council on grounds of conflict with clear or contested principles of international law, see Ian Brownlie, 'International Law in the Context of a Changing World Order', in Nandasiri Jasentuliyana (ed.), *Perspectives on International Law* (Deventer, 1995), 49.

58. See Thomas Franck, 'Clan and Superclan: Loyalty, Identity and Community in Law and Practice', *American Journal of International Law*, 90 (1996), 359, 376–82; and the jurisprudence of the Iran–US Claims Tribunal on claims by dual nationals.

59. Slaughter, 'International Law in a World of Liberal States'; Koh, 'Transnational Legal Process'; Harold Koh, 'Transnational Public Law Litigation', *Yale Law Journal*, 100 (1991), 2347; Lea Brilmayer, *Justifying International Acts* (Ithaca, NY, 1989).

60. See the judicious discussion in Oscar Schachter, 'The Decline of the

Nation-State and its Implications for International Law', *Columbia Journal of Transnational Law*, 36 (1997), 7.

61. See generally Andrew Moravsik, 'Taking Preferences Seriously: A Liberal Theory of International Politics', *International Organization*, 51 (1997), 513; Robert Keohane, 'International Liberalism Reconsidered', in John Dunn (ed.), *The Economic Limits to Modern Politics* (Cambridge, 1990), 165. As Philip Allott points out, the view of democracy as a process for the expression of interests is associated especially with the United States: he contrasts this with what he regards as a distinctive post-Marxist Western European view of democracy as 'a political system for realizing the communal interest': 'The European Community is Not the True European Community', *Yale Law Journal*, 100 (1991), 2485, 2491.

62. As Robert Boyer observes, 'asymmetry of power has definite consequences on the design of institutions, which only rarely enhance efficiency': 'The Convergence Hypothesis Revisited: Globalization but Still the Century of Nations', in Suzanne Berger and Ronald Dore (eds.), *National Diversity and Global Capitalism* (Ithaca, NY, and London, 1996), 56.

63. Robert Keohane, 'Hobbes's Dilemma and Institutional Change in World Politics: Sovereignty in International Society', in Hans-Henrik Holm and Georg Sorensen (eds.), *Whose World Order?: Uneven Globalization and the End of the Cold War* (Boulder, Colo. and Oxford, 1995), 165, 176–7. See also the discussion of 'operational sovereignty' in Keohane, 'Sovereignty, Interdependence, and International Institutions', in Linda Miller and Michael Joseph Smith (eds.), *Ideas and Ideals: Essays on Politics in Honor of Stanley Hoffman* (Boulder, Colo. and Oxford, 1993), 91.

64. David Strang, 'Contested Sovereignty: The Social Construction of Colonial Imperialism', in Thomas Biersteker and Cynthia Weber (eds.), *State Sovereignty as Social Construct* (Cambridge, 1996), 22, 25; Strang, 'Anomaly and Commonplace in European Political Expansion: Realist and Institutionalist Accounts', *International Organization*, 45 (1991), 143.

65. Kenneth Waltz, *Theory of International Politics* (New York and London, 1979). Oppenheim reflected the experience of his times in acknowledging that every now and again the odd state would disappear and new ones appear; but while the rate of new appearances has quickened, the rate of disappearances has declined to almost zero after 1945.

66. e.g. Slaughter, 'International Law in a World of Liberal States', 509–11.

67. Some of these episodes are discussed in Krasner, 'Compromising Westphalia', 115.
68. Jacob H. Hollander, 'The Convention of 1907 between the United States and the Dominican Republic', *American Journal of International Law*, 1 (1907), 287.
69. Fernando Tesón, *Humanitarian Intervention: An Inquiry into Law and Morality*, 2nd edn. (Dobbs Ferry, Md., 1994); Mario Bettati and Bernard Kouchner, *Le devoir d'ingérence: peut-on les laisser mourir?* (Paris, 1987). See also Olivier Korten and Pierre Klein, *Droit d'ingérence ou obligation de réaction?* (Brussels, 1992).
70. Ian Brownlie, 'Humanitarian Intervention', in John Norton Moore (ed.), *Law and Civil War in the Modern World* (Baltimore, 1974), 217.
71. Dan Deudney and John Ikenberry, 'The Logic of the West', *World Policy Journal*, 10 (1993–4), 17–25; and a 'Response' to commentators, *World Policy Journal*, 11 (1994), 122–4 (quotations from p. 124).
72. See e.g. Georges Abi-Saab, 'International Law and the International Community: The Long Road to Universality', in Ronald St J. Macdonald (ed.), *Essays in Honour of Wang Tieya* (Dordrecht and Boston, 1994), 31–41; and Maurice Flory, 'Mondialisation et droit international du développement', *Revue générale de droit international public*, 101 (1997), 609.
73. Max Singer and Aaron Wildavsky, *The Real World Order: Zones of Peace/Zones of Turmoil* (Chatham, NY, 1993).
74. For critical discussion, see Benedict Kingsbury, 'Whose International Law? Sovereignty and Non-State Groups', *Proceedings of the American Society of International Law*, 88 (1994), 1.
75. Martin Wight modelled this worldview as two concentric circles, the inner one being close-knit and bound by detailed rules, the outer one being looser and subject only to rather minimal rules. See Benedict Kingsbury and Adam Roberts, 'Introduction', in Hedley Bull *et al.* (eds.), *Hugo Grotius and International Relations* (Oxford, 1990), 14. A more nuanced analysis of views of the extra-European world in the writings of Alberico Gentili (1552–1608) is given in Benedict Kingsbury, *Alberico Gentili e il mondo extra-europeo: gli infedeli, gli Indiani d'America, e la sfida della differenza* (Milan, forthcoming).
76. Lorimer, *Institutes of the Law of Nations*, i. 101.
77. E.g. Keohane, 'Hobbes's Dilemma', 178–80.
78. Slaughter, 'International Law in a World of Liberal States', 516–34.
79. Jonathan Charney, 'Universal International Law', *American Journal of International Law*, 87 (1993), 529; Bruno Simma, 'From Bilateralism to Community Interest in International Law', *Recueil*

des cours, 250 (1994), 217; D. W. Grieg, 'Reflections on the Role of Consent', *Australian Year Book of International Law*, 12 (1992), 125; Pellet, 'The Normative Dilemma: Will and Consent in International Law-Making', 22.

80. Harold Lasswell and Myres McDougal, *Jurisprudence for a Free Society*, 2 vols. (New Haven, 1992).

81. Cf. Philip Alston, 'The Myopia of the Handmaidens: International Lawyers and Globalization', *European Journal of International Law*, 8 (1997), 435.

82. See Chap. 7 in this volume, and David Miller, 'The Ethical Significance of Nationality', *Ethics*, 98 (1988), 647.

NOTES TO CHAPTER 4

1. Fourth World Conference on Women, 'Beijing Declaration', adopted 15 Sept. 1995, para. 5.

2. United Nations, *The United Nations and the Advancement of Women, 1945–1995*, United Nations Blue Books Series, vol. vi (New York, 1995), 3.

3. One consequence of the UN Decade on Women (1975–85) has been the compilation of gender-aggregated data on many aspects of life. See especially *The World's Women 1995: Trends and Statistics* (New York, 1995); *Women: Challenges to the Year 2000* (New York, 1991).

4. For example, the UN-authorized action in 1990–1 to restore the 'legitimate' government of Kuwait after the invasion and occupation by Iraq was not accompanied by insistence that it become truly legitimate by enfranchising women.

5. This has once again been reduced by the failure of Benazir Bhutto to regain her position after the Pakistan elections in 1997.

6. 'On average, women represent a mere 10 per cent of all elected legislators world-wide': Fourth World Conference on Women, Platform for Action, 15 Sept. 1995 (hereafter 'Platform for Action'), para. 28.

7. Ibid. para. 182. See D. Otto, 'Challenging the New World Order: International Law, Global Democracy and the Possibilities for Women', *Transnational Law and Contemporary Problems*, 3 (1993), 371–415.

8. Platform for Action, para. 182.

9. United Nations, 'Secretary-General's Strategic Plan of Action for the Improvement of the Status of Women within the Secretariat (1995–2000)', UN Doc. A/49/587 (New York, 1994).

10. H. Charlesworth, 'Transforming the United Men's Club: Feminist Futures for the United Nations', *Transnational Law and Contemporary Problems*, 4 (1994), 421–54.

11. In 1994 the first female staff member was posted from the Royal Netherlands Army to the Field Administration and Logistics Division in the Department of Peace-Keeping Operations. Women now constitute 4% of the military personnel in the UN Secretariat: United Nations, *Women 2000* (New York, 1995).

12. Cf. 'Few Countries Treat their Women as Well as their Men', in Amnesty International, *Human Rights are Women's Rights*, vol. v; AI Index: ACT/77/01/95 (London, 1995).

13. Platform for Action, para. 16.

14. Ibid. para. 18.

15. Ibid. para. 156.

16. L. Neack and R. Knudron, 'Re-imagining the Sovereign State: Beginning an Interdisciplinary Dialogue', *Alternatives*, 21 (1996), 135–48.

17. Platform for Action, para. 153. See generally paras. 150–64.

18. Approximately 100 million children, including 60 million girls, remain without access to primary education and over two-thirds of the world's 960 million illiterate adults are women: Platform for Action, para. 70.

19. Ibid. para. 89.

20. Amartya Sen, 'More than 100 Million Women are Missing', *New York Review of Books*, 30 Dec. 1990.

21. In the developing world girls are 4 times as likely to be malnourished as boys; see further C. Chinkin and S. Wright, 'The Hunger Trap: Women, Food and Self-Determination', *Michigan Journal of International Law*, 14 (1993), 262–321.

22. Platform for Action, para. 89.

23. Ibid. para. 136.

24. UNHCR, 'Prevention of and Response to Sexual Violence among Refugees', Draft Guidelines (Geneva, 1993).

25. Tadeusz Mazowiecki [Special Rapporteur of the Commission on Human Rights], 'Report Pursuant to Commission Resolution 1992/S-1/1 of 14 August 1992', 10 Feb. 1993 E/CN.4/1993/50; SC Res. 808, 22 Feb. 1993; SC Res. 827, 25 May 1993. The International Tribunal for Rwanda also included rape as a crime against humanity: SC Res. 955, 8 Nov. 1994.

26. Despite the high incidence of rape in armed conflict, war crimes trials after World War II barely referred to it, leaving uncertainty as to its status as a war crime. See S. Brownmiller, *Against our Will* (Harmondsworth, 1975).

27. The UN Special Rapporteur on Violence against Women was ap-

pointed in 1994 by the UN Commission on Human Rights, Res. 1994/45.

28. Preliminary Report of the Special Rapporteur on Violence against Women, 'The Elimination of Violence against Women', E/CN.4/ 1995/42.

29. Platform for Action, para. 38.

30. Ibid. para. 118.

31. Claims by the International Council of Women for inclusion of women's rights in the Covenant of the League of Nations were rejected because of the consequent infringement of state sovereignty. See W. McKean, *Equality and Discrimination under International Law* (Oxford, 1983), 18.

32. The Charter provisions on sex discrimination were included at the insistence of women delegates and non-governmental organizations (NGOs): United Nations, *The United Nations and the Advancement of Women*, para. 32.

33. GA Res. 217A(III), 10 Dec. 1948.

34. International Covenant on Economic, Social and Cultural Rights, 16 Dec. 1966, 993 *United Nations Treaty Series* (hereafter '*UNTS*') no. 14531, 3–106; International Covenant on Civil and Political Rights, 16 Dec. 1966, 999 *UNTS* no. 14468, 171–346.

35. A. Byrnes, 'Equality and Non-discrimination', in R. Wacks (ed.), *Human Rights in Hong Kong* (Oxford and Hong Kong, 1991).

36. The Constitution of the International Labour Organization (1919), Art. 41 asserted the 'special and urgent importance' of the principle of equal remuneration for work of equal value for men and women.

37. ILO Convention No. 100, 20 June 1951, 165 *UNTS* no. 2181, 303–13. The Equal Remuneration Recommendation was adopted at the same time.

38. Discrimination (Employment and Occupation) Convention, 25 June 1958, 362 *UNTS* no. 5181, 31–42.

39. E.g., Treaty Establishing the European Economic Community, 25 Mar. 1957, 298 *UNTS* 3, Art. 119; Treaty on European Union (Treaty of Maastricht), 7 Nov. 1992, Art. 6. Relevant European Council Directives include: Equal Pay Directive 75/117; Equal Treatment Directive 76/207; Social Security Directive 79/7; Safety and Health of Workers during and after Pregnancy Directive 92/85. See Chris McCrudden, *Equality in Law between Men and Women in the European Community: United Kingdom* (London, 1994).

40. 14 Dec. 1960, 429 *UNTS* no. 10193, 93–121.

41. European Convention for the Protection of Human Rights and Fundamental Freedoms, 4 Nov. 1950, *European Treaty Series* No. 5.

See also Declaration on Equality of Women and Men, adopted by the Committee of Ministers, 16 Nov. 1988.

42. American Convention on Human Rights, 22 Nov. 1969, *Organization of American States Treaty Series* No. 36. The later African Charter on Human Rights and People's Rights (Banjul Charter), 27 June 1981, rep. *International Legal Material* (hereafter '*ILM*'), 21 (1982), 58–68, Art. 18(3) goes further: 'The State shall ensure the elimination of every discrimination against women and also ensure the protection of the rights of the woman and the child as stipulated in international declarations and conventions.'

43. N. Hevener, 'An Analysis of Gender-Based Treaty Law: Contemporary Development in Historical Perspective', *Human Rights Quarterly*, 8 (1986), 70–88.

44. ILO Convention No. 4 concerning the Employment of Women during the Night, 1919, rev. ILO Convention No. 41, 1934, rev. ILO Convention No. 89, 1948; ILO Convention No. 45 concerning the Employment of Women on Underground Work in Mines of All Kinds, 1935.

45. Convention Relative to the Protection of Civilian Persons in Time of War, Geneva, 12 Aug. 1949, 75 *UNTS* no. 973, 287–408; Protocol additional to the Geneva Conventions of 12 August 1949 and Relating to the Protection of Victims of International Armed Conflicts (Protocol I), 8 June 1977, 1125 *UNTS* no. 17512, 3–608, Art. 76.

46. See C. Chinkin, 'Rape and Sexual Abuse of Women in International Law', *European Journal of International Law*, 5 (1994), 320–41.

47. ICESCR, Art. 10(2).

48. Art. 68 of the UN Charter authorizes ECOSOC to set up commissions for the promotion of human rights.

49. The Division for the Advancement of Women has been located since 1992 within the Department for Policy Coordination and Sustainable Development.

50. Convention on the Nationality of Married Women, 20 Feb. 1957, 309 *UNTS* no. 65; Convention on the Political Rights of Women, 31 Mar. 1953; Convention on Consent to Marriage, Minimum Age for Marriage and Registration of Marriages, GA Res. 1763B(XVII), 1962.

51. This was not true of the ILO Discrimination (Employment and Occupation) Convention or the UNESCO Convention. For debates and expert studies on the meaning of discrimination, both within these specialized agencies and by the Sub-commission on Prevention of Discrimination and Protection of Minorities, see McKean, *Equality and Discrimination*, 8.

52. 7 Mar. 1966, 660 *UNTS* no. 9464, 195–318.

53. GA Res. 2263(XXII), 7 Nov. 1967. The CSW worked on the Declaration after a General Assembly request in Dec. 1963. An earlier draft was rejected, with disagreement centring around provisions on marriage, the family, and employment: United Nations, *The United Nations and the Advancement of Women*, 30.

54. Adopted by the General Assembly, 18 Dec. 1979, GA Res. 34/180(XXXIV), 1249 *UNTS* no. 20378, 13–142.

55. For general summaries of the Women's Convention, see McKean, *Equality and Discrimination*, chap. 10; and T. Meron, *Human Rights Law-Making in the United Nations* (Oxford, 1986).

56. Convention on the Elimination of All Forms of Racial Discrimination, adopted by GA Res. 34/180 (1979), Art. 1.

57. UN Human Rights Committee, General Comment 18 on Non-discrimination (Art. 26), 37th session, 1989.

58. ICCPR, First Optional Protocol, 16 Dec. 1966, 999 *UNTS* no. 14008, 302–48; Convention on the Elimination of All Forms of Racial Discrimination, Arts. 11 and 14. At Beijing support was expressed for the CSW work on a draft optional protocol to the Women's Convention providing for a right of petition: Platform for Action, para. 230(k).

59. Cf. the Race Convention, which provides in Art. 29(2) that a reservation shall be regarded as incompatible or inhibitive if objected to by two-thirds of the other parties.

60. Cf. the Convention on the Rights of the Child, adopted GA Res. 44/736, 20 Nov. 1989, which enumerates specific rights for children.

61. Women have, on a basis of equality with men, 'The same rights to decide freely and responsibly on the number and spacing of their children . . .': Convention on the Elimination of All Forms of Discrimination against Women, Art. 16(e). Women's reproductive rights were recognized in the Programme of Action, International Conference on Population and Development, Sept. 1994, A/CONF.171/13.

62. Convention on the Elimination of All Forms of Discrimination against Women, Art. 5(2).

63. Ibid. Art. 11(2)(d).

64. Ibid. Art. 12(2).

65. Platform for Action, para. 25.

66. See Australian Law Reform Commission, Report No. 69, Part II, 'Equality before the Law: Women's Equality' (Canberra, 1994), 49; on regional human rights jurisprudence, see A. Bayefsky, 'The Principle of Equality or Non-discrimination in International Law', *Human Rights Law Journal*, 11 (1990), 1–34.

67. S. Wright, 'Economic Rights and Social Justice: A Feminist Analysis

of some International Human Rights Conventions', *Australia Year Book of International Law*, 12 (1992), 241–64.

68. UN World Conference on Human Rights, Vienna Declaration and Programme of Action, 25 June 1993, *ILM*, 32 (1993).

69. There is an enormous literature on the impact of the public/private divide. See especially J. Elshtain, *Public Man, Private Woman* (Princeton, 1981); K. O'Donovan, *Sexual Divisions in Law* (London, 1986); C. Pateman, 'Feminist Critiques of the Public/Private Dichotomy', in S. Benn and G. Gaus (eds.), *Public and Private in Social Life* (London, 1983), 281–303; H. Charlesworth, 'Worlds Apart: Public/Private Distinctions in International Law', in M. Thornton (ed.), *Public and Private Feminist Legal Debates* (Oxford, 1995), 243.

70. H. Charlesworth, C. Chinkin, and S. Wright, 'Feminist Approaches to International Law', *American Journal of International Law*, 85 (1991), 613, 625–30.

71. C. Mohanty, 'Cartographies of Struggle: Third World Women and the Politics of Feminism', in C. Mohanty (ed.), *Third World Women and the Politics of Feminism* (Bloomington, Ind., 1991); see also K. Engle, 'After the Collapse of the Public/Private Distinction: Strategizing Women's Rights', in D. Dallmeyer (ed.), *Reconceiving Reality: Women and International Law* (Washington, DC, 1993), 143–56; S. Wright, 'Economic Rights, Social Justice and the State: A Feminist Appraisal', in Dallmeyer, *Reconceiving Reality*, 117–42, at 117; F. Olsen, 'International Law: Feminist Critiques of the Public/Private Distinction', in Dallmeyer, *Reconceiving Reality*, 157–70, at 157.

72. This primacy is seen in the language of immediate obligation in the ICCPR compared with the lesser commitment 'to take steps . . . to the maximum of . . . available resources with a view to achieving progressively' the obligations of the ICESCR. The latter also has weaker enforcement measures.

73. C. Romany, 'Women as Aliens: A Feminist Critique of the Public/Private Distinction in International Human Rights Law', *Harvard Human Rights Journal*, 6 (1993), 87–125.

74. International Law Commission, Draft Articles on State Responsibility, Art. 11, provisionally adopted by the Commission on first reading, A/CN.4/L.528/Add. 2, 16 July 1996.

75. Convention on the Elimination of All Forms of Discrimination against Women, Art. 7 asserts women's equal right 'to participate in the formulation of government policy and the implementation thereof and to hold public office and perform all public functions at all levels of government'. This is more expansive than ICCPR, Art. 25.

76. This is amplified by CEDAW General Recommendation No. 21, adopted 13th Session, Jan. 1994. Cf. ICCPR, Art. 23, which denotes the family as 'the natural and fundamental group unit of society' which is 'entitled to protection by society and the state'. The Seventh Protocol to the Convention for the Protection of Human Rights and Fundamental Freedoms, 22 Nov. 1984, Art. 5 asserts that 'Spouses shall enjoy equality of rights and responsibilities of a *private* law character between them' (emphasis added).

77. UN Charter, Art. 2(7) states that 'Nothing contained in the present Charter shall authorise the United Nations to intervene in matters which are essentially within the domestic jurisdiction of any state'. This exclusion is echoed by the general principle of non-intervention: General Assembly Declaration on Principles of International Law concerning Friendly Relations and Co-operation among States in Accordance with the Charter of the United Nations, GA Res. 2625, 24 Oct. 1970.

78. See, e.g., Convention on the Elimination of All Forms of Racial Discrimination, Convention on the Suppression and Punishment of the Crime of Apartheid, 30 Nov. 1973; South West Africa Cases (*Ethiopia* v. *South Africa*; *Liberia* v. *South Africa*), Preliminary Objections, 1962 ICJ Rep. 319; South West Africa Cases (*Ethiopia* v. *South Africa*; *Liberia* v. *South Africa*), Second Phase, 1966 ICJ Rep. 4; Legal Consequences for States of the Continued Presence of South Africa in Namibia (South West Africa) Notwithstanding Security Council 276 (1970), 1971 ICJ Rep. 16.

79. That is a peremptory norm of international law from which no derogation is permitted: Vienna Convention on the Law of Treaties, 23 May 1969, 1155 *UNTS* no. 18232, 331–512, Arts. 53 and 64.

80. R. Cook, 'The Elimination of Sexual Apartheid: Prospects for the Fourth World Conference on Women', paper given at the American Society of International Law 1995 meetings.

81. See C. Chinkin, 'Sources of International Law: Entrenching the Gender Bias', in *Contemporary International Law Issues: Opportunities at a Time of Momentous Change*, 1993 Joint Proceedings ASIL and NVIR (New York, 1993), 418.

82. Report of the World Conference to Review and Appraise the Achievements of the United Nations Decade for Women: Equality, Development and Peace, Nairobi, 1985, A/Conf.11.6/28/rev.1, 1986.

83. In an international context this was relied upon by Judge Tanaka in his classic statement on equality in South West Africa Cases (*Ethiopia* v. *South Africa*; *Liberia* v. *South Africa*), Second Phase, 1966 ICJ Rep. 4, at 305.

84. P. Cain, 'Feminism and the Limits of Equality', *Georgia Law Review*, 24 (1990), 803–47; cf. N. Lacey, 'Legislation against Sex

Discrimination: Questions from a Feminist Perspective', *Journal of Law and Society*, 14 (1987), 411–21; E. Wolgast, *Equality and the Rights of Women* (Ithaca, NY, 1980).

85. One striking example is *Geduldig* v. *Aiello*, where the State Court of California held that it was not discriminatory for disability insurance to refuse to cover maternity expenses because there is 'no risk from which women are protected and men are not': 417 US 484 (1974). See R. Graycar and J. Morgan, *The Hidden Gender of Law* (Annandale, Australia, 1990), 44–50.

86. For a good summary in the national legal context, see Australian Law Reform Commission, 'Equality before the Law'.

87. C. Gilligan, *In a Different Voice: Psychological Theory and Women's Development* (Cambridge, Mass. and London, 1982).

88. C. McKinnon, *Feminism Unmodified: Discourse on Life and Law* (Cambridge, Mass., 1987); *Towards a Feminist Theory of the State* (Cambridge, Mass., 1989).

89. Lacey, 'Legislation against Sex Discrimination', 415ff.

90. H. Charlesworth, 'What are "Women's International Human Rights"?', in R. Cook (ed.), *Human Rights of Women: National and International Perspectives* (Philadelphia, 1995), 58–84.

91. C. Smart, *Feminism and the Power of Law* (London, 1989).

92. For a good summary of the different views, see McKean, *Equality and Discrimination*, introd.

93. However, international efforts to secure the end of the slave trade were based to some extent on notions of equality: ibid. 11.

94. Treaty requirements for the protection of minorities were controversial, as they undermined the principle of sovereign equality of states in that they were only applicable to certain states. The fact that there was no general international legal obligation to protect minorities emphasized that the motivating factor was the preservation of peace, especially with respect to newly created minority populations in Europe after the collapse of the Austro-Hungarian and Ottoman Empires, rather than concern with individual rights.

95. e.g., 'Equality in law precludes discrimination of any kind; whereas equality in fact may involve the necessity of special treatment in order to attain a result which establishes an equilibrium between different situations': Minority Schools in Albania, PCIJ ser. A/B, no. 64 (1935), at 19. The PCIJ considered these clauses in a number of other cases: Rights of Minorities in Upper Silesia (Minority Schools) (*Germany* v. *Poland*), PCIJ ser. A, no. 15, Judgment No. 12 (1928); Settlers of German Origin in Territory Ceded by Germany to Poland, PCIJ ser. B, no. 6 (1923); Acquisition of Polish Nationality, PCIJ ser. B, no. 7 (1933); Access to German Minority Schools in Polish Upper

Silesia, PCIJ ser. A/B, no. 40 (1931); Treatment of Polish Nationals and Other Persons of Polish Origin or Speech in Danzig, PCIJ ser. A/B, no. 44 (1932).

96. R. Cook, 'Reservations to the Convention on the Elimination of All Forms of Discrimination against Women', *Virginia Journal of International Law*, 30 (1990), 642–716; B. Clark, 'The Vienna Convention Reservations Regime and the Convention on Discrimination against Women', *American Journal of International Law*, 85 (1991), 281–321.

97. Reservation made 6 Nov. 1984, Note by the Secretary-General, Declarations, Reservations, Objections and Notifications of Withdrawal of Reservations Relating to the Convention on the Elimination of All Forms of Discrimination against Women, CEDAW/SP/1994/2, 10.

98. GA Res. 42/60, 30 Nov. 1987, cited in A. Byrnes, *Report on the Seventh Session of the Committee on the Elimination of Discrimination against Women and the Fourth Meeting of States Parties to the Convention on the Elimination of All Forms of Discrimination against Women* (IWRAW, 1988).

99. E.g., when Kuwait acceded on 2 Sept. 1994 it entered a reservation to Art. 7(a) denying any obligation to amend the Kuwaiti Electoral Act under which the right to be eligible for election and to vote is restricted to males.

100. See A. An-Na'im, 'State Responsibility under International Human Rights Law to Change Religious and Customary Laws', in Cook, *Human Rights of Women*, 167–88.

101. Reservation made 1 June 1993, Note by the Secretary-General, Declarations, Reservations, Objections and Notifications of Withdrawal of Reservations Relating to the Convention on the Elimination of All Forms of Discrimination against Women, CEDAW/SP/1994/2, 21 Jan. 1994, 19.

102. The legal regime of reservations and objections is contained in the Vienna Convention on the Law of Treaties, Arts. 19–23.

103. Platform for Action, para. 230(c).

104. In the words of Di Otto, 'Their "citizenship" (non) status, both outside and within families, does not even entitle them to protection in the terms of the traditional equality paradigm': D. Otto, 'Holding Half the Sky, But for Whose Benefit?', *Australian Feminist Law Journal*, 7 (1996), at 26.

105. Human Rights Committee General Comment Adopted under Article 40 on Issues Relating to Reservations Made upon Ratification or Accession to the Covenant or Optional Protocol or in Relation to Declarations under Article 41 of the Covenant, 2 Nov. 1994, *ILM*, 34 (1995), 839–46.

106. Indeed, the United States and United Kingdom have already disapproved of the Human Rights Committee's General Comment.
107. Coomaraswamy lists a number of understandings of equality. In socialist states equality requires the state to 'socialize maternity' to allow women to fulfil public work responsibilities, and in others 'equality is an ideological disposition, rooted in attitudes and psychological make-up which can only be removed through strategies drawn from psychology and post structuralism': R. Coomaraswamy, 'To Bellow Like a Cow: Women, Ethnicity and the Discourse of Rights', in Cook, *Human Rights and Women*, 39, 46–7.
108. Morocco and Iraq have made similar statements. Art. 16 is one of the most heavily reserved provisions in the Convention, indicating rejection of one of the significant advances of the Women's Convention, equality in the private domain of the family.
109. Cook, 'Reservations to the Convention', 705.
110. Meron, *Human Rights Law-Making in the United Nations*.
111. *Md Ahmed Khan* v. *Shah Bano Begum* [1985] 3 SCR 844. For commentary on the case, see Coomaraswamy, 'To Bellow Like a Cow'.
112. Despite its name, this legislation excludes all Muslims from sect. 125 of the Code of Criminal Procedure and codifies the law as it was before the case.
113. Coomaraswamy, 'To Bellow Like a Cow', 54.
114. An unambiguous statement of this position is the Egyptian reservation to the Women's Convention, Art. 9. 'It is clear that the child's acquisition of his [*sic*] father's nationality is the procedure most suitable for the child and that this does not infringe upon the principle of equality since it is customary for a woman to agree that the children shall be of the father's nationality.' Note by the Secretary-General, Declarations, Reservations, Objections and Notifications of Withdrawal of Reservations Relating to the Convention on the Elimination of All Forms of Discrimination against Women, CEDAW/SP/1994/2, 12.
115. Unity Down, *The Citizenship Case* (Gabarone, 1995), 38.
116. UN World Conference on Human Rights, Vienna Declaration and Programme of Action.
117. This issue was also fought out with respect to health. The final wording of para. 9 and the removal of a footnote that asserted that actions with respect to women's health were not universally applicable but subject to different state priorities according to 'the various religious and ethical values and cultural backgrounds of its people' was accepted in return for deletion of all references to sexuality throughout the Platform: Otto, 'Holding Half the Sky', 19.

118. Ibid.
119. International Conference on Population and Development, Pro-
     gramme of Action, Principle 4.
120. Equity may be included as a source of international law under the
     Statute of the International Court of Justice, Art. 38(1)(c), 'general
     principles of law'.
121. This was in the context of Platform for Action, para. 274(d); Otto,
     'Holding Half the Sky', 14.
122. For discussion of this debate, see J. Oloka-Onyango and S. Tamale,
     'The Personal is Political or Why Women's Rights are Indeed Human
     Rights: An African Perspective on International Feminism', *Human
     Rights Quarterly*, 17 (1995), 691–731.
123. J. Cock, *Women and War in South Africa* (London, 1992).
124. G. Heng, ' "A Great Way to Fly": Nationalism, the State and Varie-
     ties of Third World Feminism', in M. Alexander and C. Mohanty
     (eds.), *Feminist Genealogies, Colonial Legacies and Democratic
     Futures* (New York, 1997), 30.
125. For histories of indigenous feminist movements and the dilemmas
     for women in national liberation movements, see K. Jayawardena,
     Feminism and Nationalism in the Third World (London, 1986); and
     J. Chafetz and A. Dworkin, *Female Revolt: Women's Movements in
     World and Historical Perspective* (Totowa, NJ, 1986).
126. Coomaraswamy, 'To Bellow Like a Cow', 51.
127. This same critique is made strongly by Black American feminists, who
     argue that white feminists assume an essential feminine existence,
     history, and condition which they do not share. See, e.g., B. Hooks,
     Feminist Theory: From Margin to Center (Boston, 1984); A. Harris,
     'Race and Essentialism in Feminist Legal Theory', *Stanford Law
     Review*, 42 (1990), 581–616; T. Morrison (ed.), *Race-ing Justice, En-
     gendering Power* (London, 1992); A. K. Wing and S. Merchan, 'Rape,
     Ethnicity, and Culture: Spirit Injury from Bosnia to Black America',
     Columbia Human Rights Law Review, 25 (1993), 1–48.
128. See, e.g., 'Platform for Action', paras. 58(a) (participation in
     macroeconomic and social policy-making); 80(d) (full and equal
     participation of women in education decision-making); 142(a) (equal
     participation and equal opportunities to participate in all forums and
     peace talks); and 190(a) (gender balance in governmental bodies and
     committees).
129. H. Eisenstein, 'Femocrats, Official Feminism and the Uses of Power',
     in S. Watson (ed.), *Playing the State: Australia Feminist Interventions*
     (London, 1990), 87–104.
130. 'Women are disproportionately victims of gender-specific abuses, the
     most obvious and egregious examples being the myriad forms of

gender-based violence': J. Connors, 'Mainstreaming Gender within the International Framework', paper delivered at the British Council Conference on Law and the Social Inclusion of Women, Warwick, Feb. 1996.

131. For examples of such violence, see the Preliminary Report of the Special Rapporteur on Violence against Women (reference at n. 28 above).

132. For example, torture is committed 'when such pain or suffering is inflicted by or at the instigation of or with the consent or acquiescence of a public official or other person acting in an official capacity': Convention against Torture and Other Cruel, Inhuman or Degrading Treatment, 10 Dec. 1984, GA Res. 39/46, Art. 1(1). The Special Rapporteur on Violence against Women has drawn attention to the similarities between extreme forms of domestic violence and torture: Report of the Special Rapporteur on Violence against Women, its Causes and Consequences, 5 Feb. 1996, E/CN.4/1996/53, para. 47.

133. See R. Cook, 'Accountability in International Law for Violations of Women's Rights by Non-state Actors', in Dallmeyer, *Reconceiving Reality*, 93.

134. *Velasquez Rodriguez* v. *Honduras*, ILM, 28 (1989), 294–334. The Court held that 'An illegal act which violates human rights and which is initially not directly imputable to a State (for example, because it is the act of a private person . . .) can lead to international responsibility of the State . . . because of the lack of due diligence to prevent the violation or to respond to it'.

135. C. Bunch, 'Women's Rights as Human Rights: Towards a Revision of Human Rights', *Human Rights Quarterly*, 12 (1990), 486–91.

136. Platform for Action, para. 118.

137. CEDAW, General Recommendation No. 19, GAOR, 47th Session, Supp. No. 38 (A/47/38), 1992.

138. UN World Conference on Human Rights, Vienna Declaration and Programme of Action, I, para. 38.

139. General Assembly Declaration on the Elimination of Violence against Women, GA Res. 48/103, adopted 20 Dec. 1993.

140. Platform for Action, paras. 112–30.

141. Ibid. para. 112.

142. C. Bulbeck, 'Less than Overwhelmed by Beijing: Problems concerning Women's Commonality and Diversity', *Australian Feminist Law Journal*, 6 (1996).

143. This compares with the Inter-American Convention on the Prevention, Punishment and Eradication of Violence against Women, adopted by the General Assembly of the Organization of American States, 9 June 1994, Belem do Pará, Brazil, which has been brought

within the mechanisms of the American Convention on Human Rights.

144. Smart, *Feminism and the Power of Law*, raises many of these issues. See also Charlesworth, 'What are "Women's Human Rights"?'.

145. 'While women are increasingly using the legal system to exercise their rights, in many countries lack of awareness of the existence of these rights is an obstacle that prevents women from fully enjoying their human rights and attaining equality': Platform for Action, para. 227.

146. A. D'Amato in a review of Cook, *Human Rights of Women*, *American Journal of International Law*, 89 (1995), 840–4; cf. F. Teson, 'Feminism and International Law: A Reply', *Virginia Journal of International Law*, 33 (1993), 647–84.

147. In September 1996 the Taliban gained control over much of Afghanistan, including Kabul. It closed girls' schools and demanded that women stay inside their homes.

NOTES TO CHAPTER 5

1. Michael Redclift, *Wasted Earth: Counting the Cost of Global Consumption* (London, 1996).

2. M. Gadgil and R. Guha, *Ecology and Equity: The Use and Abuse of Nature in Contemporary India* (London, 1995).

3. This last issue is not developed in this chapter, but it is discussed at length in Redclift, *Wasted Earth*.

4. Herman Daly, *Steady-State Economics* (London, 1992).

5. Paul Ekins, 'The Relationship between Economic Growth, Human Welfare and Environmental Sustainability', unpub. Ph.D. thesis, Birkbeck College, University of London, 1996.

6. Ekins, 'The Relationship between Economic Growth, Human Welfare and Environmental Sustainability'.

7. E. A. Brett, *The World Economy since the War: The Politics of Uneven Development* (Basingstoke, 1985).

8. I. William Zartman, *Positive Sum: Improving North–South Negotiations* (New Brunswick, NJ, 1987), 3.

9. Susan George, *A Fate Worse than Debt* (London, 1988); and Susan George, *The Debt Boomerang: How Third World Debt Harms Us All* (London, 1992).

10. Augusto Varas, 'Latin America: Toward a New Reliance on the Market', in Barbara Stallings (ed.), *Global Change, Regional Response: The New International Context of Development* (Cambridge, 1995).

11. M. Khor, 'South–North Resource Flows and their Implications for Sustainable Development', *Third World Resurgence*, 46 (1994), 14–25.

12. R. Broad and C. Melhorn-Landi, 'Whither the North-South Gap?', *Third World Quarterly*, 17:1 (1996), 7–17.

13. Ibid.

14. R. Mearns, 'Environmental Implications of Structural Adjustment: Reflections on Scientific Method', IDS Discussion Paper 284, University of Sussex Institute of Development Studies, 1991.

15. United Nations Research Institute for Social Development (UNRISD), *States of Disarray: The Social Effects of Globalization* (Geneva, 1995).

16. Anthony Giddens, *The Consequences of Modernity* (Cambridge, 1990), 64.

17. Julian Saurin, 'International Relations, Social Ecology and the Globalisation of Environmental Change', in John Vogler and Mark Imber (eds.), *The Environment and International Relations* (London, 1996).

18. R. Norgaard, *Development Betrayed: The End of Progress and a Coevolutionary Revisioning of the Future* (London, 1994).

19. S. Postel, 'Carrying Capacity: Earth's Bottom Line', in Lester R. Brown, *State of the World 1994* (London, 1994).

20. G. Conway and E. Barbier, *After the Green Revolution: Sustainable Agriculture for Development* (London, 1990), 76.

21. See R. Peet and M. Watts, 'Liberation Ecology: Development, Sustainability, and Environment in an Age of Market Triumphalism', in R. Peet and M. Watts (eds.), *Liberation Ecologies: Environment, Development, Social Movements* (London, 1996); and M. Leach and R. Mearns (eds.), *The Lie of the Land: Challenging Received Wisdom on the African Environment* (London, 1996).

22. F. Buttel and P. Taylor, 'Environmental Sociology and Global Environmental Change', in M. Redclift and E. Benton (eds.), *Social Theory and the Global Environment* (London, 1994).

23. See Peet and Watts, 'Liberation Ecology'.

24. A. Escobar, 'Constructing Nature: Elements for a Poststructural Political Ecology', in Peet and Watts, *Liberation Ecologies*, 50.

25. R. Broad, *Unequal Alliance: The World Bank, the IMF and the Philippines* (London, 1996).

26. B. DeWalt, S. Stonich, and S. Hamilton, 'Honduras: Population, Inequality, and Resource Destruction', in C. Jolly and B. Boyle Torrey (eds.), *Population and Land Use in Developing Countries* (Washington, DC, 1993); and B. DeWalt, P. Vergne, and M. Hardin, 'Shrimp Aquaculture Development and the Environment: People,

Mangroves and Fisheries on the Gulf of Fonseca, Honduras', *World Development*, 24:7 (1996), 1193–1208.

27. Bruce Rich, *Mortgaging the Earth: The World Bank, Environmental Impoverishment and the Crisis of Development* (London, 1994), 148–9.

28. S. Sandstrom, 'Participation and Sustainable Development: Applying the Lessons of Experience', keynote address to the Annual Conference of the International Association of Public Participation Practitioners, Washington, DC, 12 Sept. 1994.

29. V. Campos de Mello, 'Economic Globalization and the Contradictions of "Environmental Management": The Case of the Brazilian Amazon', Working Group on Environmental Studies Newsletter No. 16, European University Institute, Florence, 1996.

30. D. Kaimowitz, 'The Political Economy of Environmental Policy Reform in Latin America', *Development and Change*, 27:3 (1996), 433–52.

31. Kaimovitz, 'The Political Economy'.

32. D. Churchill and R. Worthington, 'The North American Free Trade Agreement and the Environment: Economic Growth versus Democratic Politics', in F. Fischer and M. Black (eds.), *Greening Environmental Policy: The Politics of a Sustainable Future* (London, 1995).

33. D. Goldrich and D. Carruthers, 'Sustainable Development in Mexico? The International Politics of Crisis or Opportunity', *Latin American Perspectives*, 19:1 (1992), 97–122.

34. C. LeQuesne, *Reforming World Trade: The Social and Environmental Priorities* (Oxford, 1996).

35. Ibid. 68.

36. Churchill and Worthington, 'The North American Free Trade Agreement'.

37. Latin America Data Base, *EcoCentral: Central American Economy and Sustainable Development*, 1:17 (10 Oct. 1996).

38. Buttel and Taylor, 'Environmental Sociology'.

39. Vira Bhaskar, 'Distributive Justice and the Control of Global Warming', in V. Bhaskar and A. Glyn (eds.), *The North, the South and the Environment: Ecological Constraints and the Global Economy* (London, 1995).

40. Anil Agarwal, 'Global Warming: Time to Take Stock', *Global Negotiator*, 1:4 (1996).

41. F. Krause, W. Bach, and J. Koomey, *Energy Policy in the Greenhouse: From Warming Fate to Warming Limit* (London, 1992).

42. Martin Parry, *Climate Change and World Agriculture* (London, 1990), 129.

43. Ibid.

44. T. Drennan and H. Kaiser (eds.), *Agricultural Dimensions of Global Climate Change* (Delray Beach, Fla., 1993), 8.
45. See Drennen and Kaiser, *Agricultural Dimensions*, and Parry, *Climate Change and World Agriculture*.
46. M. Grubb, M. Koch, A. Munson, F. Sullivan, and K. Thomson, *The Earth Summit Agreements: A Guide and Assessment* (London, 1993).
47. A. Agarwal and S. Narain, *Global Warming in an Unequal World: A Case of Environmental Colonialism* (New Delhi, 1991).
48. J. Martinez-Alier, 'Distributional Obstacles to International Environmental Policy: The Failures at Rio and Prospects after Rio', *Environmental Values*, 2 (1993), 97–124.
49. Grubb *et al.*, *The Earth Summit Agreements*, 26.
50. Ibid. 26–7.
51. Global Commons Institute, *Climate Change Economy and the Global Commons: Considerations of Efficiency, Equity and Ecology* (London, 1995), 10.
52. See Redclift, *Wasted Earth*.

NOTES TO CHAPTER 6

1. See, for example, on Latin America: John Williamson, *Latin American Adjustment: How Has This Happened?* (Washington, DC, 1990); on Sub-Saharan Africa: World Bank, *Adjustment in Africa: Reforms, Results and the Road Ahead* (Washington, DC, 1994); Gerald K. Helleiner, 'The IMF, the World Bank and Africa's Adjustment and External Debt Problems: An Unofficial View', *World Development*, 20 (1992), 779–92; P. Mosley, J. Harrigan, and J. Toye, *Aid and Power* (London, 1991).
2. See World Bank, *Adjustment Lending: An Evaluation of Ten Years of Experience* (*RAL I*), Working Paper Policy and Research Series No. 1 (Washington, DC, 1988), *Report on Adjustment Lending II* (*RAL II*) (Washington, DC, 1990), *Adjustment Lending and Mobilization of Private and Public Resources for Growth* (RAL III), World Bank Country Economics Dept., Policy Research Series 22 (Washington, DC, 1992), and *Adjustment in Africa*; T. Killick *et al.*, *The Quest for Economic Stabilisation: The IMF and the Third World* (London, 1984); M. Khan and M. Knight, *Fund-Supported Adjustment Programs and Economic Growth*, IMF Occasional Paper 41 (Washington, DC, 1985); M. Khan, 'The Macroeconomic Effects of Fund-Supported Programs', IMF Staff Papers 37 (Washington, DC, 1990); R. Faini, J. de Melo, A. Senhadji-Semlali, and J. Stanton,

Growth-Oriented Adjustment Programmes: A Statistical Analysis, Luca D'Agliano and Queen Elizabeth House, Development Studies Working Papers, 14 (Oxford, 1989); I. A. Elbadawi, *World Bank Adjustment Lending and Economic Performance in Sub-Saharan Africa in the 1980s*, Policy Research Working Papers, WPS 1001 (Washington, DC, 1992).

3. There have also been attempts to evaluate the effects of the policy changes on poverty in developing countries, e.g. G. A. Cornia, R. Jolly, and F. Stewart, *Adjustment with a Human Face* (Oxford, 1987); F. Stewart, *Poverty and Adjustment: Options and Choices* (London, 1995). These show that poverty tended to increase in the 1980s in many (but not all) adjusting countries, but the causality is unclear, since much of the rise in poverty appears to have been associated with the stabilization policies which led to the macro-economic deflation, not adjustment policies; moreover, some of the macro-deflation may have been unavoidable, following the debt and commodity price crisis.

4. See e.g. Alberto Alesina and Dani Rodrik, 'Distributive Politics and Economic Growth', *Quarterly Journal of Economics* 109:2 (1994), 465–90.

5. Moreover, absolute levels of satisfaction depend on participating in activities that are common in that society—e.g. not having a television in a society where TV is common is much more of a deprivation than in a society where other forms of entertainment prevail and TV is the exception: Amartya Sen, 'Poor, Relatively Speaking', *Oxford Economic Papers*, 35 (1983), 153–69.

6. A. Berry, F. Bourguignon, and C. Morrisson, 'Global Economic Inequality and its Trends since 1950', in L. Osberg (ed.), *Economic Inequality and Poverty: International Perspectives* (New York, 1991).

7. R. Barro, 'Economic Growth in a Cross-section of Countries', *Quarterly Journal of Economics*, 106 (1991), 407–43.

8. Lance Taylor, *Varieties of Stabilization Experience* (Oxford, 1988).

9. F. Bourgignon and C. Morrisson, *Adjustment and Equity in Developing Countries: A New Approach* (Paris, 1992).

10. In this statement we are conflating employment of assets and returns with their employment into 'returns to assets'. In the case of labour, the distinction is important because economic changes can lead to a change in the quantity of employment as well as a change in the wage rate.

11. Adrian Wood and C. Ridao-Cano, 'Skill, Trade and International Inequality', IDS Working Paper No. 47 (Sussex, 1996); Adrian Wood, *North–South Trade, Employment and Inequality* (Oxford, 1994).

12. The argument is laid out at greater length and more formally in Stewart, *Poverty and Adjustment*, chap. 2.
13. Wood and Ridao-Cano, *Skill, Trade and International Inequality*.
14. As is argued to be the case, for example, by M. E. Grosh, *From Platitudes to Practice: Targeting Social Programs in Latin America. Volume 1: Synthesis*, World Bank, Latin America and the Caribbean Technical Dept., Regional Studies Program, Report No. 21 (Washington, DC, 1992).
15. Targeting efficiency depends on errors of inclusion (covering better-off people) and exclusion (failure to cover low-income people). In many cases, reforms have reduced inclusion errors but increased exclusion errors. See G. A. Cornia and Frances Stewart, 'Two Errors of Targeting', *Journal of International Development*, 5 (1993), 459–96.
16. This trend has been described as the 'Kuznets hypothesis' since it was identified by Kuznets in a famous article: S. Kuznets, 'Economic Growth and Income Inequality', *American Economic Review*, 45 (1955), 1 ff.
17. D. Corry and A. Glyn, 'Macroeconomics of Equality, Stability and Growth', in A. Glyn and D. Miliband (eds.), *Paying for Inequality: The Economic Cost of Social Injustice* (London, 1994), 214.
18. OECD, *Employment Outlook, 1993* (Paris, 1993).
19. Anthony Atkinson, L. Rainwater, and T. Smeeding, *Income Distribution in OECD Countries: Evidence from the Luxembourg Income Study* (Paris, 1995), 47.
20. Data from Corry and Glyn, 'Macroeconomics'; see also Andrea Boltho, 'Growth, Income Distribution and Household Welfare in Industrialised Countries since the First Oil Shock', Innocenti Occasional Papers (Florence, 1992), who found worsening income distribution in each of 8 OECD countries in the 1980s compared with the mid-1970s. For more information on the UK, see T. M. Smeeding, M. O. Higgins, and L. Rainwater, *Poverty, Inequality and Income Distribution in Comparative Perspective* (Washington, DC, 1990); Anthony Atkinson, 'What is Happening to the Distribution of Income in the U.K.?', Suntory and Toyota International Centre for Economics and Related Disciplines, LSE Discussion Paper 87 (London, 1993); and Central Statistical Office, *Economic Trends*, nos. 129 and 475.
21. Boltho, 'Growth, Income Distribution, and Household Welfare', 18.
22. See table 2 and table 4 of L. Demery, B. Sen, and T. Vishwanath, 'Poverty, Inequality and Growth', ESP Discussion Paper Series 70 (Washington, DC, 1995).
23. Demery, Sen, and Vishwanath, 'Poverty, Inequality and Growth'.
24. I. Husain, 'Poverty and Structural Adjustment: The African Case',

Human Resource Development and Operations Policy, World Bank (Washington, DC, 1993), 16 argues that this was the case.

25. It is sometimes argued that poor farmers do not use fertilizers so will not be adversely affected—but this does not seem to be the case in Ghana: C. Jebuni and W. Seini, 'Agricultural Input Policies under Structural Adjustment: Their Distributional Implications', Cornell Food and Nutrition Program Working Paper 31 (Ithaca, NY, 1993).

26. For evidence on Ghana, see E. O. Boateng, K. Ewusi, R. Kanbur, and A. McKay, 'A Poverty Profile for Ghana 1987–88', *Journal of African Economics*, 1:2 (1992), 25–58; and for Côte d'Ivoire, see R. Kanbur, 'Poverty and the Social Dimensions of Structural Adjustment in Côte d'Ivoire', SDA Working Paper Series (Washington, DC, 1990); for Malawi, see J. Harrigan, 'Malawi', in Mosley *et al.*, *Aid and Power*.

27. Carol Graham, *Safety Nets, Politics and the Poor* (Washington, DC, 1994).

28. Data from Living Standard Surveys of Ghana and Côte d'Ivoire—see Kanbur, 'Poverty and the Social Dimensions of Structural Adjustment', and Boateng, 'A Poverty Profile'.

29. C. Barrett and P. Dorosh, 'Farmers' Welfare and Changing Food Prices: Non-parametric Evidence from Rice in Madagascar', mimeo, Dept. of Agricultural and Applied Economics, University of Wisconsin-Madison and Cornell Food and Nutrition Program (Madison, Wisc. and Ithaca, NY, 1994).

30. It should be noted that in a number of cases (11 countries) wage data relate to the public sector alone.

31. The 1980s saw increasing informalization of the labour market. Between 1980 and 1985, urban informal sector employment increased by 6.7% per annum, while industrial wage employment increased by only 0.1% per annum. Urban unemployment increased by 10% per annum.

32. The share of the manufacturing sector as a whole in total exports increased significantly (by 5% or more) in only 7 out of 33 countries. Among adjusting countries, half witnessed an increase in the share of manufacturing exports, but the increase was significant (exceeding 5%) only in the case of 5 countries.

33. W. Steel and L. Webster, 'How Small Enterprises in Ghana have Responded to Adjustment', *The World Bank Economic Review*, 6:3 (1992), 423–38; C. Liedholm and D. Mead, *The Structure and Growth of Microenterprises in Southern and Eastern Africa: Evidence from Recent Surveys*, GEMINI Working Paper 36 (Bethesda, Md., 1993).

34. J. P. Azam, C. Bonjean, G. Chambas, and J. Mathonnat, *Le Niger: la pauvreté en période ajustement* (Paris, 1993).

35. H. Stein, 'Deindustrialization, Adjustment, the World Bank and the IMF in Africa', *World Development*, 20:1 (1992), 83–95.

36. Expenditure on housing/social security is excluded since the extent to which such expenditure benefits the poor is questionable. It would be desirable also to include expenditure on water and sanitation, but data do not permit it.

37. E. Jespersen, 'External Shocks, Adjustment Policies and Economic and Social Performance', in G. Cornia, R. van der Hoeven, and T. Mkandawire (eds.), *Africa's Recovery in the 1990s* (New York, 1992), 37.

38. UNICEF, *State of the World's Children* (New York, 1991).

39. Evidence from Ministry of Labour, Harare. In Niger, the poor were meant to be exempt from health charges. But according to the Ministry of Health they sometimes had to pay: K. L. Tinguiri, 'Stabilisation without Structural Adjustment: The Case of Niger, 1982–9', in Cornia, *Africa's Recovery*.

40. X. P. Bethune *et al.*, 'The Influence of an Abrupt Price Change on Health Service Utilisation: Evidence from Zaire', *Health Policy and Planning*, 4 (1989); C. J. Waddington and K. A. Enyimayew, 'A Price to Pay: The Impact of User Charges in Ashanti-Akim District, Ghana', *International Journal of Health Planning and Management*, 4 (1989), 17–47; A. Creese, 'User Charges for Health: A Review of the Recent Experience', Strengthening Health Services Paper 1 (Geneva, 1990); M. Chisvo, *Government Spending on the Social Services and the Impact of Structural Adjustment in Zimbabwe* (Harare, 1993); P. Illif, *A Case for Exempting Maternity Patients from Health Service Charges*, mimeo, University of Zimbabwe (Harare, 1992); S. Reddy and J. Vandermoortele, *User Financing of Basic Social Services* (New York, 1996).

41. Richard M. Bird and R. Guillermo Perry, 'Tax Policy in Latin America: In Crisis and After', in Graham Bird and Ann Helwege (eds.), *Latin America's Economic Recovery* (New York, 1994), 21.

42. M. E. Grosh, 'Social Spending in Latin America: The Story of the 1980's', World Bank Discussion Paper 106 (Washington, DC, 1990).

43. N. Hicks, 'Trends in Government Expenditures and Revenues in Latin America 1975–1988', World Bank, LAT-IDP Report 110 (Washington, DC, 1992).

44. Most schemes fail to reach a large proportion of the poor: Cornia and Stewart, 'Two Errors of Targeting', and Reddy and Vandermoortele, *User Financing*. Furthermore, there is a danger that programmes whose only beneficiaries are the poor will not retain enough political

support to last beyond the short or middle run: Grosh, *From Plati-tudes to Practice*, 12.

45. The reforms included privatization, agricultural reform, labour and wage reform, and the reduction of taxes and public employment: Patricio Meller, *Adjustment and Equity in Chile* (Paris, 1992), 27; Economic Commission for Latin America and the Caribbean (ECLAC), *Preliminary Overview of the Economy of Latin America and the Caribbean 1996* (Santiago, 1996); Ricardo Ffrench-Davis, 'Economic Development and Equity in Chile: Legacies and Challenges in the Return to Democracy', Institute of Development Studies Discussion Paper No. 316 (Brighton, 1993).

46. Enrique A. Gelbard, 'Changes in Industrial Structure and Performance under Trade Liberalization: The Case of Argentina', unpub. Ph.D. dissertation, University of Toronto (Toronto, 1992).

47. The role of the real exchange rate is suggested by the short inverse relationship, over 1970–87, between the real exchange rate and both the real wage and the ratio of the real wage to per capita income: Albert Berry, 'The Effects of Stabilization and Adjustment on Poverty and Income Distribution: Aspects of the Latin American Experience', mimeo, University of Toronto Department of Economics (1990), 31.

48. Controls on foreign trade and capital movements were relaxed, labour markets were liberalized (S. Allen and G. Labadie, *Labor Market Flexibility and Economic Performance in Uruguay and Chile*, Report to the Tinker Foundation (New York, 1994), 12), import licensing and quotas were abolished between 1974 and 1977, the level and dispersion of tariffs was reduced, and export taxes on agricultural goods were cut.

49. Albert Berry, *The Social Challenge of the New Economic Era in Latin America*, mimeo, University of Toronto (Toronto, 1995); G. Indart, 'Trade Liberalisation and Structural Adjustment in Uruguay', Working Paper, Centre for International Studies, University of Toronto (Toronto, 1996); A. Melgar, 'El mercado de trabajo en la Coyuntura', *SUMA*, 4 (1988); A. Melgar, 'Aspectos metodológicos sobre la distribución del ingreso en Uruguay', Centro Latinoamericano de Economía Humana (CLAEH), Serie Investigaciones, No. 12 (Montevideo, 1981).

50. E. Favaro and A. Bensión, 'Uruguay', in S. Rottenberg (ed.), *The Political Economy of Poverty, Equity and Growth: Costa Rica and Uruguay* (Washington, DC, 1993), 276.

51. Jaime Ros, 'Mexico's Trade and Industrialisation Experience since 1960: A Reconsideration of Past Policies and Assessment of Current Reforms', in G. K. Helleiner (ed.), *Trade Policy, Industrialisation and Development: New Perspectives* (Oxford, 1994), 208.

52. D. Alarcon and T. McKinley, 'Widening Wage Dispersion under Structural Adjustment in Mexico', paper presented at the symposium 'El impacto del ajuste estructrural en los mercados de trabajo y en la distribución del ingreso en América Latina', San José, Costa Rica, 1994.
53. Ibid., table 6.
54. Ibid., table 5.
55. G. Hanson and R. C. Feenstra, 'Foreign Investment, Outsourcing and Relative Wages', paper presented at the conference 'Political Economy of Trade Policy', Columbia University, New York, 1994.
56. Ibid. 33.
57. Data from I. Sanatan and M. Rather, 'The Distributive Impact of Fiscal Policy in the Dominican Republic', in R. Hausmann and R. Ribobón (eds.), *Government Spending and Distribution in Venezuela* (Washington, DC, 1993), where the rise in inflation is blamed for rising inequality.
58. J. A. Ocampo, 'Trade Policy and Industrialisation in Colombia, 1967–91', in Helleiner, *Trade Policy*, 145.
59. Importantly, there was an unusually marked decline in earnings differentials across educational levels and between genders, declines especially concentrated in the late 1970s, while the economy was still growing rapidly, and in the early 1980s, when it was not: J. Tenjo, 'Evolución de los retornos a la inversión en educación 1976–89', in *Educación, mercado de trabajo y desarrollo en Colombia*, special issue of *Planeación y desarrollo* (Bogotá, 1993). The statistical evidence is matched by a growing concern in Colombia that the new 'model' is having an adverse effect on income distribution: Libardo Sarmiento, 'Reformas a la política social', *Coyuntura social*, 8 (1993).
60. Data from C. Larrea, 'Structural Adjustment, Income Distribution and Employment in Ecuador', in Albert Berry (ed.), *Poverty, Economic Reform and Income Distribution in Latin America* (London, 1998), 179–204.
61. Other possible candidates, both of which have liberalized too recently for the evidence to be clear at this time, are Peru and Jamaica. The latter case is discussed by Ashu Handa, *Structural Adjustment and Income Distribution in Jamaica, 1989–93*, mimeo (Kingston, Jamaica, 1993, 1995).
62. J. D. Trejos and P. Saumo, 'Pobreza y distribución del ingreso en el era de ajuste: Costa Rica 1980–92', paper presented at the symposium 'El impacto del ajuste estructural en los mercados de trabajo y en la distribución del ingreso en America Latina', San Jose, Costa Rica, 1994.

63. Berry, 'The Social Challenge', table 8.
64. R. Weisskoff, 'Paraguayan Agro-export Model of Development', *World Development*, 20 (1992), 10; R. Weisskoff, 'Income Distribution and Economic Change in Paraguay, 1972–1988', *The Review of Income and Wealth*, series 38:2 (1992), 165–84.
65. Calculated from Weisskoff, 'Income Distribution'.
66. Sri Lanka apparently showed a major improvement in the late 1980s, after a period in which income distribution worsened, but in part at least this appears to be due to a change in the source of data.
67. J. Fei, G. Ranis, and S. Kuo, *Growth with Equity: The Taiwan Case* (Oxford, 1979), table 7.
68. World Bank, *Structural and Sectoral Operations* (Washington, DC, 1992).
69. Albert Berry and Felicia Knaul, 'El empleo, la distribución del ingreso y los sectores sociales: lecciones para Colombia de la bonanza petrolera de Indonesia', special issue of *Planeación y Desarrollo* (1994), 4.
70. See World Bank, *Report on Adjustment*; M. Ravallion and M. Huppi, 'Poverty and Undernutrition in Indonesia during the 1980s', World Bank Policy Planning and Research Working Papers 286 (Washington, DC, 1989); according to the World Bank's *World Development Report 1993* (Washington, DC, 1993) the poverty incidence in 1991 was 17.8%.
71. Deng Xia-Ping, 'Emancipate One's Thinking, Seek Truth from Facts, Unite and Look Forward', speech delivered in Beijing, 1978.
72. K. Griffin and Z. Renwei, *The Distribution of Income in China* (London, 1993) gives a Gini for the rural areas of 0.338 in 1988, compared with Howes' 0.307 in 1988: S. Howes, *Income Inequality in Urban China in the 1980s: Level, Trends and Determinants* (London, 1993).
73. S. Howes and A. Hussein, 'Regional Growth and Inequality in Rural China', STICERD working paper, London School of Economics (London, 1993).
74. This does not tally with Howes' estimate of 0.1769 in 1990. Both Howes and Griffin *et al.* agree, however, that there was a significant rise in urban inequality from 1984 to 1988/90—see Griffin and Renwei, *The Distribution of Income in China*.
75. Griffin and Renwei, *The Distribution of Income in China*.
76. World Bank, *China: Strategies for Reducing Poverty in the 1990s* (Washington, DC, 1992).
77. Carl Riskin, 'Income Distribution and Poverty in Rural China', in Griffin and Renwei, *The Distribution of Income in China*, 135–72.
78. Berry *et al.*, 'Global Economic Inequality'.

79. Ibid. 338.
80. Ibid. 341.
81. World Bank, *World Development Report 1992* (Washington, DC, 1992), 220.
82. Berry *et al.*, 'Global Economic Inequality', 341.

NOTES TO CHAPTER 7

1. These figures are taken from World Bank, *World Development Report 1996: From Plan to Market* (New York, 1996).
2. See, for instance, D. Parfit, *Equality or Priority?*, Lindley Lecture, University of Kansas (Lawrence, Kan., 1995); J. Raz, *The Morality of Freedom* (Oxford, 1986), chap. 9.
3. For a fuller discussion, see my paper 'Equality and Justice', *Ratio*, 10 (1997), 222–37.
4. For a fuller treatment of this question, with whose conclusions I largely agree, see C. Brown, 'International Political Theory and the Idea of World Community', in K. Booth and S. Smith (eds.), *International Relations Theory Today* (Cambridge, 1995).
5. See, for example, H. Steiner, 'Territorial Justice', in S. Caney, D. George, and P. Jones (eds.), *National Rights, International Obligations* (Boulder, Colo. and Oxford, 1996); B. Barry, 'Humanity and Justice in Global Perspective', in B. Barry, *Democracy, Power and Justice* (Oxford, 1989); C. Beitz, *Political Theory and International Relations* (Princeton, 1979), pt. 3, sect. 2.
6. R. Dworkin, 'Equality of Resources', *Philosophy and Public Affairs*, 10 (1981), 283–345.
7. See R. Dworkin, 'What is Equality? Part 3: The Place of Liberty', *Iowa Law Review*, 73 (1987–8), 1–54.
8. Take a different, albeit hypothetical, case. Suppose that the Marshall Plan and the post-war German economic miracle had never happened, so that the German per capita resource base was today lower than, say, Portugal's. Could Germans argue that they should be given more resources because neither they nor their predecessors could be held responsible for the consequences of the Nazi regime? What would have to be shown to make this claim a plausible one?
9. For more on the contrast between humanitarianism and justice, see Barry, 'Humanity and Justice in Global Perspective', or B. Barry, *Liberty and Justice* (Oxford, 1991).
10. Henry Shue has put this well in the best account of basic rights known to me. 'Basic rights, then, are everyone's minimum reasonable demands on the rest of humanity. They are the rational basis for

justified demands the denial of which no self-respecting person can reasonably be expected to accept. Why should anything be so important? The reason is that rights are basic in the sense used here only if enjoyment of them is essential to the enjoyment of all other rights': H. Shue, *Basic Rights: Subsistence, Affluence and U.S. Foreign Policy* (Princeton, 1980), 19.

11. This is true, for instance, of the Universal Declaration of Human Rights, adopted by the United Nations in 1948. For discussion, see J. Nickel, *Making Sense of Human Rights* (Berkeley, 1987); M. Cranston, *What are Human Rights?* (London, 1973).

12. See the discussion of this issue in R. J. Vincent, *Human Rights and International Relations* (Cambridge, 1986), chap. 3.

13. M. Walzer, *Thick and Thin: Moral Argument at Home and Abroad* (Notre Dame, Ind., 1994), 17.

14. Someone might choose to starve himself for religious or political reasons, and in these circumstances we might be able to regard starvation as one element in a valuable life. But this must be an inner decision taken by the person himself; it would never be justifiable for an outsider to withhold food on the supposition that a starving person would be better off without it. So the basic right to food is not impugned by this case.

15. Alan Gewirth has attempted to derive recognition of basic rights from the requirements of practical rationality itself, but I do not think that the attempt succeeds. See A. Gewirth, 'The Basis and Content of Human Rights', in J. R. Pennock and J. W. Chapman (eds.), *Nomos 23: Human Rights* (New York, 1981), and for critiques, R. B. Friedman, 'The Basis of Human Rights: A Criticism of Gewirth's Theory' and M. P. Golding, 'From Prudence to Rights: A Critique' in the same volume.

16. For a fuller defence of this claim, see my discussion of ethical particularism in *On Nationality* (Oxford, 1995), chap. 3.

17. A. Sen, *Poverty and Famines* (Oxford, 1981), esp. chap. 10.

18. See, for instance, *Our Global Neighbourhood: The Report of the Commission on Global Governance* (New York, 1995), 190–201.

19. There is a dearth of recent literature on the concept of international exploitation, but see A. De-Shalit, 'Transnational and International Exploitation', *Political Studies*, 46: 4 (1998), 693–708.

20. There are other senses that I shall leave aside. For a wide-ranging discussion, see R. Goodin, 'Exploiting a Situation and Exploiting a Person', in A. Reeve (ed.), *Modern Theories of Exploitation* (London, 1987). The analysis of exploitation given here draws upon the account I presented in 'Exploitation in the Market' in the same volume.

21. For an extended discussion of vulnerability and its moral implications, see R. Goodin, *Protecting the Vulnerable* (Chicago, 1985). Chap. 6 applies the analysis to the question of foreign aid.

22. In saying this I am assuming that exploitation has individual victims even where the parties to the transaction are collectives, such as the management of a firm and the union that represents its employees. If the management exploits the union's lack of bargaining power to impose onerous working conditions, it is individual workers who will bear the brunt. Where exploitation does not create significant costs for individuals—as might be the case if a large retail firm used its market position to exploit a supplier without driving the supplier out of business—it remains unfair, but does not breach the norm I am invoking.

23. This argument is made in A. Emmanuel, *Unequal Exchange: A Study in the Imperialism of Trade* (London, 1972).

24. Further problems with the Marxist analysis are brought out in De-Shalit, 'Transnational and International Exploitation'.

25. For a general analysis of the reasons why the North–South power imbalance is unlikely to shift in favour of the South, see T. Smith, 'Changing Configurations of Power in North–South Relations since 1945', *International Organization*, 31 (1977), 1–27.

26. For an illuminating discussion of the general problems involved in rectifying historical injustices, see J. Waldron, 'Superseding Historic Injustice', *Ethics*, 103 (1992–3), 4–28.

NOTES TO CHAPTER 8

1. P. Kosonen, 'Competitiveness, Welfare Systems and the Debate on Social Competition', paper presented to the RC19 Conference on Comparative Research on Welfare State Reforms, International Studies Association, University of Pavia, Italy, Sept. 1995.

2. F. Castles, *Families of Nations* (Aldershot, 1993).

3. R. Baubock, *Transnational Citizenship* (Cheltenham, 1994).

4. D. Held, *Political Theory Today* (Cambridge, 1991) and *Democracy and the Global Order: From the Modern State to Cosmopolitan Governance* (Cambridge, 1995).

5. L. Sklair, *Sociology of the Global System* (Brighton, 1991); M. Featherstone, *Global Culture: Nationalism, Globalization and Modernity* (London, 1990).

6. Paul Hirst and Graham Thompson, *Globalization in Question* (Cambridge, 1996); Susan Strange, 'Wake Up, Krasner: The World Has Changed', *Review of International Political Economy*, 1 (1994),

209–20; A. Griffiths and S. Wall, *Applied Economics* (London, 1993); Richard Stubbs and Geoffrey Underhill (eds.), *Political Economy and the Changing Global Order* (London, 1994).

7. Fred Halliday, *Rethinking International Relations* (London, 1994); M. Shaw, *Global Society and International Relations* (Cambridge, 1994).

8. M. Kleinman and D. Piachaud, 'European Social Policy: Conceptions and Choices', *Journal of European Social Policy*, 1:1 (1993), 1–19.

9. S. Liebfried, 'The Social Dimensions of the EU: En Route to Positively Joint Sovereignty', *Journal of European Social Policy*, 4:4 (1994).

10. E. Huber and J. D. Stephens, 'The Future of the Social Democratic Welfare State: Options in the Face of Economic Internationalization and European Integration', paper presented to the Conference on Comparative Research on Welfare States in Transition, International Sociological Association, Wadham College, Oxford, Sept. 1993.

11. G. Esping-Andersen, *Welfare States in Transition* (London, 1996).

12. A. de Swann, 'Perspectives for Transitional Social Policy in Europe: Social Transfers from West to East', in A. de Swann (ed.), *Social Policy beyond Borders* (Amsterdam, 1994).

13. Esping-Anderson, *Welfare States in Transition*.

14. Bob Deacon, 'Action for Social Change: A New Facet of Preventative Peace-Keeping', report for UNPREDEP, National Research and Development Centre for Welfare and Health, STAKES (Helsinki, 1996).

15. Bob Deacon, *Global Social Policy* (London, 1998).

16. Kleinman and Piachaud, 'European Social Policy'.

17. C. Grinspin and M. A. Cameron (eds.), *The Political Economy of North American Free Trade* (London, 1993).

18. E. Meehan, *Citizenship and the European Community* (London, 1993).

19. S. Davidson, 'The European System for Protecting Human Rights', in S. Davidson (ed.), *Human Rights* (Oxford, 1993).

20. P. de Senarclens, 'Regime Theory and the Study of International Organizations', *International Social Science Journal*, 138 (Nov. 1993), 460.

21. G. Kopits, 'Social Security in Economies in Transition', in *Restructuring Social Security in Central and Eastern Europe: A Guide to Recent Developments*, ISSA Policy Issues and Options (Geneva, 1994).

22. Vito Tanzi (ed.), *Fiscal Policies in Economies in Transition* (Washington, DC, 1992); Vito Tanzi (ed.), *Transition to Market: Studies in Fiscal Reform* (Washington, DC, 1993).

23. S. E. Ahmad, 'Poverty, Demographic Characteristics and Public Policy in C.I.S. Countries', IMF Working Paper WP/93/9 (Washington, DC, 1993).

24. S. K. Chand and P. Shome, 'Poverty Alleviation in a Financial Programming Framework: An Integrated Approach', IMF Working Paper WP/95/29 (Washington, DC, 1995).
25. M. Bruno, 'Stabilization and Reform in Eastern Europe: A Preliminary Evaluation', *IMF Staff Papers*, 39:4 (1992), 741–77.
26. D. C. Hardy, *Soft Budget Constraints, Firm Commitments and the Social Safety Net* (Washington, DC, 1991).
27. IMF, *Social Dimensions of Change: The IMF's Policy Dialogue*, contribution to the World Summit on Social Development (Washington, DC, 1995).
28. S. Haggard and R. Kaufman, *The Politics of Economic Adjustment* (Princeton, 1992); E. Rodriguez and S. Griffith-Jones, *Cross-Conditionality Banking Regulations and Third World Debt* (London, 1992); D. Ghai, *The IMF and the South: Social Impact of Crisis and Adjustment* (London, 1991).
29. Tony Killick and M. Malik, 'Country Experiences with IMF Programmes in the 1980s', ODI Working Paper 48 (London, 1991).
30. IMF, 'Statement by IMF on the Realization of Economic, Social, and Cultural Rights', UN Doc. W/CN.4/Sub.2/1992/57 (New York, 1992).
31. IMF, *Social Dimensions of Change*, 1.
32. Ibid.
33. Ibid. 15.
34. Ibid. 18–22.
35. G. Kopits, 'Towards a Cost-Effective Social Security System', in *The Implications for Social Security of Structural Adjustment Policies*, ISSA Studies and Research 34 (Geneva, 1993).
36. Ibid. 103.
37. Ibid. 105.
38. Ibid. 108.
39. Ibid.
40. Ibid. 105.
41. L. W. Pauly, 'Promoting a Global Economy: The Normative Role of the I.M.F.', in Stubbs and Underhill, *Political Economy*, 120.
42. IMF, *Annual Report 1994* (Washington, DC, 1994), 120.
43. World Bank, *Investing in People: The World Bank in Action* (Washington, DC, 1995), p. v.
44. B. A. de Vries, 'The World Bank's Focus on Poverty', in J. M. Griesgraber and B. G. Gunter (eds.), *The World Bank* (London, 1996).
45. World Bank, *World Development Report 1990* (Washington, DC, 1990); 'Assistance Strategies to Reduce Poverty' (Washington, DC, 1991); *Poverty Reduction Handbook* (Washington, DC, 1992).

46. G. Cornia, R. Jolly, and F. Stewart, *Adjustment with a Human Face* (Oxford, 1987).

47. World Bank, *Implementing the World Bank's Strategy to Reduce Poverty: Progress and Challenges* (Washington, DC, 1993), p. xi.

48. World Bank, *The East Asian Miracle* (Washington, DC, 1993).

49. World Bank, *Averting the Old Age Crisis: Policies to Protect the Old and Promote Growth*, World Bank Policy Research Report (New York, 1994).

50. N. Barr, *Labour Markets and Social Policy in Central and Eastern Europe: The Transition and Beyond* (Oxford, 1994).

51. IMF, 'Social Security Reforms and Social Safety Nets in Reforming and Transforming Economies', paper presented by the IMF and World Bank to the Development Committee of the Bank and the Fund, Washington, DC, 27 Sept. 1993, p. 79.

52. Ibid.

53. Joan Nelson, 'Poverty, Equity and the Politics of Adjustment', in Haggard and Kaufman, *The Politics of Economic Adjustment*, 232–44.

54. C. Graham, *Safety Nets, Politics and the Poor* (Washington, DC, 1994).

55. S. Cleary, 'The World Bank and NGOs', in P. Willets (ed.), *The Conscience of the World* (Washington, DC, 1996).

56. M. Cichon and L. Samuel (eds.), *Making Social Protection Work: The Challenge of Tripartism in Social Governance for Countries in Transition* (Budapest, 1995).

57. OECD, *The Crisis of Welfare* (Paris, 1981).

58. OECD, 'Reforming Public Pensions', in *Social Policy Studies 5* (Paris, 1988); OECD, 'The Transition from Work to Retirement', in *Social Policy Studies 16* (Paris, 1993).

59. OECD, 'Health Care Systems in Transition: The Search for Efficiency', in *Social Policy Studies 7* (Paris, 1990).

60. OECD, 'Employment/Unemployment Study', Report by the Secretary-General, Doc. OEDE/GD(93)102 (Paris, 1993).

61. OECD, 'Challenge for the Mid-1990's: The Development Centre's Programme for 1993–1995', OECD Development Centre (Paris, 1993), 41.

62. OECD, 'New Orientations for Social Policy', in *Social Policy Studies 12* (Paris, 1994), 12.

63. Ibid. 13.

64. OECD, *Annual Report of the OECD* (Paris, 1992), 174.

65. Quoted in S. Woolcock, 'The Trade and Labour Standards Debate: Overburdening or Defending the Multilateral System?', paper for the CRUSA/RIIA Study Group (London, 1995).

66. ILO, *Report of the Director-General: Fifth European Regional Conference* (Geneva, 1995), 115.
67. D. Strang and P. M. Y. Chang, 'The ILO and the Welfare State: Institutional Effects on National Welfare Spending', *International Organization*, 47:2 (1993), 259.
68. Ibid.
69. R. Plant, 'Labour Standards and Structural Adjustment in Hungary', Occasional Paper 7, Interdepartmental Project on Structural Adjustment, ILO (Geneva, 1994), 194.
70. Ibid.
71. Ibid.
72. M. Cichon, 'Financing Social Protection in Central and East Europe: Safeguarding Political and Economic Change', in International Social Security Association, *Restructuring Social Security in Central and Eastern Europe: A Guide to Recent Developments, Policy Issues, and Options* (Geneva, 1994); M. Cichon, 'Social Protection in Transition Economies: From Improvisation to Social Concepts', ILO Policy Discussion Paper (Geneva, 1994).
73. World Bank, *Averting the Old Age Crisis*.
74. G. E. Standing, 'Restructuring for Distributive Justice in Eastern Europe', paper presented to the conference 'Towards a Competitive Society in Central and Eastern Europe: Social Dimensions', ILO, Kellokoski, Finland, Sept. 1992.
75. Cichon and Samuel, *Making Social Protection Work*.
76. Plant, 'Labour Standards'.
77. G. Rodgers (ed.), *The Poverty Agenda and the I.L.O.: Issues for Research and Action* (Geneva, 1995), 177.
78. Ibid. 174.
79. Quoted in T. Collingsworth, J. W. Goold and P. J. Harvey, 'Time for a New Global Deal', *Foreign Affairs*, 73:1 (1994), 8–20. Commission on Global Governance, *Our Global Neighbourhood* (Oxford, 1995), 10.
80. Woolcock, 'The Trade and Labour Standards Debate'.
81. Ibid. 17.
82. D. C. Esty, *Greening the Gatt: Trade, Environment and the Future* (Washington, DC, 1994).
83. Woolcock, 'The Trade and Labour Standards Debate'.
84. E. Luard, *The Globalisation of Politics* (London, 1990).
85. Cornia *et al.*, *Adjustment with a Human Face*.
86. R. Jolly, 'Adjustment with a Human Face: A UNICEF Record and Perspective on the 1980's', *World Development*, 19:12 (1991), 1807–21.
87. UNICEF, *The State of the World's Children 1995* (New York, 1995).
88. See UNDP, *Human Development Report* (New York, annual).

89. UNDP, *Human Development Report 1992*, 74.
90. UNRISD, *States of Disarray: The Social Effects of Globalization*, report for the World Summit of Social Development (Geneva, 1995).
91. Ibid. 168.
92. Commission on Global Governance, *Our Global Neighbourhood*.
93. UNRISD, *States of Disarray*.
94. Held, *Democracy and the Global Order*.
95. J. M. Griesgraber and B. G. Gunter (eds.), *Promoting Development: Effective Global Institutions for the Twenty-First Century* (London, 1995); J. M. Griesgraber and B. G. Gunter (eds.), *The World Bank: Lending on a Global Scale* (London, 1996).
96. UNRISD/UNDP, *Adjustment, Globalization and Social Development: A Report of the UNRISD/UNDP Seminar on Economic Restructuring and Social Policy, New York, 11–13 January 1995* (Geneva, 1995).
97. The *Guardian*, 2 Apr. 1996.
98. The *Observer*, 30 June 1996.
99. G7 Summit, *Communiqués* (Lyons, 1996).
100. Commission on Global Governance, *Our Global Neighbourhood*, 34.
101. Ibid. 155.
102. UNRISD/UNDP, *Adjustment, Globalization, and Social Development*.
103. H. W. Singer, 'Rethinking Bretton Woods from a Historical Perspective', in Griesgraber and Gunter, *Promoting Development*, 18.
104. Strange, 'Wake Up, Krasner'.
105. ODI, 'Rethinking the Role of the Multilateral Development Banks', ODI Briefing Papers No. 4 (London, 1996).
106. Commission on Global Governance, *Our Global Neighbourhood*, 336.
107. UNRISD, *States of Disarray*, 170.
108. Baucock, *Transnational Citizenship*.
109. Held, *Democracy*.
110. N. J. Wheeler, 'Guardian Angel or Global Gangster: A Review of the Ethical Claims of International Society', *Political Studies*, 44 (1996), 123–35.
111. C. Humana, *World Human Rights Guide*, 3rd edn. (Oxford, 1992).
112. Ibid. 8.
113. Commission on Global Governance, *Our Global Neighbourhood*, 335.
114. D. Milwood (ed.), *The International Response to Conflict and Genocide: Synthesis Report, Steering Committee of the Joint Evaluation of Emergency Assistance to Rwanda* (Copenhagen, 1996).

115. P. Willets, *The Conscience of the World* (Washington, DC, 1996).
116. World Bank Operations Evaluation Department, *1995 Evaluation Results* (Washington, DC, 1997), 1.
117. UNRISD, *Adjustment, Globalization, and Social Development*, 25.
118. Ibid. 34.
119. Hirst and Thompson, *Globalization in Question*, 191.
120. Ibid.
121. Held, *Democracy*, 279.

NOTES TO CHAPTER 9

1. See Robert W. Tucker, *The Inequality of Nations* (New York, 1977), 3–15; Hedley Bull, 'The Emergence of a Universal International Society', in Hedley Bull and Adam Watson (eds.), *The Expansion of International Society* (Oxford, 1984), 117–26.
2. See Martin Ceadel, *The Origins of War Prevention: The British Peace Movement and International Relations, 1730–1854* (Oxford, 1996), chaps. 2 and 3.
3. See Emma Rothschild, 'What is Security?', *Daedalus*, 124:3 (1995), 53–98.
4. Kenneth Waltz, *Theory of International Politics* (Reading, Mass., 1979), 143.
5. Martin Wight, *Power Politics* (London, 1979), 139.
6. Friedrich von Gentz, *Fragments upon the Balance of Power in Europe* (London, 1806), 60–1. The ambiguities between equality of power and the propensity for conflict lay at the heart of traditional conceptions of the balance of power. As Claude put it: 'War may be required for equilibrium but war may also be prevented by equilibrium': Inis Claude, *Power and International Relations* (New York, 1962), 54.
7. For a powerful refutation of this view, see David Welch, *Justice and the Genesis of War* (Cambridge, 1993), especially 10–22.
8. It is a 'principled belief' but one that is intimately connected to various 'world views', to use the categories suggested by Goldstein and Keohane. See Judith Goldstein and Robert Keohane, 'Ideas and Foreign Policy: An Analytical Framework', in Judith Goldstein and Robert Keohane (eds.), *Ideas and Foreign Policy* (Ithaca, NY, 1993), 3–30.
9. Thomas Hobbes, *Leviathan*, ed. Richard Tuck (Cambridge, 1996), 87.
10. For the classical statement of this argument, see Emerich de Vattel, *The Law of Nations*, trans. Joseph Chitty (London, 1834), p. xiv and 135. See also Andrew Hurrell, 'Vattel: Pluralism and its Limits', in

Ian Clark and Iver B. Neumann (eds.), *Classical Theories of International Relations* (London, 1996), 233–55.

11. Hedley Bull, *The Anarchical Society* (London, 1977), chap. 8.

12. J. P. Dunbabin, 'The League of Nations' Place in the International System', *History*, 78 (1993), 425.

13. 'The world wars can be seen, then, as horrific learning experiences. Most people in the developed world had gotten the point by 1918. The rest, the Japanese in particular, got it by 1945': John Mueller, *Retreat from Doomsday: The Obsolescence of Major War* (New York, 1990), 218.

14. Norman Angell, *The Great Illusion* (London, 1910), 129.

15. For a discussion of the trade-off between the benefits of large political jurisdiction and the costs of heterogeneity, see Alberto Alesina, 'On the Number and Size of Nations', *Quarterly Journal of Economics*, 112 (1997), 1027–56.

16. Karl W. Deutsch *et al.*, *Political Community in the North Atlantic Area* (Princeton, 1957), 5.

17. For a contemporary application of Deutsch's arguments, see Emanuel Adler and Michael Barnett (eds.), *Security Communities* (Cambridge, 1998).

18. Max Singer and Aaron Wildavsky, *The Real World Order: Zones of Peace/Zones of Turmoil* (Chatham, NJ, 1993).

19. There is a profound sense in which the possibility of war and conflict will always define the meaning of politics, even in apparently secure communities. See Carl Schmitt, *The Concept of the Political*, trans. Georg Schwab (New Brunswick, NJ, 1976), especially 32–5.

20. Pierre Hassner, 'Force and Politics Today', in Pierre Hassner, *Violence and Peace: From the Atomic Bomb to Ethnic Cleansing* (Budapest, 1997), 38.

21. On the prevalence and bloodiness of 'low-intensity war' and 'wars of the third kind' in the post-1945 period, see Martin van Creveld, *On Future War* (London, 1991), 20–32; and Kalevi J. Holsti, *The State, War, and the State of War* (Cambridge, 1996), chap. 2.

22. Margareta Sollenberg (ed.), *States in Armed Conflict 1994*, Report No. 39, Department of Peace and Conflict Research, Uppsala University (Uppsala, 1995).

23. For three important examples, see Richard H. Ullman, 'Redefining Security', *International Security*, 8 (1983), 129–53; Jessica Tuchman Matthews, 'Redefining Security', *Foreign Affairs*, 62:2 (1989), 162–77; and Rothschild, 'What is Security?'

24. See, for example, J. Ann Tickner, 'Re-visioning Security', in Ken Booth and Steve Smith (eds.), *International Political Theory Today* (Cambridge, 1995), 175–97.

25. See especially Mohammed Ayoob, *The Third World Security Predicament: State Making, Regional Conflict and the International System* (Boulder, Colo., 1995).

26. For reviews, see Mark Irving Lichbach, 'An Evaluation of "Does Economic Inequality Breed Political Conflict?" Studies', *World Politics*, 41 (1989), 431–70; and Jenk W. Houweling, 'Destabilizing Consequences of Sequential Development', in Luc van de Goor, Kumar Rupesinghe, and Paul Sciarone (eds.), *Between Development and Destruction: An Enquiry into the Causes of Conflict in Post-colonial States* (London, 1996), 143–69.

27. See, for example, the chapters by Dalby, Walker, and Booth in Keith Krause and Michael Williams (eds.), *Critical Security Studies* (Minneapolis, 1997).

28. John Keane, *Reflections on Violence* (London, 1996), 26.

29. Claus Offe, 'Present Historical Trends and Some Basic Design Options for Societal Institutions', paper presented to the Congress on Society and the Reform of the State, São Paulo, Mar. 1998.

30. G. John Ikenberry, 'The Myth of Post-Cold War Chaos', *Foreign Affairs*, 75:3 (1996), 79–91.

31. Jennifer A. Widner, 'States and Statelessness in Africa', *Daedalus*, 124:3 (1995), 148.

32. For a recent discussion, see Lawrence Freedman, 'International Security: Changing Targets', *Foreign Policy*, 110 (1998), 48–63.

33. World Bank figures cited by Partha Dasgupta, *An Inquiry into Well-Being and Destitution* (Oxford, 1993), 122.

34. Steven van Evera, 'Why Europe Matters, Why the Third World Doesn't: American Grand Strategy after the Cold War', *Journal of Strategic Studies*, 13:2 (1990), 1–51.

35. See, in particular, the work of Ole Waever, 'European Security Identities', *Journal of Conflict Resolution*, 34:1 (1996), 170, and 'On Securitization and Desecuritization', in Ronnie D. Lipschutz (ed.), *On Security* (New York, 1995), 46–86.

36. For example, Thomas Homer-Dixon, 'Environmental Scarcities and Violent Conflict: Evidence from Cases', *International Security*, 19:1 (1994), 5–40.

37. See David Keen, *The Economic Functions of Violence in Civil Wars*, Adelphi Paper No. 320 (London, 1998).

38. James Fairhead, 'Conflicts over Natural Resources: Complex Emergencies, Environment and a Critique of "Greenwar" in Africa', paper presented at the WIDER conference, Queen Elizabeth House, Oxford, July 1997. See also Nils Peter Gleditsch, 'Armed Conflict and the Environment: A Critique of the Literature', *Journal of Peace Research*, 35 (1998), 381–400.

39. Robert D. Kaplan, *The Ends of the Earth: A Journey at the Dawn of the 21st Century* (New York, 1997).
40. See Andrew Hurrell, 'Collective Security and International Order Revisited', *International Relations*, 11:1 (1992), 37–55.
41. Charles Krauthammer, 'The Unipolar Moment', in Graham Allison and Gregory Treverton (eds.), *Rethinking America's Security* (New York, 1992), 297.
42. For example, the idea of multi-pillared structural power propounded by Susan Strange: see *States and Markets* (London, 1998); or the importance of cultural norms and other forms of 'soft power': see Joseph Nye, *Bound to Lead: The Changing Nature of American Power* (New York, 1990).
43. See Andrew Hurrell and Ngaire Woods, 'Globalization and Inequality', *Millennium*, 24:3 (1995), 447–70.
44. On the tensions between the technological and organizational revolutions and the types of conflict in which major developed states are likely to be involved, see Lawrence Freedman, 'The Revolution in Strategic Affairs', Adelphi Paper No. 318 (London, 1998), especially chap. 3 on asymmetric wars.
45. Although this does not mean that civil wars cannot be economically rational. See Keen, *The Economic Functions of Violence in Civil Wars*.
46. 'The Concept of Cooperative Security', in Janne E. Nolan (ed.), *Global Engagement: Cooperation and Security in the 21st Century* (Washington, DC, 1994), 4.
47. For example, see van Creveld, *On Future War*, 124–6, 142–4; also Keane, *Reflections on Violence*, and Philippe Delmas, *The Rosy Future of War* (New York, 1995), chap. 9.

SUGGESTED FURTHER READING

ADLER, EMANUEL, and BARNETT, MICHAEL (eds.), *Security Communities* (Cambridge, 1998).

AGARWAL, ANIL, and NARAIN, SUNITA, *Global Warming in an Unequal World: A Case of Environmental Colonialism* (New Delhi, 1991).

ATKINSON, ANTHONY, RAINWATER, LEE, and SMEEDLING, TIMOTHY, *Income Distribution in OECD Countries: Evidence from the Luxembourg Income Study* (Paris, 1995).

AYOOB, MOHAMMED, *The Third World Security Predicament: State Making, Regional Conflict and the International System* (Boulder, Colo., 1995).

BARRY, BRIAN, *Democracy, Power and Justice* (Oxford, 1989).

BEITZ, CHARLES, *Political Theory and International Relations* (Princeton, 1979).

BERGER, SUZANNE, and DORE, RONALD (eds.), *National Diversity and Global Capitalism* (Ithaca, NY, 1996).

BHAGWATI, JAGDISH, and RUGGIE, JOHN GERARD, *Power, Passions, and Purpose: Prospects for North–South Negotiations* (Cambridge, 1984).

BHASKAR, VASKAR, and GLYN, ANDREW (eds.), *The North, the South and the Environment: Ecological Constraints and the Global Economy* (London, 1995).

BROAD, ROBIN, and MELHORN-LANDI, CHRISTINA, 'Whither the North–South Gap?', *Third World Quarterly*, 17:1 (1996), 7–17.

BULL, HEDLEY, and WATSON, ADAM (eds.), *The Expansion of International Society* (Oxford, 1984).

CASTELLS, MANUEL, *End of Millennium* (Oxford, 1998).

CHARNEY, JONATHAN, 'Universal International Law', *American Journal of International Law*, 87 (1993), 529–51.

CLAUDE, INIS L., *Power and International Relations* (New York, 1962).

Commission on Global Governance, *Our Global Neighbourhood* (Oxford, 1995).

COOK, REBECCA (ed.), *Human Rights of Women: National and International Perspectives* (Philadelphia, 1994).

DASGUPTA, PARTHA, *An Inquiry into Well-Being and Destitution* (Oxford, 1993).

DEACON, BOB, *Global Social Policy* (London, 1998).

DWORKIN, RONALD, 'Equality of Resources', *Philosophy and Public Affairs*, 10 (1981), 283–345.

FRANCK, THOMAS, *Fairness in International Law and Institutions* (Oxford, 1995).

FREEDMAN, LAWRENCE, 'The Revolution in Strategic Affairs', Adelphi Paper No. 318 (London, 1998).

GLYN, ANDREW, and MILIBAND, DAVID (eds.), *Paying for Inequality: The Economic Cost of Social Injustice* (London, 1994).

GOODIN, ROBERT, *Protecting the Vulnerable* (Chicago, 1985).

GONG, GERRIT, *The Standard of 'Civilization' in International Society* (Oxford, 1984).

GRAHAM, CAROL, *Safety Nets, Politics and the Poor* (Washington, DC, 1994).

HASSNER, PIERRE, *Violence and Peace: From the Atomic Bomb to Ethnic Cleansing* (Budapest, 1997).

HELD, DAVID, *Democracy and the Global Order: From the Modern State to Cosmopolitan Governance* (Cambridge, 1995).

HIRST, PAUL, and THOMPSON, GRAHAM, *Globalization in Question* (Cambridge, 1996).

HOLM, HANS-HENRIK, and SORENSEN, GEORG (eds.), *Whose World Order? Uneven Globalization and the End of the Cold War* (Boulder, Colo., 1995).

HOLSTI, KALEVI J., *The State, War, and the State of War* (Cambridge, 1996).

HOMER-DIXON, THOMAS, 'Environmental Scarcities and Violent Conflict: Evidence from Cases', *International Security*, 19:1 (1994), 5–40.

HURRELL, ANDREW, and WOODS, NGAIRE, 'Globalization and Inequality', *Millennium*, 24:3 (1995), 447–70.

INDEPENDENT (BRANDT) COMMISSION, *North–South: A Programme for Survival* (Cambridge, 1980).

KAPUR, DEVESH, LEWIS, JOHN, and WEBB, RICHARD (eds.), *The World Bank: Its First Half-Century*, vol. i (Washington, DC, 1997).

KRASNER, STEPHEN, 'Compromising Westphalia', *International Security*, 20 (1995–6), 115–51.

——*Structural Conflict: The Third World against Global Liberalism* (Berkeley, 1985).

MATTHEWS, JESSICA TUCHMAN, 'Redefining Security', *Foreign Affairs*, 68 (1989), 162–77.

OMAN, CHARLES, *Globalization and Regionalization: The Challenge for Developing Countries* (Paris, 1994).

O'NEILL, ONORA, *Faces of Hunger: An Essay on Poverty, Justice, and Development* (London, 1986).

OSBERG, LARS (ed.), *Economic Inequality and Poverty: International Perspectives* (New York, 1991).

RAWLS, JOHN, 'The Law of Peoples', in Stephen Shute and Susan Hurley (eds.), *On Human Rights: The Oxford Amnesty Lectures 1993* (New York, 1993).

REDCLIFT, MICHAEL, *Wasted Earth: Counting the Cost of Global Consumption* (London, 1996).

RODRIK, DANI, *Has Globalization Gone Too Far?* (Washington, DC, 1997).

RUGGIE, JOHN GERRARD, *Winning the Peace: America and World Order in the New Era* (New York, 1996).

SELIGSON, MITCHELL A., and PASSÉ-SMITH, JOHN T. (eds.), *Development and Underdevelopment: The Political Economy of Inequality* (Boulder, Colo. and London, 1997 edn.).

SEN, AMARTYA, *Inequality Re-examined* (Cambridge, Mass., 1992).

—— *Poverty and Famines* (Oxford, 1981).

SHUE, HENRY, *Basic Rights: Subsistence, Affluence and U.S. Foreign Policy* (Princeton, 1980).

SINGER, MAX, and WILDAVSKY, AARON, *The Real World Order: Zones of Peace/Zones of Turmoil* (Chatham, NJ, 1993).

SLAUGHTER, MATTHEW, SWAGEL, PHILLIP, and IMF, *Does Globalization Lower Wages and Export Jobs?* (Washington, DC, 1997).

STALLINGS, BARBARA (ed.), *Global Change, Regional Response: The New International Context of Development* (Cambridge, 1995).

STEWART, FRANCES, *Poverty and Adjustment: Options and Choices* (London, 1995).

TUCKER, ROBERT W., *The Inequality of Nations* (New York, 1977).

WILLIAMSON, JEFFREY, 'Globalization and Inequality Then and Now: The Late 19th and Late 20th Centuries Compared', NBER Working Paper No. 5491 (Cambridge, Mass., 1996).

WOOD, ADRIAN, *North–South Trade, Employment and Inequality* (Oxford, 1994).

UNITED NATIONS DEVELOPMENT PROGRAMME [UNDP], *Human Development Report* (New York, annual).

UNITED NATIONS RESEARCH INSTITUTE FOR SOCIAL DEVELOPMENT [UNRISD], *States of Disarray: The Social Effects of Globalization*, report for the World Summit of Social Development (Geneva, 1995).

VAN DE GOOR, LUC, RUPESINGHE, KUMAR, and SCIARONE, PAUL (eds.), *Between Development and Destruction: An Enquiry into the Causes of Conflict in Post-colonial States* (London, 1996).

INDEX

Abbott, K. 27
accountability 24, 25, 240–2, 245,
    246
  more equal 26
  supranational 215
Afghanistan 256
Africa 27, 158, 231
  colonialism 14, 71
  dependence on manufactures 40
  distributional changes 161–8, 174
  foreign exchange crisis 161
  real wages 132
  structural adjustment policies 224
  Sub-Saharan 18, 131, 183
  weak economic performance 183
  see also North Africa; *also under*
    various country names
African Charter of Human and
    People's Rights 113
AFTA 40, 43
agriculture 18, 132–3, 135–6, 163,
    165
  changes in productivity 144
  incomes, self-employed farmers 177
  major shifts in trade 145
  output 180
Ahmad, S. F. 220
aid 15, 17, 59
  food 88
  humanitarian 203, 213
Alexander, Tom 228
Algeria 222
alliances 227, 234, 235, 254, 265–6
Angell, Norman 256
Angola 258
APEC (Asia Pacific Economic
    Council) 43
Argentina 87, 169, 170
armaments 249
arms control 71, 254, 266, 267
Asia 49, 71, 231
  distributional changes 174–80
  exports 18
  Pacific 38, 42, 131
  South 112, 144, 258
  South-East 225, 229

  see also East Asia; *also under*
    various country names
Australia 159, 223
authority:
  collective 251
  crisis of 82
  fragmentation of 81
  legal 217
  loci of 85
  supranational 211
autocratic government 75
autonomy 27
  decision-making 89
  policy 37, 46, 57, 59
  political 220

balance of power 8, 9–10, 70, 254
  unstable 258
Bangladesh 18, 110
banks 44, 202
  international 23, 130
Bano, Shah 112, 113
bargaining 40, 205, 206, 208
  collective 235, 240
barriers:
  entry 90
  equal treatment 17–20
  health 98
  import, move to reduce 46
  inhibiting growth and welfare 16
  intra-regional 56, 57–8
  legal 97
  policy 58
  'structural' 15
  trade 20, 58
  see also tariffs
basic needs 135, 136, 203
Baubock 244
Beijing Summit (UN 4th World
    Conference on Women, 1995) 35,
    95, 97, 107
  femininization of poverty
    conceded 118
  Islamic states at 114
  Platform of Action 111, 116, 117
Beitz, Charles 14